Strategic Management Accounting

a critical exploration with a sustainability angle

Chandana Alawattage

CGA PUBLISHING

Wishaw, North Lanakshire, UK.

Copyright © Chandana Alawattage, 2024
All rights reserved.

ISBN: 9798875717826

CGA Publishing
96 Shankly Drive
Morningside
Wishaw
ML2 9QZ
United Kingdom

cgalawattage@hotmail.com

The cover page features an image generated by AI using prompts related to strategy, management accounting, and sustainability

to my family

wife Lalani

daughter Imesha

son Sajan

Preface

This book results from my years of teaching strategic management accounting (SMA) at two venerable liberal universities. My dual goal has been to present SMA as a social science while delving into its techno-managerial and professional essence. This approach renders the book somewhat paradoxical, as it strives to achieve two seemingly conflicting objectives within the constraints of limited teaching time. On the one hand, akin to the expected studies of professional accountants in strategy, the book introduces the prevalent techno-managerial aspects of SMA. Within the confines of a ten-week course, it comprehensively explores key SMA themes. These themes range from pre-Porterian strategy discourses through Porterian strategy discourses to specific topics of strategic pricing, strategic performance management, strategic management control, organizational resilience, quality costing and management, manufacturing flexibility, and strategic cost management. The book thoroughly addresses the techno-managerial nuances of these strategic themes.

On the other hand, much like how liberal university students in a college of social sciences are expected to approach the subjects they study, this book aims to provide a social science perspective on the techno-managerial aspects of the subject. As I have explored in my classrooms, this social science approach to teaching SMA involves enacting the following epistemic actions: particularizing, contextualizing, historicizing, politicizing, and theorizing.

1. **Particularizing:** In the context of this book, it refers to understanding the specific techno-managerial aspects of various SMA topics, such as strategic positioning, strategic performance management and control, organizational resilience, quality costing, and manufacturing flexibility. This epistemic act is foundational, enabling a deeper engagement with SMA's mainstream techno-managerial elements and setting the stage for other critical epistemic actions.
2. **Contextualizing:** This involves placing SMA's techno-managerial elements within the broader political-economic context of capitalism and neoliberalism to appreciate and critique their underlying political-economic logic.
3. **Historicizing:** This refers to exploring and explaining the evolution of SMA's political-economic role in tandem with the historical dynamics of capitalism. It includes examining the historical specificities that have shaped current accounting calculations and rationalizations, now recognized as SMA.
4. **Politicizing:** This act highlights the political context and historical circumstances in which SMA becomes politicized. It means recognizing how SMA techniques and methods have historically evolved to serve the interests of dominant groups, primarily owners of socialized private capital. However, these can also be challenged by other forces, such as the need to account for sustainability. In teaching SMA as a social science, it is essential to incorporate political ideologies beyond the conventional capitalist axiom of shareholder wealth maximization, acknowledging issues of social and ecological justice.
5. **Theorizing:** This involves employing social theories as a foundation for contextualizing, historicizing, and politicizing the techno-managerial aspects of SMA, leading to their interpretation and explanation

Many of these critical epistemic elements are enabled and enacted by incorporating a 'sustainability perspective' into SMA. Consequently, the global sustainability agenda serves as the broader politico-ideological foundation that contextualizes, historicizes, politicizes, and critiques SMA. Throughout the book, I discuss the sustainability implications of various SMA techniques and frameworks as opportunities arise. As such, sustainability functions as the unifying theme of the entire book.

The book is structured for a ten-session SMA course. However, it offers flexibility to shorten the course by omitting certain topics or to extend it beyond ten sessions by delving deeper into specific subjects over multiple sessions. I hope this adaptability allows others to tailor the book to their program needs.

This book represents the culmination of teaching notes I have developed for my students over many years. Nevertheless, my research publications, co-authored with my research colleague and mentor, Danture Wickramasinghe, significantly aided its transformation into this book. I must express my gratitude to him for his invaluable contributions.

Chandana Alawattage

January 2024

Contents

Dedication iii
Preface v
List of Tables xvii
List of Figures xix

1 Strategic management accounting: **emergence, definitions, and domains of operations** 1

1.1 Introduction 1
1.2 The strategic turn 3
Contextual factors 4
- Neoliberalization of politics 4
- Globalization of markets and organizational hierarchies 7
- Digitalization and virtualization of technologies and spaces 8
- Contextual factors summary 9

Epistemic factors 10
- Epistemic factors – conceptual elements 11
- Epistemic factors – institutional elements 13

Global sustainability agenda 16
- Strategic turn summary 18

1.3 Definitions and differentiations 19
Strategy discourses: military connections 20
Strategy translated into business contexts 21
- Understanding the notion of competitive terrain 22

Defining and differentiating SMA 26

1.4 Sustainablizing strategy 27
1.5 Strategizing domains and the book's structure 30

Chapter Summary 35
Test and revise your knowledge 37
Explore further 38
Develop your critical argumentation skills 39
References 39

2 Reconceptualizing competition: **discourses of competitive advantage and strategic positioning**   41

2.1. Introduction   41

2.2. From management to strategic management: organizational discourses of strategy   43

    Emergence of corporate planning   44

        Strategy as coordinating multidivisional organizations   45

        Strategy as dealing with external environmental conditions   51

        Diversification as strategy: dealing with corporate growth   52

    Bringing people and cultural factors in   53

    Summary of pre-Porterian strategy discourses   54

2.3 Porterian discourses of strategy   55

    Revising the structure-conduct-performance model   55

    The notion of competitive advantage   57

    Porter's generic strategies   59

    Porter's models of strategic analysis   61

        Porter's five forces analysis   62

        Value chain analysis   63

        Four corner analysis   64

        Porter's grand schema of strategy in summary   66

    Sustainability implications of Porterian discourses   68

    Chapter summary   69

    Test your knowledge   73

    Explore further   74

    Develop your critical argumentation skills.   75

    References   76

3 Strategizing the market: **strategic pricing decisions**   79

3.1. Introduction   79

3.2. Neoclassical economic model of pricing   80

3.3 The accounting model of pricing   86

3.4 Strategic pricing for competitive positioning   91

    Segmentation   92

        Market segment profile   95

    Targeting   95

    Positioning   96

    The strategic role of pricing in STP   96

    Other pricing considerations and techniques: Fine-tuning the pricing strategy   98

        Psychological pricing   98

        Market skimming vs penetration pricing   99

3.5 Lifecycle costing   99
    Lifecycle costing in asset management   100
    Lifecycle costing in product costing   101
3.6 Target costing   102
    The concept of survival zone   105
    Triangle of target costing   106
    Target costing process   108
    Sustainability implications of target costing   110
Dynamic pricing   112
    Chapter summary   114
    Test your knowledge   116
    Explore further   117
    Develop your critical argumentation skills   118
    Mini case study   119
    References   122

4 Strategizing the hierarchy: **strategic performance management**   123

4.1. Introduction   123
4.2 Conceptualizing performance   124
4.2. The traditional approach to performance management: responsibility accounting   128
    4.2.1 From operational to accounting logic   131
    Techniques and structure of responsibility accounting   131
    Weaknesses of responsibility accounting-based performance management   134
4.3. Strategic performance management   135
    The logic of strategic performance management   136
    Scorecards as fundamental building blocks of performance management   137
    Strategic performance as balancing between financial and non-financial   139
    Strategic performance as cascading scorecards to link operations with strategy   141
    Causalities and finalities in BSC   143
        BSC relationships causality or finality? – Norekklit's critique   145
        Other weaknesses of BSC   148
    Reimagining the BSC for sustainability   149
        Reimagining BSC as a capitalist managerial capture of sustainability – a political-economy critique   154
    Chapter summary   157
    Test your knowledge   159
    Explore further   160
    Develop your critical argumentation skills   161
    Mini case study   162
    References   163

5 Strategizing the hierarchy: **strategic management control** 167

5.1 Introduction 167
5.2 Understanding the fundamentals of management control 169
    Agency theory conception of management control 170
    Systems theory conception of management control 174
        Cybernetic perspectives on management control 175
        Beyond cybernetics 178
        Hierarchical perspectives and structural functionalism in management control 180
        Environmental perspectives on management control 184
5.3 **Strategic management control: levers of control** 187
    Simons' conception of strategic contradictions 187
    Levers of control 189
    Levers of control and integration of sustainability 195
    Chapter summary: 197
    Test your knowledge 199
    Explore further: 201
    Develop your critical argumentation skills 201
    Mini case study 202
    References 204

6 Strategizing the hierarchy: **organizational resilience** 207

6.1 Introduction: from management control to organizational resilience 207
6.2 Defining resilience: understanding the concept's diversity in applications 210
6.3 Organizational resilience and management control: analyzing consultocratic discourses 215
    Expository narratives on organizational resilience 216
        Routines, hermeneutics, and improvisation for organizational resilience 222
    Consultocratic modeling of organizational resilience 224
        Financial resilience 229
        Operational resilience 230
        Structural resilience 232
        Digital and technology resilience 233
        Reputational and environmental resilience in consultancy discourse 235
6.4 **Academic discourses on organizational resilience** 238
    Exploring the underpinning contradictions of resilience 239
    Relating contradictions to different domains of resilience strategies 241
    Chapter summary 243
    Test your knowledge 245
    Explore further 247
    Develop your critical argumentation skills 247
    References 248

7 Strategizing the point of production: **quality costing and management** 251

7.1 Introduction   251

7.2 Defining quality: multiplicity of perspectives and an operational definition   253
   Product-based approach   254
   Manufacturing-based approach   255
   User-based approach   257
   Value-based approach   258
   Transcendental approach   259
   Social constructivist approach   260
   An operational definition of quality for quality costing   261

7.3 **Quality costs**   262
   Prevention costs   263
   Appraisal costs   263
   Internal failure costs   264
   External failure costs   264

7.4 **Quality paradigms**   264
   Traditional quality paradigm   265
   Zero-defect and continuous improvement quality paradigms   269
   Post-WWII discourses   269
   Revisiting the Cost Optimization Model   270

7.5 **Quality costing system**   272
   Defining the scope of a quality costing system   273
   Costing techniques and methods   273
   Reporting and assessments of quality costs and performance   276

7.6 **Quality-centric organizational transformations**   280
   Introducing quality as a philosophical element of corporate leadership   280
   Japanization of organizational processes   281
   Chapter summary   282
   Test your knowledge   284
   Explore further   287
   Develop your critical argumentation skills   287
   References   287

8 Strategizing the point of production: **manufacturing flexibility** 289

8.1 Introduction 289
8.2 Neoliberal political rationale of flexibility 290
8.3 Flexible consumption 292
    Operational capacity for flexible consumption 293
    Informational capacity for flexible consumption 295
8.4 Flexible machines 295
8.5 Flexible labor 298
    Skill flexibility of labor 298
    Time flexibility of labor 300
8.6 Flexible manufacturing systems 302
    Different notions of flexibility in FMS 303
        Basic or element flexibilities 303
        System flexibilities 304
        Aggregate flexibilities 305
    Accounting in FMS 305
        Industry 4.0 technologies and 'smart accounting' in FMS 306
8.7 Flexible specialization and integration 310
8.8 Flexible accumulation 313
    Chapter summary 317
    Test your knowledge 319
    Explore further 320
    Develop your critical argumentation skills 321
    References 321

9 Strategizing the point of production: **strategic cost management** 325

9.1 Introduction 325
9.2 From costing to cost management: the traditional approach 327
    Standardization as a basis of traditional cost management 329
    Coupling standardization with budgeting 330
    Processual elements of traditional cost management and profit planning 331
9.3 Strategic cost management 334
    Strategic cost management as a holistic program and surveillant assemblage 336
9.4 Foundational steps toward strategic cost management: ABC/M 340
    ABC's strategic significance 343
        ABC's controllability effect 343
        ABC's strategic effect 346
9.5 Consolidating strategic cost management through target costing 349
9.6 Lean manufacturing: manufacturing philosophy that encapsulates strategic cost management 354
9.7 ERP: software infrastructure of managing contemporary organizations 357

9.8 Throughput accounting and theory of constraints 361
    Theory of constraints and throughput accounting: an example 364
    Chapter summary 366
    Test your knowledge 368
    Explore further 369
    Develop your critical argumentation skills 370
    References 371

10 Strategizing sustainability 373

10.1 Introduction 373
10.2 Political and politics of sustainability: fundamental contradictions 375
10.3 Sustainability's neoliberal political logic 380
    Rationalizing the Oxymoron 384
10.4 Management accounting's rationalization of sustainability 386
    Corporate accountability and sustainability 386
10.5 Integrating sustainability 390
    Ensuring top leadership commitment 392
    Envisioning sustainability 394
    Sustainability to postulate strategic positioning 397
10.6 Operationalizing sustainability 398
    Sustainability in capital investment decisions 399
    Sustainable value chain analysis and competitive industry analysis 400
    Sustainable performance management with balanced scorecards 402
        Integrating sustainability into BSC 403
        Establishing causal links between sustainability and financial outcomes 404
        Privileging financial over sustainability 405
    Costing sustainability 406
        Use of ABC in sustainability costing 406
        Tracing the physical flows: materials flow accounting 407
        Tracing the monetary flow: activity-based costing of environmental impact 408
    Lifecycle costing (LCC) and whole life costing (WLC) 410
    Carbon costing/accounting 413
    Environmental management systems 414
    Chapter summary and a concluding critique 416
    Test your knowledge 418
    Explore further 420
    Develop your critical argumentation skills 420
    References 421

Index 427

List of Tables

Table 1.1: Differentiating SMA   28

Table 2.1: Classical corporate planning issues and models   56

Table 2.2: Strategizing sustainability – Porter and Krammer   70

Table 3.1: Market segment profiling   95

Table 3.2: Lifecycle costing example   103

Table 4.1: Responsibility accounting – accountability centers   130

Table 4.2: Responsibility accounting regimes of performance management: key themes   134

Table 5.1: Beyond cybernetics - Hofstede's control typology   179

Table 5.2: Parson's structural functionalism and classical theory of management control systems   184

Table 6.1: Hamel and Valikangas' "Quest for Resilience" – a creed towards "zero-trauma"   220

Table 7.1: An example of quality cost variance analysis   277

Table 8.1: Flexible manufacturing integrating job shops and mass production systems   304

Table 8.2: The hierarchy of flexibility concepts   318

Table 10.1: Porter and Karammer's insertion of sustainability into value chain analysis   401

Table 10.2: Inserting sustainability into the framework of competitive advantage of a nation   402

Table 10.3: Environmental activity-cost classification scheme   411

List of Figures

Figure 1.1: The strategic turn   19

Figure 1.2: Key elements of the strategic context   24

Figure 1.3: Sustainablizing strategy   31

Figure 1.4: Structural logic of the course   33

Figure 2.1: Multidivisional organization form   46

Figure 2.2: DuPont system of financial analysis   48

Figure 2.3: Portfolio planning models   49

Figure 2.4: Ansoff's product-market matrix   52

Figure 2.5: McKinsey's 7S framework as a manifestation of structural and behavioral dynamics of strategy   54

Figure 2.6: Porterian revision of the structure-conduct-performance model   57

Figure 2.7: Porter's framework of generic strategies   60

Figure 2.8: Porter's five forces analysis   63

Figure 2.9: Value chain   64

Figure 2.10: Porter's four-corner analysis   66

Figure 2.11: Porterian strategy discourses as a biopolitical hierarchy of competitiveness   67

Figure 3.1: Neoclassical economics model of pricing   82

Figure 3.2: Accounting model of pricing   88

Figure 3.3: Market segmentation, targeting and positioning   92

Figure 3.4: Bases of market segmentation   94

Figure 3.5: Value propositions between product price and quality   97

Figure 3.6: Survival zone   106

Figure 3.7: Target costing triangle   107

Figure 3.8: Target costing process   109

Figure 4.1: Key elements of performance   127

Figure 4.2: Accountability hierarchy in responsibility accounting   129

Figure 4.3: Logic of responsibility accounting - a techno-managerial hierarchy of capital accumulation   133

Figure 4.4: Scorecards as a tool for strategic connections   138

Figure 4.5: BSC's redefinition of corporate performance in multiple dimensions   140

Figure 4.6: Processes and steps of implementing BSC: hierarchical cascading of BSC idea   142

Figure 4.7: Causalities presumed in BSC – mapping the strategic connections   144

Figure 5.1: Agency theory conception of optimum performance- compensation contracting   172

Figure 5.2: Cybernetic model of management control   176

Figure 5.3: Environment as a supra-system of external control   186

Figure 5.4: Simons' Levers of Control Framework   190

Figure 6.1: Processual and capability parameters of resilience   214

Figure 6.2: Phases and capabilities of resilience – consultancy modelling   226

Figure 6.3: Tensions and domains of organisational resilience   242

Figure 7.1: Traditional quality paradigm   266

Figure 7.2: Zero-defect and continuous improvement quality paradigms   271

Figure 7.3: Activity-based hierarchy of quality cost calculations   275

Figure 7.4: Assessing the cost efficacy of appraisal and preventive activities   279

Figure 7.5: An overview of Japanese quality-centric management   283

Figure 8.1: From traditional to flexible manufacturing business model   294

Figure 8.2: How flexible machines reduce EPQ   297

Figure 8.3: How Industry 4.0 technologies enable accounting in flexible manufacturing   308

Figure 8.4: Circulation and peripheralization of labor to enable flexible manufacturing   314

Figure 9.1: Standard costing and budgeting as cost management and profit planning   332

Figure 9.2: From ABC to ABM   347

Figure 9.3: Survival zone – how lean manufacturing doctrines are encapsulated in target costing   351

Figure 9.4: Target costing triangle – integrating three frontiers of decision-makers   352

Figure 9.5: Target costing process   354

Figure 9.6: Toyota's lean manufacturing system   356

Figure 9.7: Material requirements planning – accounting logic   358

Figure 9.8: ERP architecture   360

Figure 9.9: TOC and TA in action   363

Figure 10.1: Sustainability's Political Contradictions   377

Figure 10.2: Sustainabilizing strategy   387

Figure 10.3: Examples of corporate envisioning of sustainability   395

Figure 10.4: Environmental activity-based costing   409

Figure 10.5: WLC and LLC costs   412

CHAPTER 1
Strategic management accounting: emergence, definitions, and domains of operations

1.1 Introduction

This chapter delves into the origins, definitions, and operational aspects of strategic management accounting (SMA). It introduces fundamental concepts and themes that form the basis for critically exploring SMA. As you will discover later in this chapter, the rise of SMA is closely tied to extensive political-economic and techno-managerial changes that reshaped the management of our economic, political, and socio-cultural institutions. In exploring the contextual and epistemic reasons for SMA's emergence, these transformations can be broadly categorized as the neoliberalization of politics, globalization of markets and hierarchies, digitalization of technologies, and virtualization of spaces.

These political-economic, institutional, and techno-managerial shifts created a new set of competitive conditions. Economies underwent neoliberalization, leading to global, digital, and virtual markets, consumers, and firms. These altered competitive conditions necessitated significant changes in how we conceptualize and engage with markets, organize and manage organizational hierarchies, conduct operational activities, manage labor processes, and address various environmental dynamics and uncertainties. It is these innovative ways of conceptualizing and managing markets, organizational hierarchies, labor processes, and environmental dynamics that we now collectively refer to as strategy or strategizing.

Key point:

An initial definition of SMA to start with.

The calculative and rationalization techniques and practices that underpin these new management approaches for markets, hierarchies, labor processes, and environmental dynamics constitute what is now known as SMA.

This textbook critically examines the content and context of SMA. Its goal is to offer insights into the managerial frameworks, concepts, and techniques that make up SMA and explore their political-economic and institutional rationales and implications. To commence this critical exploration, this chapter:

Key point:

Chapter's key themes- context, definitions, differences, domains of strategic actions.

1. Clarifies the context in which SMA developed as a distinct field of study.
2. Provides a definition of SMA and highlights its differences from conventional management accounting.
3. Explores specific domains of action where strategies are implemented and facilitated.

The chapter is structured around three learning objectives:

Key point:

Learning objectives.

1. Explaining contextual conditions for SMA: This is covered in section 1.2, where the main goal is to understand the historical conditions that led to the emergence and evolution of SMA. I call this historical condition the "*strategic turn*", whereby we delve into how strategy discourses became integral to contemporary organizational management. The focus will be on two categories of factors behind the rise of strategy discourses: *contextual* and *epistemic* factors.
2. Defining and differentiating SMA: Explored in section 1.3, this objective involves exploring the concept of '*competitive conditions*', which is the foundational concept underpinning strategy formation and implementation. This discussion on competitive conditions leads to a broader definition of strategy and SMA. I also differentiate SMA from other forms of mainstream accounting, namely financial accounting and conventional management accounting. This differentiation will be extended to see how SMA must be redefined in relation to sustainability.
3. Explaining domains of strategic actions: Covered in section 1.4, this objective outlines the overall structure and logic of the textbook, relating to the key domains of strategic actions where strategies are both enabled and enacted.

1.2 The strategic turn

Since the early 1970s, there has been a widespread trend of labeling many aspects as strategic, marking a 'strategic turn' across numerous managerial disciplines. Examples encompass strategic management, strategic marketing, strategic human resource management, strategic operations management, strategic finance, and SMA. This shift is not limited to private-sector organizations but extends to public-sector and third-sector not-for-profit organizations, and all are urged to adopt a strategic approach. Consequently, these organizations actively strive to be strategic, incorporating strategic plans, strategic focus, strategic visions, strategic leadership, strategic control, and various other strategic elements.

Various aspects of strategy are frequently emphasized as critical to success, with success stories often attributing achievements to strategic thinking, strategic leadership, strategic planning and implementation, strategic control, and other strategic components. Conversely, corporate failures are often linked to firms and their managers not being sufficiently strategic. Investments are directed towards enhancing strategic thinking, strategic leadership, and strategic capabilities, with strategy consultants playing a crucial role. Strategy consultancy has evolved into a multi-billion dollar industry, with major accountancy firms taking a prominent role. Many books have been authored on being strategic in organizational processes and individual activities.

In essence, the concept of 'strategy' now encompasses techno-managerial, institutional, and political-economic elements that shape how we govern and manage our organizations. It has become ingrained in our culture as a taken-for-granted belief that strategies are essential for success. Strategy discourses are integral not only to the organization of economic enterprises but also to the management of socio-political and cultural institutions. This confluence of political-economic, cultural, and institutional significance in strategy discourses is what I call the 'strategic turn'. In simpler terms, the strategic turn represents the transformation—political-economic, techno-managerial, and institutional—that propelled various notions of strategy to the forefront in conceptualizing, analyzing, and managing contemporary economic, political, and socio-cultural institutions. The question then arises: what drives this strategic turn?

Key point:

Defining strategic turn.

Indeed, one can identify numerous factors contributing to this strategic turn. Yet, for analytical simplicity and clarity, I can categorize them into and discuss under three broad headings:

1. Contextual factors,
2. Epistemic factors, and
3. The sustainability agenda

Contextual factors

Contextual factors refer to global-scale political-economic, techno-managerial, and institutional dynamics that formed the basis for a new set of competitive conditions worldwide. These are the conditions that gave rise to global consumers, global markets, global firms, global brands, global supply chains, as well as global governance and regulatory structures. Through a multitude of techno-managerial and institutional changes, they created institutionally global, technologically digital, spatially virtual, and politically neoliberal competitive conditions. These contextual dynamics fall into four closely linked and somewhat overlapping categories:

1. Neoliberalization of politics,
2. Globalization of markets, hierarchies, governance, and regulations,
3. Digitalization of technologies, and
4. Virtualization of spaces.

Neoliberalization of politics

Before delving into neoliberalization and its impact on the emergence and popularization of strategy discourses, it's crucial to grasp the competitive conditions that existed prior to neoliberalization.

Preceding the onset of neoliberalization in the 1970s, the global economy differed significantly from its present form. Nation-states predominantly adhered to protectionist political-economic doctrines. Economies were relatively closed, and international free trade faced significant restrictions and regulations. Import/export duties and licensing systems were in place to govern global trade, aiming to safeguard domestic producers. Capital flows between nations were tightly controlled through foreign exchange mechanisms, and labor markets operated with stringent immigration controls. Essentially, the prevailing political-economic ideologies sought to shield the domestic sphere from global influences, viewing the global as a potential threat.

National economic policies were characterized by welfareism and state ownership. Public sector enterprises played a pivotal role in the economy, with major industries under nationalization and managed through centralized state planning and government bureaucracies. Extensive welfare budgets were allocated to direct nationalized industries and other state entities towards providing welfare services to the public.

During this period, markets were far from free; they were subject to heavy regulations and governed by political states and their agencies. Mechanisms such as subsidies, taxes, and direct or indirect state interventions controlled and influenced markets. Unlike today, the prevailing ideology did not view markets as the governing force for polity and society. Instead, markets were considered economic spaces to be regulated and governed by the state, sometimes even monopolized, for the benefit of the masses. In summary, nations before neoliberalization adhered to protectionism, were state-centric, focused on welfare, and heavily regulated by the state.

Key point:

Political-economic conditions before neoliberalization.

Neoliberalization refers to a shift away from liberal, state-centric welfareism, protectionism, and state regulation. With the endorsement of neoliberal economists like Milton Friedman, Friedrich Hayek, and Joseph Stiglitz, and backed by institutions like the World Bank, IMF, and OECD, the Reagan government in the US and the Thatcher government in the UK initiated a significant political change. This move veered away from protectionist, state-centric regulation and welfareism, a shift other nations quickly adopted. This resulted in global changes:

1. **Economic opening:** Facilitated by political institutional arrangements such as the European Union, economies were opened to facilitate the international movement of goods, services, capital, and labor.
2. **Privatization of industries:** Industries were privatized to minimize state involvement in economic activities. Multinational corporations became dominant globally, with their performance closely linked to capital market dynamics. Stock market performances became key indicators of corporate success.

> **Key point:**
>
> How neoliberalization changed competitive conditions.
>
> **Expand your understanding:**
>
> Read the encyclopedia entry - https://plato.stanford.edu/entries/neoliberalism/

3. **Managerial shift:** Bureaucratic administration focused on welfare was replaced by new managerial principles emphasizing shareholder value maximization and market competition. Even public and third-sector organizations adopted private-sector managerial doctrines like New Public Management (NPM), value creation, and value for money. Public administration underwent structural innovations and reforms to adopt a competition-based management regime.
4. **Ideological signification of markets:** Markets gained ideological prominence, becoming a dominant political institution governing cultural-political and economic activities. Neoliberal political doctrine advocates for markets to regulate everything, with the state's role limited to facilitating market-based governance. Neoliberalists believe that competition is the fundamental political principle, and whatever competition decides is deemed fair, just, efficient, effective, and legitimate. In accounting, this ideological transformation was evident in the standardization and institutionalization of fair value accounting.

In summary, neoliberalization represents a shift from state-centric welfareism to a private-capital-centric, market-based ideology and political governance. It replaces welfareism with market austerity to enhance the accumulation of private capital through competition.

Neoliberal connections of SMA

How did neoliberalization impact the strategic shift in management accounting? At this juncture, it's crucial to underscore a key proposition of strategy: *competition is the foundational condition that necessitates strategies, strategy discourses, and strategic calculations.* It's worth emphasizing that competition is the driving force behind the need for a strategic approach, and the type of competition dictates the strategies a firm should adopt.

> **Key point**
>
> the significance of competition in strategizing

The emergence of SMA is linked to the competitive conditions shaped by neoliberalism. The shift in politics to neoliberal principles introduced a new set of competitive conditions marked by open markets, multinational corporations, and the free and competitive flow of goods, services, capital, and labor across borders. This laid the political and ideological groundwork for the emergence of contemporary globalized competitive conditions, aptly termed 'neoliberal competitive conditions.'

These conditions necessitated a fresh set of calculations and rationalizations to manage markets, organizational hierarchies, and labor processes. Consequently, new tools emerged to analyze markets, assess performance, and manage operational processes. Examples include Michael Porter's five forces model, the value chain model, Boston Consultancy Group's growth-share matrix, activity-based costing and management (ABC/M), balanced scorecards, enterprise resource planning, target costing, lifecycle costing, and more. This collection of calculative and rationalization techniques constitutes SMA. In essence, *SMA is a phenomenon born out of neoliberal competitive conditions*.

Globalization of markets and organizational hierarchies

The second contextual factor influencing the strategic turn is the globalization of markets and organizational hierarchies. While the concept of neoliberalization, discussed in the previous section, illuminates the politico-ideological aspect of the strategic shift, globalization delves into its market, institutional, and managerial dimensions. Broadly speaking, globalization encompasses the rise of global markets, the integration of culturally diverse consumers and producers through global supply chains and marketing platforms, and the dominance of multinational firms and their global brands in the contemporary political-economic landscape.

Operational across global output, capital, and labor markets, organizational hierarchies have truly become globalized. While their headquarters are often situated in major cities like New York, London, Paris, Berlin, Tokyo, Seoul, and Beijing, their factories and call centers are dispersed across various locations. As a result, organizational hierarchies now reflect national and cultural differences, requiring management to adopt a cosmopolitan approach. Hence, globalization refers not only to the emergence of global markets but also to the rise and expansion of multinational firms and their cosmopolitan management across borders.

Likewise, globalization encompasses the establishment of a new set of regulatory and epistemic institutions. Regulation and governance have evolved beyond the confines of nation-states. The emergence of global markets, firms, brands, and supply chains necessitated a regulatory and governance regime extending beyond national boundaries. Consequently, a new set of regulatory institutions has emerged. Examples include not only political unions among nation-states like the European Union but also various industry-specific regulatory bodies

Key point:

SMA is a neoliberal phenomenon.

Expand your understanding:

Alawattage and Wickramasinghe's (2022) paper on "Strategizing management accounting: liberal origins and neoliberal trends" and their textbook (Alawattage and Wickramasinghe 2019) with the same title provide further insights into the neoliberal connections of SMA.

such as the Basel Committee on Banking Supervision, International Association of Insurance Fraud Agencies, the International Organization of Securities Commissions, and the Financial Action Task Force on Money Laundering. A set of global institutions for standardization and accreditation has also arisen, including the International Accounting Standards Board and the International Organization for Standardization. These entities were established to standardize, coordinate, monitor, and regulate global markets, firms, and supply chains.

Key point:

Globalisation encompasses market, institutional, managerial, and regulatory aspects of the strategic turn.

Globalization leads to SMA

How can we elucidate the relationship between globalization and the strategic shift in management accounting? Once again, it's crucial to reiterate the key principle regarding competition and strategy: competition is the fundamental condition that necessitates strategies and strategic calculations. Allow me to emphasize that being strategic is inherently linked to the nature of competition.

Globalization ushered in a new competitive landscape characterized by global markets, consumers, firms, brands, supply chains, and regulatory and governance frameworks. This globalized competitive environment necessitates coordinating, monitoring, and controlling organizational activities, processes, and outcomes across diverse and dispersed global sites of consumption, production, and exchange. Consequently, it calls for a new set of accounting practices, processes, calculations, and rationalizations, collectively forming SMA. Examples include cloud-based accounting, big data analytics, enterprise resource planning, and supply chain management systems.

Digitalization and virtualization of technologies and spaces

Key point:

SMA is necessitated to manage globalized markets, hierarchies, and regulations.

Over the past fifty years, we've experienced an unparalleled technological revolution. The rise of the World Wide Web, internet, emails, mobile computing, video conferencing, cloud computing, and big data analytics has shifted the world from *mechanical to digital*—from cogwheels to computer chips. This transformation has also moved us from *physical to virtual* and online realms.

These digital and virtual advancements have revolutionized how we engage in fundamental economic activities of consumption, production, exchange, saving, and investments. Computer-aided design and manufacturing, including technologies like 3D printing, have become standard, allowing flexible manufacturing and mass customization to dominate the industry.

Furthermore, the integration of digitalization and virtualization, particularly through the internet and cloud computing, has transformed marketplaces into platforms exemplified by giants like Amazon and eBay. Online transactions have become the primary mode of global trade, facilitated by services such as PayPal and Google Pay. The movement of products in global supply chains is now traceable in real-time, providing precise location information.

The internet has become a vast repository for transactions, events, and other activities, automatically recorded in mega databases like Google Analytics. Each mouse click is now trackable, offering insights and challenges for corporate managers analyzing consumer behavior.

Technology, competitive conditions and strategy

Returning to the notion of competitive conditions, the landscape has shifted with digitalization and virtualization. Competition is now virtual, digital, traceable, and analyzable online in real time. Big data analytics continuously reproduce customer and competitor profiles, making the complexities of competition visible on computer screens and dashboards. Managers can analyze and comprehend this intricate competition, allowing them to plan for different scenarios, albeit more complex than ever.

Key point:
SMA manifests an accounting response to the digitalisation and virtualization of technologies and spaces.

Digitalization and virtualization have given rise to a new set of accounting calculations providing real-time insights into market dynamics, consumer preferences, behavior, and competitive performance. These calculations, aggregated into industry averages, benchmarks, and league tables, serve as the foundation for what we now term SMA.

Contextual factors summary

The discussion so far highlights how neoliberalization, globalization, digitalization, and virtualization represent the contextual shifts driving the 'strategic turn'. Neoliberalization reflects the politico-ideological aspect, while globalization pertains to market and institutional dimensions. Digitalization and virtualization encapsulate the techno-managerial aspects.

These contextual changes have given rise to a new global order and a distinct set of competitive conditions: neoliberal, global, digital, and virtual. These contextual factors present an intricately interconnected and volatile context for current business operations, involving global consumers, firms, and regulatory institutions. In this evolving competition, the impact of any element is significant and widespread.

This shift in competitive conditions necessitated substantial changes in how we:

1. conceptualize and navigate markets,
2. manage and govern organizational hierarchies,
3. manage and control labor processes.

Key point:

An enrichment of the initial definition of strategy and SMA.

Emergent approaches to understanding and managing markets, hierarchies, and labor processes collectively form what we now refer to as strategy. The calculative and rationalization techniques and practices embedded in this strategic framework constitute what is now termed SMA.

Epistemic factors

The concept of 'episteme' or 'epistemic' pertains to how we come to know, understand, and interpret the world. Ideological doctrines, theories, concepts, models, standards, and scientific laws, and alike serve as the means through which we comprehend and assess the world around us. These elements shape our thinking, relationships, practices, behaviors, and their outcomes.

Pint in focus:

Management accounting is inherently epistemic and evolves within an epistemic context.

In management accounting, we find a similar reliance on theories, concepts, and models that influence our thinking and actions in organizational management. For instance, agency theory is often employed to explain management control issues in terms of agency and information asymmetry. Accounting standards and generally accepted accounting principles form the basis for how we account for and report organizational events and transactions. Concepts like fixed, variable, and marginal costs help determine break-even and profit-maximizing quantities and prices. Models such as balanced scorecards and activity-based costing have become popular frameworks for analyzing and managing organizational performance and costs.

These epistemic tools don't arise spontaneously; they gain acceptance as credible components of our knowledge through the support of powerful epistemic institutions. Accounting standards, for instance, owe their existence to the institutional infrastructure of the accountancy profession, where they are formulated, discussed, and eventually legalized. Similarly, management accounting innovations like balanced scorecards and activity-based costing, championed by figures like Robert S. Kaplan and his colleagues, gain prominence through their association with influential epistemic networks such as Harvard Business School and the consultancy firms they are affiliated with.

This implies two interconnected dimensions in the development of knowledge in any field:

1. Conceptual dimensions,
2. Institutional dimensions.

Epistemic factors – conceptual elements

The conceptual dimensions of the strategic turn involve the creation and widespread acceptance of various conceptual models, frameworks, and theories that form the foundation of SMA. In the upcoming chapters, you will delve into these developments in detail. Currently, I can broadly categorize these conceptual advancements into four domains:

1. **Strategic analysis of external environmental elements:** The first domain encompasses conceptual developments related to the strategic analysis of external factors. This includes industry analysis, market analysis, and competitor analysis. Numerous models have been introduced to analyze markets, industries, and the external environment. Examples include SWOT analysis, Michael Porter's five forces model, Boston Consultancy Group's Portfolio matrix, Michael Porter's four-corner analysis of competition, and Big Data analytics.
2. **Strategic analysis of organizational hierarchy and control apparatuses:** The second domain focuses on conceptual developments in the strategic analysis of organizational hierarchies and their control mechanisms. This has led to the introduction of new management control and performance management frameworks. Examples include balanced scorecards and Simon's Levers of Control framework.
3. **Calculative and analytical technologies for production systems and labor processes:** The third domain introduces a

Key point:

Four interrelated domains of SMA analyses.

plethora of calculative and analytical technologies for the strategic analysis of production systems and labor processes. This includes new costing and cost management techniques such as activity-based costing, activity-based management, throughput accounting, quality costing, flexible manufacturing, enterprise resource planning, target costing, and lifecycle costing.

4. **Accounting techniques related to sustainability:** Though still in early development, the fourth domain addresses the growing need for accounting techniques related to sustainability. Examples include carbon costing, reporting greenhouse gas emissions, and reporting on various social justice issues. These areas are gaining attention from accounting professionals and academics.

Management approach: from administration to strategy

As you will further explore in forthcoming chapters, these innovative conceptual frameworks have refined and transformed management approaches, shifting from administrative to strategic mindsets. The earlier-mentioned conceptual frameworks and tools have urged and empowered managers to recognise the neoliberal condition, asserting that competition is the fundamental doctrine of management. This doctrine serves as the basis for managerial actions and decisions.

Managers now possess a new toolkit to analyze and comprehend the competitive impact of their market activities, organizational hierarchies, and labor processes. These tools not only require but also empower managers to view every managerial situation as competitive, demanding strategic thinking and actions. The new conceptual frameworks and the calculations they incorporate establish competitive benchmarks, standards, averages, and narratives that shape our understanding of competition.

Key point:

SMA places competition at the core of managerial thinking, decisions, and actions.

Consequently, every organizational scenario is interpreted as a 'competitive situation' by linking it to these benchmarks, standards, averages, and narratives. Individual and collective performances are continuously scrutinized, compared, and evaluated competitively against them. This approach effectively introduces and sustains competition in all aspects of our organizational lives. Therefore, being strategic entails proficiency in using these new conceptual tools to confront and excel in competitive situations. Further discussions on these tools for conceptualizing competition will follow in upcoming chapters.

Epistemic factors – institutional elements

The term 'episteme' or 'epistemic' doesn't just involve concepts; it's equally tied to institutions. Knowledge is generated and sustained through specific institutions that hold sway over societies in particular historical periods. In pre-modern times, religious institutions like churches, temples, and mosques were the primary entities governing knowledge production and reproduction. However, in modern times, the institutional foundations of knowledge have significantly broadened, extending beyond religious institutions.

Poing in focus:
Epistemic is deeply intertwined with institutional structures.

In the contemporary era, a 'modern' set of institutions has taken the lead in producing, disseminating, and popularizing various forms of knowledge. These include educational establishments such as schools and universities, research institutions, professional associations in accountancy, law, engineering, and medicine, global governance institutions like the World Bank, the International Monetary Fund, the Organization for Economic Co-operation and Development (OECD), and the UN. State departments and institutions, mass and social media, consultancy firms, corporations like Google and Amazon, and market databases are also prominent players in this landscape.

Nevertheless, amid the recent surge and acceptance of strategy discourses, a noteworthy institutional development has emerged - the consultocracy. Unlike other institutional frameworks, the rise and expansion of the consultancy industry underscore the swift evolution of strategy discourses in the recent past.

The world before consultocracy

Consultocracy describes the recent emergence of a new class of intellectuals, namely consultants and management gurus, along with the specific epistemic structure they've established within contemporary organizations. To grasp its political and epistemic significance, it's crucial to contrast consultocracy with bureaucracy, the system that consultocracy has penetrated and influenced in instigating the strategic shift in management and management accounting.

Key point:
Bureaucracy predates consultocracy and establishes the legal-democratic foundations of governance and control within organisational hierarchies.

Bureaucracy became prevalent in societies during modernity, dating back to the Renaissance and the Industrial Revolution. It replaced pre-modern aristocratic systems. One fundamental doctrine of bureaucracy was that governing power should not be centered on individual charisma or traditional heritage. Instead, authority should be formally defined and attributed to specific positions in the organizational hierarchy. Bureaucracy depersonalizes power, aiming to create a governance system where actions adhere to a set of rules, laws, procedures, and codes defined by the system. Even in privately owned organizations within modern democracies, bureaucratic rules have a political link to the nation-state and the global state, adhering to legal enactments and political declarations imposed by the state on its citizens and corporations. Thus, bureaucratic rules ensure governance in line with constitutional and legal frameworks at the national and global levels.

Key point:

Bureaucracy is oriented towards regulation, control, and governance.

Another crucial aspect of bureaucratic governance is its focus on regulation and control, striving for stability, predictability, uniformity, and routinization of individual and collective actions to minimize potential risks and uncertainties. The expectation was that things should progress predictably and controllably. Administrators play a pivotal role in maintaining this uniformity, regularity, and controllability by adhering to bureaucratic rules, procedures, codes, and standards.

Key point:

Consultocracy criticises bureaucracy for its emphasis on control and regulation.

The strategic turn introduced an epistemic critique of the bureaucratic governance and control model. Consultants and management gurus critiqued bureaucracy, including its financial control mechanisms like budgeting, for being rigid, excessively control-oriented, and relatively resistant to change in response to the rapidly evolving competitive environment. Essentially, bureaucratic structures were faulted for their inability to swiftly adapt to the new competitive conditions brought about by neoliberalization, globalization, digitalization, and virtualization. Administrative approaches were criticized for prioritizing regulation, control, and governance through bureaucratic rules, standards, and procedures, thereby hindering adaptability, flexibility, and dynamism.

The growth of consultocracy

The 1970s and beyond marked an era of neoliberalization, ushering in a range of new concepts and ideologies to embrace rapid market-driven changes. Ideas like entrepreneurship, risk-taking, Japanization, learning organizations, continuous improvements, and business process reengineering became popular trends in the management lexicon. The traditional bureaucratic management style was considered inadequate for the new competitive conditions, organizational structures, and labor processes dictated by neoliberal and globalized dynamics.

In contrast to managers primarily focused on bureaucratic administration and control, a new generation of managers emerged, known by various titles such as change agents, business process reengineers, strategy consultants, risk champions, corporate entrepreneurs, intrapreneurs, strategic leaders, visionary managers, and more. Their roles were lauded for instigating change—bringing new strategic thinking, leadership, and implementation programs for continuous improvement and change management to organizations.

To replace bureaucracy, there was a search for new organizational structures, processes, and practices. The goal was to reinvent organizations to be flatter, leaner, more flexible, and adaptable. Terms like learning organizations, flexible organizations, flexible manufacturing, lean organizations, lean manufacturing, and business process reengineering became guiding principles for extensive change programs. Management gurus and consultancy firms played a dominant role in steering these transformations, giving rise to what we now call consultocracy. Consultocracy became a vital epistemic pillar in the neoliberal management landscape.

In this way, management gurus and consultancy firms emerged as crucial pillars in the epistemic structure of neoliberal management and governance systems. Figures like Michael E. Porter and Robert S. Kaplan became influential global intellectuals, and their ideas, concepts, and models were widely adopted in organizations worldwide. Consequently, consultancy evolved into a multi-trillion-dollar industry, with renowned firms like the Boston Consulting Group, McKinsey & Company, Bain & Company, and Deloitte Consulting, among others, reaching multi-billion-dollar status.

Their impact extended beyond the private sector, infiltrating public sector organizations globally. These consultancy giants now offer strategic vision, leadership, analyses, and change programs to organizations worldwide.

The ideas from these gurus and the influence of consultocracy seeped into the curricula of professional bodies and university programs in accounting and management, giving rise to a distinct field of study known as SMA. After all, perhaps ironically, this textbook is a culmination of these neoliberal epistemic developments, but it offers some critical insight into the content and context of SMA while making you aware of its managerial and technical core.

Key point:

Understanding how consultocracy became a dominant epistemic foundation in neoliberal management regimes.

Side note:

For a deeper exploration of the political-economic and strategic significance of the consulting industry, the following references are recommended: Kantola and Seeck (2011), McKenna (2006), United Nations (1993), and Werr and Stjernberg (2003).

Global sustainability agenda

The global sustainability agenda refers to a collective effort on an international scale to address and mitigate various environmental, social, and economic challenges to ensure a more ecologically and socially just and equitable future for the planet. Currently, this is characterized by UN sustainable development goals (UN SDGs). The global sustainability agenda has significant implications for management accounting, as organizations increasingly recognize the importance of integrating sustainability (often in the name of environmental, social, and governance (ESG) considerations) into their decision-making processes. Here are several ways in which the global sustainability agenda affects management accounting:

1. Reporting and disclosure: Management accountants are increasingly involved in the collection, measurement, and reporting of sustainability-related information. This includes data on carbon emissions, water usage, waste management, and social impact. Sustainability reporting standards, such as the Global Reporting Initiative (GRI) and the Sustainability Accounting Standards Board (SASB), guide organizations in disclosing relevant ESG information. Management accountants play a crucial role in aligning financial and sustainability reporting.

2. Performance measurement: Organizations are integrating sustainability metrics into their key performance indicators (KPIs). Management accountants are involved in developing and tracking these metrics to assess the organizational performance from a sustainability perspective. For example, developing sustainability-balanced scorecards that include sustainability indicators (in addition to the conventional financial and non-financial indicators) helps organizations evaluate their sustainability performance alongside traditional financial measures.

3. Costing and resource allocation: Sustainability initiatives often require investments in renewable energy, eco-friendly technologies, and social responsibility programs. Management accountants need to accurately allocate costs associated with these initiatives and assess their impact on overall profitability. For example, activity-based costing may be employed to understand the true costs of products and services,

Key point:

Some ways in which the global sustainability agenda affects SMA.

including their environmental and social costs. In effect, there is a greater need for management accounting techniques to internalize the costs that were traditionally considered 'externalities'.
4. **Risk management and resilience:** The global sustainability agenda introduces new risks related to climate change, supply chain disruptions, and reputational damage. Management accountants are involved in identifying, assessing, and mitigating these risks. For example, scenario analysis and stress testing may be used to evaluate the financial impact of various sustainability-related risks on the organization. You will delve into these aspects more in the forthcoming chapter on organizational resilience.
5. **Regulatory compliance:** Management accountants need to stay informed about evolving sustainability regulations and standards to ensure organizational compliance. This includes understanding the implications of regulatory changes on financial reporting and disclosure requirements.
6. **Incentive structures:** Management accountants are involved in designing incentive structures that align employee behavior with sustainability goals. This may include incorporating sustainability performance into bonus and compensation schemes.
7. **Supply chain management:** Sustainability considerations are increasingly important in supply chain management. Management accountants play a role in evaluating and improving the sustainability performance of suppliers, which can impact cost structures and overall supply chain resilience.
8. **Integration with strategic planning:** Sustainability is becoming a core component of strategic planning. Management accountants contribute by ensuring that sustainability goals are integrated into the overall business strategy and that the necessary financial resources are allocated.

In summary, the global sustainability agenda has transformed the role of management accounting by requiring organizations to consider and account for a broader set of factors beyond traditional financial metrics. This shift reflects a growing recognition that sustainable business practices are not only ethically responsible but also contribute to long-term financial success and resilience. As I will further discuss in the forthcoming chapters, strategizing management accounting now includes considering sustainability as a strategic priority and then developing specific calculative and rationalization techniques to plan, implement, monitor and control organizational activities towards sustainability goals. And it should be noted that this sustainability agenda encompasses the contextual and epistemic factors I mentioned above. Management accounting should now deal with sustainability as a strategic priority.

Strategic turn summary

This marks the conclusion of Section 1.2, and a summary will be beneficial at this point. The primary goal of this section was to comprehend the circumstances that led to the 'strategic turn' in management accounting. The 'strategic turn' encompasses broader political-economic, techno-managerial, and epistemic dynamics, forming the foundation for the emergence and widespread acceptance of strategy discourses. These dynamics fall into two main categories: contextual and epistemic.

Contextual factors pertain to global political-economic and techno-managerial transformations that created a new global competitive landscape. They are classified into three main headings: (a) neoliberalization of politics, (b) globalization of markets and hierarchies, and (c) digitalization of technologies and virtualization of spaces. These contextual factors materialize in three interconnected dimensions of the 'strategic turn': neoliberalization (politico-ideological), globalization (market and institutional), and digitalization/virtualization (techno-managerial and spatial).

On the other hand, epistemic factors involve conceptual and institutional advancements that introduced new theories, concepts, models, technologies, and practices related to strategic analyses of markets, firms, and operational processes. These developments are categorized into two sections:

1. Conceptual developments: encompassing new theories, concepts, models, and techniques that populate SMA.
2. Institutional developments: focusing on the emergence of consultocracy as a crucial pillar within the epistemic infrastructure of the neoliberal management and governance regime.

Extend your understanding:

Visit https://sdgs.un.org/goals to expand your understanding of UN SDGs.

The global sustainability agenda is the third element that underpins the contemporary evolution of management accounting, which has implications for how we manage markets, organizational hierarchies and labor processes.

For a visual representation of how the strategic turn is conceptualized in this chapter, refer to Figure 1.1.

Figure 1.1: The strategic turn

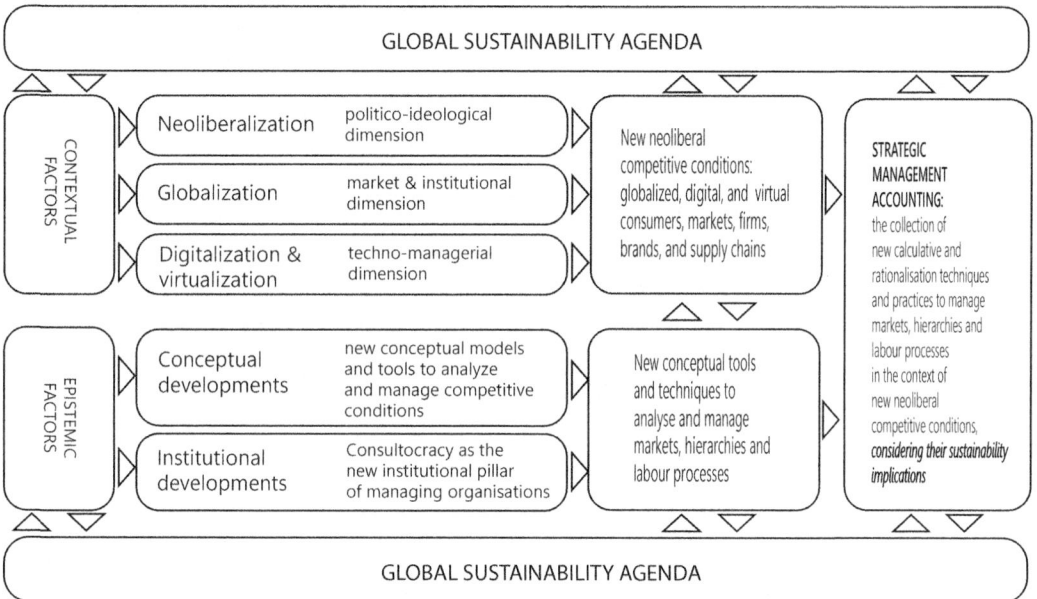

1.3 Definitions and differentiations

A meaningful definition of SMA should center on its primary focus: strategy. The concept of strategy distinguishes SMA from traditional management accounting. Strategy, or the act of being strategic, becomes imperative in response to competitive or wartime conditions. It is the exigencies of competition or war that necessitate strategic approaches. Therefore, it is crucial to delve deeper into this aspect, as a comprehensive understanding of the concepts of 'competitive conditions' forms the bedrock of strategy and SMA definitions. You will do that by first delving into the strategy discourses' military connections because military conceptions of strategy have always been a popular thread of interpreting strategy, even in the business contexts.

Strategy discourses: military connections

Side note:

Sun Tzu's Art of War is an ancient Chinese text supposedly written 5th century BC, and is considered one of the oldest and greatest texts on military strategies (see http://classics.mit.edu/Tzu/artwar.html). General von Clausewitz's "On War" is a European classic on military strategies, originally published in 1832.

Key point:

Different ways strategies can be seen and explained.

Before strategy gained popularity in the context of business management, it was primarily utilized in military sciences and campaigns. Timeless classics such as Master Sun Tzu's "Art of War" (see Tzu 2009 [circa 5th century BC]) and General Carl von Clausewitz's "On War" (see von Clausewitz 2007 [1832]) articulated strategic concepts in a military context. The shift towards neoliberalism in the 1970s and intense global competition led to markets being considered "battlefields," and strategic rhetoric and theories gained traction in the business press.

Whether in military sciences or business management, understanding and defining the concept of strategy should be in relation to the notions of 'competitive conditions', which can be markets, industries, or battlefields. In a broader sense, strategy is the approach people adopt to engage with a particular competitive condition, positioning themselves in the competitive terrain to gain an advantage over rivals. As Mintzberg (1987) elucidates, strategies may take the form of **plans**, exemplified by 'strategic plans,' or they may manifest as ploys, seen in 'game plans' or 'tactical plans.' These strategies can stem from rational and deliberate thought and discussions. Alternatively, strategies may be implicit and emergent, appearing as historically evolved **patterns of actions**—gradually developed and consistent approaches organizations adopt in navigating short and long-term competitive challenges. Strategies can also represent broader **perspectives** on competition and war. In any of these scenarios, strategy invariably revolves around '**positioning**'—how organizations plan, employ tactics, shape their actions, or cultivate a standpoint to position themselves and their resources in the competitive arena. The ultimate goal is to secure victory, sustain one's position, survive, avert losses, or achieve any other strategic objectives relevant to the competitive conditions they face.

However, **positioning** stands out as a central concept in defining and elucidating strategies. The concept of positioning is commonly interpreted in terms of engagement and deployment. For instance, as elucidated in the military classics of Sun Tzu and Carl von Clausewitz, strategizing involves deciding when, where, and how to deploy resources (such as commanding officers, military units, equipment, weapons, and diplomats) to interact (or abstain from interaction) with enemies, allies, and civilians. The role of the strategist (such as military generals, political leaders, and corporate leaders) is to determine how their resources should be gathered, organized, deployed, and engaged. To accomplish this, they employ epistemic devices (i.e., tools for knowing and understanding) such as satellites, binoculars, maps, scouts, spies, messengers, and even fortune tellers and crystal ball readers, as depicted in medieval war films illustrating warfare strategies.

Key point:

Positioning as the focal concept of strategy.

Therefore, *as a form of positioning, strategizing entails determining the time-space distribution of resources to achieve specific territorial, political, economic, or cultural-symbolic goals.* In military contexts, historical records from around the world often reveal that such strategic objectives frequently involved rather inhumane, immoral, and terrifying aims, such as the capture and ownership of land, the enslavement of people, the accumulation of wealth and power, and even the annihilation of particular groups through genocide. These alarming and dreadful aims are frequently intertwined and obscured, justified through rhetoric and propaganda proclaiming emancipation, freedom, and civilization. Nevertheless, essential takeaways from military definitions of strategy include:

1. Strategy as positioning involves time-space distribution, deployment, and engagement of resources, connecting strengths and weaknesses with opportunities and threats.
2. Strategizing requires epistemic tools for understanding the time-space nature of the competitive terrain, essentially "mapping the territory" for decision-making.
3. Strategic mapping involves actively defining the competitive terrain by associating it with enemies, allies, citizens, etc.
4. Strategizing encompasses determining ways to achieve specific short and long-term objectives in multiple dimensions of territorial, political, economic, or cultural-symbolic ends.

Strategy translated into business contexts

A parallel emerges when these militaristic conceptions of strategy are transposed into business contexts. Much like the military commanders referenced earlier, corporate strategy luminaries such as Michael Porter and Henry Mintzberg endorse the concept of positioning as a pivotal component of business strategies. This perspective is frequently elucidated through various strategic management tools like the BCG Growth-Share Matrix and the GE nine-cell matrix (to be explored in the subsequent chapter). The essence of strategizing lies in orchestrating and guiding a company's resources within a competitive terrain—aligning the firm's strengths and weaknesses with the opportunities presented and threats posed by prevailing competitive conditions.

Moreover, the concept of the competitive landscape assumes a central role in the business interpretation of strategy. Consequently, to perceive business strategy as positioning, one must initially grasp how the notion of competitive terrain is conceptualized in corporate strategy discourses.

Understanding the notion of competitive terrain

Markets or industries serve as the specific contexts within which competition is defined in both management and economics literature. Traditionally, particularly in neoclassical economic theory, the market is perceived as a structural determinant influencing a firm's conduct, particularly in determining prices and production quantities. Standard economic analyses categorize different competitive scenarios or 'market structures' based on variables such as the number of producers in a given market, the uniformity of the products offered, and the feasibility of free entry and exit, among others. Consequently, economists commonly classify a firm's competitive environment into four primary structural conditions: perfect competition, imperfect competition, oligopoly, and monopoly.

Key point:

How neo-classical economics conceptualise competitive conditions.

It is presupposed that these structural conditions dictate a firm's ability to establish prices and quantities. In perfect competition, firms are deemed mere "price takers," whereas, in other market conditions, firms possess varying degrees of monopolistic power to influence prices. The neoclassical economic models of market structures and firm behavior offer a somewhat reactive approach to strategy, where firms respond to market demand based on their marginal costs with the primary aim of maximizing profit. In this framework, strategy is simplified to the economic doctrine that a firm's prices and quantities should be determined by equating marginal cost to marginal revenue – deemed 'optimal decisions' because they ostensibly maximize the firm's profits.

This neoclassical economic thinking underpinned traditional management accounting calculations, primarily geared towards production optimization. It assumed that the competitive conditions, often reflected in demand forecasts, were a predetermined constraint. Subsequently, managerial decision parameters, such as production volume, capacity utilization, labor usage, and material usage, were subject to this demand constraint. Techniques such as budgeting, cost-volume-profit analysis, limiting factor analysis, and linear programming were employed to determine these parameters. Therefore, within conventional management accounting, strategies, at their zenith, have typically been operational or tactical, with a primary emphasis on enhancing operational efficiency.

This focus on operational efficiency stemmed from the perception that demand forecasts represent the competitive condition, and demand is deemed an uncontrollable or 'given' factor around which other operational parameters must be configured. Consequently, strategizing in conventional management accounting was narrowly conceptualized as achieving operational efficiency and effectiveness through these established methods of calculation and rationalization.

Epistemic dynamics associated with the 'strategic turn' discussed in the preceding section significantly altered the neoclassical economic perspective on competition in the 1980s and 1990s. Strategy experts like Michael Porter introduced novel conceptual frameworks and epistemic tools for analyzing and interpreting competitive conditions. Moving beyond the traditional neoclassical economic viewpoint on markets and competition, they embraced a more comprehensive systemic and territorial outlook.

In this new paradigm, competition was perceived not only as a structural aspect but also as a dynamic interplay of competitive forces, encompassing factors like inter-firm rivalry, the threat of new entrants, substitutes, bargaining power of buyers, and bargaining power of suppliers. Likewise, the concept of competition took on a territorial dimension, where markets and industries were analyzed and categorized into distinct segments based on factors such as consumer demographics, psychographics, competitor profiles, the profitability of each segment, and the degree of rivalry.

In essence, the understanding of competition, markets, and industries underwent a shift towards a pluralistic perspective, analyzed across multiple dimensions. This evolution gave rise to a new set of analytical tools, including big-data analytics and Porter's five forces model of industry analysis. These tools enabled managers to recognize the

Side note:

See to Porter (1996) for a critique of viewing strategy solely through the lens of operational effectiveness.

Key point:

Conventional economics and accounting offer a restricted definition of strategy, primarily centred on operational efficiency.

Key point:

The necessity of seeing competition as a complex pluralistic condition.

existence of a 'strategic context' for their decisions, emphasizing that these decisions must align with this context to be strategically viable and competitively advantageous. The strategic context, as revealed through these tools, encompasses both immediate competitive conditions and broader infrastructural and regulatory dynamics.

Figure 1.2 summarizes the key elements of a strategic context.

Figure 1.2: Key elements of the strategic context

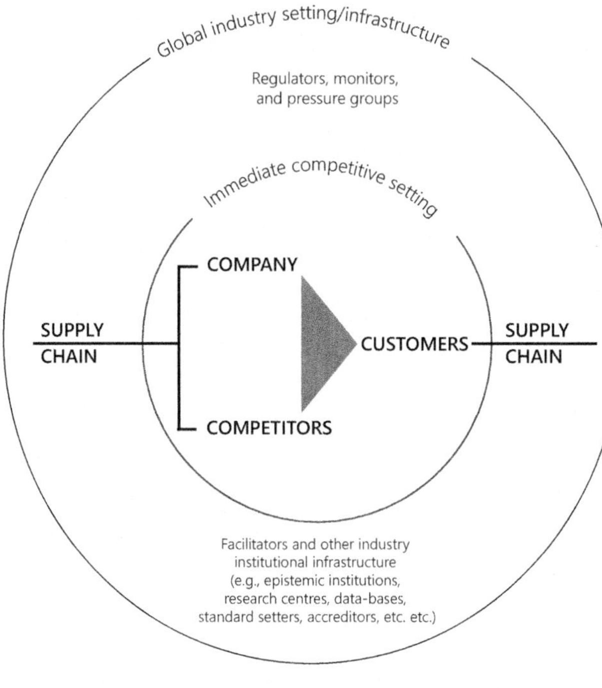

Key point:

Strategy is positioning within the competitive terrain to attain competitive advantages.

In traditional management accounting, operational decisions are primarily grounded in demand forecasts, linking them to prevailing market conditions. Consequently, the competitive landscape towards which operations are oriented becomes evident through these demand forecasts. In SMA, however, the approach shifts significantly. Competitive condition is no longer merely acknowledged through demand forecasts; competition should be meticulously profiled and mapped across various dimensions. Strategic maps, exemplified by tools such as the BCG growth-share matrix and sophisticated profiling techniques like big data analytics, now form the foundation for managers to make and rationalize their competitive positioning decisions. In this context, strategy entails a thoughtful and rationalized placement within a competitive landscape to secure a competitive advantage.

Furthermore, the identification of strategies by firms hinges on their conceptualization and understanding of the competitive terrain in which they operate. Therefore, it is crucial to emphasize that the transition from traditional management accounting to SMA is underscored by a profound change in how we conceptualize and analyze competition. In this context, strategizing revolves around decisions on strategically positioning oneself in a competitive terrain to achieve a competitive edge.

At this juncture, it would be beneficial to revisit the four pivotal points previously discussed regarding the military conception of strategies, examining how they translate into business contexts.

1. **Strategic positioning:** Strategy as positioning encompasses the temporal and spatial allocation, deployment, and utilization of resources. It entails aligning strengths and weaknesses with the opportunities presented and threats posed by competitive conditions. In the business context, this necessitates analyzing the market, industry, and the broader political-economic and institutional landscape in which the firm operates.
2. **Epistemic tools for strategizing:** Effective strategizing requires epistemic tools to comprehend and appreciate the temporal and spatial nature of the competitive terrain in which resources are deployed. Essential to this is mapping the territory when deciding on positioning. In a business context, this involves analyzing the market, industry, and the macro-political-economic and institutional context in which the firm operates.
3. **Strategic mapping:** Strategic mapping goes beyond perceiving the terrain as a passive space; it defines the 'competitive terrain' by associating it with the enemy, allies, citizens, and regulators. In a business context, this entails dynamic analyses of competitors, supply chain connections, customer or market profiling, and regulatory infrastructure. It also involves the discursive construction and reconstruction of the firm's competitors, allies, customers, and regulatory institutions.
4. **Setting objectives in multiple dimensions:** Strategizing entails defining specific short and long-term objectives across terri-

Key point:

Drawing parallels between militaristic strategies and their equivalence in the business realm.

torial, political, economic, or cultural-symbolic dimensions. In a business context, this involves establishing the corporate vision, mission, strategic goals, and a broader spectrum of operational objectives, including key performance indicators (KPIs). Normative elements of strategizing should pluralistically encompass various dimensions, such as financial perspectives, customer perspectives, internal business processes, and learning and growth, as illustrated in models like Johnson and Kaplan's balanced scorecards. Additionally, these normative elements should incorporate eco-justice and eco-efficiency dimensions of sustainability.

Defining and differentiating SMA

Key point:

SMA definition further enhanced.

In terms of the discussion thus far, *SMA can be defined as an ever-evolving set of calculative, analytical, and rationalization techniques and practices employed to analyze competitive conditions, enabling the definition, decision-making, implementation, and control of strategies in four interconnected domains of strategic actions: the market, the point of production, the organizational hierarchy, and the social and environmental aspects.* This definition encapsulates several critical points about SMA:

1. **Dynamic field of study:** SMA is dynamic, with its techniques and practices evolving in response to the analytical demands imposed by changing competitive conditions. As competitive conditions dictate the strategic analyses a firm should conduct and the strategies it should pursue, the techniques within SMA are subject to continual adaptation.

2. **Analytical focus:** The primary analytical focus of SMA is to understand and comprehend the competitive conditions faced by a strategic entity (e.g., a nation, firm, division, or product). Regardless of the techniques employed, SMA's central aim is to appreciate the time-space nature of the terrain in which the strategic entity's resources are deployed. It essentially involves mapping the territory to determine strategic positioning.

3. **Comprehensive strategic mapping:** Strategic analysis or mapping goes beyond perceiving the competitive terrain as a passive space. Instead, it defines competitive conditions by associating the terrain with potential actions and reactions of competitors, suppliers, customers, and other relevant par-

ties that constitute the competitive landscape (refer to Figure 1.2).
4. **Strategy as positioning:** Strategy as positioning entails the distribution, deployment, and engagement of resources in the most appropriate segments of the competitive terrain. It also involves building an entity's capacity and competence to position itself advantageously. SMA should empower managers to decide on the most suitable positioning of the firm's resources and enhance its capacity and competence for achieving strategic positioning that ensures competitive advantage.
5. **Strategic pluralism and uncertainties:** Strategizing involves determining specific short and long-term objectives across various dimensions, such as territorial, political, economic, or cultural-symbolic ends. Hence, SMA techniques should address strategic uncertainties and the pluralistic nature of strategic goals and objectives.
6. **Domains of strategic actions:** Strategies are enacted and enabled in four interrelated domains of strategic actions: markets, points of production, organizational hierarchies, and social and environmental arenas.

To better understand SMA, one can compare it with conventional management accounting and financial accounting. Table 1.1 provides this comparison, including an additional column for "sustainability-driven SMA," which is the thematic focus of the next section.

1.4 Sustainablizing strategy

Preceding discussions primarily centered around concepts of market competition and positioning. Despite occasional references, there has been a notable lack of substantive attention to sustainability issues—an indispensable dimension that contemporary organizations must earnestly incorporate into their strategic formulations.

When situating strategy within the context of sustainability discourses, it becomes imperative to acknowledge ontologically fundamental contradictions extending beyond mere market competition. Accordingly, four foundational structural categories must be considered—economy, polity, society, and ecology. These forces are inherently contradictory, illustrating that economic pursuits geared towards profit maximization can frequently compromise our shared world's social, political, and ecological dimensions. In essence, strategic decisions

Key point:

Fundamental contradictions that a sustainable organisation has to deal with.

Table 1.1: Differentiating SMA

	Financial Accounting	Management Accounting	SMA	Sustainability driven SMA
What do you analyse?	Financially measurable past events and transactions	Financial impacts of various operational decisions, analysing their costs, revenues, contributions, risks, etc.	Competitive conditions that the firm is facing and will be facing in the future.	In addition to economic conditions that the firm has to deal with, political, social and ecological justice issues.
What is your analytical focus/aim?	**Financial reporting:** Providing a fair and faithful representation of outcomes of the company's financial events and transactions for the accounting period. Assessing aggregate impacts of financial events and transactions of the accounting period on: • Net income • Financial position • Cash flows	**Operational optimization:** Analysing possible outcomes of operational decisions to be made, i.e. to assess financial impacts and risks associated with short-term *operational decisions* on resource allocations. Assessing current values of future cash flows arising from capital investments.	**Strategic positioning:** Determining strategic perspectives and positions that the firm should take amid the current or future competition, i.e. to determine companies long-term vision and mission. Determining *appropriate strategic moves or positions* the company should adopt in its competitive conditions. Developing and deploying appropriate strategic performance and control measures to ensure the company's strategic intentions are achieved as planned.	**Sustainabilizing strategic position.** Considering sustainability as a critical element of strategic positioning. Incorporating ecological and social justice issues into the company's long-term vision and mission. Integrating Integrating sustainability issues into the operational and strategic performance management and control systems.
Where does the data for analysis come from?	Companies accounting system – transaction processing system. Internal data.	Company's accounting system and other operational data systems (e.g. production and marketing). Primarily internal data or internal looking data: standard costing; budgeting; production planning and engineering worksheets; supplier information, and so on.	Internal data as well as external data stemming from databases, big data analytics, market surveys, consultancy and other forms of 'research', own surveys and research, brainstorming sessions, and consultants. Industry forums and reports, epistemic institutions And also the experiences, intuition and opinions of experts and corporate leaders.	Expanding and enhancing analytical techniques and data sources to understand and explain the sustainability implications of the firm's strategies and actions. UN SDGs and other related global sustainability information.

	Financial Accounting	Management Accounting	SMA	Sustainability driven SMA
What are the typical or popular tools of analysis?	Financial statements. Ratio analysis Comparative financial statement analysis Cash flow analysis Debt analysis (debt age analysis).	Budgeting Standard costing and variance analysis Marginal costing and cost-volume-profit analysis Contribution analysis, including limiting factor analysis and linear programming Discounted cash flows	Five forces model of industry analysis. Swot analysis. Four corner analysis of competitors Market segment analysis Value chain analysis Supply chain management Quality costing. Big data analytics. Activity-based costing and activity-based management. Balanced scorecards. Levers of control analysis.	Carbon costing. Ecosystem analysis. Ecological footprint analysis. UN SDG compliance analysis. GRI compliance analysis. Compliance with related environmental and social laws, including Modern Slavery Acts.
Who is involved in the analysis and decision-making?	Financial accountants and auditors	Management accountants and other operational managers	Plural multidisciplinary forums often consisting of internal and external parties. Strategy groups, special task forces, and steering committees.	Plural multidisciplinary forums often consisting of internal and external parties, including sustainability experts. Strategy groups, special task forces and steering committees.
Where do the analytical principles, rules, and wisdom come from?	Accounting standards and GAAPs, auditing standards and principles. Company law and other related legal provisions	Neoclassical economics, especially microeconomic theory of the firm, statistics and mathematics. Industrial engineering. Organisational sciences.	Strategic management, technology fields such as big data analytics, marketing, organisational studies, Industry-specific expertise Regulatory bodies and other epistemic institutions, including consultancy.	Environmental sciences. UN SDGs. Global Reporting Initiative.
To whom are the accounts provided?	Mainly to the shareholders	Operational managers	Top management and other parties involved in the strategic decision-making and implementation processes.	Top management and other parties involved in strategic decision-making and implementation processes. Wider stakeholder groups.
What is the time orientation of the analyses?	Past	Current and short-term future or predictable future for capital investment decisions.	Long-term uncertain and competitive future as well as short-term strategic scenarios.	Long-term future in terms of ecological and social conditions to which the firm contributes positively or negatively.

within economic domains such as markets, organizational hierarchy, and production points can have diverse implications for political, social, and ecological justice issues currently grappling with the contemporary world. This encompasses concerns such as carbon emissions, global warming, gender disparities, ethnic and racial discrimination, and modern slavery, among various others, with which companies are compelled to engage actively. Frameworks like the United Nations Sustainable Development Goals (UN SDGs) and sustainability reporting protocols outlined by the Global Reporting Initiative (GRI) encapsulate some of these critical issues that companies must meticulously consider while formulating their market, production, and operational strategies.

The crux of the matter lies in the imperative for contemporary strategic considerations to encompass a more expansive array of factors beyond those traditionally emphasized in classical strategy discourses (as explored in previous sections). In this context, strategic planning must transcend the confines of mere market positioning for competitive advantage. Instead, it should be perceived as an endeavor to forge sustainable connections between the economy, polity, society, and ecology, guided by the decisions made regarding our operations in markets, organizational hierarchies, and labor processes. In light of the imperative for sustainability, one might redefine *SMA as an ever-evolving suite of calculative and analytical techniques and practices oriented towards conceptualizing and evaluating an organization's competitive and contradictory conditions in enabling and enacting strategies within the realms of markets, organizational hierarchies and labor processes with the aim of not only competitive positioning for a competitive advantage but also addressing broader ecological and social justice issues.*

Key point:

Further enhancement of SMA definition to capture sustainability.

This sustainability-based reconception of strategy is illustrated in 1.3.

1.5 Strategizing domains and the book's structure

The ongoing discussion in this chapter has led us to identify several critical aspects of strategizing:

1. **Competitive conditions:** This is the foundation upon which strategies are conceived and executed.
2. **Competitive advantage:** The ability to surpass competitors in

Figure 1.3: Sustainablizing strategy

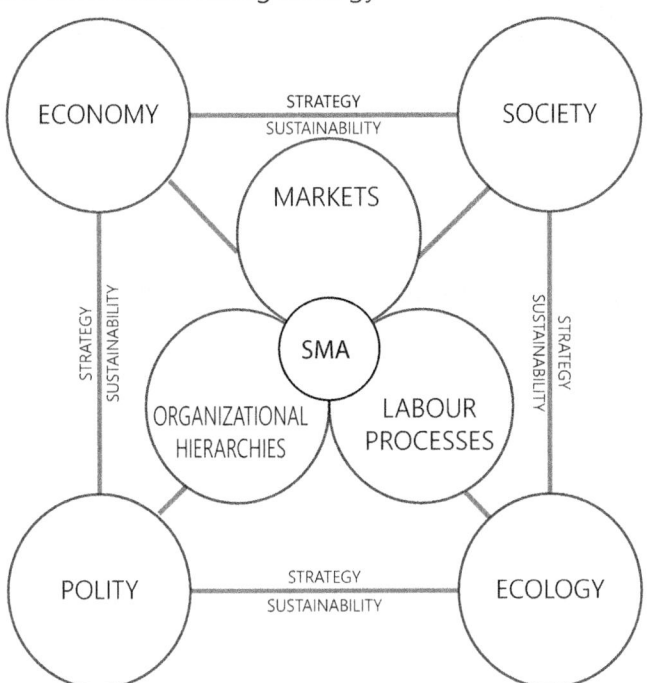

the market, achieved through a distinctive strategic positioning that the company actively pursues. The ultimate goal of strategizing is to attain a sustainable competitive advantage.
3. Positioning: This encompasses an overarching plan/ploy, perspective, and a coherent pattern of action and thinking that a firm adopts to secure a specific competitive position and advantage.
4. Rationalizations/calculations: These involve analyses, calculations, and rationalizations essential for comprehending, appreciating, and responding to competition. The frameworks, techniques, and processes employed in such analyses, calculations, and rationalizations collectively constitute SMA.
5. Ecological and social justice: In the contemporary business landscape, effective strategizing requires attention to broader social and ecological justice issues that characterize the modern world. This involves considering aspects such as the UN SDGs and reporting protocols of GRI.

Key point:

Key elements of strategizing.

These five crucial elements can significantly bolster a company's ability to compete in the market by reshaping and reconfiguring its structures, relationships, processes, practices, and outcomes. Strategizing entails reinvention and reconfiguration of a firm's internal conditions and results to align with external competitive conditions and environmental demands. Essentially, strategizing is an ongoing effort to keep pace with the ever-evolving competitive landscape – a continual endeavor to establish and sustain a viable alignment between the demands posed by competition and the company's capacity to meet those demands. As depicted in Figure 1.3, this underscores the imperative of establishing and sustaining a viable and enduring alignment across various domains of strategic actions. Strategizing occurs within these interdependent domains of strategic action.

Key point:

Domains of strategic actions.

1. **Strategizing the market:** In this realm, the company engages in strategic positioning through the implementation of pricing and other marketing strategies.
2. **Strategizing the labor process (or Value Chain):** This domain of strategic action requires the company to ensure that its productive system, the value chain, can generate and deliver the strategic positioning it aims to achieve in the market.
3. **Strategizing the organizational hierarchy:** Within this sphere of strategic action, the company transforms its organizational hierarchy, control systems, and performance management to establish and maintain essential strategic connections between the market and its operations/labor processes. This also involves enhancing and maintaining the capabilities of being resilient in adverse conditions.
4. **Strategizing the social and environmental:** This domain encompasses strategic decisions and actions where the company can contribute to the global sustainability agenda. This involves addressing ecological and social justice issues outlined in the UN SDGs.

In a wider context, this entails formulating strategies for the company's production, management control systems, marketing activities, and sustainability agenda. The structural framework of this textbook underscores the interconnectedness of these four areas of strategic action. As depicted in Figure 1.4, the book delves into nine topics associated with these strategic domains across nine chapters (in addition to the content discussed in this chapter).

Figure 1.4: Structural logic of the course

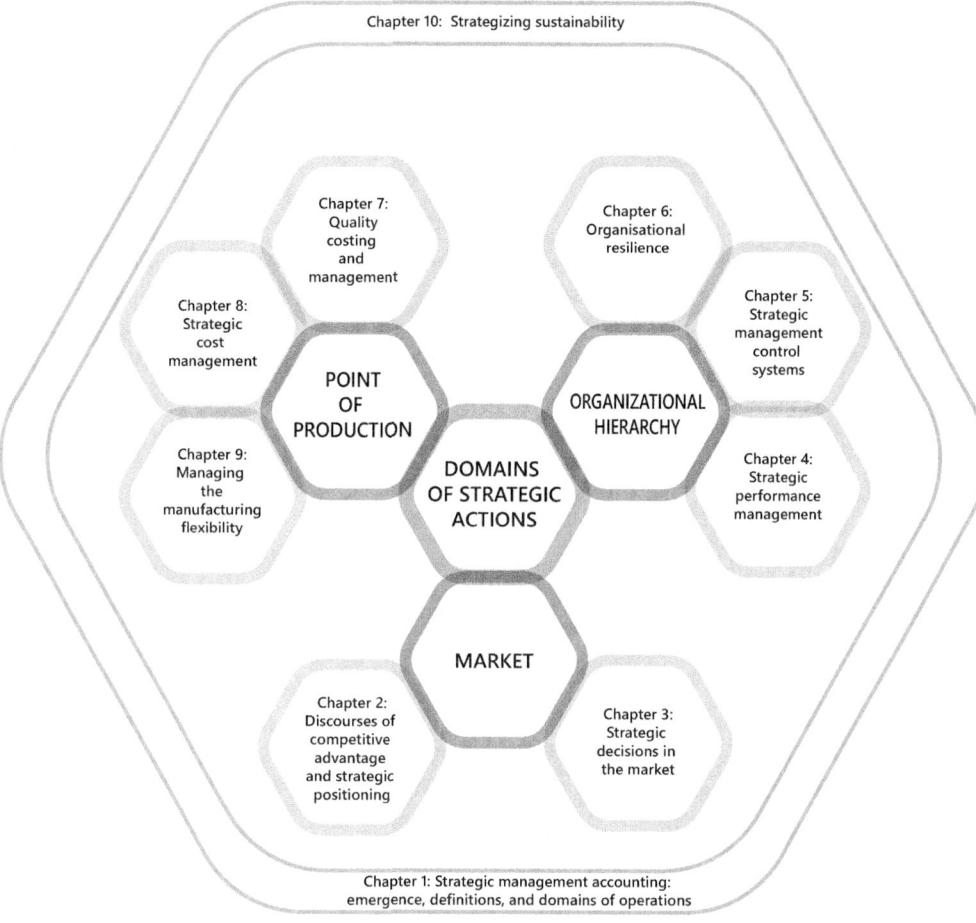

1. Chapter 1: Strategic management accounting - emergence, definitions, and domains of operations

    In this chapter, as you have already gone through, we delved into the contextual conditions that underpin the emergence of SMA and the foundational concepts that constitute and differentiate SMA from other branches of accounting.

2. Chapter 2: Reconceptualizing competition - discourses of competitive advantage and strategic positioning

    This chapter explores how strategy discourses, including Michael E. Porter's discussions on strategy, provide new conceptual bases for understanding and managing contemporary organizations. This chapter will trace the evolution of strategy concepts from Alfred Chandler to Michael Porter and beyond, laying the conceptual foundation for subsequent chapters on strategizing in the market, organizational hierarchy, and the factory.

3. Chapter 3: Strategizing the market - Strategic pricing decisions

    This chapter delves beyond conventional accounting and economic paradigms and discusses how contemporary competitive conditions and analytical tools complicate pricing decisions. Special attention is given to marketing elements underpinning strategic pricing decisions, including market segmentation, targeting, positioning, and specific pricing techniques such as target costing and lifecycle costing.

4. Chapter 4: Strategizing the hierarchy - Strategic performance management

    Focusing on Johnson and Kaplan's Balanced Scorecard (BSC) discourses, this chapter explores the new strategic focus BSC brought to performance management. This chapter will discuss the competitive conditions necessitating the multidimensional conception of performance and how BSC provided a conceptual framework linking performance management with strategy. Additionally, Kaplan and colleagues' recent attempts at reimagining the BSC for sustainability are explored.

5. Chapter 5: Strategizing the hierarchy - Strategic management control

    This chapter centers on management control systems, particularly Simons' Levers of Control (LOC) framework, offering a strategy-based conception of management control systems. It will discuss specific competitive conditions or strategic imperatives that require a new strategic perspective on management controls.

6. Chapter 6: Strategizing the hierarchy - organizational resilience

    Extending the strategic control theme from Chapter 5, this chapter explores how the concept of 'organizational resilience' has entered the management control lexicon as a strategic imperative, especially during and after the COVID-19 pandemic and recent financial crises.

7. Chapter 7: Strategizing the point of production - quality management and costing

    Corporate managers must address three strategic imperatives when strategizing labor processes and the factory floor: quality, flexibility, and cost. This chapter focuses on the first imperative – quality costing and management – examining how various strategic notions penetrate the operational elements of managing the labor process to deliver quality.

8. Chapter 8: Strategizing the point of production - managing flexibility

    This chapter explores the strategic imperative of flexibility, discussing various micro-organizational and macro-political elements of manufacturing flexibility.

9. Chapter 9: Strategizing the point of production - strategic cost management

    Exploring the strategic imperative of managing costs, this chapter focuses on both intra-organizational techniques and processes of cost management and extra-organizational arrangements for managing costs across supply chains.

10. Chapter 10: Strategizing sustainability

    Sustainability has become a critical strategic intent in contemporary organizations. This chapter examines how the global sustainability agenda has affected management accounting, especially its performance management and control systems. Special attention is given to contemporary ESG (environment, social, and governance) discourses.

Chapter Summary

This chapter provided an introduction to SMA and was structured around three primary elements. Firstly, it elucidated the contextual and epistemological backdrop in which the strategic turn' unfolded. Concerning contextual dynamics, three principal global political-economic and techno-managerial trajectories underpinned the strategic shift: (a) the neoliberalization of politics, (b) the globalization of markets and hierarchies, and (c) the digitalization and virtualization of technologies and spaces. Regarding epistemological dynamics, the chapter explored the interplay between the strategic turn and a new set of institutional and conceptual developments. These encompass various conceptual models of strategy and institutional phenomena, such as consultocracy and the emergence of management gurus.

The second section of this chapter delved into basic definitions, distinguishing SMA from other forms of accounting. To grasp the essence of strategy, central to SMA, attention was first given to how strategy is defined and conceptualized in military contexts. Drawing insights from military strategy, the understanding emerges that strategy entails positioning in conditions resembling warfare competition: the temporal-spatial distribution, deployment, and engagement of resources with key actors and factors defining the competitive terrain. Consequently, strategic analyses involve mapping the competitive terrain to ascertain optimal approaches for distributing, deploying, and engaging resources. This military perspective on strategies is then applied to business contexts, introducing a spatial and time-based conception of the market and industry. Crucially, the nature of competitive conditions shapes strategic analyses and choices.

Key to strategic analyses are the notions of competitive or contradictory conditions and competitive positioning. Consequently, SMA is characterized as an ever-evolving set of calculative and analytical techniques and practices aimed at conceptualizing and evaluating the competitive and contradictory conditions faced by a firm and its strategic units. Accordingly, SMA guides decisions on the strategies they should pursue in relation to market competition, as well as broader ecological and social justice issues. Distinctions from conventional management accounting and financial accounting were highlighted on multiple dimensions.

In conclusion, four interconnected and interdependent domains of strategic actions were identified: markets, organizational hierarchies, labor processes, and the social and environmental spheres. The essence of strategizing lies in establishing a sustainable alignment between actions and outcomes across all these domains.

Test and revise your knowledge

These questions assess your comprehension of key concepts and elements discussed in the chapter:

1. What is meant by the term 'strategic turn'? Provide a brief explanation.
2. Populate the table below with the factors underpinning the 'strategic turn.'

Factors underlying the strategic turn		Meaning of the subcategory	Collectively how did they lead to the evolution of SMA
Major categories	Subcategories		

3. Provide a brief explanation of military connections in conceptualizing business strategies.
4. Compare and briefly explain how the concept of 'competitive terrain' is conceptualized in military and business contexts.
5. Define what is meant by strategy in relation to the idea of 'competitive terrain.'
6. Characterize and differentiate SMA from conventional management accounting based on the following dimensions:
   a. What is analyzed?
   b. What is the analytical focus/aim?
   c. Where does the data for analysis come from?
   d. What are the typical or popular tools of analysis?
   e. Who is involved in the analysis and decision-making?
   f. Where do the analytical principles, rules, and wisdom come from?
   g. To whom are the accounts provided?
   h. What is the time orientation of the analyses?
7. Briefly explain how sustainability-driven SMA may reconfigure these dimensions.
8. Enumerate fundamental contradictions that 'sustainable strategic management' must address.

9. Populate the table below in relation to the domains in which strategies are enabled and enacted.

Domains of strategic action	Strategic imperatives to deal with

Explore further

1. To familiarize yourself with sustainability issues, visit the United Nations Sustainable Development Goals website (https://sdgs.un.org/goals) and reflect on why the UN had to develop such an extensive framework to address sustainability issues on a global scale. Consider how far conventional management accounting and emerging strategy discourses might have contributed to creating contemporary 'unsustainable' methods of managing economic enterprises.

   Develop some brief notes on these issues for a classroom discussion forum.

2. The International Federation of Accountants (IFAC) issued a statement titled "Accounting for Sustainability: From Sustainability to Business Resilience." In introducing this document, the IFAC declares that it "clarifies the important role accountants can, and must, play in embracing sustainability to ensure that the organizations they serve are resilient by linking sustainability to a broader business agenda and strategy." The document begins with a visionary statement that "accountants will save the world."

   Download this document from the IFAC site (www.ifac.org).

   Critically think about the ways in which management accounting, as a practice and body of knowledge, should change to help "save the world." Do you think the parameters this document sets will be sufficient for "accountants saving the world"?

Develop your critical argumentation skills

1. Write an argumentative essay on the following theme:

   "The emergence of SMA is due to a set of interconnected political-economic, institutional, techno-managerial, and epistemic dynamics, all of which, one way or another, created new competitive and contradictory conditions in which 'strategizing' became a necessity."

2. Write an argumentative essay on the following theme:

   "Strategy discourses encapsulate a militaristic reconception of competition where time-space distribution, positioning, and deployment of resources to engage with enemies and allies are considered strategy."

References

Alawattage, C., and D. Wickramasinghe. 2019. Strategizing management accounting: liberal origins and neoliberal trends. London: Routledge.

———. 2022. Strategizing Management accounting: liberal origins and neoliberal trends. Accounting, Auditing & Accountability Journal 35 (2):518-546.

Kantola, A., and H. Seeck. 2011. Dissemination of management into politics: Michael Porter and the political uses of management consulting. Management Learning 42 (1):25-47.

McKenna, C. D. 2006. The World's Newest Profession: Management Consulting in the Twentieth Century: Cambridge University Press.

Mintzberg, H. 1987. The strategy concept I: five Ps for strategy. California Management Review 30 (1):11-24.

Porter, M. E. 1996. What is strategy? Harvard Business Review 1996 (November-December):61-78.

Tzu, S. 2009 [circa 5th century BC]. The art of war [translated by Lionel Giles]. Translated by L. Giles. www.PaxLibrorum.com: Pax Librorum Publishing House.

United Nations. Management consulting: a survey of the industry and its largest firms. United Nations 1993 [cited. Available from https://books.google.co.uk/books?id=81C1AAAAIAAJ.

von Clausewitz, C. 2007 [1832]. On war. Translated by M. Howard and P. Paret. Oxford: Oxford University Press.

Werr, A., and T. Stjernberg. 2003. Exploring M=management consulting firms as knowledge systems. Organisation Studies 24 (6):881-908.

CHAPTER 2
Reconceptualizing competition: **discourses of competitive advantage and strategic positioning**

2.1. Introduction

The preceding chapter highlighted that competition is the driving force underpinning and necessitating strategies and strategy discourses. We elucidated how global competitive conditions underwent a transformation due to a set of broader contextual and epistemic factors, thereby perpetuating the imperative nature of strategies and strategic discourses as a central pillar in the management of contemporary organizations. Additionally, we noted that the concept of strategy boasts a lengthy history in military science and war histories. This 'militaristic' conceptualization of strategy has been transposed into business management, facilitating the reimagining of industries and markets as competitive arenas.

Key point:

A reminder of the strategic turn.

We comprehend that the formulation of strategic management accounting is an outcome of this reimagining of markets and industries as strategic arenas, wherein firms must adopt a 'strategic' approach to thrive. Furthermore, we explored how broader social and ecological sustainability issues have permeated the realm of strategic considerations.

In this chapter, the overarching aim is to explore the evolution of discourses surrounding business strategy within the context of SMA over the past five decades or so. We observe two interconnected discourses at play. The first pertains to strategy discourses associated with business management disciplines, encompassing organizational theory, marketing, operations management, and strategic manage-

> **Key point:**
>
> SMA encapsulates the accounting elements of the convergence of two forms of strategy discourses: organisational study strategy discourses and industrial economics strategy discourses.

ment. The second involves strategy discourses that originated from industrial economics, particularly those linked with Alfred Chandler and Michael Porter. Essentially, contemporary strategy discourses amalgamate these two schools of thought. SMA seeks to capture the calculative or accounting elements arising from this convergence.

This chapter delves into various strategy concepts and tools introduced by these interconnected discourses. Specifically, it focuses on essential concepts and tools such as generic strategies, corporate planning, portfolio planning, and industry analysis. It also explores the specific political-economic and institutional conditions necessitating the use of these concepts and tools. Accordingly, the chapter establishes the following learning objectives:

1. Explain the different ways competition and strategy are conceptualized in classical business policy and corporate planning models.
2. Explain how Porterian discourses of strategy have transformed our understanding and approach to concepts of competition and strategy.
3. Explain the various modes of calculation and rationalization introduced by these strategy discourses.
4. Explain how emerging sustainability discourses implicate these conceptions.

> **Key point:**
>
> Structure of the chapter and key themes of learning.

The chapter is structured around these learning objectives. Section 2.2 explores how strategy is conceived in business policy and corporate planning, discussing strategy concepts and frameworks such as SWOT analysis, portfolio planning models, long-term goal setting, and strategic diversification. Section 2.3 forms the core of this chapter and focuses on learning objectives 2 and 3. It examines how Porterian discourses have redefined the notions of competitiveness and strategy, signifying them simultaneously as macro-level political-economic and organizational-level managerial problems. This section also directs attention to a set of Porterian concepts and frameworks of strategic analysis, including competitive advantage, generic strategies, the five forces model of industry analysis, the four-corner model of competitor analysis, and value chain analysis. Finally, as a concluding remark, section 2.4 discusses the modes of calculation and rationalization that such strategic discourses have popularized in managing contemporary organizations.

2.2. From management to strategic management: organizational discourses of strategy

The rise of modern management can be traced back to the emergence of two institutional apparatuses of production during modern times, particularly during the Industrial Revolution: the creation of the 'factory' and the 'corporation'. These two elements provided institutional impetus for the development of modern management, notably the so-called 'scientific management'. Initially, modern management centered around the organization and rationalization of labor processes into mechanized large-scale mass production.

In its early developmental phase, the evolution of 'scientific management' primarily revolved around a series of inventions attributed to Frederick W. Taylor and other industrial engineers of that era. During this initial period of shaping modern management, their focus was on the rationalization and systematization of labor processes. A labor process is the specific "set of relations into which men and women enter as they confront nature, as they transform raw materials into objects of their imagination" (Burawoy 1979, 15). In simpler terms, these are the relations in production through which a particular product or service is produced and constitute the point of production. They include techno-managerial and social relationships between men and women as co-workers and supervisors. They also encompass relationships between workers and the tools they use to carry out their work activities, comprising not only physical elements like tools, machinery, and raw materials but also conceptual aspects such as rules, procedures, standards, and processes. Therefore, as an engineering task, management involves deciding, defining, implementing, and controlling such relationships to improve and enhance production efficiency.

Key point:

Scientific management and Fordism are the genesis of modern management; their emphasis was on rationalising labour processes to enhance production efficiency.

Division, planning, delegation, monitoring and control of work, and motivating workers through appropriate incentives were the key functions of scientific management. During the era of 'scientific management,' management was predominantly a function directed towards the factory floor to enhance the efficiency and profitability of operational activities. Marketing and market positioning were not as crucial since there was a readily available market for industrial products if produced as inexpensively as possible.

Subsequently, the Fordist assembly line emerged to streamline labor processes for efficiency and profitability further, marking the evolution of 'scientific management' into Fordist mass production systems. Scientific management and Fordism were strategic only to the extent that strategies were implicit and directed towards operational efficiency. There was neither explicit discussion about strategy nor texts, and gurus focused on strategy. Implicit in scientific management and Fordism, the strategy was to manufacture products as inexpensively as possible through the most efficient use of labor, machinery, and materials. Consequently, there were only budgets and standards, not strategic plans; only work schedules, rules, routines, and procedures, not strategies. The concept was to design, deploy, and control work processes, methods, schedules, and payment schemes in a way that synchronized labor with machinery to generate maximum efficiency through economies of scale.

Emergence of corporate planning

Key point:

Historical and contextual conditions that necessitated 'corporate planning', representing the early form of strategic management.

When capitalism transitioned from industrial capitalism to what later became known as 'monopoly capitalism', managerial emphasis shifted from the factory floor to the corporation and the organizational hierarchy. This transformation occurred at the onset of the 20th century, particularly in the US, as companies endeavored to establish monopolies through mergers and acquisitions. Concurrently, the political state sought to mitigate the adverse economic consequences of such monopolies by enacting anti-monopolistic laws.

During this period, the imperative of *'managing the organization as a totality'* became equally or even more crucial than overseeing the factory floor. The constant pursuit of capital accumulation, defined by sustained growth in sales and profits to ensure an abnormal return on capital, necessitated corporations to expand into various regions, markets, and technological or industrial fields through mergers and acquisitions. Particularly before and during the *third wave of mergers*, companies aimed to broaden their production and distribution capacities and the scope of market operations. This phenomenon led to the emergence of multidivisional corporate conglomerates, exemplified by entities such as DuPont and General Electric.

Side note:

The third wave of mergers, known as the period of conglomerate mergers, refers to the merger wave during the 1960s. The first and second waves occurred during the late 1890s to mid-1900s and late 1910s to mid-1920s, respectively (see Gaughan 2007).

In this context, strategic and corporate planning emerged as a distinct field of expertise attributed to top management. In the early stages, as evidenced by strategy discourses in the 1960s (e.g., Ansoff

1965; Chandler 1962), notions of corporate strategy or corporate planning evolved in relation to three interrelated issues:

1. Coordination between business units in multidivisional organizational forms.
2. External environmental legitimacy.
3. Market and product diversification.

Strategy as coordinating multidivisional organizations

Chandler (1962) vividly elucidated in his seminal work, *"Strategy and Structure: Chapters in the History of the Industrial Enterprise"*, that by the 1950s, industrial organizations in the US had undergone a transformation into decentralized and multi-division enterprises. DuPont, General Motors, Standard Oil, and Sears Roebuck were among the influential companies analyzed by Chandler in his exploration of multidivisional decentralized corporations. These corporations played a pivotal role in shaping numerous concepts and frameworks within the field of strategic management.

Key point:
The establishment of multidivisional firms as the foundation for corporate planning.

As depicted in Figure 2.1, these multidivisional enterprises comprised multiple businesses organized into decentralized divisions, each dedicated to a specific product or service line or a particular region. In contemporary strategy discourses, these decentralized divisions are commonly referred to as *strategic business units* (SBUs). Each SBU is considered to possess a unique competitive condition distinct from other SBUs. They autonomously handle their production, sales, distribution, and other core functions, operating independently of other units.

In the realm of multidivisional organizations, commonly referred to as M-Form organizations, *corporate planning and strategy emerge as the predominant functions of the corporate head office,* also known as the General Office in Alfred Chandler's terminology. In this context, the formulation of strategy becomes the primary responsibility of the corporate head office, involving the integration and coordination across Strategic Business Units (SBUs) to establish a unified corporation. This entails the development of institutional mechanisms through which otherwise quasi-independent and dispersed divisions are consolidated into a cohesive managerial entity referred to as the 'corporation'.

Figure 2.1: Multidivisional organization form

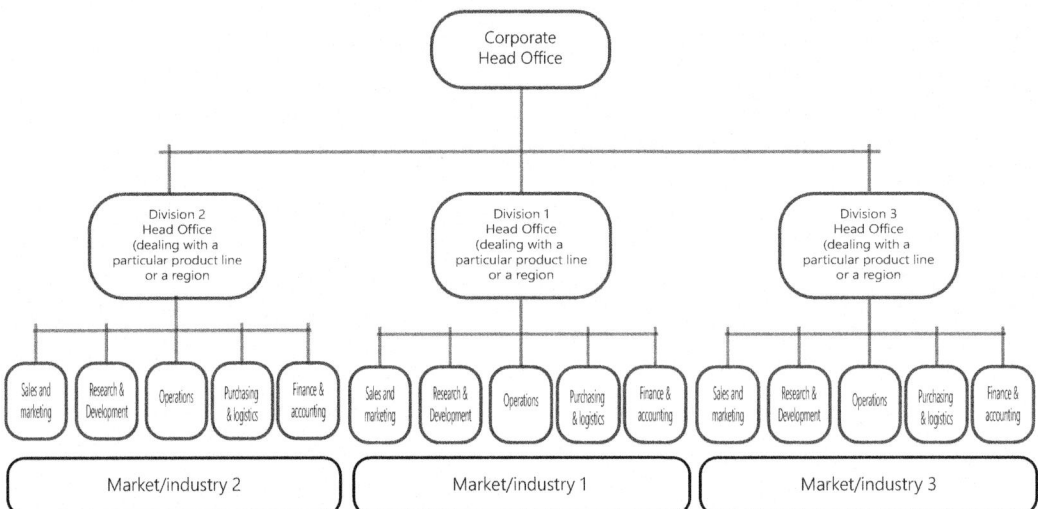

The overarching objective of corporate planning and strategy is to ensure the overall growth of the corporation as a collective entity of SBUs. Consequently, the strategic imperative of corporate planning and strategy formulation lies in the coordination and integration of SBUs into a singular corporation. To achieve this goal, three interrelated and overlapping functions characterize corporate planning and strategy formulation:

1. **Setting long-term goals:** Establishing long-term goals or growth targets for the corporation as a whole and its SBUs, and determining the appropriate courses of action to achieve them.
2. **Formulating policies:** Developing business or corporate policies to standardize and control activities across SBUs.
3. **Resource allocation:** Allocating and reallocating resources among SBUs, which involves deciding how investments should be prioritized among them.

The significance of these three elements as constituting the corporate strategy is vividly evident in the following quote from Chandler's classic work (1962, 13):

The thesis that different organisational forms result from different types of growth can be stated more precisely if the planning and carrying out of such growth is considered a strategy, and the organisation devised to administer these enlarged activities and resources, a structure. *Strategy can be defined as the determination of the basic long-term goals and objectives of an enterprise, and the adoption of courses of action and the allocation of resources necessary for carrying out these goals. Decisions to expand the volume of activities, to set up distant plants and offices, to move into new economic functions, or become diversified along many lines of business involve the defining of new basic goals.* New courses of action must be devised and resources allocated and reallocated in order to achieve these goals and to maintain and expand the firm's activities in the new areas in response to shifting demands, changing sources of supply, fluctuating economic conditions, new technological developments, and the actions of competitors. As the adoption of a new strategy may add new types of personnel and facilities, and alter the business horizons of the men responsible for the enterprise, it can have a profound effect on the form of its organisation.

Key point:

Corporate head office functionalities constitute strategy formulation in the early phase of strategy discourses.

Accounting calculations in corporate planning

Accounting played a crucial role in the functionality of corporate planning. Firstly, particularly through consolidated financial statements, accounting provided the calculative foundation upon which corporate and divisional performances could be assessed. Consequently, decisions in corporate planning were made based on these assessments. Secondly, during the era of monopoly capitalism, the effectiveness of corporate growth was gauged through a specific accounting calculation: return on investment (ROI) or return on equity (ROE). This was then associated with the structural frameworks of 'responsibility accounting', where Strategic Business Units (SBUs) were considered, in accounting terms, as 'investment centers'. The success of SBUs was judged based on their ROI.

Key point:

How accounting calculations supported corporate planning as strategizing

As the primary criterion for performance management and investment, ROI was dissected into operational sub-elements (refer to Figure 2.2). The DuPont Corporation pioneered this decomposition of ROI by analyzing how it was influenced by profitability, asset utilization, and leverage. Other performance elements, such as revenue and market share, operating expenses, and so forth, can effectively be linked to ROI, elucidating how a target ROI is achieved. ROI thus emerged as the ultimate accounting indicator of corporate performance, or, as per Bryer (2012), a "signature of monopoly capitalism". Long-term growth targets or goals for the corporation and its SBUs were primarily outlined and measured through ROI.

Figure 2.2: DuPont system of financial analysis

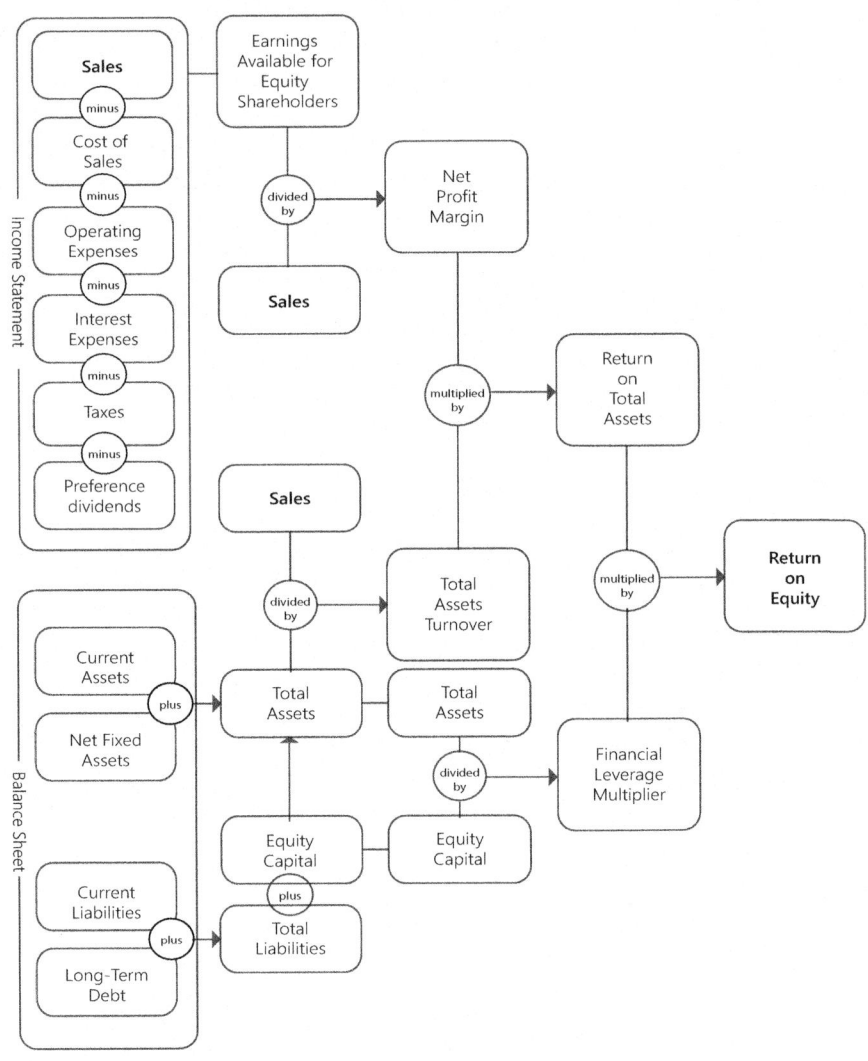

Business portfolio models in corporate planning

As previously mentioned, the reallocation of resources was one of the three functions of corporate planning. In this context, a key managerial consideration was determining which Strategic Business Units (SBUs) should receive funds for further growth through investment and which SBUs should be considered for divestment, serving as a source of corporate funds. When making such decisions, corporate planners in large corporations, such as General Electric, began viewing a corporation as a portfolio of businesses. Within this framework, decisions on resource allocations and reallocations need to be carefully determined on the basis of the investment attractiveness of each SBU. In essence, the managerial task involved making strategic investment and divestment decisions across SBUs. Portfolio planning models, initially introduced by the Boston Consultancy Group (BCG) as the Growth-Share Matrix, and later refined by General Electric through the Nine-Cell Matrix, were rationalization techniques that popularized the investment-divestment logic of corporate planning (see Figure 2.3).

Figure 2.3: Portfolio planning models

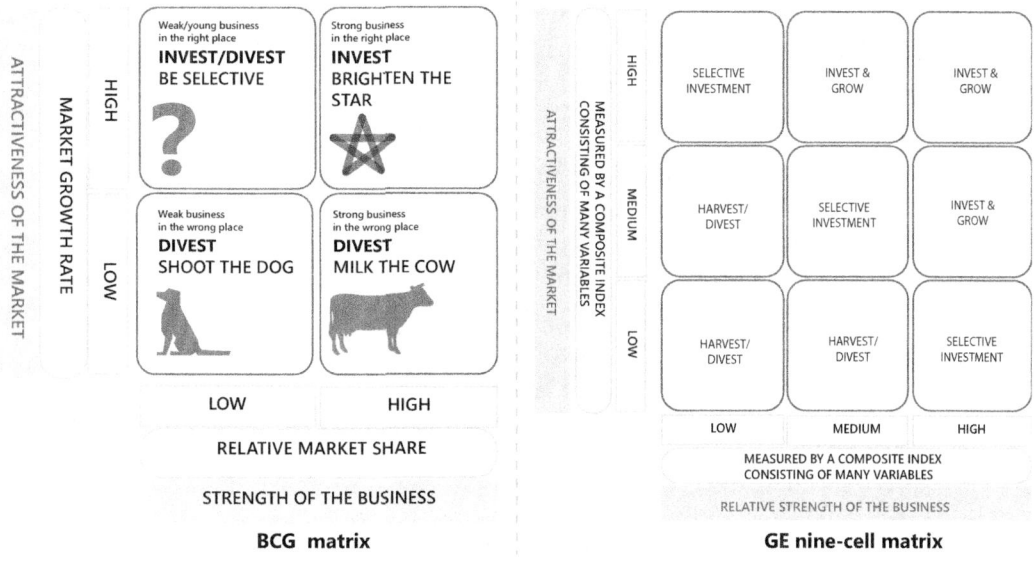

These business portfolio planning models offer a two-dimensional 'strategic map' for evaluating Strategic Business Units (SBUs) in terms of strategic investments and divestment decisions, guided by the following criteria:

1. Market Attractiveness: Assessing whether a business operates in an attractive market with growth potential is a crucial factor. In the BCG Growth-Share Matrix, this was gauged through a singular indicator of market or industry growth rate. General Electric enhanced the BCG model by incorporating a composite index of multiple indicators to measure industry attractiveness and growth potential. In both cases, the evaluation revolves around the 'location' of the business, determining if the industry or market it operates in is sufficiently attractive in terms of growth potential. This dimension aims to determine if the business is strategically positioned to receive corporate funding.

2. Competitive Strength: Evaluating whether a business is strong or weak compared to its competitors is another key consideration. The BCG Growth-Share Matrix uses a singular indicator of relative market share (= business market share/best competitors market share) for this assessment. General Electric, once again, advances this dimension by using a composite index of multiple indicators of business strength. The focus remains on assessing the relative strength of the business to determine if it is robust enough to warrant corporate funding.

Key point:

Criteria for corporate resource (re)allocation using portfolio planning models.

When viewed through these business portfolio models, corporate strategy involves making investment and divestment decisions regarding SBUs in the corporate portfolio. This entails determining the flow of corporate funding from some SBUs to others. This concept is often expressed through metaphors such as "killing dogs", "milking cows", "brightening stars", and being selective about "question marks". The underlying idea is that corporate growth is achieved by reallocating capital from weaker or saturating businesses in less attractive markets to businesses with the potential to become stronger in attractive markets. Such allocation and reallocation of funds among divisions aim to maximize the corporation's positive cash flows and long-term Return on Investment (ROI).

An additional analytical framework closely associated with portfolio planning models is the product lifecycle framework. This framework traces a product's lifecycle from development through introduction, growth, and maturity to decline. Investment and divestment decisions are often aligned with the product's lifecycle stage. This model is frequently linked with the BCG growth-share matrix: the introductory phase of a product is associated with a "question mark", growth with a "star", saturation with a "cash cow", and the decline stage with a "dog".

Strategy as dealing with external environmental conditions

The external environment emerged as the second focal point around which strategy discourses evolved. Particularly in the 1970s, under the epistemic influence of general systems theory, the external environment gained recognition as a critical aspect for managers to factor into corporate growth planning. Concepts of political-economic, legal, and socio-cultural legitimacy permeated the literature on business management. Envisaging organizations as subsystems of a broader political-economic and socio-cultural system, corporations were characterized as "environment-serving organizations" or ESOs (Ansoff 2007 [1979]). Consequently, strategic management is perceived as a boundary-spanning activity, aiming to establish an optimal alignment between the organization's internal and external environments. The following quote from Ansoff's (2007 [1979], 25) renowned text of that era on strategic management vividly elucidates this environmental perspective of strategy:

Key point:

Strategizing as dealing with the issue of external environmental legitimacy

> "... the commercial results realised by an ESO are largely determined by an alignment of certain attributes. [...] Part of this alignment is external, between the level of environmental turbulence and what we shall call the strategic thrust of the ESO. Another part is internal, between the strategic thrust and three attributes of the ESO: its strategic culture, its managerial capability, and its logistic capability. [...] When the attributes are properly matched, the potential performance is optimised; when they are not, the potential deteriorates proportionally to the mismatch. [...] The performance is also influenced by the resource commitment, the strategic budget, which the ESO makes to its strategic thrust. The theory defines for each environment a strategic budget

level, called critical mass, below which the ESO cannot hope to realise a positive net commercial exchange with the environment. Above the critical mass, the ROI rises for a while as the budget is increased, but eventually levels at a maximum."

In this quote, it is evident that, despite the inclusion of certain sociological and behavioral elements, corporate strategy was still perceived as a pursuit of corporate growth through ROI. However, in contrast to the portfolio planning models discussed earlier, this behavioral perspective underscored the importance of a proper alignment between external environmental attributes and internal organizational attributes. To achieve this alignment, specific techniques such as SWOT analysis and Political-Economic-Social-Technological (PEST) analysis (or even PESTEL analysis recently, incorporating two additional elements of Ecological and Legal) gained popularity in strategy discourses.

Diversification as strategy: dealing with corporate growth

Diversification entered the managerial lexicon in the 1960s as a 'strategy' for companies seeking corporate growth and improved ROI. For instance, its early prominence is evident in Igor Ansoff's strategic writings. Faced with escalating competition and expanding global market opportunities post-World War II, companies sought to augment their ROI through various forms of product and market expansions. Ansoff's product-market matrix emerged as a widely embraced analytical framework during this period (see Figure 2.4).

Figure 2.4: Ansoff's product-market matrix

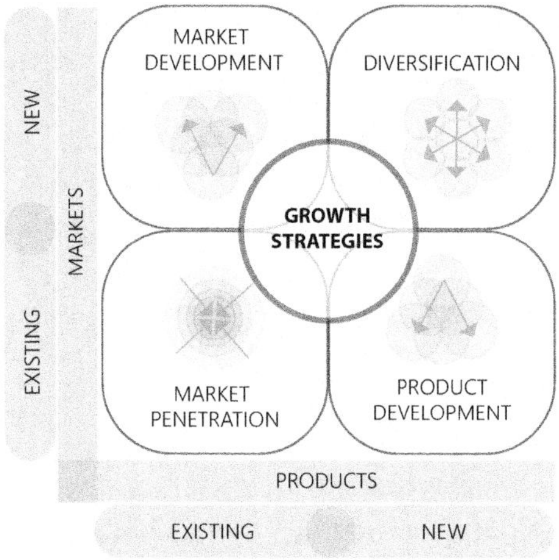

In line with the other perspectives discussed, Ansoff also prioritized the firm's growth to maintain a robust ROI. He delineated a specific path for firms to pursue growth. The least perilous strategy is "market penetration", where the firm aims to maximize profit potential in existing markets with existing products. Operational tactics such as new pricing strategies, intensified sales efforts, targeted marketing, improved quality, and efficient distribution are deployed to implement a market penetration strategy.

In terms of potential risks, the next viable option is "market development", involving the introduction of existing products to new markets. As this entails more effort, cost, and ventures into uncharted operational territories, market development is riskier than market penetration. The third option, riskier than the two mentioned so far, is "product development", which necessitates significant investments in research and development, production capacity enhancement, and so forth. Finally, the riskiest yet potentially more rewarding option is "diversification", where a firm enters new markets with new products, often facilitated by mergers and acquisitions.

Key point:

Various diversification strategies to facilitate corporate growth.

Bringing people and cultural factors in

During the 1960s and 1970s, corporate strategy discourses were predominantly characterized by creating and reinstating rational models. However, in the 1980s and 1990s, attention swiftly shifted towards the behavioral and institutional aspects of strategy implementation. The emphasis was placed on the structural and behavioral dynamics that either hindered or facilitated strategy implementation, specifically in managing the change process envisioned by corporate strategies. Consequently, change management gained popularity as a prominent agenda in strategy consultancy.

Books such as "In Search of Excellence" by Peters and Waterman (1982), Peter Senge's "Fifth Discipline: The Art and Practice of the Learning Organization" (1990), and similar works became essential readings in the field of strategy. Concepts such as mission and vision, learning organizations, corporate culture, strategic and visionary leadership, and business process reengineering gained widespread acceptance among strategy consultants and gurus. McKinsey's 7S framework (see Figure 2.5) is a vivid example of how these behavioral and structural dimensions were expressed in strategy discourses.

Key Point:

Strategy discourses also involve considering behavioural and cultural dimensions.

Figure 2.5: McKinsey's 7S framework as a manifestation of structural and behavioral dynamics of strategy

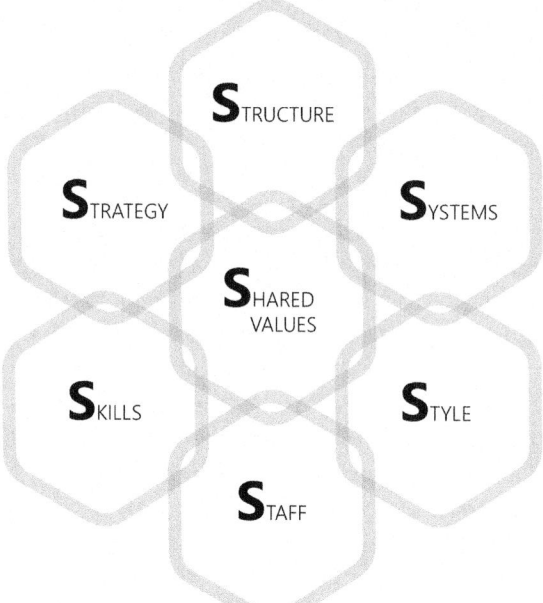

Another critical issue to address was the integration of performance measurement and management with corporate strategies. Two key strategy models gained popularity in this context: Johnson and Kaplan's Balanced Scorecards and Simons' Levers of Control Framework (LOC). Chapters 4 and 5 will provide detailed discussions of these models.

Summary of pre-Porterian strategy discourses

This section outlined the broader issues from which corporate and strategic planning ideas began to emerge. At the beginning of the 20th century, during the Scientific Management and Fordist era of management, the primary managerial focus was on the systematization and rationalization of the labor process—specifically, on deskilling and synchronizing labor with machinery.

However, as corporations expanded through mergers and acquisitions into new markets and product lines, they evolved into M-form or multidivisional enterprises. In this institutional evolution of the firm, core managerial attention shifted to managing the corporation as a totality. Comprising Strategic Business Units (SBUs) with their own core-functional departments and facing unique competitive conditions, corporate head offices were established to manage their interconnection and integration. Corporate planning, corporate strategy, or business policy, as it was then popularly known, constituted the set of functions that these corporate head offices carried out in addressing three interrelated issues: (1) coordinating and consolidating SBU operations; (2) aligning internal environmental factors with external environmental dynamics for legitimation, survival, and growth; and (3) sustaining continuous corporate growth through product and market expansion and diversification.

Various strategic planning models and frameworks emerged to address these issues. Since the late 1970s, managerial attention has shifted toward strategy implementation and change management problems. The institutional logic of strategy models should be explained by relating them to the key issues corporate managers faced at that time. Table 2.1 summarizes this explanation.

2.3 Porterian discourses of strategy

Michael Porter has exerted significant influence on strategy discourse during neoliberal times, shaping a distinct epistemic trajectory of competitiveness and strategy formulation. This section critically examines the strategy schema he has popularized.

Revising the structure-conduct-performance model

The strategy models and frameworks discussed thus far have emerged from management, organizational studies, and management consulting backgrounds. In contrast, Michael Porter's contributions are rooted in an industrial-economics context. In his early writings, he began formulating his concept of strategy by revising the then-prevalent structure-conduct-performance model. This model was commonly used to elucidate how the structural conditions faced by firms would determine their conduct (i.e., strategy) and collective performance.

As depicted in Figure 2.6, this model conceptualizes strategy as conduct, involving the decisions firms make regarding prices, production quantities, capacity usage, levels of quality, etc. However, this model is rather deterministic, assuming a linear causality between market/industry structural conditions and a firm's conduct. It posits that

Table 2.1: Classical corporate planning issues and models

Issue	Strategy models and concepts that dealt with the issue
Coordination and consolidation of independent business divisions (SBUs).	
Setting long-term goals and objectives.	• Vision and mission statements. • Corporate objectives. • Long-term divisional objectives. • Return on investment/equity as a long-term objective.
Developing and implementing corporate and business policies.	• Accounting policies. • Pricing policies. • Advertising policies. • Investment policies and criteria, including ROI specifications.
Resource allocations among divisions.	• Portfolio planning models: • BCG Growth-Share Matrix • GE Nine-Cell Matrix
Creating and maintaining a strategic fit between external environmental dynamics and internal environmental factors.	• SWOT analysis • PEST and PESTEL analysis
Sustaining corporate growth through product and market developments.	• Igor Ansoff Product-Market Matrix of growth strategies
Strategy implementation and change management.	• Various theories, concepts and frameworks that brought behavioural, cultural, institutional and structural factors into consideration. Examples include: • Learning organisations; business process reengineering; continuous improvements. • McKinsey's 7S framework put together some of these factors.

structural conditions determine the firm's conduct, and the notion of performance, as per this model, encompasses collective outcomes at the industry and market levels, often measured by indicators like allocative efficiency, distributive efficiency, and innovation levels.

A fundamental flaw in this neoclassical economic model is its failure to provide any strategic agency to the firm. The firm is conceptualized as a passive and reactive economic entity conditioned by market or industry structure. Porter addressed this weakness in his revision. According to Porter (1981), as depicted in Figure 2.6 (panel B), while

Figure 2.6: Porterian revision of the structure-conduct-performance model

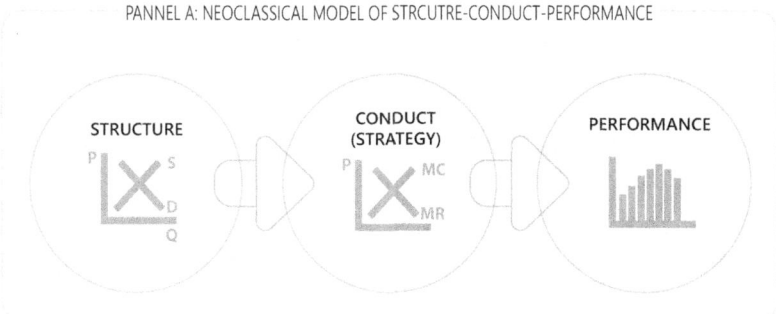

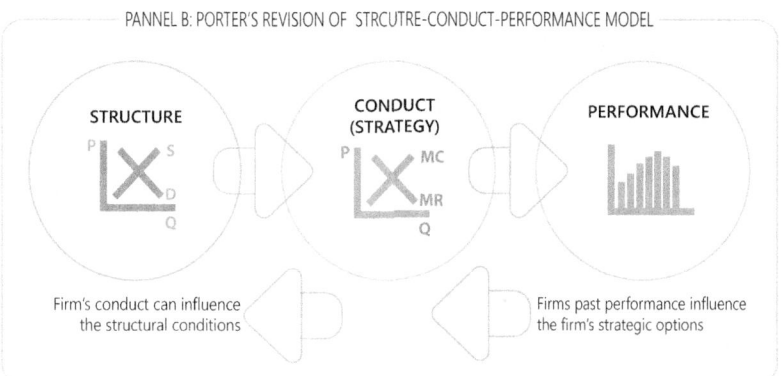

structural conditions such as the number of rival firms, entry barriers, and demand elasticity do influence a firm's conduct, the firm's past performance can offer strategic options for innovation and initiating actions to alter structural conditions.

Depending on the firm's resource capabilities and how strategies are designed and implemented, these actions can influence structural conditions, presenting opportunities to uniquely position the firm for a 'competitive advantage' and abnormal returns. For Porter, strategizing involves this distinctive positioning of the firm within the competitive structure to gain a competitive advantage.

Key point:

The structure-conduct-performance model reflects a neoclassical economic understanding of corporate strategies.

Key point:

Porter's revision of the structure-conduct-performance model attributes strategic agency to the firm.

The notion of competitive advantage

Porter's overarching framework for strategy commences with a foundational economic concept: competitive advantage. In Porter's view, competitive advantage pertains to a firm, or in the context of a nation, the ability to surpass competitors consistently over an extended period. As an economic and managerial inquiry, it seeks to address how a firm or nation can outperform rivals. Economists traditionally tackled this question through theories of absolute advantage, comparative advantage, and factor endowment, which hinge on resource availability (i.e., factors of production) and the opportunity costs associated with producing goods and services. Nonetheless, Porter's concept of competitive advantage offers an alternative perspective, emphasizing strategies over factor endowment and opportunity costs.

> **Key point:**
> The centrality of competitive advantage in Porter's strategic discussions.

In contrast to traditional economic theories, Porter contends that the competitive advantage of both firms and their respective nations is determined by the strategies they pursue. In his seminal work, "Competitive Advantage of Nations", Porter introduced his renowned "diamond model", outlining six pivotal factors influencing a nation's competitive advantage:

1. Related and supporting industries or the industrial and institutional infrastructure
2. Factor conditions.
3. Demand conditions.
4. Firms' strategy and structure of rivalry
5. political role of the government
6. mere chance

> **Key point:**
> Factors influencing a nation's competitive advantage and the pivotal role of firms' strategies and structure of rivalry play therein.

Porter identifies 'firm strategy and structure of rivalry' as the most critical among these factors. According to him, the effectiveness of adopted strategies and the competitive landscape within which a nation's firms operate are paramount in determining national competitive advantage.

Porter introduces the concept of competitive advantage in two interconnected contexts: the macroeconomic and political landscape of a nation and the micro-organizational context of firms. Within the nation's political context, Porter emphasizes competitiveness as "The Looming Challenge of Competitiveness", identifying it as the foremost and fundamental problem faced by nation-states today. Porter and other Harvard academics frame this challenge as a "biopolitical problem" (see Alawattage and Wickramasinghe 2019), wherein competitiveness becomes the primary criterion against which various social and political elements should be assessed. In essence, the political effectiveness of elements like taxation, education, democracy, employment rights, trade unions, and political administration is judged based on their contribution to the global competitiveness of the nation's firms. For instance, Porter (2013), in his testimony to the US House of Representatives, argued that the "challenge is competitiveness, not jobs per se".

When viewed as a national problem, competitiveness requires measurement at macropolitical and economic dimensions to gauge a nation's competitiveness. Over the last few decades, attempts have been made to develop a "global competitiveness index", with the Global Competitiveness Report by the World Economic Forum, in which Michael Porter played a prominent role, standing out as a notable example (see https://www.weforum.org).

By positioning competitiveness as a national predicament, Porter elevates the status of business strategy and strategy discourses beyond the realm of management to a political-economic concern. Acquiring and maintaining a competitive advantage are now considered not only a managerial challenge at the firm level but also a political-economic one for the nation. Consequently, Porter's strategic framework imparts political significance to strategy, presenting it not just as a managerial tool but as a political-economic instrument. Once competitiveness is discursively framed as the "most critical problem of our times", the concept of strategy gains macropolitical significance beyond its managerial applications. Strategy is conceived as the fundamental means through which the problem of competitiveness can be addressed at both organizational and national levels.

Key point:

How Porterian discourses on strategy raise the issue of strategy to the political arena as a national and global concern.

It's noteworthy that, according to Porter, it is not nations themselves that compete in the global markets, but rather the firms within a given nation. Therefore, enhancing a nation's competitiveness, in Porter's view, is achievable only through improving the competitive capabilities of its firms.

Porter's generic strategies

At the firm's level, according to Porter's strategy framework, there exist two generic strategies that a firm may adopt. As depicted in Figure 2.7, a firm possesses strategic options, namely 'cost leadership' or 'differentiation', which can be applied in either a broader or narrower market context. According to Porter, it is crucial to underscore that strategy involves distinctively positioning the firm's brand and products to set them apart from competitors' offerings. Whether pursuing 'differentiation' or 'cost leadership', the central strategic objective is to distinguish the firm's brand, products, or services from those of com-

Key point:

Porter identifies two generic competitive strategies: cost leadership and differentiation.

Key point:

Cost leadership and differentiation can be applied within a broader or narrower market scope.

petitors. If this distinction is achieved based on cost and pricing, it is termed 'cost leadership'. In contrast, if the differentiation is achieved through means other than cost or price, this positioning approach is referred to as 'differentiation'.

Figure 2.7: Porter's framework of generic strategies

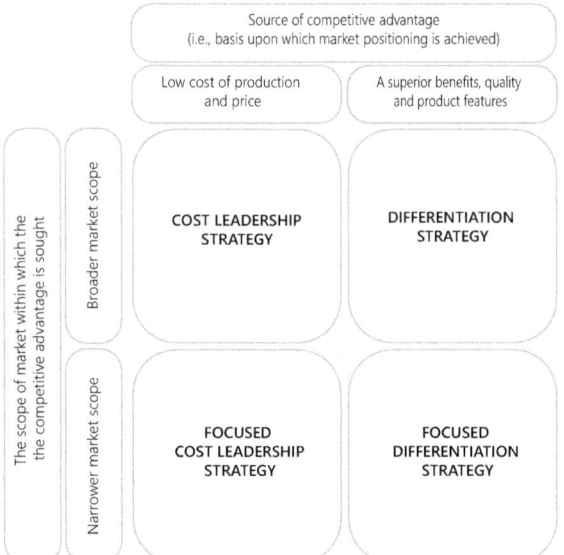

Source: based on Porter's various writings

Value for money

One way to comprehend the distinction between cost leadership and differentiation strategies is by elucidating them using the concept of 'value for money'. The economic concept of value for money underpins the decision-making process of how a customer selects alternative products and the firm's ability to reach a particular market segment. The value for money can be expressed by the formula:

value for money = value/price.

In this formula, the numerator, the value, encompasses the package of benefits, qualities, and features that a consumer can access by owning, using, or consuming a product. The denominator, the price, encompasses the consumer's sacrifice to own, consume, or use the product. Consequently, a firm has two interrelated approaches to enhance the value for money and influence consumers' purchasing decisions.

1. The first approach, cost leadership, primarily deals with the denominator, the price. While maintaining the value package at an acceptable level for consumers in general, the firm can focus on reducing the costs of bringing the product or service to the market, allowing the firm to offer the product at a lower price than competitors. The primary focus is on cost management to enable the firm to lower the price as much as possible and generate a higher value for money for the consumer. However, this requires advanced and sophisticated cost management techniques, including, for example, a well-coordinated supply chain and a just-in-time (JIT) inventory management system. Classic examples of successful implementation of this strategy include Japanese car manufacturers, especially Toyota. This strategy is most effective in markets or market segments where consumers are more price-sensitive and willing to accept an 'acceptable level of value' rather than seeking a superior premium value.
2. The second approach, the differentiation strategy, primarily deals with the numerator, the value package. The strategy is to offer superior quality, benefits, and product features at a higher price but still with a greater value-for-money ratio. In other words, the value package the firm offers customers should be greater than what competitors offer to justify the extra price that the firm demands from the customer: the extra price tag should justify the additional features and benefits offered by the product. Products targeting 'high-end segments' of the market exemplify this strategy. For example, in the digital camera market, at the time of writing this chapter, Sony follows this by offering A9, while Canon and Nikon offer R5 and Z9, respectively, with higher pixel size, frame rates per second, stabilization features, wider ISO ranges, and autofocus features, dual card slots, and so on.

Key point:
Porter's generic strategies can be elucidated through the notion of value for money.

Porter's models of strategic analysis

According to Porter, decisions on whether to adopt a cost leadership strategy or a differentiation strategy, within a broader or narrower market scope, should be based on three interconnected strategic analyses:

1. Analysis of the Structure of Rivalry – Macro-Industrial Analysis
2. Analysis of the Value Chain – Micro-Organizational Analysis
3. Analysis of the Competitor Response Profile – Competitive Context Analysis

Porter's five forces analysis

Porter presents his renowned Five Forces Framework for industry analysis. According to this framework, the competitive intensity of an industry (the central point of the model, as illustrated in Figure 2.8) is determined by four fundamental forces: the bargaining power of buyers, the bargaining power of suppliers, the threat of new entry, and the threat of substitutes. A firm's ability and necessity to pursue a specific generic strategy depend on how these five forces influence the firm. For instance, in a market where non-price competition dominates inter-firm rivalry, the necessity and capacity to pursue a 'differentiation' strategy for competitive advantage depend on:

1. Whether customers possess bargaining power over the firm and whether they exercise that power to demand premium product features and quality. In such a scenario, a differentiation strategy has a better chance of winning customers.
2. Whether the firm has significant bargaining power over its suppliers, enabling it to dictate specific terms regarding the quality and special features of raw materials and components they supply. The firm's bargaining power over suppliers is crucial in pursuing a differentiation strategy since quality and product features are vital differentiators.
3. Whether the specific quality and product features offered by the company are not easily imitated or substituted by others in the market or new entrants.

Similar conditions apply if the company is following a 'cost leadership' strategy, with the variation that:

1. Customers enjoy bargaining power over the company to demand standard acceptable products at lower prices than competitors.
2. The firm has bargaining power over its suppliers to dictate prices of raw materials and components, along with their time-scheduled delivery, to manage operational costs effectively.
3. Competitors or new entrants cannot easily imitate the firm's cost advantage.

Key point:

How the Five Forces Model Can Rationalise Generic Strategies.

Figure 2.8: Porter's five forces analysis

Source: based on Porter's various writings

In an overall sense, a firm's ability to pursue a particular strategy depends on the nature and degree of bargaining power that its customers have over the company, the bargaining power the firm has over its suppliers to dictate costs, delivery timing, quality, product features, and payment terms, and whether existing competitors or potential new entrants can easily imitate and undermine the cost-leadership or differentiation advantage that the firm enjoys in the market.

Value chain analysis

While the Five Forces model endeavors to encompass external macro-industrial conditions, the value chain analysis concentrates on internal factors and processes that a firm must establish and uphold to achieve a successful strategic position in the market. The notion is that a firm's ability to pursue a differentiation or cost-leadership strategy, whether in a narrower or broader market scope, relies on the nature of its value chain. Here, the term "value chain" denotes the interconnectedness of the inbound supply chain, internal conversion and managerial processes, and the outbound supply chain to generate value for customers while ensuring a satisfactory return on investment (ROI). Figure 2.9 illustrates Porter's conception of a value chain. The fundamental proposition is that differentiation and cost-leadership strategies necessitate distinct value chain configurations. To pursue a cost-leadership strategy, the value chain should be configured, managed, and controlled in a way that all elements of the value chain are focused on minimizing the cost of their activities and operations while delivering an acceptable benefit package to the customer. Core activities and all supporting or infrastructural functions must be consistently re-evaluated to enhance processes and activities, thereby reducing costs. Similarly, when a firm seeks to pursue a differentiation strategy, every aspect of the value chain must be configured to consistently innovate and produce quality, flexibility, and new product features that can create a distinctive appeal in the market.

Key point:

How generic strategies can be related to the value chain model

Figure 2.9: Value chain

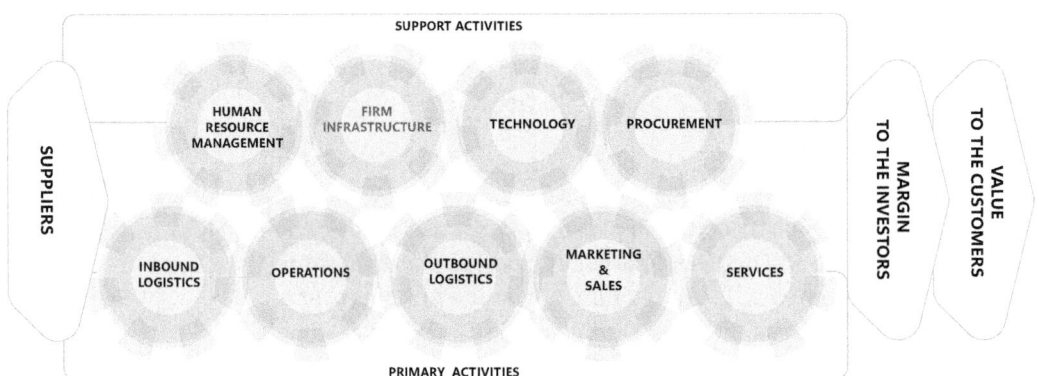

Source: based on Porter's various writings

Four corner analysis

This represents Porter's third analytical model, conceived as a tool for evaluating the probable strategies of key competitors in the medium-term future. This model can be envisioned as a more nuanced examination of competitive dynamics. In contrast to the broad evaluation of competitive structure in the aforementioned five forces model, the four-corner model offers a more targeted analysis of potential strategic responses from key competitors. Its specific objective is to formulate what Porter terms a "competitor's response profile," encompassing an evaluation of four interconnected elements underpinning the competitor's future strategy (see Figure 2.10):

1. **Strategic drivers:** This involves an examination of the factors propelling the competitor, encompassing financial and non-financial goals, vision, mission, and business philosophy, the top management team and leadership, corporate culture, organizational structure, and external and internal constraints.
2. **Strategic assumptions about itself and the industry:** This dimension encompasses the competitor's perceived strengths and weaknesses, cultural and value systems, as well as perceptions of industry forces.
3. **Current strategy:** This delves into the competitor's existing actions and competitive approaches. It includes an assessment of market positioning strategies (e.g., cost leadership or differentiation), market scope, value creation methods, investment areas, and the relationships and networks the competitor has cultivated.
4. **Capabilities:** This involves an evaluation of the competitor's strengths and weaknesses, considering aspects such as marketing skills, product and service quality, workforce skills and training levels, patents and copyrights, financial strength, and leadership qualities of top management.

Key point:

Four key parameters of developing a competitor's response profile

According to Porter, an analysis of these 'four corners' should construct the 'competitor's response profile,' addressing the following questions (see Porter 2004, 49):

1. Is the competitor content with its current position?
2. What probable moves or shifts in strategy might the competitor undertake?
3. Where is the competitor susceptible?
4. What actions are likely to trigger the most significant and effective retaliation from the competitor?

Figure 2.10: Porter's four-corner analysis

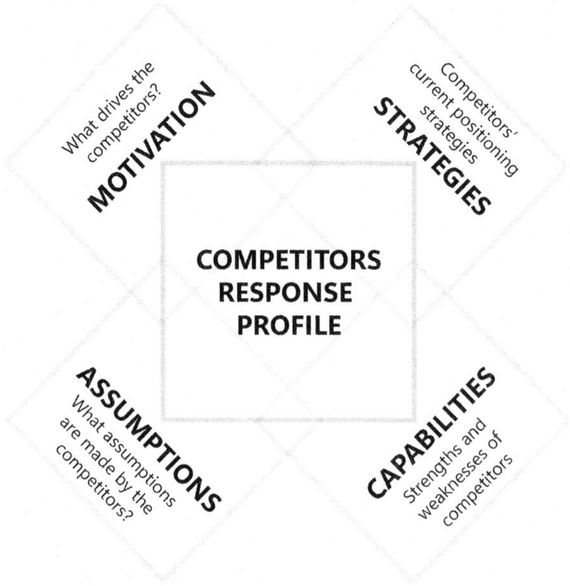

Source: based on Porter's various writings

Porter's grand schema of strategy in summary

When considering the Porterian strategy concepts discussed thus far, it becomes evident that he has propagated a 'grand schema of strategy' that spans from macro-political to micro-organizational dimensions, interconnecting various institutional facets of strategizing. This schema establishes a "biopolitical hierarchy of competitiveness" (see Alawattage and Wickramasinghe 2019, 2022). As depicted in Figure 2.11, the apex of this hierarchy is the concept of competitive advantage, discussed as both a challenge and a normative goal within the domain of the nation-state or population (i.e., the biopolitical realm). It is perceived as a pathological issue for the nation-state, necessitating attention from the political state through neoliberal political-economic policies that support the global economic strategies of the nation. Porter's diamond model then delineates the factors influencing a nation's ability to attain a competitive advantage over others. In Porterian discourses, particular emphasis is placed on "firm strategy, structure, and rivalry". This serves as the nexus between the macro-political (i.e., biopolitical realm) and the micro-organizational (i.e., anatomico-political). In the domain of competitiveness within orga-

Key point:

How Porter's diverse conceptual elements and frameworks materialise into a comprehensive strategy schema.

nizations and management, Porterian discussions have popularized four interconnected frameworks for strategic analysis: the five forces model, the model of generic strategies, the value chain model, and the four-corner model for analyzing competition.

Figure 2.11: Porterian strategy discourses as a biopolitical hierarchy of competitiveness

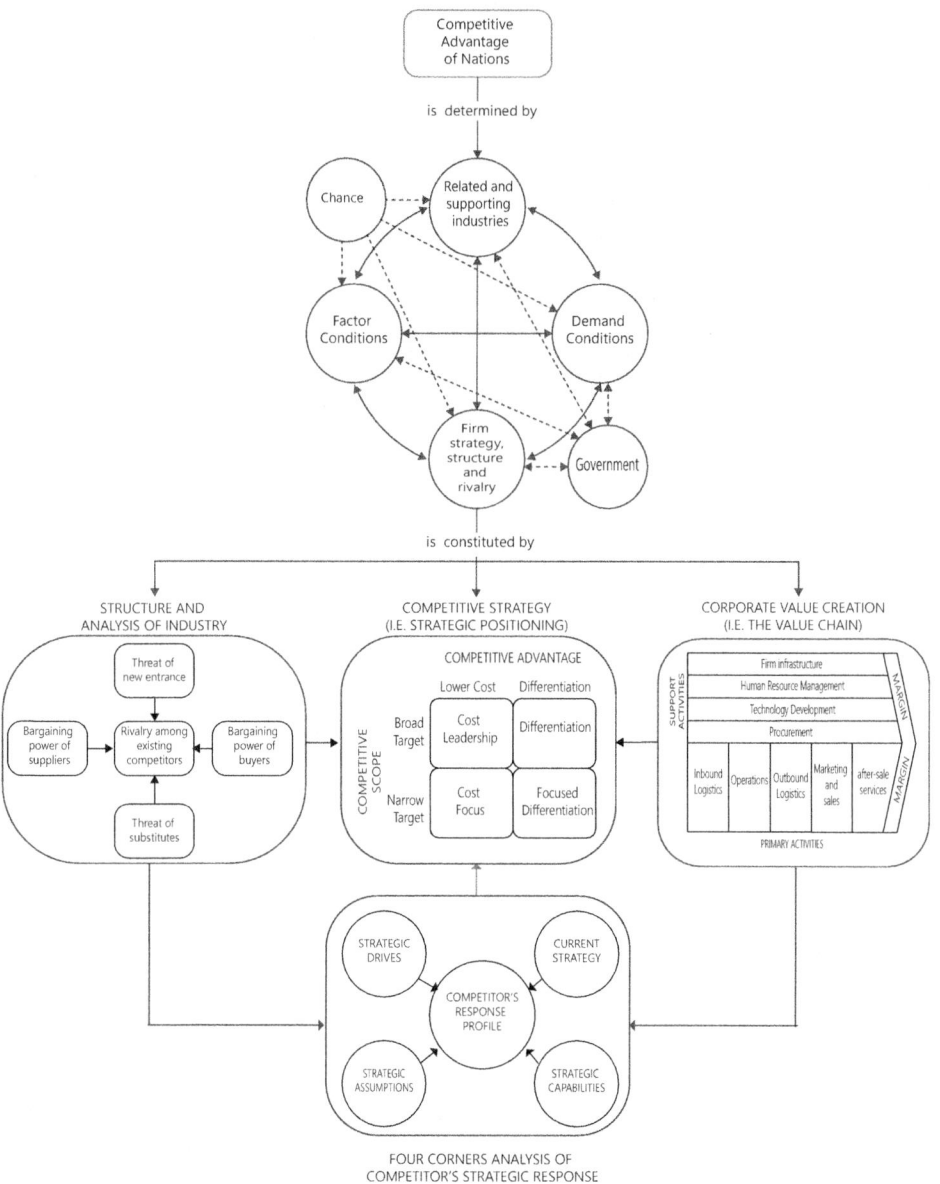

Sustainability implications of Porterian discourses

You should note that the strategic discussions mentioned in the preceding sections conspicuously overlook ecological and social justice concerns, i.e., sustainability in a broader sense. Within these discussions, strategy has consistently been conceptualized within a narrow organizational and industrial scope, disregarding the broader social and ecological implications that corporate strategies can entail.

Key point:

Strategy experts like Porter view sustainability as a "value proposition" – a specific conditionality that firms can use to improve their competitive positioning and advantage.

Nevertheless, there has been a recent global-scale recognition of sustainability, particularly with the United Nations' sustainable development goals (SDGs). Corporations are now increasingly embracing UN SDGs, and sustainability reporting has become a crucial aspect of corporate reporting practices. Companies are adopting reporting standards and schemas, such as the Global Reporting Initiative (GRI). In response to this trend, strategy experts like Michael Porter are refining and redefining their frameworks to incorporate sustainability (see, for example, Porter and Kramer 2006).

However, even in these efforts, the primary focus has been on how sustainability concerns can augment companies' strategic positioning and competitive advantage. A close examination of recent endeavors by strategy experts into sustainability reveals that their primary concern is not sustainability itself but how the emerging global discourses on sustainability can be leveraged to further enhance their competitive positioning – the strategic instrumentality of sustainability discourses. For example, Porter and Kramer (2006, 13) explain:

> "Creating a social dimension to the value proposition. At the heart of any strategy is a unique value proposition: a set of needs a company can meet for its chosen customers that others cannot. The most strategic CSR [corporate social responsibility] occurs when a company adds a social dimension to its value proposition, making social impact integral to the overall strategy."

In developing such a 'sustainability value proposition', Porter and Kramer (2006) suggest new applications for Porter's traditional strategic frameworks (discussed earlier) of value chain analysis and industry analysis (i.e., the five forces model): using them to map social opportunities by identifying 'inside-out linkages' and 'outside-in linkages.' Mapping "inside-out linkages" involves identifying potential negative or positive social impacts of a firm's value-chain activities, while outside-in linkages refer to the social dimensions dictated by the firm's competitive context. They propose a revised version of Porter's industry analysis model to perform these mappings, which includes four key dimensions: the context for firm strategy and rivalry, factor (input) conditions, local demand conditions, and related and supporting industries. Table 2.2 summarizes Porter and Kramer's integration of sustainability into their tools of strategic analyses.

Key point:

Mapping "inside-out-linkages" and "outside-in-linkages" with five forces and value chain models are Porter and Kramer's proposals for strategizing sustainability.

Chapter summary

This chapter traced the evolution of managerial discourses on strategy. While the concept of strategy has a longstanding history in military sciences and campaigns, it gained prominence in business management only in the early 1960s. During the initial phase of modern management's evolution, strategy was not an explicit concern. In the era of 'scientific management,' managerial focus centered on the point of production and the labor process. The primary objective was to enhance efficiency by synchronizing labor with machinery, thereby subordinating it to the interests of capital accumulation. The implicit strategy during this period involved the systematization and rationalization of labor through deskilling and mechanization, as seen in Taylorist and Fordist management regimes.

Nevertheless, a series of mergers and acquisitions that commenced in the late 19th century paved the way for the necessity of strategic thinking. Corporations began expanding into conglomerate entities through mergers, acquisitions, and the establishment of factories and offices across various regions and markets. This led to the rise of multidivisional or M-form organizations like DuPont and General Electric. With the emergence of such organizations, managerial attention shifted from the labor process to the holistic management of the corporation. Three fundamental managerial challenges surfaced: (a) coordinating business units in multidivisional forms, (b) establishing external environmental legitimacy, and (c) addressing the need for diversification for corporate growth. Corporate planning and strategy emerged as mechanisms to tackle these challenges.

Long-term corporate goal-setting, corporate policies, and resource allocation among divisions became essential means for achieving coordination. Corporate planning incorporated concepts such as corporate vision statements, mission statements, corporate goals, and

Table 2.2: Strategizing sustainability – Porter and Krammer

Model	Model dimensions	CSR examples
Value-chain analysis (inside-out linkages)	Inbound logistics	Transportation impacts (e.g. emissions, congestion, logging roads)
	Operations	Emissions & waste Biodiversity & ecological impacts Energy & water usage Worker safety & labour relations Hazardous materials
	Outbound logistics	Packaging use and disposal (McDonald's clamshell) Transportation impacts
	Marketing and sales	Marketing & advertising (e.g. truthful advertising, advertising to children) Pricing practices (e.g. price discrimination among customers, anti-competitive pricing practices, pricing policy to the poor) Consumer information Privacy
	After-sales services	Disposal of obsolete products Handling of consumables (e.g. motor oil, printing ink) Customer privacy
	Procurement	Procurement & supply chain practices (e.g. bribery, child labor, conflict diamonds, pricing to farmers) Uses of particular inputs (e.g. animal fur) Utilisation of resources
	Technology development	Relationships with universities Ethical research practices (e.g. animal testing, GMOs) Product safety Conservation of raw materials Recycling
	Human resource management	Education & job training Safe working conditions Diversity & discrimination Health care & other benefits Compensation policies Layoff policies
	Firm Infrastructure	Financial reporting practices Government practices Transparency Use of lobbying

Industry analysis (outside-in linkages)	Context for Firm Strategy and Rivalry (The rules and incentives that govern competition)	Fair and open local competition (e.g. the absence of trade barriers, fair regulations) Intellectual property protection Transparency (e.g. financial reporting, corruption: Extractive Industries Transparency Initiative) Rule of law (e.g. security, protection of property, legal system) Meritocratic incentive systems (e.g. antidiscrimination)
	Factor (Input) Conditions (Presence of high quality, specialised inputs available to firms)	Availability of human resources (Marriott's job training) Access to research institutions and universities (Microsoft's Working Connections) Efficient physical infrastructure Efficient administrative infrastructure Availability of scientific and technological infrastructure (Nestlé's knowledge transfer to milk farmers) Sustainable natural resources (GrupoNueva's water conservation) Efficient access to capital
	Local Demand Conditions (the nature and sophistication of local customer needs)	Sophistication of local demand (e.g. appeal of social value propositions: Whole Foods' customers) Demanding regulatory standards (California auto emissions & mileage standards) Unusual local needs that can be served nationally and globally (Urbi's housing financing, Unilever's "bottom of the pyramid" strategy)
	Related and Supporting Industries (the local availability of supporting industries)	Availability of local suppliers (Sysco's locally grown produce; Nestlé's milk collection dairies) Access to firms in related fields Presence of clusters instead of isolated industries

Source: based on Porter and Kramer (2006, 5-6)

corporate policies to provide overarching directions for divisions. Portfolio planning models, particularly the BCG growth-share matrix and GE nine-cell matrix, gained popularity as techniques for rationalizing investment and divestment decisions. Concerning environmental legitimacy, corporate planners began viewing their corporations as environment-serving organizations (ESOs) and emphasized maintaining a viable fit between external environmental dynamics and internal organizational factors. Analytical models such as SWOT, PEST, and PESTEL were developed to address environmental congruence. The issue of diversification was addressed through rationalization techniques like Igor Ansoff's product-market diversification matrix.

The behavioral school of strategy emerged in the mid-1970s, focusing on strategy implementation and change management issues. Discourses such as "in search of excellence," "learning organizations," lean manufacturing, business process reengineering, and continuous improvement gained popularity.

Since the mid-1970s, with the advent of neoliberalization, globalization, digitalization, and virtualization of markets and hierarchies, managerial attention shifted to market positioning. Strategizing in the market became more critical than managing the hierarchy and labor process. Consequently, the concept of strategy acquired a new meaning – strategy as positioning. Michael Porter's contributions became pivotal in this regard.

Porter provides an overarching schema of strategy that presents strategy and competitive advantage simultaneously as macro-political issues pertaining to the nation-state and managerial issues related to micro-organizational dynamics of positioning. Porter revised the neoclassical economic model of structure-conduct-performance, attributing strategic agency to the firm. He argued that a firm could influence the structural conditions within which it operates through strategies and performance, making strategy a fundamental factor in determining competitive advantage.

According to Porter, a firm may adopt two generic strategies: cost leadership or differentiation in a narrow or broader market scope. The strategic decision should stem from three interrelated strategic analyses: (1) industry analysis, for which Porter suggests the Five-Forces model; (2) an analysis of internal production and marketing processes, for which Porter provides the value-chain analysis framework, and (3) an analysis of competitor response profiles, for which Porter introduces the Four-Corner analysis of competition framework.

Finally, the chapter explored how sustainability discourses have influenced the reconception of strategy, particularly recent attempts to rebrand Porter's old strategic analysis tools in the light of corporate social responsibility (CSR).

Test your knowledge

1. What was the implicit strategic focus of managing modern organizations during scientific management and Fordism?
2. Briefly explain the contextual and historical conditions underpinning the emergence of 'corporate planning'.
3. List the three interrelated issues that 'corporate planning' aims to address.
4. What is a multidivisional firm? What are the critical managerial functionalities of the corporate head office (or the General Office, as Chandler identified it) in a multidivisional firm?
5. Explain the key elements of Chandler's definition of strategy.
6. Coordination between business units (SBUs) is a crucial functionality to be carried out under corporate planning. List and explain three managerial functionalities that fall under this coordination role of the corporate head office.
7. Briefly explain which accounting techniques, in which ways, were mobilized to aid the corporate planning functionality of coordinating and consolidating SBUs' performances.
8. What is a portfolio planning model? Use examples of the BCG growth-share matrix and GE nine-cell matrix to explain. Also, focus on the fundamental criteria upon which resource allocations among SBUs were decided with such business portfolio planning models.
9. Dealing with the external environment is also considered a key functionality of strategic management or corporate planning. Explain the concept of "environment serving organizations". How do you explain strategic management in relation to this functionality? What are the key strategic analysis frameworks that deal with this external environmental dimension of strategizing?
10. Briefly explain how Ansoff's product-market matrix identifies different strategies for corporate growth.
11. Using McKinsey's 7S framework as an example, explain key behavioral and cultural dimensions that strategy formulation and implementation must consider.
12. What is the structure-conduct-performance model? Explain how Michael Porter revised this and enabled a new economic understanding of firms' strategic agency and capabilities.
13. Briefly explain the notion of competitive advantage and how it occupies a central position in Porterian strategy discourses.

14. What are the key factors affecting a nation's competitive advantage? Explain using Porter's diamond model.
15. What are the two fundamental competitive strategies that Porter conceptualized? In which ways can they be operationalized in relation to the scope of their deployment?
16. Explain how Porter's generic strategies can be related to the concept of value for money.
17. Porter provides three frameworks to analyze competitive conditions. List them.
18. Briefly explain Porter's five forces model and explain how it can be related to the choice of cost-leadership or differentiation strategies.
19. Briefly explain Porter's value chain model and how it can be related to the choice between cost-leadership and differentiation strategies.
20. Explain the key parameters according to which competitors' response profiles can be analyzed. Use Porter's four-corner analysis as a guide.
21. Explain Porter and Kramer's ideas of strategizing sustainability.

Explore further

1. Visit the website of a large multidivisional corporation, where you can find a good deal of information on the company's strategic choices and declarations. Carefully study the website information and make notes on the following:

   - The means through which the company communicates its strategic intents, especially its long-term directions and guiding principles.
   - Its major strategic business units and the competitive market conditions within which it operates.
   - Study its history and try to identify the manner in which it diversified its business over time.
   - Select one of its key products or product lines and see whether it adopts a differentiation or cost leadership strategy regarding that product or product line.
   - See whether and how its higher-order strategic statements and objectives (e.g., vision and mission statements, long-term goals, guiding principles, etc.) capture sustainability. In which

ways do UN SDGs appear in their website information? What specific programmes is the company implementing to achieve UN SDGs?

2. Visit the website https://www.imd.org and/or https://www.weforum.org. These two organizations publish policy views and rankings related to nations' competitiveness.

- Read carefully how they conceptualize and measure the idea of 'competitiveness'. Try to see how their conceptualization is based on Porterian ideas of a nation's competitive advantage.
- Look into the key themes that they prioritize over time. Based on the changes in the thematic structure of their reports, can you think of how the notion of competitiveness is evolving?
- See to what extent and in which ways UN SDGs appear in these competitiveness themes.

3. Visit the OECD competition assessment toolkit website: https://www.oecd.org/daf/competition/assessment-toolkit.htm. There are three volume sets you can download there: volume 1 - principles, volume 2 - guidance and volume 3 – operational manual. Read volume 1 of this and

- Explain the purpose of this competition assessment toolkit. What level of competition does this toolkit try to assess (organizational, industry/market, national)? Why does the OECD think that competition needs to be assured through regulation?
- Explain the conditions under which this competitiveness assessment toolkit is to be used.
- Drawing on other relevant materials on neoliberalism (e.g., Harvey 2005; Alawattage and Wickramasinghe 2022), can you think of how this competition assessment toolkit operationalizes neoliberalism? Write a brief note on the neoliberal conditionality of this toolkit.

Develop your critical argumentation skills.

1. Compose an argumentative essay on the theme:

   "The evolution of strategy discourses, frameworks, and techniques, from Alfred Chandler to Michael Porter and beyond, signifies the emerging managerial and institutional challenges posed by transformations in organizational structures, competitive landscapes, and environmental conditions".

Utilizing the strategy frameworks discussed in this chapter, elucidate the specific managerial challenges these frameworks evolved to tackle.

2. Draft an argumentative essay on the theme:

"The popularity of Porter's strategy discourse can be ascribed to its conceptualization and integration of competitiveness and competitive advantage across an analytical spectrum that encompasses macro-political to micro-organizational dynamics of strategizing and policy-making."

When building this argument, focus on how Porter's various models and concepts interconnect through diverse layers of managerial and policy analysis.

3. Construct an argumentative essay on the theme:

"Owing to their hyper-capitalistic nature, contemporary strategy discourses and frameworks exhibit limited capacity to provide genuinely effective approaches for addressing pressing sustainability issues in our times."

Explain this assertion with particular reference to Porter's recent endeavor to incorporate sustainability into his strategic frameworks.

References

Alawattage, C., and D. Wickramasinghe. 2019. Strategizing management accounting: liberal origins and neoliberal trends. London: Routledge.

———. 2022. Strategizing management accounting: liberal origins and neoliberal trends. Accounting, Auditing & Accountability Journal 35 (2):518-546.

Ansoff, I. 1965. Corporate strategy: an analytical approach to business policy for growth and expansion: New York: McGraw-Hill.

———. 2007 [1979]. Strategic management. Basingstoke: Palgrave Macmillan.

Bryer, R. 2012. Americanism and financial accounting theory – Part 1: Was America born capitalist? Critical Perspectives on Accounting 23 (7–8):511-555.

Burawoy, M. 1979. Manufacturing consent: changes in the labor process under monopoly capitalism. Chicago; London: University of Chicago Press.

Chandler, A. D. 1962. Strategy and structure: chapters in the history of the industrial enterprise. Cambridge, Mass.: M.I.T. Press.

Gaughan, P. A. 2007. Mergers, acquisitions, and corporate restructurings. 4th ed. ed. Hoboken, N.J.: Wiley.

Peters, T. J., and R. H. Waterman. 1982. In Search of Excellence: lessons from America's Best-run Companies: Harper & Row.

Porter, M. E. 1981. The contributions of industrial organization to strategic management. The Academy of Management Review 6 (4):609-620.

Porter, M. E. 2004. The competitive strategy: techniques for analyzing industries and competitors. London: Simon & Schuster.

Porter, M. E., and M. R. Kramer. 2006. Strategy and society: the link between competitive advantage and corporate social responsibility. Harvard Business Review 2006 [Reprint R0612D] (December):1-15.

Senge, P. M. 1990. The fifth discipline: the art and practice of the learning organization: Doubleday/Currency.

CHAPTER 3
Strategizing the market: strategic pricing decisions

3.1. Introduction

As discussed in previous chapters, a firm has three interconnected domains or sites of strategic action to enable and enact its strategies: the market, the point of production, and the organizational hierarchy. In a managerial sense, the market holds the utmost significance among these domains of strategic action. According to prevailing strategy discourses (e.g., Porter 1985, 1996), business strategy fundamentally revolves around the competitive market positioning of the firm's brand and products. In this context, strategy entails creating, maintaining, and enhancing a competitive market position to gain a competitive advantage. In pursuing such a strategic position, the firm may adopt, as per strategy experts like Michael Porter, cost leadership or differentiation strategies within narrow or broader market scopes. While following these strategies, pricing emerges as a critically important strategic consideration.

Key point:

The strategic importance of pricing – price constitutes value for money, and hence, pricing is a strategic calculation through which competitive positioning is achieved.

The centrality of pricing in strategy arises from two interrelated aspects. Firstly, it is linked to the 'value for money' equation, where the price is the denominator, underscoring its pivotal role in determining the firm's value proposition. Price becomes a crucial variable through which customers comprehend and assess the *'value for money'* a brand or product provides. Consequently, pricing becomes a strategic calculation through which firms rationalize, enable, and enact their competitive market positioning.

Side note:

$$\text{value for money} = \frac{\text{value}}{\text{price}}$$

Side note:

The marketing mix encompasses the totality of the product, price, place (distribution channels), and promotion (advertising, sales promotions, publicity, personal selling), often abbreviated as 4Ps.

Key point:

Pricing is the strategic marketing decision that ensures the firm's financial viability.

Key point:

Chapter structure and learning objectives.

Secondly, pricing is financially fundamental, as it is the sole variable in the *marketing mix* that generates revenue and ensures that firms earn adequate profits and return on investment. On the one hand, the price must capture market dynamics and enable strategically advantageous market positioning. On the other hand, it should allow the firm to earn sufficient profits and achieve an adequate return on investment. This dual functionality of pricing as both a strategic and financial decision makes it a crucial element in strategic decision-making. Viewing pricing as the most critical strategic decision to be made in relation to market positioning, this chapter is structured around three main themes or learning objectives.

1. Firstly, before delving into the specific factors and processes of strategic pricing, the chapter will explore how pricing is conceptualized in neoclassical economics and conventional management accounting pricing models. This establishes the traditional conceptual framework against which strategic pricing needs to be compared and understood.
2. Secondly, the chapter will examine the processes and dynamics of strategic pricing. Emphasis will be on how pricing is practiced as an element of competitive market positioning, alongside other marketing approaches, such as market segmentation, targeting, and positioning.
3. Thirdly, the chapter will delve into three important topics related to strategic pricing: life cycle costing, target costing, and dynamic pricing.

Consequently, after perusing this chapter, you should be capable of explaining and critiquing neoclassical economics and accounting pricing models, elucidating the strategic pricing process and dynamics, and detailing target costing, life cycle costing, and dynamic pricing as strategic pricing techniques.

3.2. Neoclassical economic model of pricing

One of the most discussed pricing models is the neoclassical economic model of pricing, which you may have studied in your introductory economics courses. Therefore, this section may revisit what you have learned elsewhere. However, refreshing the neoclassical economics pricing model is crucial as it provides a comparative basis against which strategic pricing can be compared and better understood.

The starting point of the neoclassical economics model is its assumption that the firm's primary objective is to maximize profit. Hence, the profit maximization rule is used as the operational doctrine and the criterion for deciding the best price for a product. Mathematically speaking, the 'profit function' becomes the objective function that needs to be maximized subject to relevant constraints.

Given that the profit function is composed of two key elements, revenue and costs, the profit maximization objective is operationalized through a mathematical proposition: *at the point of profit maximization, the marginal revenue should be equal to the marginal cost.* In other words, to be at the profit maximization point, the extra revenue generated by producing and selling an extra unit of production should equal the extra cost incurred to produce and sell that extra unit. This profit maximization proposition is explained by the numerical example below. Figure 3.1, which you should have seen many times in introductory economics books and some management accounting books you read for your previous courses, further illustrates the numerical example.

Key point:

Neoclassical economics pricing is based on marginal analysis of revenue and costs to maximise profit. Accordingly, the optimum price is where marginal revenue equals marginal cost.

A numerical example of the neoclassical economics model of pricing.

Demand function: $p = 100 - 5q$, where p is the price and q is the quantity produced.

Total cost function: $TC = 100 + 0.05q^3 - 0.25q^2 + 5q$, where TC is the total cost and q is the quantity produced

(Note: q is in millions)

Given these cost and demand functions, the requirement is to calculate the profit maximizing price and quantity.

The profit function can be stated as $\pi = TR - TC$, where TR is the total revenue function

Given that $TR = pq$, TR can be derived by multiplying the demand function by q

$TR = (100-5q)q; \quad TR = 100q - 5q^2$

As stated earlier, when profit is maximized, $MR = MC$, where MR is the marginal revenue and MC is the marginal cost, which can be derived by differentiating the TR and MR, respectively.

$MR = dTR/dq = 100 - 10q$
$MC = dTC/dq = 0.15q^2 - 0.5q + 5$

Equating *MR* to *MC*, we have $100 - 10q = 0.15q^2 - 0.5Q + 5$

And solving this, we have *q* = 8.782203665038656 (in millions)

Substituting *q* in p, we have *p* = 56.08898 or 56.09

With these values

Total revenue: 492.5848604 (millions)

Total cost: 158.4965386 (millions)

Maximum profit: 334.0883219 (millions)

Figure 3.1: Neoclassical economics model of pricing

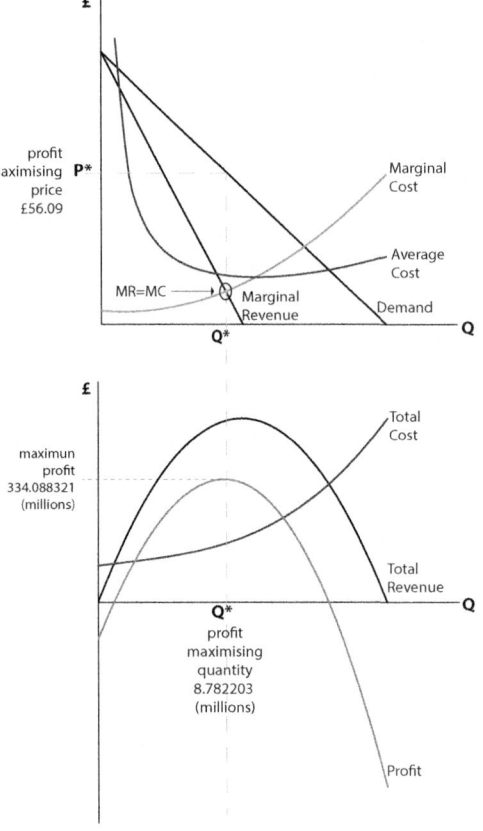

According to this neoclassical economics model, the demand curve approximates, estimates, and integrates the market into the decision-making framework. As discussed in previous chapters, the market is where a firm should strategically position its brands and products. It forms a complex nexus between consumer behavior and a firm's marketing strategies. However, it is the demand curve which singularly represents the market in this neoclassical economics pricing model. Furthermore, demand is conceptualized as the causal link between price and quantity. As you learned in your economics courses, assuming other factors remain constant, the quantity a firm can sell decreases when the firm sets a higher price. Conversely, if the firm sets a lower price, it can sell a higher quantity. The demand curve illustrates potential price-quantity combinations available to the firm. These combinations, outlined by the demand curve, determine the firm's revenue, expressed in accounting or economic terms as total revenue = price * quantity (TR= PQ). The marginal revenue curve is also derived from the demand curve (note MR= dTR/dQ).

Key point:
The demand curve delineates market dynamics as a price-quantity relationship and encapsulates the revenue aspect of the profit function.

The demand curve only considers the revenue or market side of the profit-driven decision-making formula. The other facet is the point of production, where production is carried out and costs are incurred. Accordingly, cost curves encapsulate the point of production in determining the optimal or profit-maximizing price and quantity, which occurs when marginal cost equals marginal revenue.

Key point:
Cost curves represent the point of production in the profit formula.

Nonetheless, the neoclassical economics model can only offer a relatively narrow and problematic understanding of how firms establish their prices as a strategic variable. The following outlines the fundamental limitations of the neoclassical economics model of pricing:

1. Problematic assumption of profit maximization: The presumption of profit maximization becomes questionable when examining real-world decision-making scenarios. In practical terms, managers do not necessarily aim for profit maximization; instead, they strive to achieve specific profit targets outlined in their budgets and incentive plans. The application of 'maximization' logic or calculations, as expected by economic theories, is not commonly observed. Perhaps there is an underlying concept of attaining the maximum possible profit, but not necessarily 'profit maximization'.

   Depending on a firm's position in the market, variables such as sales growth, market share, and strategic objectives like

Key point:
Economic's problematic profit maximisation assumption

market penetration and skimming take precedence in determining product prices, as opposed to a focus on profit maximization. For instance, companies may be willing to incur certain losses during the introductory period of a product. They might establish 'introductory prices' that are not sufficiently high to generate a substantial profit or even fail to yield any profit at all.

Even in the mature stages of a product, a firm may not be oriented towards profit maximization. Instead, companies may find contentment in achieving a target profit and a satisfactory return on investment.

2. **Limited market conceptualization:** Secondly, the neoclassical economics model conceptualizes and integrates the market into the decision-making model exclusively through the demand curve. Consequently, the market is envisioned solely as the causal link between price and quantity. This reflects a limited understanding of the market and the competitive landscape. As discussed in previous chapters, from a strategic standpoint, the competitive landscape is far more intricate than the price-quantity relationship represented by the demand curve.

Key point:

Economic model of pricing narrowly conceives the market through the demand curve.

Moving beyond this price-quantity dynamic, one should consider a wider range of factors in a strategic conceptualization of the competitive landscape. These factors may encompass the strengths and weaknesses of the firm, its perspectives on achievable and desirable competitive positioning, the strengths and weaknesses of competitors, and potential strategic moves by competitors. Additionally, profiles of customers should be considered in terms of their demographic, political, economic, legal, and cultural characteristics (refer to Figure 1.2 in Chapter 1). Various dynamics associated with the supply chain, as well as the broader regulatory and governance infrastructure, also come into play.

Therefore, in strategic terms, the competitive landscape in which price must be determined as a positioning variable is considerably more complex than what this economic model can operationalize.

3. Limited strategic agency attributed to the firm: According to the neoclassical economics model, the firm is perceived to have limited or no strategic agency. Aligned with the structure-conduct-performance model discussed in the preceding chapter, neoclassical economics assumes structural determinism. Demand is regarded as a condition determined by the structural properties of the market, and the firm, at best, determines the price based on the price-quantity relationship dictated by demand. Consequently, demand is perceived as a structural imposition, and pricing decisions must be made accordingly. Thus, it is posited that the firm lacks strategic capacity or agency; its only option is to adjust its price-quantity relationship on the curve with the profit-maximizing rule MR = MC.

Key point: Neoclassical economics attributes very limited or no strategic agency to firms.

This issue of neoclassical economics' structural determinism was explored in the previous chapter when elucidating the "structure-conduct-performance" model. The preceding chapter also examined Michael Porter's revision, which attributes strategic agency to the firm. Porter argues that firms can shape and reshape markets based on their past performances and strategic moves. This implies that firms possess the ability to create, recreate, and reproduce the structural conditions within which they operate through the strategies they implement and facilitate. In essence, the neoclassical economic model does not acknowledge such strategic agency for the firm.

4. Isolation of pricing decision: The neoclassical economics model perceives product pricing as an independent, singular decision. However, in a strategic sense, pricing is just one element of a 'marketing mix' that firms should decide to pursue a competitive market positioning. As a critical variable in this marketing mix, pricing cannot and should not be isolated from other marketing variables; pricing should always be considered alongside other marketing mix variables - the product, place, and promotion. All these marketing mix decisions collectively determine the firm's competitive market positioning.

Key point: Neoclassical economics mistakenly considers pricing as a singular decision isolated from other strategic decisions in the market.

In summary, the neoclassical economics pricing model utilizes 'marginal analysis' to maximize profit based on the rule that profit is maximized when marginal revenue equals marginal cost. Critically, this model can be contested for its problematic assumptions about profit maximization, limited conceptualization of the market, restricted strategic agency attributed to firms, and the isolated consideration of pricing as a singular decision separate from other marketing mix variables.

3.3 The accounting model of pricing

The second pricing model we need to discuss is the conventional accounting model, commonly known as cost-plus pricing, a concept you should have already encountered in your prior management accounting courses. In simple terms, this model determines the price by adding a required or desired profit margin to the cost. The accounting challenge here lies in calculating the full cost of a product, which comprises two elements: direct and overhead costs. The calculation of direct costs, encompassing direct labor costs, direct material costs, and direct expenses—costs directly and readily attributable to the relevant cost object—is relatively straightforward. Transaction processing systems and other operations management information systems furnish the relevant information to capture and calculate these direct cost items.

Key point:

Conventional accounting deploys a simple cost-plus pricing model.

Key point:

Cost calculation, especially overhead absorption, is the most daunting task in accounting's cost-plus pricing model.

However, the more substantial challenge emerges in overhead allocation and absorption—the computation of the specific portion of overheads relevant to a given cost unit. Numerous overhead expenses are incurred throughout the organization, predominantly at the upper echelons of the organizational hierarchy. Over the past decades, the relative significance of overhead expenses (i.e. overhead as a percentage of the total organizational cost) has witnessed a significant increase. The unit price of a given product should encompass all these costs incurred across the organization.

For this purpose, traditional absorption costing techniques may be employed. For example, you may use direct labor hours, direct labor cost, direct material cost, or prime cost as the basis of overhead absorption. Alternatively, you may opt for activity-based costing, a more refined, advanced, and accurate method of tracing overhead costs to relevant cost units. In activity-based costing, activities performed in producing a given cost unit are deemed the most accurate 'cost drivers.' Therefore, overheads need to be absorbed based on such activities, rather than arbitrary bases like direct labor hours or prime cost used in conventional absorption costing. Consequently, overhead expenses are allocated to relevant cost units based on a set of activities that underpin the cost incurrence on each cost unit.

Management accounting consultants such as Norton and Kaplan argue that activities provide a superior basis for capturing the 'cost incidence' and accurately tracing overhead costs to cost objects. In other words, activities are the real drivers behind the cost; hence, tracing costs based on activities associated with a particular cost unit or cost object provides a more precise cost estimation that can be utilized to manage the activities driving the costs. The following simple numerical example and Figure 3.2 illustrate the accounting's cost-plus pricing model.

Key point:
Activity-based costing is considered a superior method of absorbing overheads to cost units.

A numerical example of cost-plus pricing (activity-based costing)

Basic data:

	Product A budget For the budget period
Direct materials cost	£2,250
Direct labour cost	£3,000
Direct expenses	£1,500
Budgeted production units	400
Direct labour hours	90
Number of setups	6
Number of orders	8
Machine hours	180
Kilowatt-hours	90

The breakdown of overhead expenses for the budget period is given in the table below

Overhead Item	Expected Cost	Relevant activity driver	Expected activity volume for the budget period
Setup costs	£150,000	Number of setups	1,200
Ordering costs	£40,000	Number of orders	10,000
Maintenance	200,000	Machine hours	16,000
Power	20,000	Kilowatt-hours	100,000
Total	£410,000		

The profit margin required is 30%

Cost and price calculations are provided in the table next page:

Figure 3.2: Accounting model of pricing

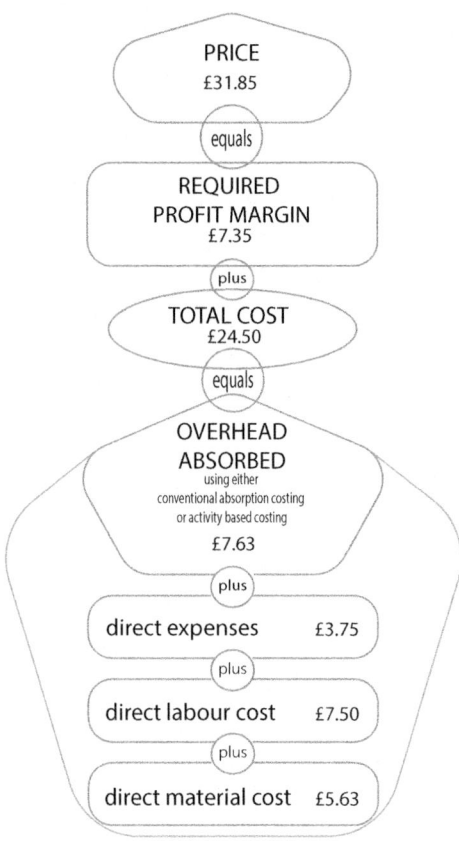

Strategizing the market: strategic pricing decisions | 89

						Product A	
	Total organisational-wide costs for the budget period						
Overhead Item	Expected Cost	Activity Driver	Expected activity volume	Activity cost driver rate	Activity volume for the period		Total overhead attributed
Setup costs	150000	Number of setups	1200	£125.00	6		£750.00
Ordering costs	40000	Number of orders	10000	£4.00	8		£32.00
Maintenance	200000	Machine hours	16000	£12.50	180		£2,250.00
Power	20000	Kilowatt-hours	100000	£0.20	90		£18.00
Total overhead cost	**410000**						**£3,050.00**
Budgeted production for the period							£400.00
Overhead cost per unit							£7.63
Direct material cost per unit (= 2250/400)					£5.63		
Direct labour cost per unit (= 3000/400)					£7.50		
Direct expenses per unit (=1500/400)					£3.75		£16.88
Total cost per unit							£24.50
PLUS: Profit margin 30%							£7.35
Selling price per unit							**£31.85**

The cost-plus pricing model is straightforward to comprehend and has enjoyed widespread use in organizations for numerous decades, if not centuries. Additionally, accounting and other corporate operational management information systems are frequently configured to operationalize a cost-plus pricing model, providing rudimentary information and calculations for strategic pricing. However, in terms of the strategic dynamics of pricing, this model possesses a set of fundamental weaknesses:

1. Market consideration absent: This model lacks consideration for the market, the ultimate arena where strategies are enacted and enabled. It does not contribute to determining a price that captures the intricacies of market dynamics. A sound strategic approach should meticulously analyze the competitive terrain, taking into account factors such as rivalry among existing firms, the threat of new entrants, the threat of substitutes, the bargaining power of suppliers and customers, etc. Yet, this pricing model fails to consider such market dynamics.

2. Production-driven and push strategy: Cost-plus pricing is inherently production-driven or production-based, embodying a push strategy. This implies that pricing originates from the factory floor rather than the market, with product cost estimated based on resources used and activities performed. Costs so calculated, topped up with a required profit margin, are then pushed onto the customers. However, these costs represent not strategic targets but merely the accounting value of resources used or activities performed, which are to be recovered from the customers through the price the firm charges. This can render the product strategically less competitive in the market. This pricing strategy is effective only in situations where the firm holds relatively higher monopoly power in the market, characterized by an inefficient market where customers have no choice but to accept the price imposed by the producer. In a highly competitive market, the firm must reverse this push strategy and adopt a 'pull strategy', starting from the market with a price that aligns with market dynamics and working backwards to manage costs, ensuring the firm can deliver the price demanded by the market with a desired profit margin. In this regard, adopting a Target Costing system, as discussed in section 3.6, becomes crucial.

Key point:

Fundamental weaknesses of cost-plus pricing.

3. **Firms' inefficiencies are passed on to the customers:** Accounting costs encompass all the inefficiencies of the firm, including wastages, suboptimal capacity utilizations, and various others. Cost-plus pricing incorporates these inefficiencies into the price as implicit cost elements. Furthermore, when calculating the price as a percentage of cost and adding a profit margin, cost-plus pricing permits these inefficiencies to be factored into the profits, enabling the firm to gain from its own inefficiencies. This renders the firm strategically less competitive and raises moral-economic concerns about transferring one's inefficiencies to others for a profit.
4. **Incompatibility with highly competitive conditions:** The cost-plus pricing model may falter in highly competitive conditions where:

    a. Customers exhibit price sensitivity and wield bargaining power over firms.
    b. Competitors can manage costs more efficiently and effectively than the company.
    c. The company is striving to pursue a 'cost leadership' strategy.

In summary, the cost-plus pricing model, as part of the conventional accounting model of pricing, exhibits fundamental weaknesses when confronted with the complexities of modern market dynamics.

3.4 Strategic pricing for competitive positioning

The pricing models discussed earlier, rooted in neoclassical economics and conventional accounting, assume a mass production and mass marketing paradigm. This perspective envisions the market as an undifferentiated expanse of demand, aiming to create a universal marketing package that can broadly appeal to all consumers, irrespective of demographic, psychographic, geographic, and behavioral distinctions. During the early stages of industrial capitalism, particularly during the zenith of the Ford Motor Company, mass production prevailed as the standard. The focus was on achieving economies of scale to make products available to the market at the lowest possible cost. This production philosophy was famously epitomized by Henry Ford's statement, "Any customer can have a car painted any color that he wants so long as it is black," reflecting his overarching vision for the company:

"I will build a motor car for the great multitude. It will be large enough for the family but small enough for the individual to run and care for. It will be constructed of the best materials, by the best men to be hired, after the simplest designs that modern engineering can devise. But it will be so low in price that no man making a good salary will be unable to own one - and enjoy with his family the blessing of hours of pleasure in God's great open spaces." (see Crowther and Ford 2015 [1922], 73)

Key point:

For mass production and marketing to succeed, a monopoly or near-monopoly condition is essential. In highly competitive market conditions, a market-driven STP approach becomes crucial.

While such a marketing strategy thrived at that time due to near-monopoly conditions enjoyed by Ford and others, contemporary markets are vastly different. Neoliberalized, globalized, digitalized, and virtualized markets are now highly fragmented and segmented. They necessitate more than a mass marketing strategy centered around a universal marketing package. As explored in preceding chapters, achieving a 'competitive advantage' requires strategic positioning. Therefore, in the current competitive landscape, a market-driven positioning strategy, as opposed to Ford's factory-driven approach, is imperative. Such a market-driven approach encompasses market segmentation, targeting, and positioning – in short, STP marketing. Figure 3.3 illustrates the key elements of this strategic approach.

Figure 3.3: Market segmentation, targeting and positioning

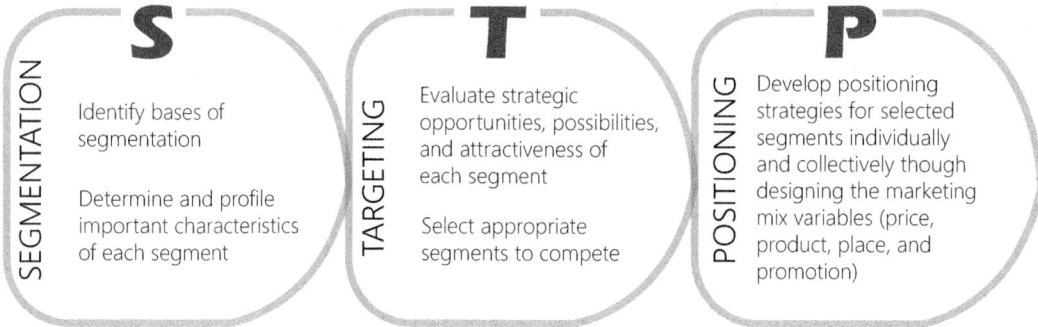

Segmentation

The concept of segmentation revolves around the idea that distinct customer groups require unique strategies to persuade them to purchase the firm's products. Each of these customer categories has specific demands from the company. Segmentation, therefore, entails the analytical process of profiling the market to identify strategically crucial bases on which it can be segmented into different customer categories, each requiring different positioning strategies. The initial step in this process is to identify potential segmentation bases that differentiate and characterize market segments. Market surveys and other methods of understanding the market, such as big data analytics, assist in determining these segmentation bases. The critical analytical question in market segmentation is identifying the forms of segmentation among customers that necessitate different pricing, product characteristics, distribution channels, and promotional themes and media. According to prevalent marketing and strategic management discourses, there are four key sets of variables based on which the market can be segmented (refer to Figure 3.4).

1. **Geographic segmentation** involves considering geographic differences between customers when designing distinct marketing strategies. Examples include legal and regulatory standards and cultural disparities between regions or countries (e.g., Asia vs Europe vs America; or country differences). Similarly, geographic differences may matter due to consumption patterns influenced by urban vs rural distinctions, climatic conditions in different zones, population density, and transportation facilities.
2. **Demographic segmentation** plays a strategically vital role when variables such as age, gender, ethnicity, race or skin color, religion, family size, and family life cycle demand differences in product design, pricing decisions, choice of distribution channels, and the mobilization of promotional themes and channels.
3. **Psychographic segmentation** relates to market conditions where differences in psychological or trait characteristics of consumers are critical in promoting the company's products. This could include factors such as risk-taking vs risk aversion, lifestyles, color preferences, taste preferences, inclination towards displaying social status, and the AIO concept (activities, interests, and opinions).
4. **Behavioral segmentation** focuses on different behavioral patterns related to customers' purchasing decisions, considering factors such as:
    a. Benefit orientation (i.e., benefits sought through the product),

b. Occasion orientation (e.g., one-off purchases, regularly repeated purchases),
c. Usage orientation (e.g., heavy, moderate, minor usage; home vs office usage),
d. Loyalty orientation (i.e., customer retention rate, whether customers tend to stick to one product/brand for a long time or shift brand loyalty).

Key point:

Market segmentation can be conducted based on four different categories of variables, with certain mixtures between them also possible.

It is important to note that these segmentation bases are not necessarily mutually exclusive; they can be used in combination, for example, to create geodemographic and geopsychographic segmentations. Such combinations of segmentation variables are becoming more accessible and popular due to the availability of geographic, demographic, and psychographic databases, along with technologies such as big data analytics.

Figure 3.4: Bases of market segmentation

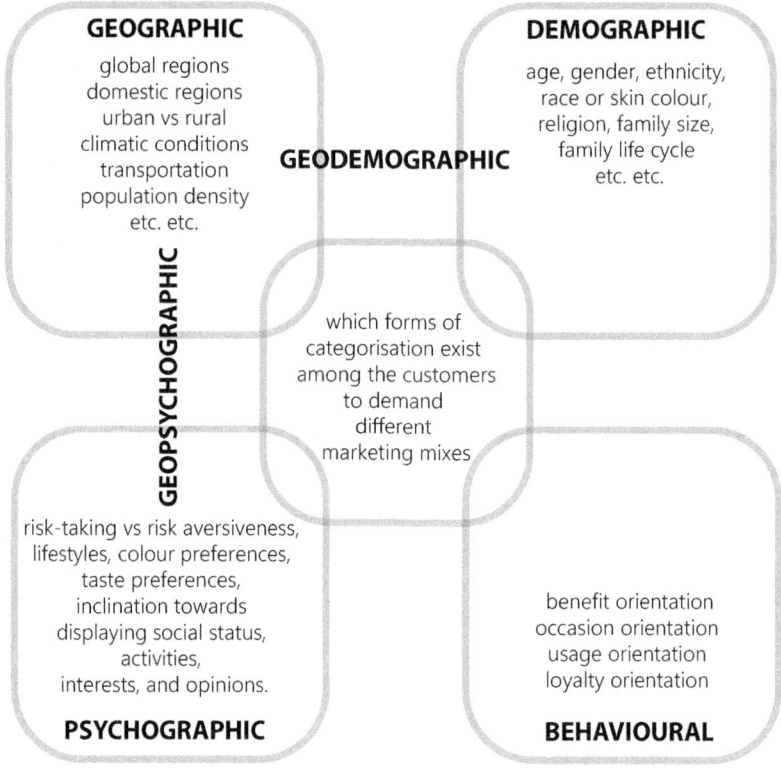

Market segment profile

The analytical outcome of segmentation analysis is to develop detailed market segment profiles. These profiles provide a comparative view of each segment in terms of a selected set of segmentation variables. For illustrative purposes, Table 3.1 provides a possible template for developing segment profiles.

Key point:
Market segmentation should result in developing a market segment profile.

Table 3.1: Market segment profiling

	Segment 1	Segment 2	Segment 3
KEY MEASURES			
Segment size			
Segment growth			
The proportion of the overall market			
CONSUMER BEHAVIOR			
Main consumer needs			
Usage level			
Level of brand loyalty			
Price sensitivity			
Product involvement levels			
Retailer preferences			
DESCRIPTION			
Geographic spread			
Demographic description			
Psychographic description			
COMPETITION/COMMUNICATION			
Main competitive offerings			
Main media choices			

Targeting

Once the market segment profiles have been developed, appropriate segments should be selected for targeting. In deciding which market segments to target, the firm needs to assess the following:

1. Whether the segment is substantial enough and suitable for the company's strategic objectives.

2. Whether the segment is uniquely identifiable in terms of differences that it demands compared to the marketing mix offered to other segments.
3. Whether the segment is reachable by the company.
4. Whether the segment is profitable.
5. Whether the segment is responsive to the firm's new offerings.

> **Key point:**
> The key analytical question to answer in deciding which segments to target.

Depending on the segment assessments, targeting could range from a single segment concentration to full market coverage, offering different marketing mixes for each segment.

Positioning

Positioning refers to the strategic act of creating specific conceptions of the product/brand in the minds of customers in the selected market segments. Although it includes the managerial use of various marketing tools, it is ultimately directed towards a cognitive-psychological outcome - 'owning a word in the mind of the customer.' The answers to the following fundamental questions can better explain the notion of positioning:

> **Key point:**
> Positioning is a brand-developing exercise where a particular cognitive-psychological profile in the customer's mind is built using marketing mix variables.

1. Where do you position? In the mind of the customer. This means that the company brand/product should be able to cater to the targeted market segment's specific customer needs or desires.
2. What do you position? You position an idea, concept, image, benefit, status, etc., to define your brand. Following the American Marketing Association, a brand can be defined as "a name, term, sign, symbol, or design, or a combination of them, intended to identify the goods or services of one seller or group of sellers and to differentiate them from those of competitors."
3. How do you position? Positioning is carried out creatively using all the marketing mix elements, i.e., the 4Ps: product, price, promotion, and place.

The strategic role of pricing in STP

The accounting and economic models discussed earlier consider pricing a singular decision made in isolation, considering only revenue and cost. In contrast, pricing decisions in the STP framework are interdependent with the firm's other marketing mix decisions. None can be considered in isolation but should be treated as elements of a total marketing package. They should all be directed towards the specific positioning propositions the firm is trying to achieve in specific market segments.

For example, suppose the firm is trying to achieve a superior differentiation positioning strategy in a particular market segment with a high-quality product and corresponding distribution channels and promotional campaigning. In that case, the pricing decisions should also manifest this positioning strategy with relatively higher prices. In such a differentiation strategy, the price may not be the most critical variable in the marketing mix, but the superior quality of the product and how that quality is communicated and conveyed to the customer.

In contrast, if the firm's positioning strategy is 'cost leadership' directed towards mass marketing a standard product, then pricing should manifest this with a competitive price tag. There should be a clear connection between the price and the quality proposition the firm is trying to realize in the market. Figure 3.5 illustrates the possible positioning concepts (i.e. value propositions) arising from the possible connection between price and product quality.

Key point:

The price is a critical element in constructing the strategic value proposition in the market.

Figure 3.5: Value propositions between product price and quality

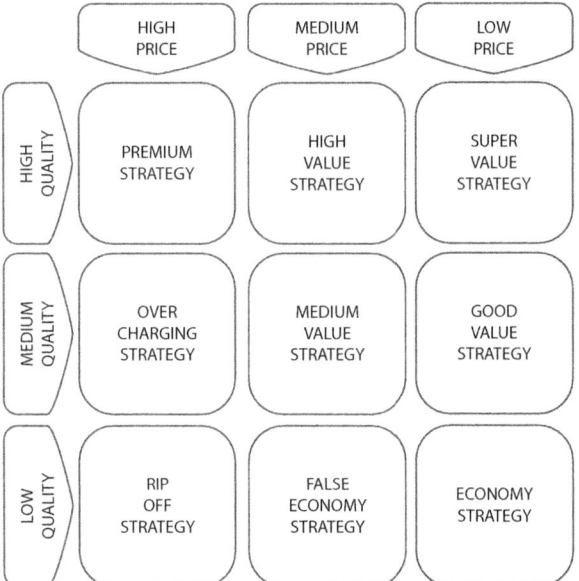

Nevertheless, price is a special element in the marketing mix because it is the only marketing mix variable that generates revenues, while all other marketing mix variables contribute to costs. Hence, the financial viability of any positioning strategy depends on the price's capacity to generate sufficient revenue to guarantee the desired return on investment. To that end, accounting calculations still play a critical role.

Other pricing considerations and techniques: Fine-tuning the pricing strategy

Once the specific price or price range is identified for each market segment, the price needs to be adapted and communicated to create cognitive appeal and impact. To that end, firms often adopt what is now popularly known as 'psychological pricing'. Psychological pricing is, in effect, the subtle use of the price tag and other associated information to 'push' the customer to make the purchasing decision. This often includes the following techniques.

Psychological pricing

Key point:

Subtle ways to adapt and communicate the final price to push the customer to make the purchasing decision.

1. **Charm pricing:** This involves using, for example, £1.99 instead of £2.00. The idea here is that the customer sees the 1 first in the price tag and perceives the price to be closer to £1.00 than to £2.00. It should also be noted that the prevalence of this price tagging has created the opposite effect. Accordingly, prices ending in 9 now tend to connote a 'value price'. Conversely, prices ending in 0 can now connote a 'prestigious price'. So, for valuable or high-class products, like expensive jewelery, for example, it might be better to have a price tag ending with a 0 to give customers the impression that they are paying for something expensive and worthy.
2. **Artificial time constraining:** This is the practice of associating a time-limited special value with the price. For example, "today only" or 'today's special price'.
3. **Innumeracy:** This is the practice associated with, for example, "buy one get one free" rather than saying "50% off two items".
4. **Price appearance:** This refers to the specific attempt to make the price 'appear small'. This is often used by fancy restaurant menus where prices are stated in a small font without £ sign and penny values (i.e. just 12, instead of "£12.00").

Market skimming vs penetration pricing

These two pricing techniques are especially useful when a new product is introduced to a market. They manifest two different, if not opposing, approaches to introducing a product and depend on the manner in which the market is stratified and the appeal that the product can make in the market.

Market skimming is more suitable for a condition where:

1. the market is vertically stratified with layers of different purchasing power or status groups where top layers are relatively price insensitive, and;
2. the product is relatively new and innovative and, hence, can demand a higher price initially.

In such a condition, market skimming pricing first 'skims' the top layer of the market with a higher price and then gradually, over time, drops the price to 'skim' the lower layers in sequence. In a broader sense, this captures Porter's idea of 'differentiation'.

On the other hand, market penetration is more suitable when the market is 'flat' and relatively saturated by existing competitive offers, and the product the firm offers is generic with marginal advantages over the others. In such cases, firms may offer the product at a relatively low competitive introductory price to capture the largest possible market share. In a broader sense, this captures Porter's idea of 'cost leadership'.

Key point:
Market skimming and penetration are two alternative strategies in introductory pricing.

3.5 Lifecycle costing

Typically, economic and accounting pricing models discussed in the initial section of this chapter adopt a short-term time perspective, mainly capturing costs incurred during a specific accounting period. In contrast, lifecycle costing introduces a long-term viewpoint to strategic pricing. In essence, the concept of lifecycle costing is straightforward: when calculating the cost of a product and consequently determining its price, all costs already incurred or anticipated throughout the entire lifecycle must be considered. In accounting and related literature, lifecycle costing is addressed for two distinct purposes or within two different contexts:

1. Asset Management
2. Product Costing

Lifecycle costing in asset management

The asset management perspective evaluates the total lifecycle cost of owning and utilizing a specific asset. This viewpoint is seen from the perspective of a product user or purchaser. For instance, when employing lifecycle costing to decide on purchasing a car, considerations should encompass:

a. Purchase price
b. Interests or borrowing costs (if applicable) during its useful life
c. Estimated running costs, such as fuel, repairs, insurance, tax, MOT tests, services, parking charges, etc., over the intended usage period
d. Ultimately, at the end of its useful lifespan, its disposal or sales value, etc.

Following recommendations from the European Commission and the European Union (e.g., 2014 EU procurement rules), lifecycle costing has become a crucial element in the procurement procedures of public authorities. It is utilized in assessing the "most economically advantageous tender" (MEAT), where, according to the European Commission, all costs incurred throughout the product lifecycle should be considered when purchasing a product or undertaking a work or service. The lifecycle cost of an asset includes:

Key point:

Lifecycle costing can be embraced as an asset procurement and management technique, and in some instances, it is a regulatory requirement in asset procurement and management within public authorities.

a. Purchase price and all associated costs (delivery, installation, insurance, etc.)
b. Operating costs, encompassing energy, fuel and water use, spares, and maintenance
c. End-of-life costs (such as decommissioning or disposal) or residual value (i.e., revenue from the sale of a product)

The European Commission also provides specific guidelines on situations and conditions under which the 'cost of externalities' (e.g., greenhouse gas emissions) may be included in the assessment of the lifecycle cost of an asset. Overall, the adoption of lifecycle costing in asset procurement and management is imposed to encourage the following:

- Savings on energy, water, and fuel usage
- Savings on maintenance and replacement
- Savings on disposal costs

Lifecycle costing in product costing

As a technique in product costing, lifecycle costing adopts the perspective of a seller determining the selling price of a product, considering all the lifecycle costs associated with that specific product. From a production and costing standpoint, the lifecycle can be categorized into three major phases:

1. **Pre-production phase:** Costs incurred during this phase typically involve research and development (R&D), market surveys, product design and prototyping, process and technology designs, licensing, networking, development of supply chain connections, acquisition of capital assets related to production, and various other similar activities. All these costs must be factored into the calculation of the product cost and price.
2. **Production or operational phase:** This phase encompasses the actual production, distribution, and selling of the product. All variable and fixed costs associated with production, distribution, selling, and general administrative costs should be taken into consideration. The calculation of these costs should extend beyond a single accounting period to cover the entirety of the accounting periods in which the product is produced and sold.
3. **Disposal and decommissioning phase:** This marks the conclusion of the lifecycle, involving estimated disposal and decommissioning costs.

Key point:

Lifecycle costing must encompass all costs incurred or expected to be incurred throughout the entire product lifecycle, from design to decommissioning.

It is essential to note that lifecycle costing is most effectively applied to products with a definite lifecycle. Examples include high-tech products, such as specific car models, computer chips, laptops, etc., that require periodic updates and replacement with more technologically advanced models. In contrast, products like Coca-Cola have no utility for lifecycle costing.

The concept of the lifecycle cost of a product can be expressed using the following formula:

$$\text{average cost per unit} = \frac{\text{total cost incurred and estimated to be incurred during the entire life cycle of the product}}{\text{total number of units to be sold during the entire lifecycle of the product}}$$

$$\text{Price} = \text{average cost per unit} + \text{required profit margin per unit.}$$

A mini case study illustrating the application of lifecycle costing is provided in the appendix of this chapter. Before delving into that at the end of this chapter, Table 3.2 (next page) offers a simplified example of calculating a product's lifecycle cost and price.

It should be noted that the price calculated using this method represents the average for the entire lifecycle. In this context, lifecycle cost and price establish a long-term target. This means the price can then be effectively adjusted according to specific strategic requirements of competitive market conditions. For instance, during the introductory phase of the product, if competitive conditions necessitate it, a slightly lower price may be set as an introductory or market penetration price. Meanwhile, at the mature stages, higher prices can be applied, still ensuring that the average lifecycle price is attained. Conversely, if market conditions permit, the product can be launched with a relatively high market skimming price to target the top layers initially, followed by subsequent price reductions to capture the lower layers.

Key point:

Lifecycle costing necessitates a long-term perspective on various activities, from the pre-production phase through the production phase to the post-production.

As a cost management technique, lifecycle costing requires a long-term perspective on various activities, spanning from the pre-production phase through the production phase to the post-production. In this regard, it offers a more comprehensive understanding of long-term cost management. Consequently, it can have positive sustainability effects by compelling management to carefully consider future resource usage, disposal, and decommissioning costs. However, on the flip side, the accuracy of cost, price and profit calculations dangerously depends on the precision of cost estimates for activities scheduled in the distant future. It also necessitates a multidisciplinary approach that facilitates collaborative information-sharing among various departments across the organization.

3.6 Target costing

Initially pioneered by Japanese companies, notably Toyota, target costing represents a market-driven approach to product pricing and cost management. The costing and pricing methodologies discussed thus far, including lifecycle costing, embody a 'push strategy'. This involves determining costs based on activities and resource consumption during production and distribution, subsequently passing these costs, alongside a desired profit margin, onto customers. Consequently, conventional cost-plus pricing hinges on resource consumption at the production stage and within administrative hierarchies.

Table 3.2: Lifecycle costing example

This model/version is expected to be replaced after three operating years, and the management requires a 35% profit margin on cost.

	pre-production	operating years 1st	operating years 2nd	operating years 3rd	post-production	total
Estimated sales (units)		50,000	60,000	40,000		150,000
Costs						
Research and development	£200,000	£25,000	£10,000			£235,000
Licensing and other preparatory costs	£25,000					£25,000
Variable cost per unit		£300	£325	£350		
Total variable cost = per unit VC * estimated sales		£15,000,000	£19,500,000	£14,000,000		£48,500,000
Fixed overheads attributable to the product		£5,000,000	£5,500,000	£6,000,000		£16,500,000
product decommissioning and disposal costs					£30,000	£30,000
After-sales service commitment costs not included in the three operating years					£50,000	£50,000
TOTAL LIFECYCLE COST						£65,340,000
AVERAGE LIFECYCLE COST PER UNIT = TOTAL COST (i.e. 65,340,000)/TOTAL UNITS (i.e. 150,000)						£435.60
Required profit margin per unit (35%)						£152.46
AVERAGE LIFECYCLE PRICE PER UNIT = AVERAGE COST + REQUIRED PROFIT MARGIN						£588.06

In contrast, target costing embodies a 'pull strategy,' initiating pricing from the market perspective. It begins by evaluating market competition and customer attributes to establish a competitive price aligned with market conditions—one that customers are willing and able to pay. This market-dictated price, conceived as the strategically optimal price, serves as the starting point. The firm then works backwards, deducting the desired profit margin to calculate the cost at which the product should be produced and distributed. Therefore, the target costing pricing formula is:

Price – Profit Margin = Target Cost

This approach is conceptually and operationally distinct from the conventional formula "cost + profit margin = price," as *it shifts from a 'push strategy' to a 'pull strategy,' aligning market demands with production targets.*

Key point:
Conventional cost-plus pricing manifests a 'push strategy', whereas target costing manifests a 'pull strategy'.

Crucially, target costing deviates from other costing techniques like activity-based costing, absorption costing, and process costing. It is not merely a product costing technique but an overarching managerial approach to strategically manage costs. Originating in the 1970s, target costing gained popularity in the 1980s and 1990s as a pivotal component of Japanese management systems, influencing the Japanization of Western management practices. It forms an integral part of the comprehensive Japanese management package, alongside methodologies such as total quality management (TQM), lean manufacturing, continuous improvement (kaizen), quality circles, etc. According to Cooper and Slagmulder (1997), target costing, coupled with value engineering, establishes a strategic link between the price, quality, and functionality of firms' market offerings.

Key point:
Target costing is not a specific costing or pricing technique but an overarching managerial approach to cost management.

Our discussion of target costing here can be built around three interconnected themes:

1. The survival zone
2. The triangle of target costing
3. The target costing process

Key point:
Three foundational concepts in explaining target costing as a managerial approach.

In essence, target costing is not confined to a specific costing or pricing technique but represents a holistic managerial approach to cost management, emphasizing its strategic importance.

The concept of survival zone

As an overarching managerial framework for value engineering and cost management, target costing, as defined by Cooper and Slagmulder (1997), ought to be grounded in a delineation of the 'survival zone' for the company. The survival zone, also referred to as the 'triangle of survival', as elucidated by Cooper and Slagmulder (1997), represents the competitive realm within which a firm must operate; straying beyond this zone may imperil its competitive viability. Essentially, this delineates a specific manner of defining the competitive landscape or conditions in terms of value engineering and target costing parameters. It constitutes a competitive space determined by three closely interconnected variables shaping competition: price, quality, and product functionalities. Illustrated in Figure 3.6, the survival zone is demarcated by upper and lower limits for each variable, with the objective being to operate within this designated space. Consequently:

1. Concerning price, there exists a maximum allowable price; any price exceeding this may lack competitive viability and sustainability, given insufficient market demand for such elevated pricing. Correspondingly, there is a minimum allowable price; any pricing below this is financially unviable as it falls below production costs.
2. Functionalities pertain to the specific capabilities of a product or the specific customer needs it can fulfill. For instance, a high-end digital SLR camera is designed to capture high-quality full-frame images in 4K, 6K, or even 8K videos at a higher frame rate (e.g. 60, 120, 150 frames per second). There is a technically and financially viable upper limit to the number of functionalities a product can incorporate. Similarly, a product should be able to perform a must-have set of functionalities as a lower limit. For instance, a camera lacking at least HD capabilities may not garner sufficient market demand in the current technological landscape.
3. Quality, on the other hand, refers to how proficiently the product executes its functionalities. For example, a high-end digital SLR camera may be capable of recording 4K or 8K videos but only for a limited time, as the camera can overheat and automatically shut down—a problem high-end Canon cameras faced compared to high-end Sony cameras. There is

Key point:

The concept of the survival zone elucidates the domain within which a firm should operate in terms of price, product quality, and product functionalities.

a minimum allowable quality, below which a product is not competitive at any price and may be considered defective by the market. The upper limit is the maximum feasible quality that is technically and financially viable.

Figure 3.6: Survival zone

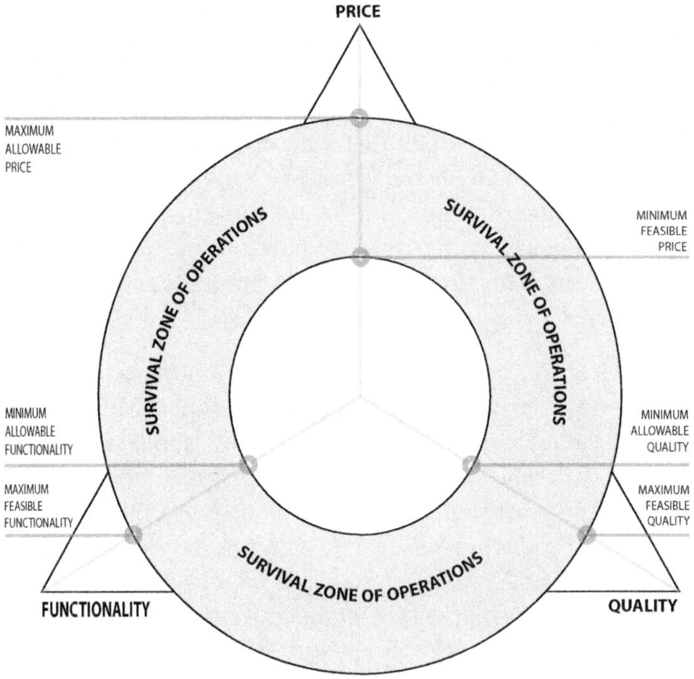

Source: Adapted from Cooper and Slagmulder (1997, p. 5)

Triangle of target costing

While the survival zone defines the sphere within which the firm should operate, the firm's operation within this survival zone depends on how it connects and integrates three critical strategic actors: customers, suppliers, and product designers. The target costing triangle conceptualizes these interconnections between customers, suppliers, and product designers. As depicted in Figure 3.7, the network of connections and interactions the firm establishes among them determines the various cost elements that a target costing system should address. Together, these elements constitute the firm's profit management regime.

Figure 3.7: Target costing triangle

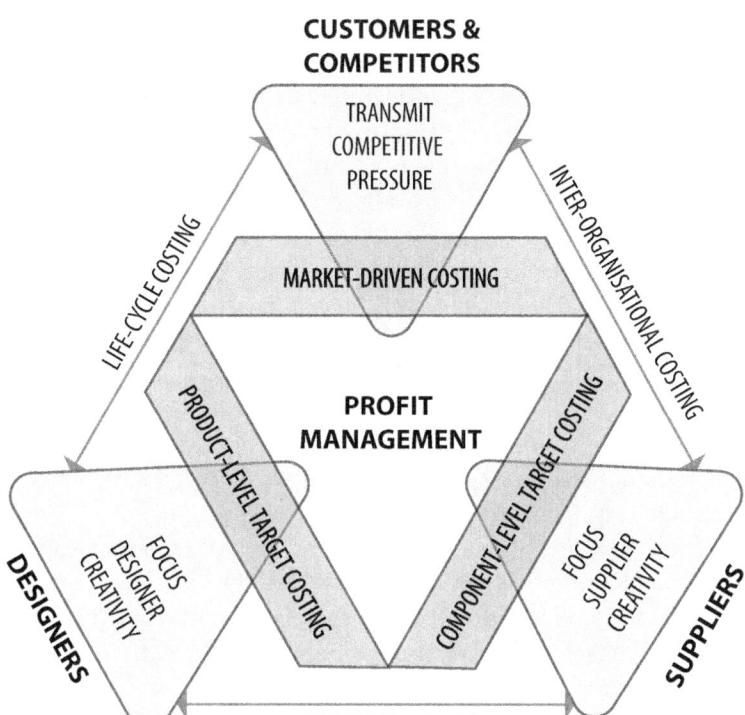

Source: adapted from Cooper and Slagmulder (1997, 9)

As shown in Figure 3.7, target costing can be broadly understood as a system of profit management that integrates customers, suppliers, and product designers through a series of costing and value engineering processes. Accordingly, target costing-based profit management comprises the following key elements:

1. **Market-driven target costing** operates on the frontier between the company and its customers, transmitting customer requirements and competitive pressures as specific cost targets to suppliers and product designers. Market conditions dictate the strategically optimum price the firm should adopt—subtracting the desired profit margins from the price results in the target cost. Inter-organizational costing across the supply chain intensifies competitive pressure on suppliers, requiring them to be innovative in meeting those cost requirements.

Key point:

The target costing triangle consolidates customers, designers, and suppliers into a profit management system through lifecycle costing, inter-organisational costing, and value engineering.

Lifecycle costing connects customers with product designers and ensures that the target profit margins consider upfront investments in product development and any future cost incurrence or savings anticipated over the product's life, including disposal and decommissioning costs (Cooper and Slagmulder 1997, 9). The use of lifecycle costing in target costing can also provide opportunities to address sustainability issues, such as costs associated with carbon offsetting.

2. **Component-level target costing** operates on the frontiers between the company and its suppliers to stimulate supplier creativity. Here, the focus is on ensuring that specific components delivered by contracted suppliers meet quality requirements at specified target costs. Inter-organizational costing (e.g., open-book accounting and enterprise resource planning systems running across the supply chain) establishes operational and accounting connections between suppliers and the firm.

3. **Product-level target costing** stimulates designers' creativity, demanding product and process designers to meet product quality and functionalities at specified target costs. It requires a high degree of collaboration between product designers and suppliers. Target costing needs to be complemented by value engineering to create strategic optimality between product quality, functionalities, and price.

Viewed through this set of relationships and costing techniques, target costing is defined as *"a structured approach to determining the lifecycle cost at which a proposed product with specified functionality and quality must be produced to generate the desired level of profitability over its life cycle when sold at its anticipated selling price"* (Cooper and Slagmulder 1997, 10).

Target costing process

Target costing is a meticulous procedure that determines, oversees, regulates, and enhances functional, component, and activity-level target costs. This process commences with establishing a competitive market price and extends to the production points within and outside the firm, namely suppliers. Figure 3.8 illustrates the target costing process.

Figure 3.8: Target costing process

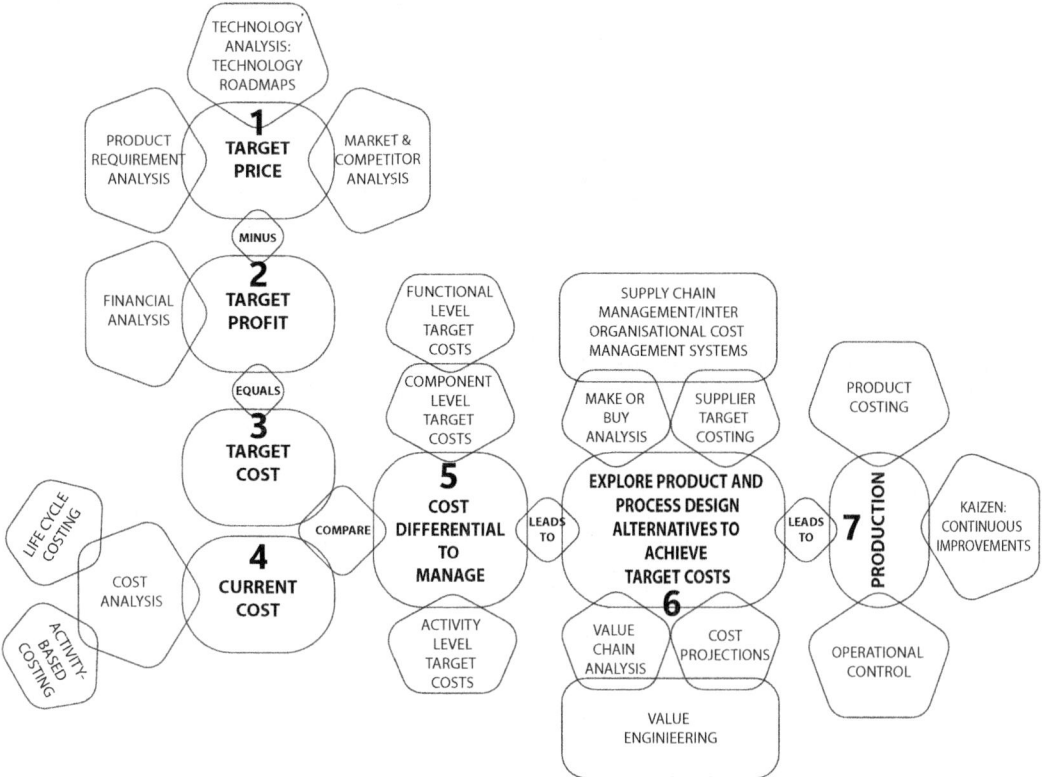

The process initiates with the *target price*. Establishing the target price necessitates a thorough analysis of product requirements, technology roadmaps (i.e. the product's historical and future technological direction), and market and competitor analysis (e.g. market segments and competitor profiles). These analyses are essential to ascertain how the firm operates in the survival zone, striking an optimal balance between product price, quality, and functionalities (refer to the discussion on the survival zone above).

Once the target price is determined, deducting the *target profit* margin reveals the target unit cost. This requires a financial analysis of how well the target profit margin aligns with financial expectations, including the cost of capital, return on investments, future cash flows, etc.

Next, the target cost should be compared with the *current cost*. Calculating the current cost necessitates a comprehensive cost analysis. Product costing techniques such as lifecycle and activity-based costing can be utilized to estimate the current cost. A comparison between the target and current costs highlights the *cost differential* that needs management, representing the full cost reduction required within a specified time limit.

The cost differential should then be allocated to its sub-elements. *Functional-level target costs* often encompass measures to reduce overhead costs associated with various functional departments, such as factory management and administration, selling and distribution, human resource management, accounting and finance, etc. These include the 'support activities' in Porter's value chain framework. *Component-level target costs* pertain to specific cost targets set for components composing the final product. They involve cost management activities aimed at fostering supplier creativity, including inter-organizational costing and value-chain engineering. *Activity-level target costs* are the most fundamental elements relating to specific cost (and time) targets for distinct activities (e.g. material handling, machining, molding, painting, finishing, etc.). This is often operationalized through activity-based costing and management.

Identifying functional-level, component-level, and activity-level cost targets leads to exploring product and process design alternatives to meet the target costs. Such alternatives can be categorized into s*upply chain or inter-organizational cost management systems and value engineering*. Supply chain-related issues encompass make-or-buy decisions and the imposition of supplier target costs. Value chain analysis and cost projections constitute value engineering.

The actual production marks the final step of the target costing process, requiring continuous evaluation through appropriate product costing techniques, monitoring via production control systems, and improvement through continuous improvement systems, known in Japanese management terminology as kaizen.

Sustainability implications of target costing

The sustainability implications of target costing can present a paradox. Collaborations within target costing systems involving customers (market-driven target costing), suppliers (component-level target costing), and product and process designers (product-level target

Key point:

Target costing encompasses a sequential process of analysis and management, ranging from understanding market requirements to the continuous improvement of production systems.

costing) should incorporate the growing market demands for sustainable product features. This integration allows the system to convey these demands to designers and suppliers. In this regard, a target costing system can facilitate market pressures for more energy-efficient and environmentally friendly product features and functionalities. In essence, heightened customer awareness and market demand for eco-friendly products can redefine the 'survival zone,' compelling firms to integrate new features and qualities into their products and processes to enhance ecological sustainability. Furthermore, the system's use of lifecycle costing to assess the entire lifecycle cost, considering factors like energy usage, water consumption, and carbon emissions, can aid in identifying and addressing sustainability issues.

Similarly, inter-organizational costing and value engineering within target costing systems can encourage creativity among the firm's product and process designers and suppliers in addressing sustainability concerns.

However, on the flip side, target costing, as a management system, transmits market pressure down the supply chain, from influential customers to vulnerable laborers at the distant end, often situated in 'third-world' peripheries. Target costing can exert unequivocal pressure and a substantial managerial burden across the supply chain to continuously reduce costs. It is at the terminus of the global supply chain – the sweatshops on the periphery of global capitalism – that this pressure is ultimately unleashed, impacting the impoverished laborers earning wages below subsistence levels. As (Burawoy 1983, 588) notes, "despotic regulation of the labor process is constituted by the economic whip of the market ... anarchy in the market leads to despotism in the factory." Such despotism can manifest as human trafficking, modern slavery, and similar despotic labor control practices.

In response to these possibilities of despotism at the periphery, modern slavery has become a burgeoning research issue among accounting and management scholars. They have documented various ways in which accounting contributes to the perpetuation of modern slavery or similar despotic labor control practices across the supply chain (Neu et al. 2014; New 2015; Christ and Burritt 2021; Christ et al. 2020; Christ et al. 2019; Crane 2013; Crane et al. 2022; Islam and Van Staden 2022). Such practices have become increasingly prevalent, a problem that global regulatory institutions such as the United Nations

Key point:
The sustainability implications of target costing can be dual-faceted – offering opportunities for product and process improvements for sustainability on the one hand, while on the other, potentially fostering highly despotic relations in production, if not modern slavery.

(UN) and the International Labor Organization (ILO) now identify as a significant social injustice issue concerning global sustainability. Consequently, the UK and Australian governments have enacted anti-modern slavery laws (UK Modern Slavery Act, 2015, and Australia's Modern Slavery Act, 2018) to impose specific accountabilities and reporting requirements on large corporations regarding their supply chain connections.

Dynamic pricing

Dynamic pricing is a strategy that adjusts the prices of products or services based on market demand, competitive conditions, customer behavior, firms' supply and inventory levels, competitor actions, and any other relevant dynamic variable on which a differential price can be charged. This approach can assist businesses in optimizing revenue, managing inventory levels, enhancing customer satisfaction, and strategically outperforming competitors. However, implementing dynamic pricing demands a substantial and robust data and information infrastructure supported by data analytics and algorithms, often running on web-based data conditions such as enabled cookies. In economic terms, the following are preconditions for a company to deploy dynamic pricing, which is essentially an advanced and technologically enabled form of extreme price discrimination:

1. The firm's bargaining power over buyers.
2. Consumers or consumer segments with different elasticities of demand and willingness to pay.
3. The firm's techno-managerial capacity to gauge how demand fluctuates over variables that underpin consumer decision choices of prices, quantities, and timing.
4. Minimal possibilities of reselling between prices by buyers.

However, more than anything else, the contemporary form of dynamic pricing manifests technological innovation; it revolves around how technology has enabled firms to practice automated and continuous price discrimination using real-time data, data analytics, and algorithms to capture the essence of such real-time data. The following definitions of dynamic pricing, sourced from my web search, illustrate this technological conditionality:

- "The (fully or partially) automated adjustment of prices" (McKinsey).
- "A strategy in which the price of an item is constantly and automatically adjusted in response to real-time changing demand" (Inc.com).
- "The main idea behind dynamic pricing is that it is flexible and based on real-time data" (Business.com).
- "A strong dynamic pricing strategy relies on the power of the algorithm used to generate pricing" (Wall Street Journal, Deloitte).

Here are some examples of dynamic pricing in different industries and how they operate:

- Airlines use dynamic pricing to set the fares of their flights based on factors such as demand, seasonality, time of day, route, and competition. They change their prices frequently to match the changing market conditions and customer preferences. For example, Delta Airlines uses dynamic pricing to charge higher prices for flights that have no direct competitors or for frequent fliers who are more likely to pay more.
- E-commerce platforms use dynamic pricing to adjust the prices of their products based on factors such as demand, supply, customer behavior, and competitor prices. E-commerce platforms can use data and algorithms to monitor market trends and customer preferences and change prices accordingly. For example, Amazon uses dynamic pricing to change product prices based on the customer's purchase history, browsing patterns, location, and other factors.
- Ride-sharing services use dynamic pricing to adjust the fares of their rides based on factors such as demand, supply, traffic, and peak hours. Ride-sharing services can use data and algorithms to calculate the optimal price for each ride based on the current and expected market conditions and customer willingness to pay. For example, Uber uses dynamic pricing to apply surge pricing when the demand for rides exceeds the supply of drivers or when special events or weather conditions affect the demand.
- Sports teams use dynamic pricing to set the prices of their tickets based on factors such as demand, team performance, opponent, and seat location. Sports teams can use data and

algorithms to analyze market trends and customer behavior and change prices accordingly. For example, Major League Baseball teams use dynamic pricing to charge higher prices for popular games, premium seats, or last-minute purchases.

While dynamic pricing is a powerful and flexible strategy, it comes with challenges and limitations:

1. It can impact customer perception of product or service value and fairness, leading to confusion or frustration.
2. Dynamic pricing may increase competition and price wars among businesses, necessitating constant monitoring and matching of competitor prices.
3. Implementation requires a large amount of data and sophisticated technology, leading to potential complexity, cost, and risk for businesses.
4. Businesses may also have to deal with the legal and ethical issues that may arise from dynamic pricing, such as antitrust laws, price discrimination, or price gouging.

Chapter summary

This chapter delved into the neoclassical economics model of pricing, accounting models of pricing, and strategic pricing. The neoclassical economics pricing model employs 'marginal analysis' to determine the profit maximization price by equating marginal revenue with marginal cost. Criticism is directed at its narrow understanding of market dynamics, capturing them solely through the assumed relationship between price and quantity (i.e. demand function). The accounting model of pricing adopts a cost-plus approach, adding a desired profit margin to the cost to determine the selling price. It is critiqued for neglecting market dynamics and promoting a 'push strategy'.

Strategic pricing is an intricate process involving market segmentation, targeting, and positioning, requiring collaboration with other marketing mix decisions. Segmentation identifies strategically important market stratifications necessitating distinct positioning strategies for product, place, promotion, and price. Four key sets of segmentation variables—geographic, demographic, psychographic, and behavioral—were discussed. With advancements in information technologies like big data analytics, a subtle mix of these variables, such as geodemographics and geopsychographics, is possible. The outcome of segmentation is the development of segment profiles for a comparative understanding of market segments and their differing demands for positioning strategies.

Once a comparative understanding is reached, the firm can decide which segments to target, ranging from full market coverage to a single segment concentration. A targeted market segment should be substantial, identifiable, reachable, profitable, and responsive. Positioning involves strategically shaping perceptions of the product/brand in the minds of customers through the subtle use of marketing mix variables. This requires answers to questions such as where, what, and how to position.

Lifecycle costing was discussed as a strategic pricing technique; it can be deployed as an asset management or product costing technique. As an asset management technique, taking the customer's perspective, it considers the total cost of owning and using a product from acquisition through operational deployment to disposal, including environmental costs. As a product costing technique, taking the producer's perspective, it calculates the average lifecycle cost of a product, considering all costs associated with pre-production, production, and post-production phases.

The chapter also explored target costing as a comprehensive cost and profit management system, contrasting with push strategies of accounting and economics pricing models. Target costing employs a pull strategy with three conceptual themes: survival zone, target costing triangle, and target costing process. It encompasses customer-driven target costing, product-level target costing for enhanced creativity, and component-level target costing to foster supplier creativity. Within a target costing system, lifecycle costing facilitates connections between customers and product designers, while inter-organizational costing establishes connections between customers and suppliers. Value engineering connects product designers with suppliers to enhance strategic optimality between price, product functionalities, and quality. Despite its advantages, target costing may have paradoxical implications for sustainability.

Test your knowledge

1. Provide a brief explanation of the neoclassical economic model of pricing.
2. What are the primary weaknesses of the neoclassical economic model of pricing?
3. Briefly outline the conventional accounting model of pricing.
4. Identify the most challenging element of the conventional accounting model of pricing and discuss how activity-based costing improves this aspect within the traditional cost-plus pricing model.
5. Enumerate the critical weaknesses of the conventional accounting model of pricing.
6. Explain strategic or competitive positioning as the primary objectives towards which strategic pricing should be directed.
7. List the three critical elements in strategic pricing.
8. Briefly describe the four principal bases for segmenting a market with examples.
9. Enumerate the key parameters for developing a market segmentation profile.
10. List the criteria for selecting a market segment for targeting.
11. Explain the concept of 'positioning' using the key questions of what, where, and how.
12. In relation to the concept of 'value proposition', explain the strategic role of price.
13. Illustrate the adoption of 'psychological pricing' with specific examples.
14. Differentiate between market penetration and market skimming pricing.
15. Distinguish the use of lifecycle costing as an asset management technique and as a product costing technique.
16. Considering it as a product costing technique, provide the generic formula for calculating lifecycle cost and price.
17. Differentiate target costing from conventional costing techniques such as process or job costing.
18. Briefly explain the concept of a survival zone.
19. Outline the target costing triangle, emphasizing:

    a. Key parties or forces integrated
    b. Key strategic capabilities developed and enhanced

c. Specific costing and engineering systems facilitating integration.

20. Briefly explain the key stages of the target costing process, focusing on the managerial analyses required at each step.
21. Briefly explain the practice of dynamic pricing, paying special attention to the centrality of technology therein.

Explore further

1. Investigate product development, promotion, and pricing strategies in the toothpaste market, considering:

    a. Segmentation based on benefits sought.
    b. Design of product promotions, especially advertisements, based on specific themes (benefits).
    c. Manifestation of specific segmentation variables (benefits) in product design.

2. Visit the European Commission website pages on lifecycle costing, exploring:

    a. Guiding principles for adopting lifecycle costing in procurement and asset management.
    b. Conditions mandating lifecycle costing as regulatory compliance.
    c. Administrative procedures and accounting calculations prescribed by the European Commission.
    d. Explain how lifecycle costing contributes to the global sustainability agenda.

3. Read Robin Cooper and Regine Slagmulder's book "Target Costing and Value Engineering" to explore case studies on the techno-managerial core of target costing and variations in its use by world-leading corporations.
4. Read the report "Discrimination, Artificial Intelligence and Algorithms" published by the Directorate General of Democracy - Council of Europe (Borgesius 2018).

    Summarise the key ethical and legal challenges of using AI and algorithms in business decisions, including dynamic pricing.

Develop your critical argumentation skills

1. Craft an argumentative essay on the theme:

   "Contemporary competitive conditions demand a more sophisticated and market-driven approach to pricing than what neoclassical economic and accounting models offer."

2. Write an argumentative essay on the theme:

   "Target costing is not merely a technique for determining product costs but a comprehensive profit management system connecting customers, product designers, and suppliers through inter-organizational costing, lifecycle costing, and value engineering."

3. Develop an argumentative essay on the theme:

   "Concerning sustainability, target costing can address certain issues positively through costing and value engineering but may also contribute to social injustice, including despotic labor controls and modern slavery."

4. Write an exploratory essay articulating the techno-managerial as well as legal-ethical issues of using dynamic pricing.

Mini case study

GreenGig roduct Development and Pricing Strategy: Lifecycle Costing Illustrative Case Study

This hypothetical case has been crafted to elucidate specific strategic management accounting concepts, primarily limiting factor analysis, life cycle costing, and target return pricing.

ABC Plc, a high-tech chemical company operating in a highly research-sensitive industry, relies historically on patent rights for market success. These rights confer a temporary monopoly, shaping the company's organizational culture and leadership style that emphasizes significant investments in research and development (R&D). R&D expenses, a substantial element of corporate overheads, have risen notably in recent years due to efforts in recruiting leading scientists and establishing state-of-the-art laboratories. Despite the cost, this commitment has positioned ABC Plc as a profitable industry leader, setting benchmarks for R&D, new product development, and successful marketing. With a global presence, ABC Plc employs approximately 60,000 people worldwide and boasts a diverse product portfolio. Its recent financial performance indicated a 20% increase in pre-tax profits, representing around 35% of turnover, with a 10% growth in dividends per share.

The strategic challenge for ABC Plc lies in sustaining R&D efforts to launch new patented products as older patents expire. A significant portion of revenue, approximately 30%, has been derived from one product over the last four years. However, as the underlying technology loses its competitive edge, sales are expected to decline sharply. To address this, a new product, GreenGig, boasting superior technical efficiency, has completed its development and testing phase and is poised for global marketing. Product testing has demonstrated that it is 200% more technically efficient than the best competitor (Gif-Chem) in its intended use, providing a superior competitive advantage regarding quality and reliability. The company intends to use this tested superiority in its product positioning strategy.

The retail market price (i.e. manufacturer's recommended price) of GifChem is £12.00 a liter can. It is understood that GifChem's bought-in cost for the retailer per can is £9.00. GreenGig's total activity costs (excluding R&D and other overheads described in the next paragraph) of taking the product to the retailer is estimated to be £3.00 a liter, which the company's cost accountant considers the total variable cost. However, the new product must be in 1.5-liter cans as the recommended use quantity is 1.5 times larger than that of GifChem. Availability of shelf space is a critical limiting factor for most retailers. The shelf area occupied by each can of GifChem is 18 square centimeters, while that of GreenGig is 24 square centimeters. The holding cost of each can for the retailer is estimated as £0.40 and £0.50, respectively, for GigChem and GreenGig. Market analysis indicates that the average weekly sales volume for retail outlets stocking both products will be 120 cans of GreenGig and 20 cans of GifChem if the company can offer GreenGig to retailers at a price that provides them with a better contribution to their limited shelf space. Marketing Director for GreenGig argues that it can offer many incentives for retailers even if its price is equal to that of GifChem.

ABC Plc has invested £20 million in R&D for GreenGig, with an additional £5 million committed for further refinement and patent protection over the next five years. Annual marketing and overhead costs are estimated at £4 million. None of these costs have been absorbed into the full activity cost of £3.00 mentioned above.

The Marketing Director has envisaged two alternative strategic moves for the new product: supreme value strategy and supreme quality strategy. Under the supreme value strategy, the company will set GreenGig price either equal to or slightly above the price of GifChem. Accordingly, the price needs to be in the range of £12 to £15 per liter. The marketing mix will be directed to convey the message that the customers get superior quality for a competitive price. The supreme quality strategy will set the price much higher than the GifChem price (in the price range between £15 to £18). The marketing mix will be directed to convey the idea that the product is costly but extremely superior in quality and functionality.

Demand and market share forecasts under each strategy are as follows:

	Supreme value strategy		Supreme quality strategy	
	Sales (Litres)	Relative market share	Sales (Litres)	Relative market share
Year 1	800,000	32.00%	700,000	28.00%
Year 2	1,200,000	48.00%	1,100,000	44.00%
Year 3	1,500,000	60.00%	1,300,000	52.00%
Year 4	1,400,000	56.00%	1,300,000	52.00%
Year 5	1,000,000	40.00%	900,000	36.00%
Year 6	50,000	2.00%	30,000	1.20%
Total for six years	5,950,000		5,330,000	

Required:

1. Explain the company's strategic scenario using relevant strategic management concepts, such as the product/market life cycle and BCG growth-share matrix.
2. Explain the two strategic options using Porter's framework of generic strategies.
3. Calculate the minimum contribution GreenGig should offer the retailer to ensure that retailers prefer shelving GreenGig to GifChem. Hint: carry out a limiting factor analysis using shelf space as the limiting factor.
4. The company needs a 30% return on investment over the total expenditures on the product over its lifespan of six years. The company wishes to replace the product in year six with a new one. There is no decommissioning or removal cost at the end of the six years. Calculate the minimum price for each strategy to meet this target rate of return. The company management does not wish to consider the time value of money. Hint: use lifecycle costing combined with target return for this. Lifecycle costing considers the total expenditures spent or committed to be spent in the future for the product's entire lifecycle in pricing decisions.
5. Which strategy should the company adopt regarding GreenGig?

References

Borgesius, F. Z. 2018. Discrimination, artificial intelligence and algorithms. Strasbourg: Directorate General of Democracy - Council of Europe, 1-94.

Burawoy, M. 1983. Between the labor process and the state: the changing face of factory regimes under advanced capitalism. American Sociological Review 48 (5):587-605.

Christ, K. L., and R. L. Burritt. 2021. Accounting for modern slavery risk in the time of COVID-19: challenges and opportunities. Accounting, Auditing & Accountability Journal 34 (6):1484-1501.

Christ, K. L., R. L. Burritt, and S. Schaltegger. 2020. Accounting for work conditions from modern slavery to decent work. Accounting, Auditing & Accountability Journal 33 (7):1481-1504.

Christ, K. L., K. K. Rao, and R. L. Burritt. 2019. Accounting for modern slavery: an analysis of Australian listed company disclosures. Accounting, Auditing & Accountability Journal 32 (3):836-865.

Cooper, R., and R. Slagmulder. 1997. Target costing and value engineering. Portland: Productivity Press.

Crane, A. 2013. Modern slavery as a management practice: exploring the conditions and capabilities for human exploitation. The Academy of Management Review 38 (1):49-69.

Crane, A., G. LeBaron, K. Phung, L. Behbahani, and J. Allain. 2022. Confronting the business models of modern slavery. Journal of Management Inquiry 31 (3):264-285.

Islam, M. A., and C. J. Van Staden. 2022. Modern slavery disclosure regulation and global supply chains: insights from stakeholder narratives on the UK Modern Slavery Act. Journal of Business Ethics 180 (2):455-479.

Neu, D., A. S. Rahaman, and J. Everett. 2014. Accounting and sweatshops: enabling coordination and control in low-price apparel production chains. Contemporary Accounting Research 31 (2):322-346.

New, S. J. 2015. Modern slavery and the supply chain: the limits of corporate social responsibility? Supply Chain Management: An International Journal 20 (6):697-707.

CHAPTER 4

Strategizing the hierarchy: **strategic performance management**

4.1. Introduction

As emphasized in preceding chapters, firms enable and enact strategies within three interconnected domains of strategic action: markets, organizational hierarchies, and labor processes. Previous chapters primarily delved into the market dynamics of strategizing, focusing on competitive positioning and other related calculative practices such as lifecycle costing, target costing, and dynamic pricing. In the forthcoming three chapters, attention is directed towards how strategies unfold within organizational hierarchies, aiming to link markets with labor processes through performance management and management control. This chapter centers on performance management, while the subsequent two will address strategizing management control and organizational resilience. Performance management, management control, and organizational resilience are indeed three inseparable, overlapping, and interdependent themes of strategizing. There are lots of elements that confusingly overlap under these three themes. However, I differentiated them into three chapters for analytical and pedagogical reasons so that I could cover specific management accounting frameworks in separate chapters.

Reminder:
Three arenas of enabling and implementing strategies—markets, organizational hierarchies, and the point of production.

The theme of strategizing performance management is examined here by addressing two fundamental questions: what is meant by performance, and how is performance managed? Answers to these questions hinge on the approach taken, and two approaches to managing performance can be identified: traditional and strategic. Consequently, this chapter is structured around three key themes and related learning objectives.

1. The traditional approach to managing performance: This section explores philosophies, concepts, structures, techniques, tools, and procedures constituting the traditional approach to managing performance. Understanding the traditional approach serves as a basis for comparing and contrasting with strategic approaches, particularly by grasping the fundamental weaknesses of the former that the latter seeks to rectify.
2. A strategic approach to managing performance: This section, primarily based on Johnson and Kaplan's Balanced Scorecard (BSC) approach, explores philosophies, concepts, structures, techniques, tools, and procedures that constitute the strategic approach to managing performance and how they address perceived weaknesses in the traditional approach. Potential drawbacks of this approach are also examined.
3. Sustainability implications of performance management: Finally, the chapter delves into how contemporary strategic approaches to performance management may or may not address more profound and broader social and ecological justice issues prevalent in the contemporary world.

Consequently, upon completing this chapter, you should possess a critical understanding of both traditional and strategic approaches to managing performance and their sustainability implications.

Key point

Learning objectives.

4.2 Conceptualizing performance

As this chapter revolves around managing performance, the most rational starting point for this discussion is to consider what constitutes performance. Performing differs from doing, acting, or producing things. We engage in many activities, such as reading, studying, singing, dancing, and running. In our workplaces, we write, type, and word process, operate machines, talk in meetings, make decisions, and produce things. Such activities are integral to performing but do not necessarily constitute it. For these actions to become performance, they themselves or the outcomes they produce must be goal-directed and subjected to observations, evaluations, and judgments. You may sing or dance on your own, hidden from everyone else; in this case, it is merely singing or dancing, not performing. However, if you do the same on Britain's Got Talent to win a prize, your singing and dancing become performances because they are goal-directed and are subjected to observations, evaluations, and judgments. In your university courses, you read books and papers, attend lectures and tutorials, take notes, and study them in preparation for examinations and assessments; such examinations and assessments transform your actions, behavior, and their outcomes into performances. When your classroom presentations are observed, assessed, and graded, they become performances. Similarly, when the manner in which managerial decisions are made and the outcomes they produce are subjected to various observations, assessments, and rankings, they become performance outcomes. In this sense, *performances are actions, behaviors, and their outcomes that are goal-directed and subjected to observations, evaluations, and judgments.* Furthermore, such observations, evaluations, and judgments lead to accreditations, rankings, rewards, and punishments. Performances, thus, constitute the basis upon which status, opportunities, privileges, resources, and power are distributed and redistributed.

Key point:
Performance defined.

Performances are rather context-specific. The manner in which actions, behaviors, and their outcomes are conceptualized, observed, evaluated, judged, rewarded, and punished depends on the specific political, legal, socio-cultural, and institutional context within which they occur and, therefore, the specific manner in which they are supposed to perform are context specific. In a context-specific manner, performance management sets out the parameters within which people's individual or collective actions, behaviors, and personal attributes (such as skills, aptitudes, knowledge, and so on) and their outcomes are goal-directed and observed, assessed, judged, rewarded, and punished. For example, your subject-specific knowledge and skills in a university setting may be observed and assessed individually or in groups through coursework, presentations, or examinations to achieve a good grade or class. By providing details of individual coursework, group work, examinations, marking schemes, and so on, university courses should specify the manner in which your performances are assessed and rewarded. Similarly, corporate performance management systems should specify how individual, workgroup, departmental, divisional, and corporate performances are related to the organization's long or short-term goals and objectives and are measured, evaluated, and rewarded. The context-specificity of performance management arises due to the following:

Key point:
Context specificity of performance.

1. The entity whose performance is to be managed: individuals, groups, departments, divisions, corporations, organizations, industries, nations, and transnational entities such as the UN, World Bank, IMF, etc.
2. The subjective-objective nature of the observed actions, behaviors, personal attributes, and outcomes. They may be conceptualized through objective measures such as the number of units produced, the speed at which a particular task is completed, the number of defective items, correct answers in a multiple-choice question set, and so on. Alternatively, on other occasions, they can be rather subjective and rely upon subjective narratives provided by relevant parties.
3. The underlying basis of legitimacy for performance. That is the basis upon which one's actions, behaviors, personal attributes and outcomes can be subjected to observations, evaluations, and judgments. Such bases could be legal, institutional, economic, political, and cultural-religious.

Key point:

Performance definition extended.

With all these context-specific variations, *performance means how a particular entity (individuals, groups, departments, corporations, nation-states, and so on) contributes to a larger schema of things or higher-order principles.* These higher-order principles could be things such as productivity, efficiency, costs, revenue, profitability, return on investment, quality, flexibility, competitiveness, innovativeness, corporate vision and mission, individual and collective well-being, democracy, sustainability, and global peace. Relevant higher-order principles define the larger schema of things towards which performance is directed. In that sense, performance is the extent to which and the manner in which one would contribute to such higher-order principles. Performance management thus observes, assesses, and judges how a particular entity/body would contribute to a relevant set of higher-order principles. In a corporate setting, these higher-order principles are captured and communicated through elements such as corporate mission and vision, corporate goals and objectives, etc. In university teaching and educational settings, these higher-order principles or the bigger schema of things are captured by what UK universities often call "graduate attributes".

Performance is, in effect, the hybridity between the actual and expected. On the one hand, performance is what people individually or collectively produce from their actions, behaviors, and personal attributes. On the other hand, they get observed, assessed and judged on the basis of a predetermined set of expectations and desires often embedded in organizational elements such as goals, objectives, targets, standards, benchmarks, guidelines, grading schemes, rating schemes, laws, regulations, policies, rules, procedures, protocols, and so on. These are the forms in which collective desires and expectations of organizational actors (mainly of those dominant and powerful actors) are institutionalized. In that sense, performance means the extent to which and the manner in which one's actual actions, behavior, attributes, and outcomes meet those predetermined sets of institutionalized expectations and desires. Considering both these dimensions, as illustrated in Figure 4.1, performance management constitutes organizational attempts to enhance the overlapping space between the actual and desired.

Key point:

Performance as hybridity of actual and desired.

Figure 4.1: Key elements of performance

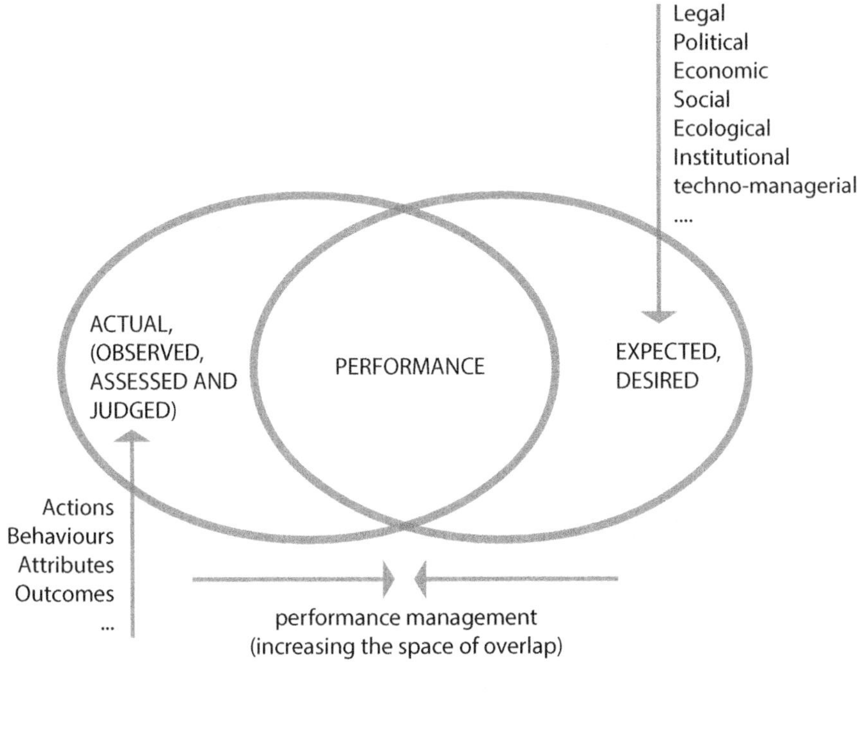

4.2. The traditional approach to performance management: responsibility accounting

The traditional approach to performance management is based on 'responsibility accounting'. Developed over centuries in Western organizational settings, responsibility accounting manifests the manner in which accounting calculations are institutionalized in performance management by translating techno-managerial centers of performance into accountability centers. For instance, a machine workshop managed by engineers or a sales department overseen by marketing professionals is considered an accountability center for which a specific set of accounting calculations is prescribed to observe, assess, and judge performance. The overarching philosophy behind responsibility accounting can be summarized in three main points:

Key point:

Operational philosophy of responsibility accounting.

1. Hierarchy of accountability centers: To manage performance effectively, different sites where organizational activities occur and managerial decisions are made should be redefined as specific types of responsibility or accountability centers. This ensures that their performances become the accountability and responsibility of the managers leading those centers. Four types of accountability centers are identified for this purpose: cost centers, revenue centers, profit centers, and investment centers. They should be hierarchically organized and linked, with cost centers at the bottom, revenue centers and profit centers in the middle, and investment centers at the top.

2. Accounting calculations: The performances of each center should be defined by a specific set of accounting calculations, hierarchically arranged in line with the responsibility centers. These calculations enable managers to assess whether investment centers achieve the required rates of return on investment and how profit centers, revenue centers, and cost centers contribute to earning those required rates of return. These accounting calculations are commonly managed through budgeting, standard costing, variance analysis, and ratio analysis.

3. Concept of controllability: The accountability holder for each responsibility center should be held accountable only for the performance that falls under their direct control. When assessing and judging a responsibility center manager's perfor-

mance, uncontrollable cost, revenue, profit, and investment return variances should be excluded from that manager's scope of performance.

Figure 4.2 and Table 4.1 summarize the accountability hierarchy that responsibility accounting constructs. Return on investment occupies the pinnacle of this hierarchy, the most dominating higher-order principle, and other centers are directed towards this end, reflecting a capitalistic logic of accumulation (note that return on investment is the rate at which capital is accumulated).

Key point:

Prominence of ROI in responsibility accounting system.

Figure 4.2: Accountability hierarchy in responsibility accounting

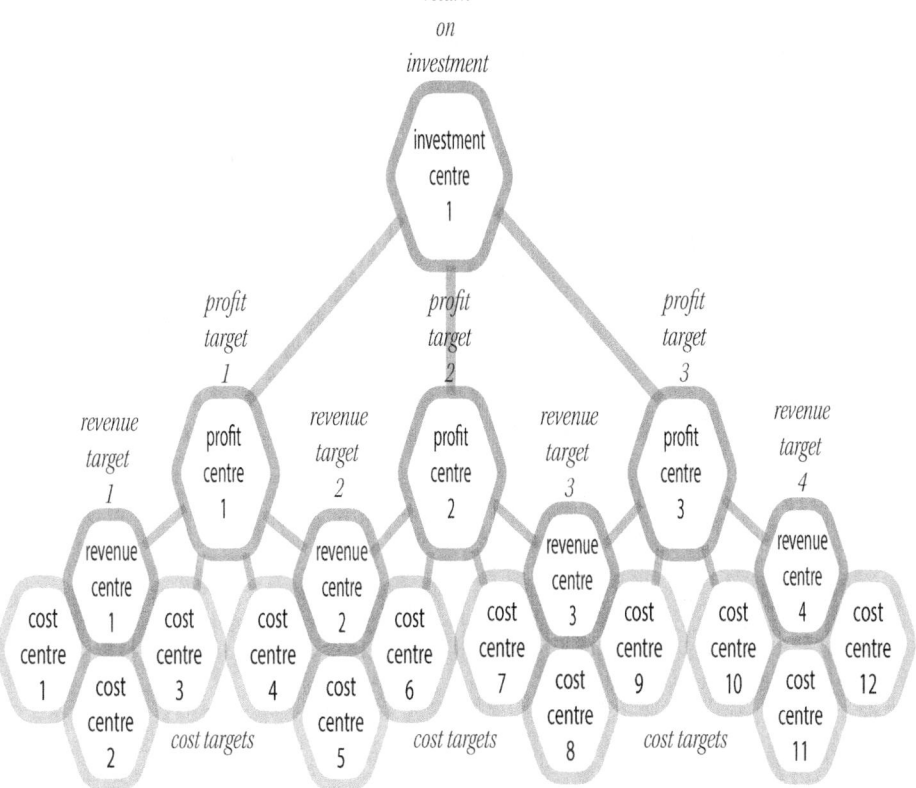

Table 4.1: Responsibility accounting – accountability centers

Hierarchical element	Accountability focus	Popular techniques and measures
Cost centers Performance is conceptualised and assessed through various cost measures.	Operates often at the bottom of operational, techno-managerial and administrative hierarchy, performing the basic operational activities that drive costs. In a manufacturing setting, classic examples are job shops, workshops, or machine centers, which constitute the majority of the operational activities needed to produce goods and services.	Operational budgeting, especially material usage budgets, labour usage budgets, and production budgets. Enterprise resource planning schedules. Inventory control techniques. Standard costing and variance analysis related to production, materials usage, labour usage, and factory overheads.
Revenue centers Performance is conceptualised and measured through various revenue measures	Represents the departments responsible for selling and distributing a particular line of goods or services. These centers can be connected to several cost centers that constitute the production of that particular good or service.	Operational budgeting, especially sales budget and sales variances (sales price variances and sales quantity/volume variances) Sales growth rates. Market share statistics.
Profit centers (performance is conceptualised and measured through various profit and profitability measures).	Profit centers consolidate cost and revenue centers so that their combined outcomes become a responsibility of a particular manager. These represent higher-level accountability holders who hold cumulative responsibility for the costs and revenues of one or more product lines. They command and direct relevant cost centers and revenue centers for profit targets.	Master budgeting, especially budgeted profit and loss accounts, balance sheets and cash flow statements. Profit variances. Profit margins: gross profit ratio, net profit ratio.
Investment centers Performances are measured through various investment efficiency criteria.	These represent the top level of management that is responsible for investment decisions pertaining to a set of profit centers, often SBU managers and the board of directors, etc.	Assessments of investment efficiency in terms of: Return on investment Stock market performance (share prices) Cost of capital, discounted cash flows, internal rate of return, payback period, etc. Return on total assets. Total assets turnover.

4.2.1 From operational to accounting logic

It should be noted that organizational hierarchies are operational or techno-managerial before they become accounting or financial. Organizational hierarchies are, in effect, techno-managerial and administrative arrangements for the division of work and hierarchical supervision. For example, in an automobile company, the division of work is primarily based on specific engineering, administrative, and marketing dimensions. Divisions and departments are formed on that basis and are managed and controlled by experts in those specific aspects of operations. Similarly, in a university, the division of work and organizational hierarchy will primarily be on academic grounds; colleges, faculties, and departments are often organized according to academic disciplines and are headed by experts in those specific disciplines.

Key point:

Accounting transforms otherwise non-accounting hierarchies into accounting hierarchies.

Responsibility accounting systems superimpose a financial logic and financial hierarchy over these otherwise non-accounting organizational hierarchies. They require that the non-accounting operational logic and measures of running an organization (e.g. production efficiency, economies of scale, economies of scope, innovations, market positioning, brand loyalties, and so on) are translated into financial and accounting measures so that the company can be managed with accounting and financial logics of return on investments. In that way, responsibility accounting superimposes an accounting logic for managing industrial organizations. It imposes a logic of assessing the techno-managerial efficiencies and outcomes through accounting numbers.

Techniques and structure of responsibility accounting

This accounting logic of managing corporations is achieved through a set of conventional management accounting techniques: budgeting, standard costing, and variance analysis, often supplemented by a system of accounting analysis highlighted by DuPont's system ratio analysis. Collectively, these management accounting techniques institutionalize a hierarchical system of performance management and control by:

1. Establishing a system of planning in which organizational activities' efficacy is conceptualized and planned by their contribution to profits and returns on investment. Budgeting is the fundamental technical tool here. As you should have learned in your previous management accounting cours-

es, budgets are prepared to form a hierarchy of accounting calculations, starting from bottom-level operational budgets related to material usage, material purchases, labor usage, production overheads, and fixed overheads. They then accumulate into master budgets (i.e. the budgeted profit and loss account, the budgeted balance sheet, and the budgeted cash flow statement).

2. Establishing a comparative basis against which actual performances are compared, evaluated, judged, and rewarded. First, together with budgeting, standard costing and variance analysis play a critical role here. Various cost and operational standards provide the calculative bases for preparing cost targets and budgets. In that sense, they provide the comparative bases for performance management, upon which organizational actors' collective actions, behaviors, and outcomes are observed, assessed, and judged. Secondly, variance analysis highlights the extent to which and the manner in which actual performances deviate from the standard or planned performance, creating the possibilities of corrective or control actions.

3. Conceptualizing and operationalizing capital accumulation as the primary purpose of an economic enterprise. Collectively, techniques and tools used in responsibility accounting make all other techno-managerial and broader social purposes secondary to the purposes of capital accumulation (note: profit is the rate at which capital is accumulated in a given accounting period). As illustrated in Figure 4.3, such techniques collectively create a hierarchy of accounting measures of which the pinnacle occupies the idea of profitability, especially the return on investment. All the other operational elements are then directed towards that end.

Key point:

The technical functionalities of responsibility accounting – institutionalising capital accumulation through planning and control.

In a broader context, as depicted in Figure 4.3, responsibility accounting represents the traditional framework for performance management, wherein performances are chiefly conceptualized and evaluated through financial metrics encompassing costs, revenues, sales, and returns on investment. These metrics are systematically allocated to cost, revenue, profit, and investment centers to facilitate the delegation of responsibility and accountability. Standard costing and variance analysis, in conjunction with operational and master budgeting,

Figure 4.3: Logic of responsibility accounting - a techno-managerial hierarchy of capital accumulation

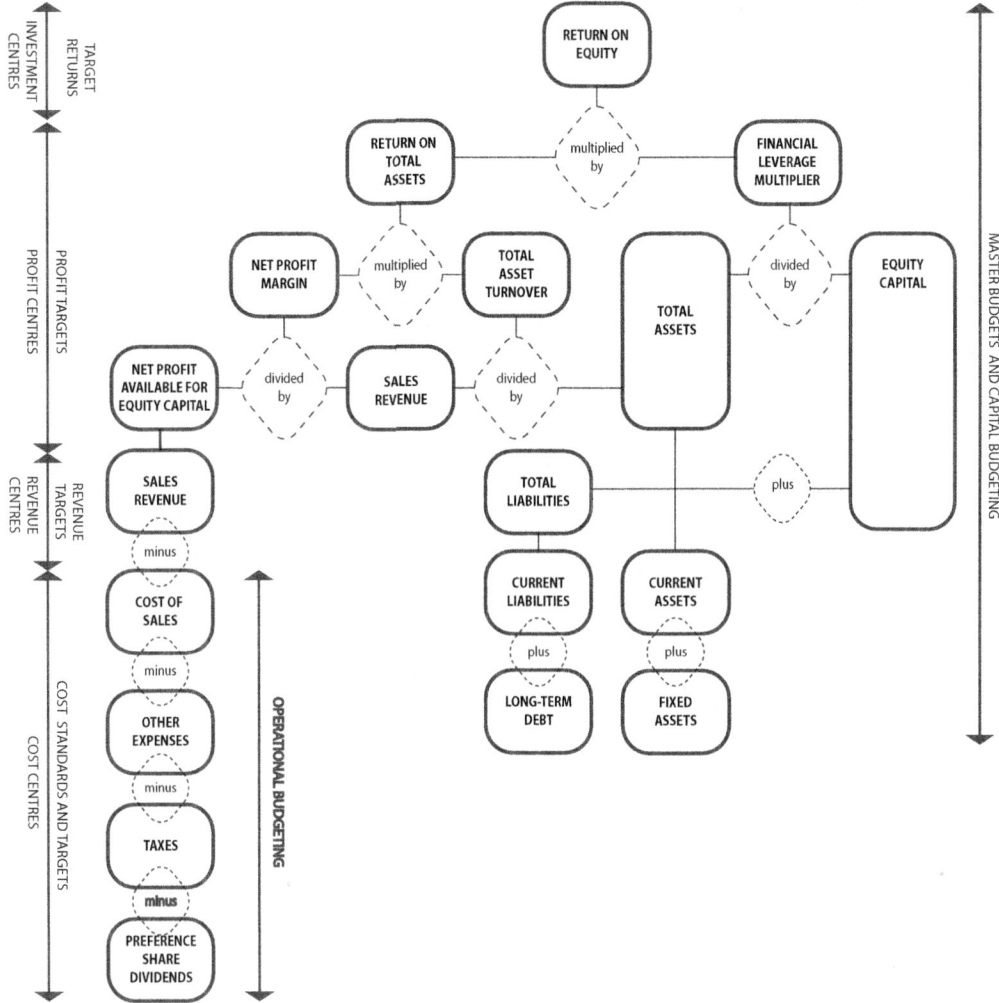

serve as the primary planning and control techniques within this framework. Ratio analysis frameworks, such as the DuPont system, break down the return on investment to scrutinize how various accounting measures ultimately contribute to the overarching goals of capital accumulation, with return on investment serving as the ultimate gauge for assessing the rate at which capital is amassed.

The fundamental principles of conventional responsibility accounting systems in performance management are succinctly outlined in Table 4.2.

Table 4.2: Responsibility accounting regimes of performance management: key themes

Theme	Description
Logic	To enhance and ensure the operational efficiency measured through accounting indicators of costs, revenues, profits and returns on investment. Return on investment is considered the ultimate measure of performance, all other measures being assessed as to how they contribute to it.
Structure	Operational centers of the organisations are redefined as cost centers, revenue centers, profit centers, and investment centers to construct a hierarchy of financial performances leading to return on investment.
Process	Standards and budgetary targets are to be defined as the bases against which actual performances are observed, assessed, judged and rewarded/punished. Techniques of variance analysis and ratio analysis are used to assess the degree to which and the manner in which standards and budgetary targets are met.
Tools and techniques	Mainly budgeting, standard costing and variance analysis, and DuPont system of ratio analysis supported by other decision-making techniques such as cost-volume-profit analysis, limiting factor analysis and inventory controls.

Weaknesses of responsibility accounting-based performance management

With the advent of strategic discourses, this traditional responsibility regime has faced various critiques. The following outlines the critical issues in this context:

1. Responsibility accounting has a tendency to foster excessively centralized hierarchical organizations, dominated by accountants who frequently lack techno-managerial expertise in crucial operational matters.
2. Placing a significant emphasis on budgets, cost standards, and their hierarchical and centralized structure, the resulting accountability regime tends to be rigid and inflexible.
3. Operational inefficiencies can arise because managers of accountability centers often incorporate 'budgetary slacks' into their budgets and targets. These slacks consist of additional elements that managers may include in the budgetary tar-

gets beyond what is realistically necessary. This may involve overestimating costs and underestimating revenue and profits, providing a safety net for cost, revenue, and profit center managers when their actual performances are compared with the budgeted figures.
4. Given that budgeting serves as the primary technique for performance planning and management, managers often rely on incremental values based on the previous period's accounting figures without adequately considering internal and external factors. For instance, they may frequently overlook market conditions.
5. Most importantly, as strategy gurus such as Robert Kaplan argue, responsibility accounting suffers from a problem of balance and a problem of strategic connection. I will discuss this in the next section.

Key point:

Among others, the most fundamental weaknesses of responsibility accounting are the issues of balancing and linking.

4.3. Strategic performance management

In response to the strategic shift discussed in Chapter 1, there have been notable developments in the concepts and tools of performance management systems over the last few decades. They aimed to 'strategize' performance management by

a. imparting strategic meanings and connections to performances and
b. diversifying the dimensions of performance management beyond the narrow financial focus of conventional systems.

The most significant innovation in this realm is the 'balanced scorecards' system, popularized by Kaplan and Norton (see Kaplan 2008; Kaplan and Norton 1993, 1996a, 1996b, 2000). This section explores the logic, concepts, and tools of strategic performance management primarily based on Kaplan and Norton's balanced scorecards (BSC).

Side note:

For a critical analysis of how BSC became a globally popular discourse in strategic management, see Cooper et al. (2017).

A note of caution is warranted. In popular strategy and management accounting discussions, Kaplan and Norton's BSC approach is often hailed as the pioneer of multidimensional performance management that extends beyond conventional responsibility accounting measures to encompass non-financial metrics. However, as Cooper et al. (2017) elucidate, Kaplan and Norton's positioning and networking played a crucial role in the global popularization of multidimensional performance management. Yet, the multidimensional nature of corporate performance has long been recognized by many organizations worldwide. Notably, the French performance management system known as "*tableau de bord*" introduced the concept of a 'dashboard' as early as the 1930s. See Bessire and Baker (2005) and Bourguignon et al. (2004) for a comparative discussion of French tableau de bord and American BSC.

The logic of strategic performance management

As originally conceived by Kaplan and Norton, the logic of strategic performance management systems aims to rectify the narrow operational and financial focus of conventional responsibility accounting-based corporate performance management systems. This is achieved by:

1. Balancing between financial and non-financial dimensions of performance: Strategic performance management systems seek to diversify corporate performance management by integrating multiple strategically critical dimensions beyond conventional accounting and financial measures.
2. Linking the performance management system to corporate strategies: This is accomplished by creating a 'cascading system of scorecards' that connects operational-level performance with the organization's strategic goals.

Key point:

Strategic performance management aims to address issues of balancing and linking.

In this sense, balancing and cascading are the two pivotal analytical and managerial actions underpinning Kaplan and Norton's BSC approach to strategizing performance management. Unlike the conventional responsibility accounting approach, which focuses on operational efficiency, strategic approaches to performance management underscore the need to broaden analytical attention to multiple dimensions underlying an organization's strategic success. Strategic performance management entails establishing a system that encourages understanding and appreciation of the organization's strategic priorities, devising strategies to contribute to these aims, and assessing one's success in contributing to the organization's strategic processes and objectives.

Scorecards as fundamental building blocks of performance management

Scorecards are the fundamental building blocks of Kaplan and Norton's strategic approach to performance management, hence the term BSC. Scorecards are designed to replace budgets and be prepared for all managerial levels, from overarching corporate scorecards to lower-level individual managers' scorecards. A fundamental distinction between a budget in the classical accounting sense and scorecards used in strategic performance management is that budgets only capture the financial dimensions of performance, whereas scorecards provide an open template to incorporate any critical performance dimensions. Scorecards are promoted as a flexible, simple, yet powerful tool serving to:

1. Identify multiple dimensions for framing and assessing performance, allowing managers to think beyond financial metrics and integrate critical non-financial dimensions.
2. Link operational actions and initiatives with corporate strategies and objectives and communicate these down the organizational hierarchy.
3. Identify how specific localities (departments, groups, and individuals, etc.) can contribute to corporate strategies and goals through objectives and initiatives related to their own scope of operations. Scorecards operate as a means of 'cascading' corporate objectives and strategies downward.

Kaplan and Norton (1996b, 81) provide an example of how this happens:

> The exploration group of a large oil company developed a technique to enable and encourage individuals to set goals for themselves that were consistent with the organisation's. It created a small, foldup personal scorecard that people could carry in their shirt pockets or wallets. ... The scorecard contains three levels of information. The first describes corporate objectives, measures, and targets. The second leaves room for translating corporate targets into targets for each business unit. For the third level, the company asks both individuals and teams to articulate which of their own objectives would be consistent with the business unit and corporate ob-

Key point:

Scorecards enable balancing and linking.

jectives, as well as what initiatives they would take to achieve their objectives. It also asks them to define up to five performance measures for their objectives and to set targets for each measure. The personal scorecard helps to communicate corporate and business unit objectives to the people and teams performing the work, enabling them to translate the objectives into meaningful tasks and targets for themselves. It also lets them keep that information close at hand – in their pockets.

Proponents of the BSC approach suggest that scorecards should operate as a techno-managerial tool connecting individuals' and groups' day-to-day operations and thinking to the corporation as a whole. Each scorecard is intended to embed a hierarchical connection between the local and the corporate, incorporating the possibility of conceptualizing performance in multiple dimensions beyond conventional financial measures. Figure 4.4 illustrates this functionality of a scorecard (see also Kaplan and Norton 1996b).

Figure 4.4: Scorecards as a tool for strategic connections

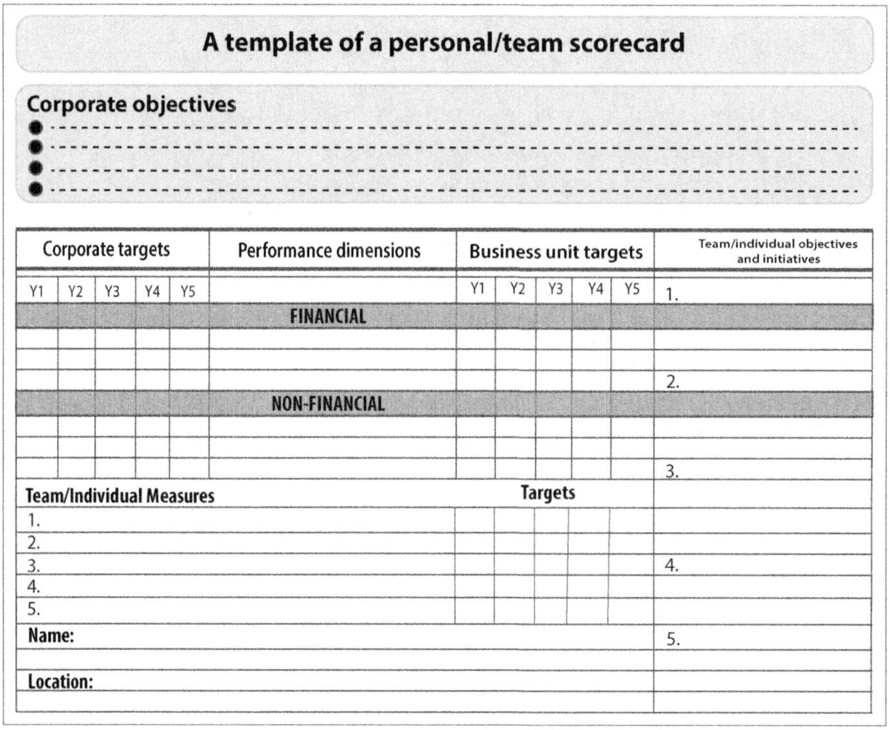

Corporate targets	Performance dimensions	Business unit targets	Team/individual objectives and initiatives
Y1 Y2 Y3 Y4 Y5	FINANCIAL	Y1 Y2 Y3 Y4 Y5	1.
			2.
	NON-FINANCIAL		
			3.

A template of a personal/team scorecard

Corporate objectives
- ....
- ....
- ....
- ....

Team/Individual Measures / Targets
1.
2.
3.   4.
4.
5.
Name: 5.
Location:

Source: based on Kaplan and Norton (various publications)

If effectively mobilized, this straightforward performance template can wield significant influence by compelling and enabling organizational actors to consistently consider the measures and objectives imposed upon them from above (e.g., corporate objectives, corporate targets, and business unit targets) and then determine how their thinking and actions can contribute to them. Scorecards offer a much more flexible, open, and personalized managerial space compared to conventional budgets. However, these scorecards still embody a strong top-down approach to managing performance. One's performance must always be framed within the parameters set by higher-order strategies and objectives established by top-level executives.

Strategic performance as balancing between financial and non-financial

The popularity of the Balanced Scorecard (BSC) as a strategic performance management system can be attributed to its proponents' claims that BSC can rectify the narrow financial focus of conventional management accounting and incorporate strategically critical non-financial dimensions of performance. This is referred to as the 'balancing' aspect of BSC: achieving equilibrium between financial and non-financial measures of performance. For this purpose, Kaplan and Norton propose a framework for defining corporate performance in terms of four key performance dimensions, each requiring the development of separate 'key performance indicators' (KPIs). As illustrated in Figure 4.5, these four key performance areas have been identified as four critical strategic questions, answers to which Kaplan and Norton believe should clarify the organization's strategic posture and establish the strategic connection of performance management. BSC is considered a strategic performance management system because, as argued by its proponents, these questions and the resulting performance measures and indicators enhance the organization's capacity to realize its corporate strategies and objectives by balancing between the financial and non-financial measures of performance.

Key Point:

Balancing between financial and non-financial dimensions of performance.

For Kaplan and Norton (see 1993, 1996a, 1996b, 2000), the starting point in developing a strategic performance management system is the organizational strategy, especially the corporate vision, mission, and long-term goals. Using these as the fundamental higher-order principles towards which organizational performances should be directed, they identify four key 'critical performance dimensions' (i.e.

Figure 4.5: BSC's redefinition of corporate performance in multiple dimensions

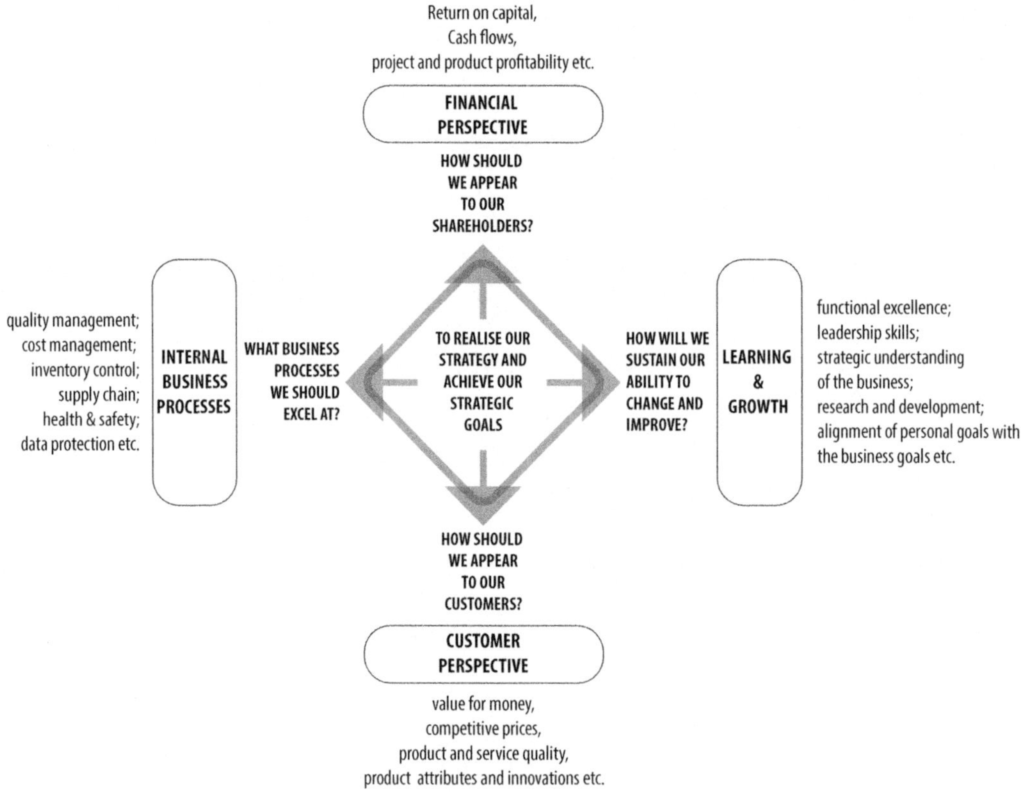

Return on capital,
Cash flows,
project and product profitability etc.

FINANCIAL PERSPECTIVE

HOW SHOULD WE APPEAR TO OUR SHAREHOLDERS?

quality management;
cost management;
inventory control;
supply chain;
health & safety;
data protection etc.

INTERNAL BUSINESS PROCESSES — WHAT BUSINESS PROCESSES WE SHOULD EXCEL AT?

TO REALISE OUR STRATEGY AND ACHIEVE OUR STRATEGIC GOALS

HOW WILL WE SUSTAIN OUR ABILITY TO CHANGE AND IMPROVE? — **LEARNING & GROWTH**

functional excellence;
leadership skills;
strategic understanding of the business;
research and development;
alignment of personal goals with the business goals etc.

HOW SHOULD WE APPEAR TO OUR CUSTOMERS?

CUSTOMER PERSPECTIVE

value for money,
competitive prices,
product and service quality,
product attributes and innovations etc.

Source: based on Kaplan and Norton (various publications)

Key point:

Identifying critical success factors is key to strategic performance management.

financial, customer, internal business processes, and learning and growth), in which critical success factors need identification. In this context, critical success factors refer to the specific conditions firms should achieve to successfully answer the four strategic questions proposed by Kaplan and Norton for managing a corporation. For instance, within the financial dimension, a critical success factor could be a target return on investment. Similarly, value for money, quality management, and functional excellence can respectively be critical success factors in customer, internal business processes, and learning and growth perspectives. These critical dimensions and success factors should then be incorporated into relevant scorecards as measurements, targets, and initiatives (see the previous section scorecard template).

Strategic performance as cascading scorecards to link operations with strategy

The second strategizing act that BSC promotes is linking operational (i.e. lower-level managerial actions, initiatives, and outcomes) with corporate strategies and objectives. Linking is to be achieved through the downward cascading of scorecards through the organizational hierarchy. Drawing on various 'successful cases' with which they had consultancy relationships, Kaplan and Norton propose a consultocratic approach (seemingly in heavily top-down bureaucratic organizational structures) to developing a chain of scorecards, starting from the corporate scorecard to individual scorecards for every manager and supervisory employee. They conceptualize the managerial acts of cascading and linking into four key managerial processes:

1. Translating the vision: This involves building a consensus around the organization's vision and strategy, expressing vision and mission statements as "an integrated set of objectives and measures, agreed upon by all senior executives, that describe the long-term drivers of success" (Kaplan and Norton 1996b, 76).
2. Communicating and linking: In implementing a BSC, according to Kaplan and Norton, communicating the corporate strategy elements (vision, mission, long-term objectives, etc.) up and down the organization and linking it to departmental and individual objectives play a critical role. For Kaplan and Norton (1996b, 76), "scorecard gives managers a way of ensuring that all levels of the organization understand the long-term strategy and that both departmental and individual objectives are aligned with it".
3. Business planning: Under this title, Kaplan and Norton discuss integrating financial and non-financial aspects of planning an organization. Business planning is, in effect, a process of investment or business rationalization by eliminating non-strategic investment and initiating change management programs. All are to be supported by external and internal consultants and other business experts.
4. Feedback and learning: This is what Kaplan and Norton also call "strategic learning", the processes through which managers evaluate strategy in the light of recent performance in the four key dimensions. Their argument is that strategy reviews

Key point:

Cascading processes of linking operations with strategy.

based on scorecards let managers reflect upon the extent to which they achieve their objectives in those four key performance areas.

A careful reading of Kaplan and Norton's celebrated writings on BSC, where they explain and prescribe BSC implementation processes mostly based on the experiences of well-resourced large corporations, will tell you that implementation is not easy, and it takes time, often more than 24 months in the initial process. Then, it demands continuous monitoring and reviews, often with expensive external consultants' involvement. Based on their consultancy engagements, Kaplan and Norton (1996b) outlined a 10-step process that a company followed in implementing BSC over 24 months. For brevity, these ten steps and how they are connected to the four key processes mentioned above are illustrated in Figure 4.6.

Key point:

Implementing BSC takes time, and it is costly.

Figure 4.6: Processes and steps of implementing BSC: hierarchical cascading of BSC idea

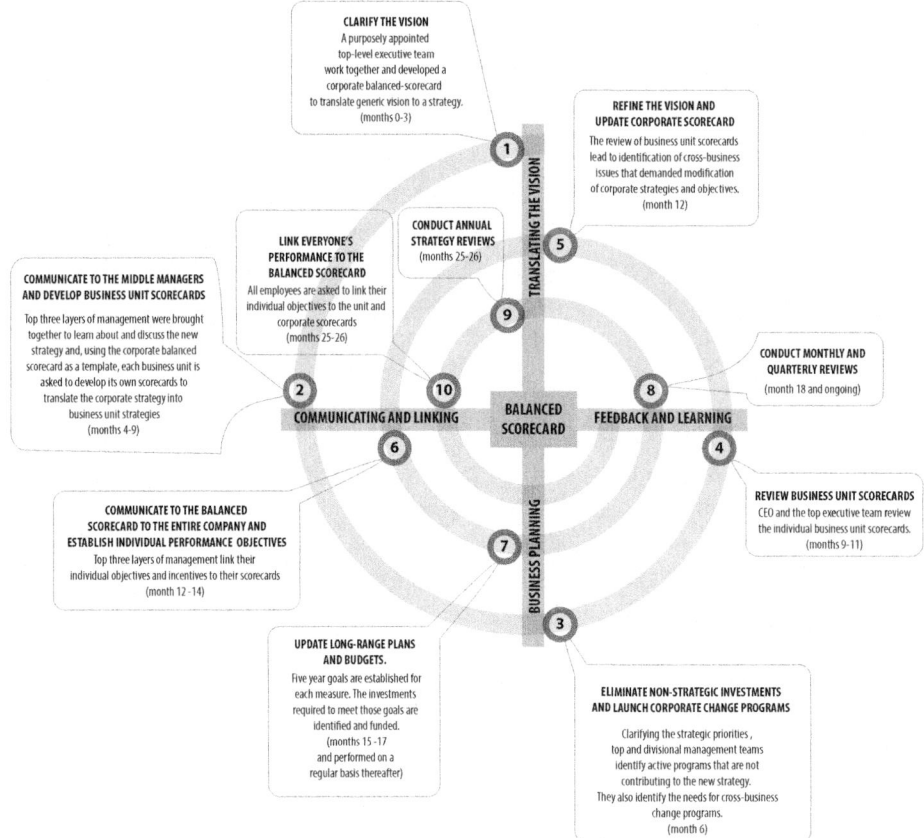

Source: based on Kaplan and Norton (various publications)

Causalities and finalities in BSC

In the background of these strategic acts of balancing and linking, proponents of the Balanced Scorecard (BSC) assume a specific set of causalities. Kaplan and Norton (1993, 1996a, 1996b, 2000) have dedicated considerable effort to clarify that the non-financial dimensions of performance (namely, learning and growth, internal business processes, and customer perspectives) are not merely a random assortment of arbitrary dimensions or variables. According to Kaplan and Norton, these performance dimensions represent a fundamental set of causal relationships. Once carefully mapped and operationalized through scorecards, they assert that these dimensions can propel the organization towards generating enhanced shareholder value. Consequently, Kaplan and Norton underscore that the BSC should not encompass a haphazard collection of measures but instead demonstrate causality between outcome measures and the performance drivers leading to those outcomes. For instance, they elucidate:

> The Balanced Scorecard, unlike ad hoc performance measurement systems, articulates the 'theory of the business'. By having an explicit set of linkages among the scorecard measures, managers can test informally, if not statistically, the business theory's hypothesised causal chain of strategic initiatives, performance drivers, and outcomes (Kaplan and Norton 1996a, 261).

Key point:

The Balanced Scorecard is propagated as a system of cause-and-effect relationships

Their fundamental assumption is that learning and growth should result in improved internal business processes, subsequently providing the company with better capabilities to satisfy customers than competitors. This sequence, according to Kaplan and Norton, should ultimately lead to improved shareholder value. Tracing these causalities in an organization-specific manner through relevant performance measures constitutes one of the core pillars of Kaplan and Norton's strategic approach to performance management, referred to as "creating strategy maps" (see Kaplan and Norton 2000). The operational details of how these presumed causalities function are inherently organization-specific. Nevertheless, Figure 4.7 provides a generic conception of them.

Figure 4.7: Causalities presumed in BSC – mapping the strategic connections

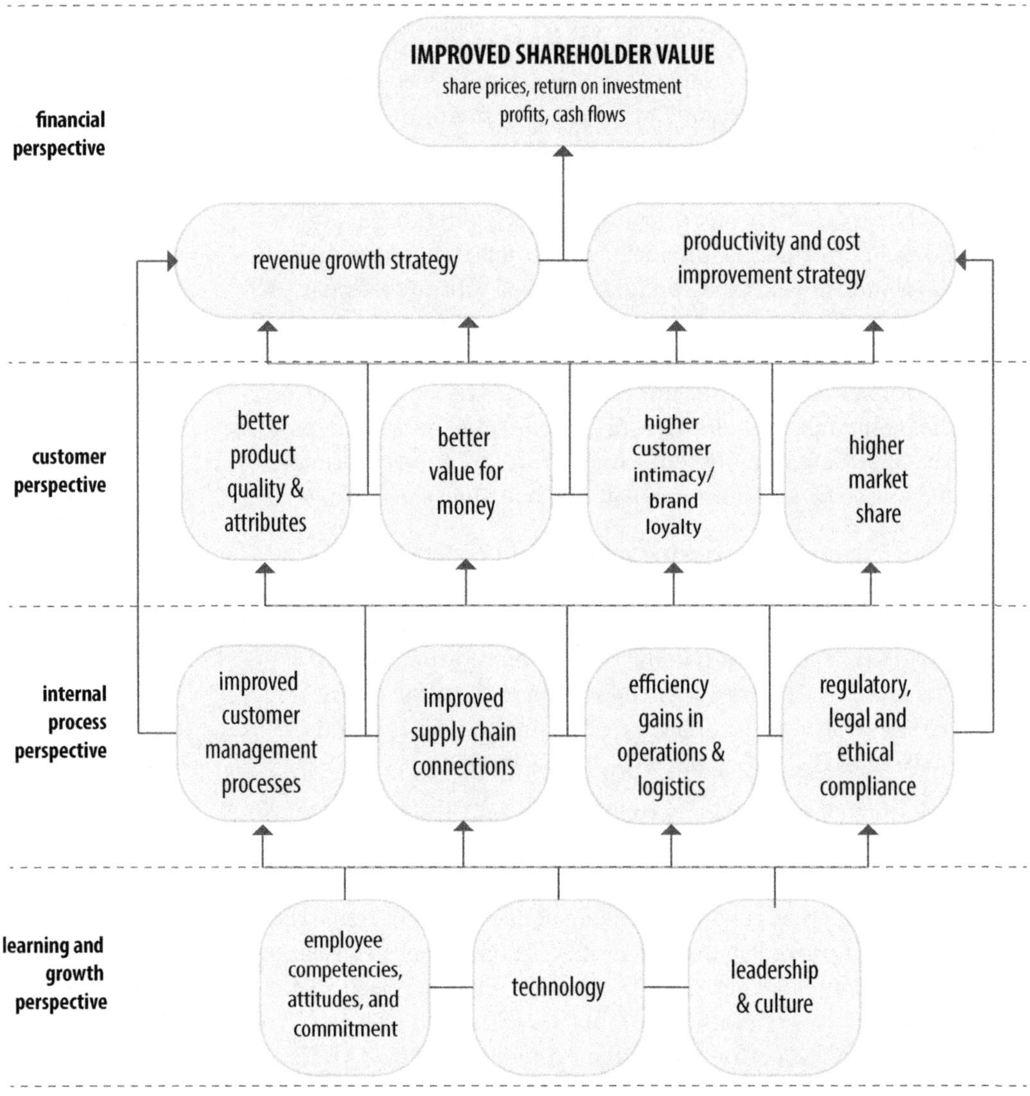

financial perspective

IMPROVED SHAREHOLDER VALUE
share prices, return on investment
profits, cash flows

- revenue growth strategy
- productivity and cost improvement strategy

customer perspective

- better product quality & attributes
- better value for money
- higher customer intimacy/ brand loyalty
- higher market share

internal process perspective

- improved customer management processes
- improved supply chain connections
- efficiency gains in operations & logistics
- regulatory, legal and ethical compliance

learning and growth perspective

- employee competencies, attitudes, and commitment
- technology
- leadership & culture

Source: based on Kaplan and Norton (various publications)

BSC relationships causality or finality? – Norekklit's critique

As previously mentioned, causal relationships among these performance dimensions are to be analyzed and tested in a company-specific manner. According to Kaplan and Norton's discussions on 'strategy mapping', strategizing involves conceptualizing and establishing specific connections between the variables captured by the scorecards at different levels. These presumed causal relationships make the BSC approach more than a mere ad-hoc collection of financial and non-financial performance measures. These relationships transform the BSC into a feed-forward control system where non-financial measures, in sequence, drive the financial measures towards shareholder value optimization (see Norreklit 2000). Kaplan and Norton explain the interconnections between four performance dimensions as essentially 'causalities' that drive the firm towards enhanced returns on investment and shareholder values, but Norreklit (2000, 2003) is critical of whether the BSC framework actually holds such a 'causal relationship' between financial and non-financial measures. For her, there are some fundamental issues pertaining to the presumed causalities of the BSC approach.

Norreklit advances her critique of BSC's presumed causality on three interrelated grounds.

1. Neglect of time dimensions: A time lag between the cause and effect often binds causal connections. The BSC encompasses a problematic causal connection because it does not sufficiently capture and conceptualize such a time lag between causes and effects, especially between the non-financial and financial. Kaplan and Norton's minimal discussions on the time dimensions of BSC (i.e. statements that the strategic objectives have to be broken down into budgetary targets and reached over time and be followed up) only constitute 'static' descriptions of the causality between the performance measures. For example, as the discussion so far revealed, Kaplan and Norton capture the causality between various performance measures through what they call 'strategic mapping', where a map so-developed, in effect, manifests a space of timeless connections between them. Norreklit (2000, 71) argues:

the effect of the measures will occur at different points of time because the effects of the different areas involve different time scales. While the introduction of more efficient processes may yield more satisfied customers within a period of 3 months, innovation may not affect the financial results until a few years have passed. The effect of some efforts will be almost immediate and that of others very slow. ... One argument for not measuring at different points of time could be that the time lag between an effort and its effect is very short. If this is the case, however, then the balanced scorecard ceases to be relevant since the full consequences of a company's actions would appear from its accounting figures.

2. **Problematic relationship between measures:** Norreklit argues that the relationship between the measures on the BSC is ambiguously explained. On the one hand, Kaplan and Norton assume a causal linear relationship which starts from learning and growth and leads to financial outcomes through internal processes and customer perspectives. That means a higher return on investment is necessarily, or highly probably, occurring if learning and growth, internal processes and customer perspective measures are achieved. In that sense, learning and growth, internal business processes and customer perspectives are independent or driver variables that themselves should produce the financial outcomes they are supposed to produce. However, on the other hand, Kaplan and Norton's explanations demand the use of accounting calculus to decide whether and how a firm should invest in such non-financial measures. In that sense, the accounting calculus precedes the non-financial measures. Norreklit also argues that, for example, there is no empirically testable guarantee that satisfied customers or loyal customers will necessarily lead to higher financial returns.

3. **Interdependence of the four perspectives:** For Norreklit, instead of a linear causal connection among the BSC measures, there is an interdependency, a possible or logical circular relationship among BSC measures.

Key point:

Elements of Norreklit's critique of BSC's presumed causality.

Considering these foundational issues, Norreklit (2000) perceives the connections that Kaplan and Norton discuss in their BSC literature as 'finality relationships' rather than 'causal relationships'. Finality relationships are logical and normative connections that people desire or believe should occur, as opposed to empirical conditions that underpin causal connections. According to Norreklit (2000, 76), finality relationships delineate how human actions, desires, and perspectives interrelate. They are shaped by people's beliefs that a specific action is the most effective means to an end and that a particular outcome can indeed be achieved through that action. The attainment of that outcome then reinforces the conviction that it is brought about by that action and not by any other means. Actions are undertaken because they align with an individual's views and desires. Hence, a reciprocal relationship exists between ends and means. Each specific means is just one of several that can be employed to achieve the end, and each may have various other consequences.

For instance, a favorable financial outcome may be attained by initially marketing a product at what marketers commonly refer to as an 'introductory price,' attaching a lower margin than required to secure a larger market share. While this might initially result in a suboptimal return on capital, it could create opportunities to raise prices and boost profits. This is not causality in itself but rather a 'possible' outcome (as opposed to a 'probable' outcome of causal relationships in science) under specific market conditions that a particular strategic action may generate. Conceptualizing such finalities as 'causal relations' may have imparted a 'scientific appearance' to BSC discourses and established the notion that BSC possesses an underlying scientific "theory of the business" (see Kaplan and Norton 1996a, 261). Consequently, any effort to expound, clarify, or rectify the relationships that BSC assumes as finalities rather than causalities could significantly impact the academic and scientific credibility of the Kaplan and Norton BSC project. It is enlightening to quote Norreklit (2000, 77) here to comprehend this effect.

Key point:

Causalities vs finalities and BSC as encompassing finalities rather than causalities.

> There are indeed indications that Kaplan and Norton want to refer to finality and not to causality. In one of Kaplan and Norton's figures, the arrows point in both directions …, indicating assumed finality. Nevertheless, in both text and figures, an assumption of causality plays a dominant role, relationships among events being assumed to be unidirectional … So, in this respect, too, the

text is ambiguous. And even though Kaplan and Norton may sometimes intend to refer to finality, the idea of cause and effect pervades the balanced scorecard. Giving up the assumption that cause-and-effect relationships are involved has major consequences for their entire argumentation and for the techniques suggested for the balanced scorecard, which may not be valid. Finality is fundamentally different from cause-and-effect relationships. The consequence of assuming finality is that the relationships among the various perspectives become more ambiguous and less simple – complexity increases and many of the techniques suggested for the balanced scorecard will be impracticable. Furthermore, if Kaplan and Norton are assuming finality instead of causality, then the balanced scorecard is no different from many other approaches. Altogether, the power of the instrument to make statements and to serve the purposes of management control will be greatly reduced.

Other weaknesses of BSC

In addition to the issue of causality, the BSC approach is often criticized for the following reasons:

1. The implementation of BSC is a highly autocratic top-down process. Kaplan and colleagues, through their consultocratic engagements and experiences, explain that it commences with the creation of top-level corporate scorecards, which must then be cascaded and imposed throughout the organizational hierarchy.
2. It assumes a rather apolitical, resistance-free organizational setting where the wisdom and thinking of top management and consultocrats are unquestionably accepted by those working at lower levels.
3. The implementation of BSC demands a substantial investment, which often fails to justify the managerial benefits it creates.
4. The process takes an extended period (for example, in Kaplan and Norton's cited instance, more than two years) to complete a project, during which conditions may have drastically changed. This is a reason why many BSC projects are abandoned midway through implementation.

5. Once implemented, the BSC system can become rigid and inflexible because altering scorecards necessitates rerunning expensive redesigning and cascading processes.

Reimagining the BSC for sustainability

There have been numerous attempts to redesign the BSC framework to address ecological and social justice issues highlighted by the global sustainability agenda (e.g. Figge et al. 2002; Hansen and Schaltegger 2016; Kalender and Vayvay 2016; Kaplan and McMillan 2021). These efforts appear to encompass two interconnected approaches:

1. Incorporating specific sustainability measures and initiatives within the existing four key dimensions of the BSC framework. The concept here is that organizations should undertake their current activities with sensitivity and a commitment to sustainability issues.
2. Introducing a new perspective, and consequently, a new set of causal relationships, to integrate sustainability into the BSC framework. The notion is that the current activities and measures inadequately capture sustainability, necessitating the addition of a new perspective or dimension to the framework.

Key point:

Two interrelated methods of creating a sustainable BSC framework.

As the originator of the BSC framework, Kaplan's paper with a colleague may be the best example of how the BSC framework is "reimagined for the ESG era" (ESG stands for environmental, social, and governance). In typical Kaplan fashion and that of similar consultocratic management gurus, the rationale for this "reimagining of the BSC" derives from their experiences and engagement in corporate experiments. This reimagining commences with Kaplan's and his colleagues' 2018 Harvard Business Review paper, "Inclusive Growth: Profitable Strategies for Tackling Poverty and Inequality" (Kaplan et al. 2018)/. In this paper, their central message is that successful corporate strategies for sustainability require the creation of "inclusive, sustainable, and profit-generating ecosystems" (Kaplan et al. 2018, 5). To achieve this, they identify and recommend three strategies, which a potential fourth principle should support.

1. The first involves the pursuit of systemic multi-sector opportunities. Their consultocratic recommendation is that companies should surpass the conventional corporate social responsibility (CSR) budgeting approach and seek opportunities that generate economic benefits for themselves while

fostering socioeconomic gains for all other actors in the new ecosystem. As a prelude to their "reimagined balanced scorecard approach to sustainability," they critique the conventional CSR budgeting approach, arguing that:

> such programs typically benefit a relatively small number of people and don't fundamentally change the community's socioeconomic conditions. What's more, they are generally funded from a sustainability budget, not embedded in the company's local business strategy. That means they are often the first programs to be cut during lean times. The traditional corporate sustainability approach ultimately has a limited impact because it is positioned as a social or an environmental program, not a profit-generating one (Kaplan et al. 2018, 5).

Key point:

Kaplan and colleagues promote a neoliberal ideology that asserts sustainability needs to be profitable to be sustained.

The corporatist argument that profit is a fundamental prerequisite for sustainability is blatantly implicit in this critique. I will return to this point later in this section after first explaining the key principles upon which Kaplan and his colleagues constructed their "reimagined balanced scorecard."

2. The second strategy involves mobilizing complementary partners as "catalysts." Here, Kaplan and colleagues steer the corporate consultocracy in a different direction by collaborating with civil society organizations and global development capital institutions. The goal is to provide essential access to, and, more importantly, trust and legitimacy within, the so-called 'new inclusive ecosystem'. Such a catalyst could be an NGO or a project management and consulting company. The paper specifically mentions the global consultancy firm Palladium, to which Kaplan and his authoring colleagues are affiliated as managers or consulting advisors. Palladium's website asserts that they allocate 1.5% of their profits to humanitarian relief efforts, community projects nominated by employees, and an annual Challenge Fund to address major global problems. The ideology and strategy here are explicitly evident in their argument:

> A CSO or a country manager who wants to create transformative change is unlikely to get much

traction, let alone a budget sufficient to provide proof of concept. Nor does he or she have the authority to add sustainability objectives to line managers' operational responsibilities and performance assessments. And local managers, under pressure to deliver short-term financial results, lack the authority, legitimacy, trust, capabilities, and resources to support more than incremental feel-good projects.

Whoever recognises an opportunity, one thing is certain: Without the involvement of a profit-seeking corporation, no program is likely to go far. For an industrial ecosystem to be sustainable, it must be credible to businesses searching for competitive advantage and able to scale up. Governments are attracted to public-private partnerships for improving local socioeconomic conditions because they can harness the resources and innovation capabilities of profit-seeking companies (Kaplan et al. 2018, 6).

Key point:

how Kaplan and colleagues signify a consultocratic, profit-seeking approach to sustainability.

I will revisit this point later in the chapter when advancing a political-economy critique of this "reimagining the balanced scorecard project."

3. Their third strategy involves acquiring seed and scale-up financing. Ironically and paradoxically, corporatist guru Kaplan and his colleagues recognize and acknowledge the ideological and institutional incapacity of corporate capitalism to address sustainability when they declare that:

> The corporate partner would seem to be a natural supplier of seed financing for an ecosystem transformation. After all, a corporation has resources to invest in positive net present value projects and will be a prime beneficiary when projects succeed. … But few companies are prepared to finance this type of risky investment, especially with their limited sustainability and CSR budgets. Corporate investment funds favor safe projects with short payback periods, not projects that require disrupting

an existing equilibrium and creating new relationships across multiple sectors far from headquarters. All the organizational, incentive, and cultural hurdles that make disruptive innovation so hard become amplified when implementing projects designed to create new, socially inclusive business models and ecosystems (Kaplan et al. 2018, 6).

Key point:

Private sector profit-seeking capital is advised to exploit the "poverty capital."

Their strategy is to assist corporations in overcoming this challenge by exploring ways and means of tapping into what they refer to as the growing "pool of impact investment," which Ananya Roy (Roy 2010) alternatively calls "poverty capital": the types of finance that underpin poverty management and poverty alleviation, especially in the poverty-ridden global south. This is the pool of capital sourced not only by development funding agencies such as the United Nations, World Bank, US Aids, Japanese Agency for International Cooperation (JAICA), Asian Development Bank, African Development Bank, and so on but also by philanthropic and charity money contributed wholeheartedly by millions of individuals through charities and NGOs (I am thinking of school children like my son and daughter walking many miles to raise such money to help the poor in Africa!). Moreover, this poverty capital also involves the money that less developed country states allocate from their national budgets for various development agendas such as UN SDGs. So, it is this pool of poverty capital that Kaplan and colleagues aim to tap into in developing their "new ecosystem" (which I will elaborate on shortly). Kaplan and his colleagues here are not at all different from Prahalad (2005), another leading corporate strategy guru, who also advises corporations on how to seek "the fortune at the bottom of the pyramid" (which is the title of his book with the subtitle, eradicating poverty through profits and enabling dignity and choice through markets).

4. The fourth principle or strategy involves implementing a new measurement and governance system to foster commitment, monitor progress, and sustain alignment among key stakeholders in creating the new ecosystem. This entails reimagining the BSC to accommodate the first three principles/strategies mentioned earlier. Kaplan and colleagues delve into this concept in their subsequent publications (Kaplan and McMillan 2021), drawing on their consultocratic engagements

and experiences. They assert that the BSC can be "reimagined for the ESG era" by

a. Redefining the company's long-term strategic intents, particularly the corporate vision and mission, to incorporate Environmental, Social, and Governance (ESG) elements. Particular emphasis should be placed on how the company aligns with the construction of the "new inclusive ecosystem." Illustrated through the example case study of Riau Cocoa, they articulate visions encompassing a unique sustainable and inclusive cocoa supply chain, the integration of multiple breakthrough innovations, and the disruption of the traditional cocoa paradigm.

b. Introducing a new layer of "triple bottom line perspective" or "positive impact outcomes" atop the financial perspective. This introduces a new causality from the financial perspective to the triple bottom line perspective. As previously expounded in their work on "inclusive growth" (Kaplan et al. 2018), the underlying doctrine suggests a dual facet. Firstly, sustainability is deemed achievable only through profits or returns on investment for private capital. The idea is that profit-seeking corporate involvement is imperative for sustainability, with these ventures eventually benefiting other stakeholders. Secondly, there are profit "opportunities at the bottom of the pyramid," and corporate managers should display ambition and creativity to tap into such opportunities emerging from the global sustainability agenda. However, given the high-risk nature of such ventures for corporate capital, which demands higher returns, the necessary capital should be sourced from the "pool of impact investments", as Kaplan and colleagues call it. Private capital, lacking essential social, political, and symbolic capital, should collaborate with other "ecosystem players," including providers of "poverty capital" (cf., Roy 2010), NGOs, charities, and community groups. Once this collaboration is established, the financial perspective can be relabeled as the "stakeholder perspective," within which the dominant financial aspect is now tactically and rhetorically disguised.

Key point:

How BSC is reimagined to incorporate social and environmental issues but with a profit motive.

c. Embedding sustainability concerns into the lower levels of BSC causality, either as a separate perspective or as measures integrated into the internal processes and learning and growth perspectives. The Amanco example provided by Kaplan and colleagues incorporates a "social and environmental perspective" between the internal process and learning and growth perspectives (labeled as human resources). Measures such as transparency, social impact, water usage, and occupational health and accident prevention are identified within this perspective. In the Riau Cocoa example of strategy mapping, sustainability elements are integrated into the process perspective, relabeled as "sustainable and innovative processes." Additionally, the learning and growth perspective is renamed as "key enablers and resources." These two causal layers/perspectives collectively encapsulate the idea of the "new ecosystem" discussed earlier, highlighting the processes and practices through which the company can tap into the "poverty capital" infrastructure.

Reimagining BSC as a capitalist managerial capture of sustainability – a political-economy critique

Key point:

The critical notion of 'managerial capture'.

Kaplan and colleagues' endeavors to "reimagine the BSC for the ESG era" embody what critical accounting scholars (see, for example, Alawattage et al. 2022; Baker 2010; O'Dwyer 2003; Owen et al. 2000) often term as capitalistic "managerial capture." Managerial capture involves the discourses, processes, and practices through which wider socio-political and ecological justice issues are "recast in ways that pose no moral or emotional challenge to the dominant logic of shareholder [wealth] maximization" (Baker 2010, 847). Thus, as explicitly demonstrated in Kaplan and colleagues' aforementioned writings, the pursuit of profit or even profiteering is framed as a necessary condition for addressing ecological and social justice issues created by shareholder capitalism (or its predecessor, colonial capitalism) in the first place. In my view, embedded in this overarching capitalistic managerial capture, Kaplan and colleagues' "reimagining the BSC for the ESG era" faces the following fundamental issues:

Key point:

Reimagined BSC's problematic finality.

1. Its sustainability connection is built on a problematic assumption of causality (or 'finality' as discussed above). It assumes and unquestioningly propagates that capitalistic economic value creation should necessarily lead to social and

ecological elements of sustainability. Sustainability, according to their perspective, can only be achieved through profits. As mentioned earlier, they assert that corporations' profitable engagements are crucial to creating a sustainable world. This demonstrates either a blatant ignorance or a neglect of colonial, industrial, and natural history. Anyone with a sensible understanding of economic and natural history would acknowledge that colonial and modern industrial capitalism played a significant role in creating an unsustainable world. As Kaplan and colleagues ironically acknowledge in their cited writings, entrusting corporate capital with the socially and ecologically responsible function of creating a sustainable world is challenging and even perilous. According to natural scientists such as Donna Haraway and Jason Moore, the '*capitalocene*' has been a fundamental historical movement underpinning global unsustainability through profit-driven destruction of ecological and social balances (see Haraway 2015; Moore 2015).

2. Kaplan and colleagues' notion of an 'ecosystem' is rather narrow and misconceived. As discussed in Chapter 1, sustainability should encompass the ways in which the fundamental contradictions between the economy, polity, society, and ecology are addressed. In a sustainability context, the idea of an ecosystem should encompass all these elements and contradictions; it should not be mislabeled as another 'economic system'. Intentionally or ignorantly, Kaplan and colleagues appear to misuse the term 'ecosystem' for the economic system or a new supply chain. Perhaps they know that the term 'ecosystem' carries more sustainability appeal and legitimacy than economic system or supply chain, but their use of the term is dangerously and misleadingly economic. Upon careful and critical examination of their publications, it becomes apparent that their "new ecosystem" is nothing more than a set of 'profitable' connections with the poor through so-called 'catalysts' so that corporations can tap into the "poverty capital," to use Ananya Roy's terminology, which is "the pool of impact investments," as per Kaplan and colleagues' terminology, and create a 'sustainability image' for them.

3. The empirical picture of inclusive capitalism they portray in their publications is problematic when considering the realities in the global south, where 'inclusive capitalism' is

Side note:

Capitalocene is a term used to describe the current historical epoch in which capitalism has become the dominant force shaping the world and its ecosystems. The term highlights the negative impact of capitalism on the environment and argues that the pursuit of profit has led to the exploitation of natural resources, pollution, and climate change. The Capitalocene concept argues that the current crisis in the world's ecosystems is a direct result of the capitalist system and that radical changes to this system are necessary to ensure a sustainable future for the planet.

Key point:

A strategically misconceived idea of 'ecosystem'.

experimented with the corporate ideology of profit-seeking and entrepreneurship. As extensively discussed in various sociological, anthropological, and critical accounting scholarship (see Alawattage et al. 2019; Brett 2006; Jacobs et al. 2012; Roy 2010; Weber 2006; Fernando 2011), ground realities are worsening. For instance, consider the microfinance industry today. Initially launched as a noble social movement to assist poor women in Bangladesh in improving their financial inclusiveness and literacy, manifesting an instance of capitalistic or managerial capture, it has evolved into a highly profitable global industry. This transformation has created corporate opportunities to seek the "fortunes at the bottom of the pyramid," if I use Hamel Prahalad's book title. Since this transformation, microfinance has become a social disaster in peripheral villages in India, Sri Lanka, Bangladesh, and many other countries, leading to a higher rate of suicides among "micro-financially indebted" poor women in rural areas. These women find themselves in conditions of perpetual indebtedness, with microfinance institutions lending money to them at rates of around 5% to 10 % per month (yes, per month! not annual rates). This situation results in microfinance companies collecting a large majority of their income as interest payments perpetually because these poor women are unable to pay the loan principals, thereby perpetually continuing to pay the interest. Although these women are now 'included' in the formal market economy (i.e. inclusive capitalism and the "new inclusive ecosystem," as Kaplan and others talk about), they are paying insanely high-interest rates and reproducing their poverty more than ever before. They have neither become nor will become the so-called 'entrepreneurs' that this 'new inclusive ecosystem' promises to develop. Nevertheless, based on the mere fact that they have taken loans, these poor women are 'statistically reported' in glossy industrial and policy reports as new entrepreneurs 'included' in the formal economy with financial literacy.

Key point:

Inclusive capitalism or profiting from poverty?

4. As evident in Kaplan and colleagues' own case studies, the poor have acquired a new identity – entrepreneurs (not laborers). In this 'new ecosystem' that Kaplan and his colleagues advocate, the poor are less likely to secure fixed-income jobs as workers or laborers; instead, they are presented with the "opportunity to become entrepreneurs" but with a high-inter-

est loan. However, unlike wage workers, they must bear the risks of running a business and pay significantly higher interest rates than corporations or wealthy business people would pay as their cost of capital. The large majority of the income they can generate by being a so-called entrepreneur running a tiny business in a rural village goes to the corporations in terms of interest. In assuming business and financial risk, these individuals then produce cheap raw materials for global companies. Therefore, in this new ecosystem, poor laborers are transformed into entrepreneurs to bear the business and financial risks that capital should otherwise bear. Hence, in this 'new ecosystem', corporations can earn a return for which someone else bears the real risks (see Alawattage et al. 2019). The strategy for doing this is termed "inclusive growth" and "reimagining the BSC for the ESG era"; the underlying theme is tapping into what Ananya Roy called "poverty capital." In effect, it resembles 'poverty capitalism' more than inclusive capitalism.

Key point:

Kaplan and colleagues' new ecosystem shifts the risk to the labour and provides the capital with the opportunity to earn a return for which it bears no risk at all.

Chapter summary

This chapter explored performance management within traditional and strategic frameworks. It commences with a broad definition of performance as goal-directed behavior, actions, and outcomes subject to observations, evaluations, assessments, and rewards/punishments.

The traditional approach to performance management is responsibility accounting, of which operational philosophy comprises a hierarchy of accountability centers, accounting calculations to conceptualize and measure the performance of such accountability centers, and the principle of controllability. Responsibility accounting formalizes performance by structuring organizations hierarchically into cost, revenue, profit, and investment centers. Aligned with this hierarchy, accounting techniques are employed to conceptualize, measure, and evaluate center managers' performance, subsequently linked to return on investment. Budgeting, standard costing, variance analysis, ratio analysis, and other costing and decision-making techniques play crucial roles in responsibility accounting. The DuPont system, exemplifying the breakdown of return on investment, illustrates responsibility accounting's calculative hierarchy.

Despite its widespread use, responsibility accounting faces criticism for two fundamental weaknesses: its financial overemphasis (i.e. imbalance between financial and non-financial measures of performance) and its operational overemphasis (i.e. lack of strategic connections).

Kaplan and Norton's Balanced Scorecard (BSC) emerged as a solution to these shortcomings. BSC is acknowledged as a strategic performance management system because it 'balances' financial and strategically vital non-financial measures and 'links' operations with strategy. The foundational elements of Kaplan and Norton's BSC approach are 'scorecards,' which are recording templates combining objectives, measures, indicators, and initiatives. Balancing occurs through the incorporation of multiple performance dimensions, with a balanced scorecard encompassing learning and growth, internal business processes, customer, and financial dimensions at the organizational level. Linking is achieved by cascading scorecards from top-level organizational scorecards to bottom-level individual managers' scorecards.

BSC assumes a set of underlying causalities: non-financial performance in learning and growth and internal business processes leading to financial performance through customer satisfaction. However, for Hanna Norreklit, this assumed causality is a major weakness of the BSC framework, resembling more like 'finalities' than 'causalities.'

Recent endeavors by Kaplan and colleagues aim to reimagine BSC for the ESG era, envisioning an "inclusive, sustainable, and profit-generating ecosystem." They propose four interrelated strategies: searching for systemic multi-sector opportunities, mobilizing complementary partners as catalysts, obtaining seed and scale-up financing, and implementing a new measurement and governance system. These strategies, framed within the discourse of inclusive capitalism, constitute a neoliberal capitalist ideology suggesting sustainability can only be achieved through profit-seeking ventures. This perspective is subject to political-economy and pragmatic critique, highlighting potential issues such as "managerial capture." Kaplan and colleagues' "reimagining BSC for the ESG era" and the concept of a "new inclusive ecosystem" demonstrate a disregard or strategic neglect of the fundamental contradictions and historical dynamics underlying the evolution of unsustainability.

Test your knowledge

1. How would you define performance in generic terms?
2. Enumerate three factors that underlie the context specificity of performance.
3. Elaborate on the role that 'higher-order principles' play in defining performance.
4. Define performance management in generic terms.
5. Responsibility accounting is considered the traditional approach to performance management. Briefly elucidate three elements that constitute the operational philosophy of responsibility accounting.
6. Briefly explain the hierarchy of responsibility/accountability centers in a responsibility accounting system. Offer examples of measuring performance at these responsibility/accountability centers.
7. Clarify how accounting transforms otherwise non-accounting hierarchies into an accounting hierarchy. You may use examples of budgeting systems or the DuPont system of ratio analysis.
8. Draft a concise note on the techniques and structures of responsibility accounting.
9. Summarize the key features of responsibility accounting under the following themes:

    a. Logic
    b. Structure
    c. Process
    d. Tools and techniques

10. Define a strategic performance management system.
11. Enumerate key weaknesses of responsible accounting as a performance management system.
12. Which of these weaknesses does Kaplan and Norton's BSC attempt to rectify?
13. List and elucidate the performance measurement dimensions advocated by BSC.
14. Explain the process that BSC deploys to link operational performance with corporate strategies.
15. Outline the role that scorecards play in the managerial acts of balancing and linking.

16. Describe the process suggested by Kaplan and Norton for implementing a BSC project.
17. Expound on the causal connections that BSC upholds.
18. Elaborate on Hanna Norreklit's critique of the causalities assumed by Kaplan and Norton's BSC.
19. How do you differentiate between causality and finality?
20. List the major weaknesses of BSC as a system of performance management.
21. Briefly discuss the key propositions of Kaplan and his colleagues' attempt to reimagine the BSC for the ESG era.
22. Briefly explain the notion of 'managerial capture'.
23. Using managerial capture literature as an example, explain the political-ideological issues of Kaplan and colleagues' neo-liberal reimagination of sustainability through BSC.

Explore further

1. Select a large for-profit corporation and visit its website to explore the following:

    a. How has the company communicated its long-term strategic ambitions and goals (where and in which type of statements)?
    b. What performance dimensions are captured in such strategic statements that you discussed in part (a) above?
    c. How does the company assess their achievement in those areas? What indicators and measures are used in key statements of corporate performance review (e.g. chairman's review) for the public?

2. Select a public organization like the National Health Service, for example, and explore their websites. Examine the manner in which their performance dimensions and targets are communicated and reported to the public at large. Pay special attention to the key performance indicators (KPIs) the organization highlights as key to its successful public service delivery.

3. Visit the UN SDGs website and explore the 17 SDGs. Then, assess a for-profit organization's corporate reports and website information to see the extent to which and the manner in which UN SDGs are incorporated into various strategic statements of the corporation.

Develop your critical argumentation skills

1. Write an argumentative essay on the following theme:

   "From Kaplan and Norton's BSC perspective, strategizing performance management involves managerial acts of balancing and linking."

   Explain why balancing and linking are strategically important and how strategic balancing and linking are to be carried out with scorecards.

2. Write an argumentative essay on the following theme:

   "Kaplan and colleagues' project of reimagining the balanced scorecard for the ESG era leaves more problems than solutions for sustainability."

   With a thorough reading of their recent articles on sustainability and connecting them to relevant critical accounting literature on managerial capture, critically assess arguments and propositions that Kaplan and his colleagues propose for reimagining the BSC for ESG.

Mini case study

A Balanced Scorecard for an NGO

Sarvodaya is among the largest and oldest non-governmental organizations (NGOs) operating in a less developed country. With over 60 years of operational history, it stands as the largest and most extensively integrated people's organization, boasting a network spanning 15,000 villages, 345 divisional units, 34 district offices, and 10 specialist Development Education Institutes across the country. The organization has successfully mobilized over 100,000 youth for peacebuilding and rural development.

Rural development and welfare form the core focus of Sarvodaya. Engaging in a diverse range of activities and businesses, it aims to address the developmental needs of rural villages nationwide. The organization operates one of the country's largest micro-credit (microfinance) organizations, with a cumulative loan portfolio exceeding one billion LKR (the domestic currency). Furthermore, it administers a significant welfare service program catering to over 1,000 orphaned and destitute children, underage mothers, and elders. Additionally, Sarvodaya oversees 4,335 pre-schools, benefiting more than 98,000 children.

Apart from profits generated by its microfinance operations, Sarvodaya receives development funding (grants) from international donor agencies such as UNICEF, the World Bank, and the UN. A major recurrent grant scheme is slated for review in three years.

To enhance its case during grant renewal discussions with funding agency officers, the finance director at Sarvodaya has decided to present a balanced scorecard demonstrating the NGO's performance. Accordingly, he intends to advocate for the adoption of a balanced scorecard as the NGO's performance management system in the upcoming Board of Directors Meeting. As the senior management accountant, you have been tasked with assisting him. Given that many board members include eminent philanthropists, leading politicians, religious leaders, and senior government officers who may be unfamiliar with the balanced scorecard concept, it is crucial to provide a comprehensive briefing.

Required

1. Briefing on the concept of a balanced scorecard for the management board

   For the benefit of the Management Board, it is essential to outline the concept of a balanced scorecard, emphasizing its utility for the NGO compared to a conventional budgeting-based performance management system.

2. Development process and examples of measures for the balanced scorecard

   Discuss the process employed to develop a balanced scorecard for the NGO and provide examples of measures that can be incorporated.

3. Addressing concerns about suitability

   Respond to the concern raised by a colleague about the balanced scorecard being primarily developed for for-profit organizations and built upon the idea of causality leading to financial perspectives, especially the enhancement of return on investment. Clarify how the balanced scorecard is adaptable to a legendary not-for-profit organization like Sarvodaya, highlighting its relevance and benefits in measuring and improving performance in the non-profit sector.

References

Alawattage, C., C. Graham, and D. Wickramasinghe. 2019. Microaccountability and biopolitics: microfinance in a Sri Lankan village. Accounting, Organizations and Society 72:38-60.

Alawattage, C., C. Jayathileka, R. Hitibandara, and S. Withanage. 2022. Moral economy, performative materialism, and political rhetorics of sustainability accounting. Critical Perspectives on Accounting:102507.

Baker, M. 2010. Re-conceiving managerial capture. Accounting, Auditing & Accountability Journal 23 (7):847-867.

Bessire, D., and C. R. Baker. 2005. The French Tableau de bord and the American Balanced Scorecard: a critical analysis. Critical Perspectives on Accounting 16 (6):645-664.

Bourguignon, A., V. Malleret, and H. Norreklit. 2004. The American balanced scorecard versus the French tableau de bord: the ideological dimension. Management Accounting Research 15 (2):107-134.

Brett, J. A. 2006. "We sacrifice and eat less": the structural complexities of microfinance participation. Human Organization 65 (1):8-19.

Cooper, D. J., M. Ezzamel, and S. Q. Qu. 2017. Popularising a management accounting idea: the case of the balanced scorecard. Contemporary Accounting Research 34 (2):991-1025.

Fernando, J. L. 2011. The political economy of NGOs

State formation in Sri Lanka and Bangladesh: Pluto Press.

Figge, F., T. Hahn, S. Schaltegger, and M. Wagner. 2002. The sustainability balanced scorecard – linking sustainability management to business strategy. Business Strategy and the Environment 11 (5):269-284.

Hansen, E. G., and S. Schaltegger. 2016. The sustainability balanced scorecard: a systematic review of architectures. Journal of Business Ethics 133 (2):193-221.

Haraway, D. 2015. Anthropocene, capitalocene, plantationocene, chthulucene: making kin. Environmental Humanities 6 (1):159-165.

Jacobs, K., M. Habib, N. Musyoki, and C. Jubb. 2012. Empowering or oppressing: the case of microfinance institutions. In Handbook of Accounting and Development edited by T. Hopper, M. Tsamenyi, S. Uddin and D. Wickramasinghe. Cheltenham: Edward Elgar Publishing 162-181.

Kalender, Z. T., and Ö. Vayvay. 2016. The Fifth Pillar of the Balanced Scorecard: Sustainability. Procedia - Social and Behavioral Sciences 235:76-83.

Kaplan, R. S. 2008. Conceptual foundations of the balanced scorecard. In Handbooks of management accounting research, edited by A. G. H. Christopher S. Chapman and D. S. Michael: Elsevier, 1253-1269.

Kaplan, R. S., and D. McMillan. 2021. Reimagining the balanced scorecard for the ESG Era. In Harvard Business Review, 1-12.

Kaplan, R. S., and D. P. Norton. 1993. Putting the balanced scorecard to work. Harvard Business Review 1993 (September-October):134-147.

———. 1996a. The balanced scorecard: translating strategy into action. Boston, Mass.: Harvard Business School Press.

———. 1996b. Using the balanced scorecard as a strategic management system. Harvard Business Review 1996 (January-February):75-85.

———. 2000. Having trouble with your strategy? then map it. Harvard Business Review 2000 (September-October):3-11.

Kaplan, R. S., G. Serafeim, and E. Tugendhat. 2018. Inclusive growth: profitable strategies for tackling poverty and inequality. Harvard Business Review 2018 (January-February):3-9.

Moore, J. 2015. Capitalism in the web of life: ecology and the accumulation of capital: Verso.

Norreklit, H. 2000. The balance on the balanced scorecard a critical analysis of some of its assumptions. Management Accounting Research 11 (1):65-88.

———. 2003. The balanced scorecard: what is the score? a rhetorical analysis of the balanced scorecard. Accounting, Organizations and Society 28 (6):591-619.

O'Dwyer, B. 2003. Conceptions of corporate social responsibility: the nature of managerial capture. Accounting, Auditing & Accountability Journal 16 (4).

Owen, D. L., T. A. Swift, C. Humphrey, and M. Bowerman. 2000. The new social audits: accountability, managerial capture or the agenda of social champions? European Accounting Review 9 (1):81-98.

Prahalad, C. K. 2005. The fortune at the bottom of the pyramid: eradicating poverty through profits, enabling dignity and choice through markets. New Jersey: Wharton School Publishing.

Roy, A. 2010. Poverty capital: microfinance and the making of development: Taylor & Francis.

Weber, H. 2006. The global political economy of microfinance and poverty reduction: locating local 'livelihoods' in political analysis In Microfinance: Perils and Prospects, edited by J. L. Fernando. London: Routledge.

CHAPTER 5

Strategizing the hierarchy: **strategic management control**

5.1 Introduction

Let me refresh your mind on the overarching thematic structure of this textbook. Previous chapters highlighted that strategies are implemented and activated in three interconnected sites or domains of strategic actions: the market, the organizational hierarchy, and the point of production. As elucidated in the initial three chapters, the market serves as the arena where strategic positioning is implemented and brought into effect. Three forthcoming chapters will delve into how the point of production facilitates and executes these market positioning strategies by producing what the market demands, encompassing three critical strategic imperatives: quality, cost, and flexibility.

In a broader context, the organizational hierarchy furnishes the institutional and administrative infrastructure that manages, regulates, and governs the strategic linkage between the market and the point of production while ensuring that the organization complies with ethical, legal, and regulatory obligations imposed by external environmental elements. Within this context, three strategic themes associated with the organizational hierarchy are delineated: performance management, management control, and organizational resilience. The preceding chapter addressed strategic performance management, while the current chapter focuses on strategic management control. Following this, the subsequent chapter will explore organizational resilience as a further extension of the discussions on strategizing organizational hierarchy.

Reminder:

Three sites for enabling and implementing strategies – markets, organizational hierarchies, and the point of production.

The chapter is structured around the following key themes:

1. Firstly, section 5.2 will examine the generic meaning of 'control' and the fundamental conditions that necessitate different forms of control. The discussion in this section will primarily revolve around the conventional manner in which control was conceptualized in management accounting and control literature before the notions of strategic management control started to penetrate and populate our field of study. This section begins with a brief discussion of how agency theory, a popular theoretical framework in mainstream accounting research, frames our understanding of management control. Then, as system theory-based conceptions of management control laid the initial conceptual groundwork for the subsequent development of strategic management control frameworks, this section will specifically highlight the various ways system theory underpins our comprehension of management control. After reading this section, you should be able to elucidate the conditions that necessitate control and the different conceptual frames according to which control is conceptualized in conventional management accounting literature.

2. Secondly, in section 5.3, using Simons' levers of control framework (LOC), you will explore the strategic management control dynamics, systems, and processes. The LOC framework enables us to understand how management control underpins broader strategic considerations, such as defining the organization's beliefs and core values, establishing boundaries for risk-taking, managing critical performance variables through diagnostic control systems, and addressing strategic uncertainties through interactive control systems. This section will also address the possibilities and challenges of utilizing the LOC framework for sustainability. After reading this section, you should be able to expound on the key propositions and concepts of strategic management control using Simon's LOC framework and assess the extent to which and the ways in which the LOC framework can be applied to promote sustainability.

3. Finally, section 5.5 concludes the chapter with a summary.

Key point:

Chapter's key themes and learning objectives.

5.2 Understanding the fundamentals of management control

The conceptualization of management controls can manifest in various forms, often delineated by dichotomies, such as operational versus strategic control, bureaucratic versus cultural controls, external versus internal control, cybernetic versus non-cybernetic controls, and so forth (see Berry et al. 2005). However, amidst the potential variations in the manifestation of control issues, they all stem from a fundamental ontological condition – namely, *control is mandated and defined by contradictory or conflicting conditions and situations.*

How control is conceptualized and how control systems, processes, and procedures are designed and implemented depend on the specific contradictory conditions to which these controls are linked. For instance, control may be necessitated by transnational contradictions and conflicts between nations involving conflicting political, ideological, and economic interests. In such instances, various global governance and control mechanisms, such as international treaties and accords and global governance institutions like the UN and EU, play a crucial role in mitigating potential crises arising from such conflicts. Similarly, contradictions may arise between organizations, parties involved in market transactions, supply chain arrangements, etc. In such cases, laws, regulations, and contracts are essential control mechanisms to maintain order among conflicting and competing parties. Alternatively, contradictions may be intra-organizational, occurring between different levels or departments of management emphasizing divergent managerial priorities. In such cases, various management control techniques, including budgets, policies, regulations, procedures, protocols, and guidelines, may constitute control practices to foster coordination and cooperation among conflicting priorities. Contradictions can also be interpersonal, requiring specific human resource policies, procedures, and ethical codes of conduct to address such interpersonal contradictions and conflicts. Alternatively, they may be intra-personal, necessitating various 'self-control' or psychological control mechanisms.

Key point:

Contradictions underpin and necessitate different forms of control.

In an overall sense, control may thus involve the regulation of actions and outcomes, the mitigation of risks and losses, the exploitation and domination of one party by another, compliance with norms, and so on. However, the specific form that control takes depends on the specific manner in which the control situation (i.e., the contradictory condition) manifests and is conceptualized. Therefore, the theoretical framing of contradictory conditions is critical in understanding and interpreting control.

Let us consider two prevalent conceptual/theoretical frameworks to observe how contradictory conditions, and hence management control, are differently conceptualized in management accounting literature: agency theory and systems theory.

Agency theory conception of management control

In its various iterations, such as the agent-principal model, transaction cost theory, and the Rochester model (see Baiman 1990, 2006), agency theory incorporates neoclassical economic perspectives on management control. It conceptualizes management control as the means by which a company addresses potential inefficiencies and losses arising from the agency problem. The agency problem, central to this theory, represents a contradiction between two parties in a contract or transaction. In the agent-principal model, the firm is viewed as a series of hierarchically arranged agency relationships where the principal hires an agent to delegate responsibilities under a mutually agreed-upon employment or managerial contract. This contract outlines compensation arrangements, accountabilities, information systems, allocation of duties, ownership rights, and any other conditionality relevant to the relationship to be controlled. Examples of such relationships include those between owners (principals) and managers (agents), estate owners (principals) and stewards (agents), superior managers (principals) and subordinates (agents), and clients (principals) and service providers such as physicians, lawyers, or accountants (agents).

Side note:

The discussion here focuses on the generic principal-agent model; for nuanced differences between agency theory variants, see Baiman 1990, 2006.

These agency relationships can exist within an organization (intra-organizational) or between firms (inter-organizational). Organizational hierarchies and inter-firm arrangements, such as franchising, licensing, and subcontracting, are examples of agency relationships.

Key point:

Agency relationship and contract as the basis of management control in neoclassical economic interpretations.

The 'contract,' whether explicit or implicit, serves as the primary control tool regulating the relationship between the agent and principal and their performance outcomes. It outlines specific objectives, duties, responsibilities, authorities delegated to the agent, compensation arrangements, information and communication arrangements, and allocation of ownership rights. Various managerial techniques and tools, such as management by objectives, budgeting and responsibility accounting, balanced scorecards, and human resource management practices of job descriptions, job prescriptions, and letters of appointment, constitute complementary methods of contractual arrangements between agents (employees) and the principal (the firm). Such contractual arrangements define the agency relationships between the firm and its employees and construct the organization as a nexus of contracts (Fama 1980; Fama and Jensen 1983).

Any agency relationship is contradictory and conflicting because, as agency theorists commonly assume, the agents are self-interested, and their interests and behaviors are not naturally consistent with the principals' or firms' interests in profit maximization. A self-interested agent is assumed to be work-averse and risk-averse and possesses private information about the agent's own actions, work, risks, and returns, which the principal cannot costlessly access. It is this contradictory or conflicting conditionality that is identified as the 'agency problem': the possibility that the self-interested, risk-aversive, and work-aversive behavior of the agent, coupled with information asymmetry between the principal and agent, can undermine corporate goals.

It is this agency problem, according to agency theorists, which necessitates management control because if 'self-interested,' risk-aversive, and work-aversive individual is the 'nature', then 'controls' are necessary to make agents' behavior comply with corporate goals. Such controls define the nature of agency relationships within economic enterprises. Responsibility accounting systems involving budgeting, standard costing, and balanced scorecards, for example, may define the parameters within which agency relationships are to be defined and controlled so that possible efficiency losses due to the agency problem are minimized, and shareholders' wealth is maximized.

Key point:

Management control as mitigating the agency problem.

From the agency theory perspective, the management control challenge is designing a 'performance and compensation contract' incentivizing agents to exert effort to maximize the firm's (principal's) profit. Wages and rents represent opposing forms of compensation, and a combination of both is likely to maximize the principal's payoff.

A wage-only contract, where the principal agrees to pay a fixed monthly wage irrespective of effort and performance by the agent, provides no monetary incentives for the agent to exert greater effort and take more risks to perform better. In that case, the principal bears the total risk of the business. On the other hand, in a total rent con-

Key point:

Agency theory sees management control as optimum performance-compensation contracting.

tract, where the principal rents out the business for a fixed monthly payment which the agent agrees to pay irrespective of performance so that any extra net income (or loss) generated from the business goes to the agent, it is the agent who bears the total business risk as principal's return is fixed. Although a rent contract motivates the agent to perform better, his/her performance brings no additional gains for the principal. As such, a particular combination of wage and rent compensation most likely maximises the principal's payoff.

Figure 5.1 illustrates the agency theory conception of optimum performance-compensation contracting.

Figure 5.1: Agency theory conception of optimum performance- compensation contracting

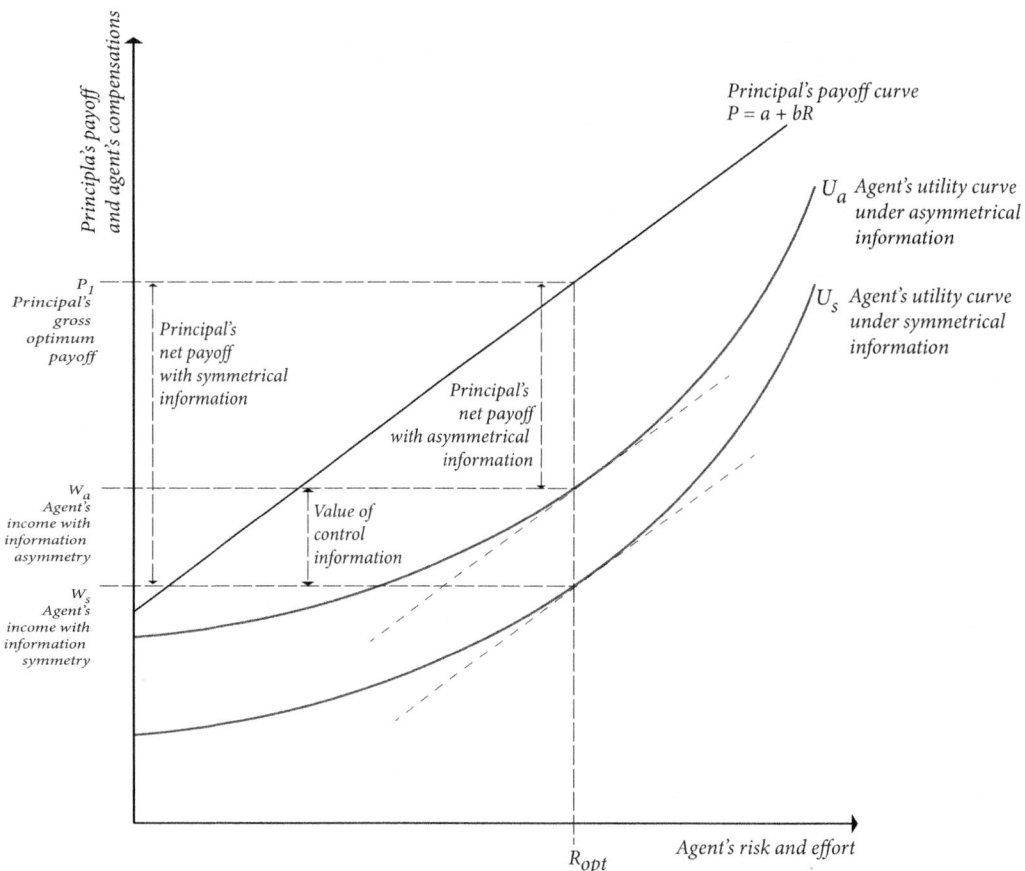

Reading Figure 5.1: the vertical axis signifies the dependent variables of the principal's payoff (P) and the agent's remuneration/compensation (W). The horizontal axis denotes the independent variables of risks undertaken and the effort exerted by the agent. The principal's payoff is determined by the amount of risk and effort shouldered and exerted by the agent, encapsulated in the linear function represented as $P=a+bR$, where:

- '*P*' represents the principal's payoff (i.e., profit before deducting payments for the agent).
- '*a*' represents the principal's payoff when the agent assumes no risks, equivalent to the compensation under a fixed-wage contract, making it a risk-free arrangement for the agent.
- '*b*' signifies the marginal contribution of the agent's additional risk and effort to the principal's payoff, indicating the increment in the principal's payoff due to a one-unit increase in the agent's risk and effort propensity.
- '*R*' denotes the level of risk and effort the agent undertakes.

The agent's risk-return preference or utility is denoted by U and is illustrated through indifference curves (U_a and U_s). These curves portray different risk-return combinations for the agent, reflecting the expectation that a higher return is anticipated for assuming higher risks and exerting more effort. The agent is indifferent at any point on a given *U* curve, thus termed an 'indifference curve.' U_a and U_s present possibilities for indifferent risk-return combinations, distinguishing agents with or without private information (i.e., information asymmetry). With asymmetric information, the agent can demand higher returns for a given level of risk and effort.

The principal's net payoff is the difference between their gross payoff (the P curve) and the agent's utility curve (*U*) at any given level of risk/effort assumed by the agent. As depicted in Figure 5.1, the net payoff is maximized at R_{opt}. Two utility curves are displayed, one for information asymmetry and the other for information symmetry. A condition of information symmetry opens the agent's private information to the principal, prompting the agent to accept the R_{opt} level of risk/effort for a lower wage level (W_s) compared to what they could obtain under information asymmetry (W_a). Consequently, the principal attains greater profit with information symmetry (i.e., $P_1 - W_s$) than with information asymmetry ($P_1 - W_a$). From the principal's standpoint, the solution to the agency problem under information symmetry is considered the first-best solution, while the solution under information asymmetry is termed the second-best solution. The difference between these two solutions signifies the value of control information, making agency relationships symmetrical and the agent's behavior and outcomes more predictable and manageable.

Key point:

Optimality of performance contracts and economic value of control information.

Control information makes the principal aware of agents' activities, efforts, and outcomes and is instrumental in their manageability. From an agency theory perspective, the value of control information lies in enhancing the principal's (i.e., shareholders') wealth maximization prospects. In Figure 5.1, the economic value of control information equates to the difference between W_a and W_s, which is the difference between the principal's optimum pay with and without asymmetric information. According to agency theory, a firm should not expend more resources than this value to obtain accounting and control information.

Systems theory conception of management control

Systems theory pervades the management control literature more dominantly and extensively than the neoclassical economic concepts of management control discussed earlier. Noteworthy works in management control, such as Berry et al.'s (2005) Management Control: Theories, Issues and Performance and Anthony et al.'s (2014) Management Control Systems, are fundamentally expositions of management control based on system theory. Even recent innovations in strategic management control, such as Simons' "Levers of Control", are essentially conceptions of management control rooted in system theory.

Key point:

Recognizing organizations as open systems is the basis for a system theory-based understanding of management control.

The foundation of these system theory-based conceptualizations of management control lies in acknowledging that any organization functions as an open system. An open system is defined as an assembly of interacting and interdependent components collaborating and engaging with its environment to achieve a common set of goals. These components are often identified as subsystems. By recognizing organizations as open systems, the core challenges addressed by management control are systemic contradictions and conflicts, which not only exist among various subsystemic elements but also extend to the interactions between the organization and its external environment. Consequently, system theory-based perspectives on management control encompass and appreciate a broader spectrum of situations and dynamics than the agency theory's agency problem-based understanding of management control.

Taking a broader view, a system theory-based conceptualization of management control encompasses three interconnected perspectives:

1. Processual, programmatic, or cybernetic perspective
2. Hierarchical perspective
3. Environmental perspective

Cybernetic perspectives on management control

The cybernetic approach envisions the organizational system as a programmable input-conversion-output process, subject to regulation and control through feedback information. Cybernetic controls may target inputs, conversion processes, or outputs, representing three modes of control: feedback control (output-driven), concurrent control (conversion process-driven), and feedforward control (input-driven). However, as depicted in Figure 5.2, their controllability hinges on four necessary conditions:

1. Objectives for the system being controlled (related to inputs, conversion processes, and outputs).
2. Means of measuring results along the dimensions defined by the process objectives. Such measurements often encapsulate three generic dimensions – effectiveness (the extent to which a system achieves its intended transformation), efficiency (the extent to which the system achieves its intended transformation with minimum use of resources or energy), and efficacy (the extent to which the system contributes to the purpose of a higher-order system of which it is a subsystem).
3. A predictive model of the system being controlled.
4. Choices of relevant corrective actions available to controllers.

Key point: Critical elements of a cybernetic control system.

Cybernetics emphasizes the inherent interdependence of control and communication. As highlighted by Baecker (2001, 59), "control cannot be discussed without referencing communication. Every control act is inherently a communicative act and achieves success only when communication is effective". Echoing this sentiment, Otley and Berry (1980, 236) assert that "control can only exist when knowledge of outcomes is available." The predictive model serves as the controlling component, executing this communicative function. It is the conduit through which the targeted system is conceptualized, comprehend-

Key point: Inseparability of control and communication.

Figure 5.2: Cybernetic model of management control

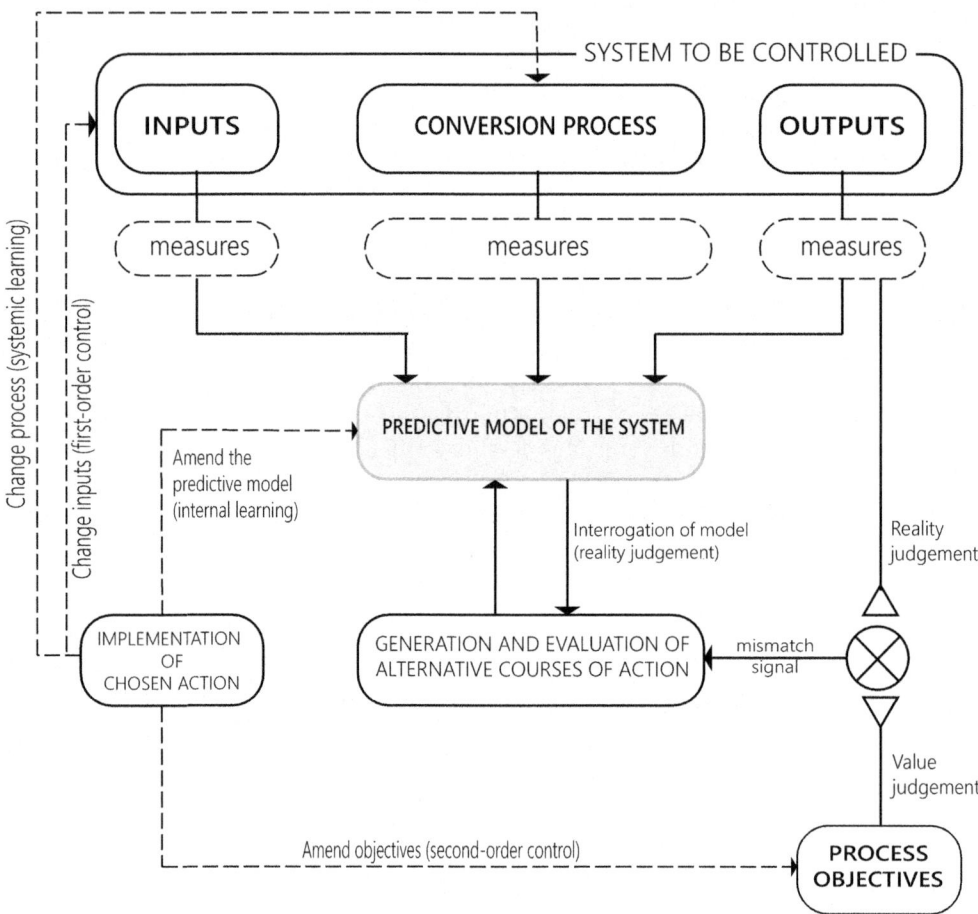

Source: Adapted from Otley and Berry (1980, 236)

ed, measured, and understood. In essence, predictive modeling constitutes a communicative endeavor whereby the system to be controlled is perceived, and the efficacy of control is contingent upon the success of communication facilitated by this model. As elucidated by Otley and Berry (1980, 236), "In the absence or malfunction of such a model, control becomes unattainable, and efforts to enforce control may prove counterproductive." Ultimately, the predictive model becomes the means through which potential outcomes of diverse courses of action are ascertained.

The **predictive model** is pivotal as the performer of three essential cybernetic functions: *detector, comparator,* and *effector*, all of which are communicative functionalities. In essence, the predictive model within a cybernetic system serves as the central epistemic tool or the conceptual framework according to which the system to be controlled is conceived, designed, and controlled in terms of inputs, conversion process, and outputs. It spells out the underlying processual logic according to which detection, comparison, and execution of corrective actions are to be designed and implemented. It establishes the performance measures pertaining to inputs, conversion processes, and outputs; it establishes data collection and testing methodologies according to which actual performances are monitored, recorded, and evaluated; it establishes the comparative benchmarks and standards against which actual performances are compared for corrective actions.

Key point: Centrality of a predictive model in cybernetic control.

Various forms of recording, counting, accounting, seeing, and understanding constitute the *detection*. The control system effectively detects the actual system status through counting, accounting, costing, testing, and various other modes of seeing, recording, and understanding. Hence, for an effective cybernetic control system to operate, there needs to be an effective system that captures and meaningfully records system inputs, conversion processes, and their outputs/outcomes. Transaction processing systems, including bookkeeping, constitute the basic element of this detector functionality of a control system. Such systems of detection interrogate the system to formulate *reality judgments* as to how it operates and performs.

Key point: Detector functionality in cybernetic control system.

Reality judgment then leads to the second functionality of cybernetic control: *comparator*. This involves comparing the reality judgment on the actual system performance with the predetermined process objectives to formulate a *value judgment*. A classic illustration of this process is found in standard costing and variance analysis. Substantial variances between actual performance and standards (objectives) trigger the *effector*—the process of implementing corrective actions. This encompasses generating and evaluating alternative courses of action, selecting the optimal one, and implementing it. Such corrective actions may be directed towards changing input (i.e., *first-order control*), amendments to the process objectives (i.e., *second-order control*), amendments to the predictive model of process (i.e., *internal learning*), changes to the productive process (i.e, *systemic learning*) or any combination thereof.

Key point: Detector, comparator, and effector are three key functionalities of a cybernetic system of control.

So, this is the essence of the cybernetic conception of management control, and you should recognize that it is rather technical and mainly captures control of techno-operational processes.

Beyond cybernetics

Not all control systems can be effectively distilled into a cybernetic framework. Control mechanisms may encompass both cybernetic and non-cybernetic elements, with various management control scenarios exhibiting the latter. Acknowledging this diversity, Hofstede (1981) devised a typology of management control that recognizes both cybernetic and non-cybernetic attributes.

Hofstede's typology is grounded in four key questions assessing the cybernetic nature of a control environment:

1. Clarity of objectives: whether objectives are unambiguous.
2. Measurability of outputs: whether outputs are measurable.
3. Known effects of interventions: whether the effects of interventions are known.
4. Repetitive nature of activity: whether the activity is repetitive.

Based on the extent to which these four cybernetic characteristics are evident in a given control system, Hofstede identified six possible types of management control, as summarized in Table 5.1.

As summarized in Table 5.1 and elaborated in the upcoming sections, strategic management control is distinctly 'political', involving negotiations among conflicting political-economic, social, and ecological values. This complexity is particularly pronounced in the emerging global sustainability agenda, where management control must reconcile contradictions between the economy, polity, society, and ecology.

Dermer (1988), in his exploration of the relationship between control and organizational order, critiques the cybernetic conceptualization of organizations. According to him:

> "Conventional thinking about order has been dominated by two concepts: strategy and cybernetics. As management's definition of what the organization is and what it should be doing, strategy articulates, shapes, and justifies the context of organizational activity for all concerned. This activity is then regulated cybernetically,

Table 5.1: Beyond cybernetics - Hofstede's control typology

Control type	Whether the objectives are unambiguous or if not, whether the ambiguity can be resolved	Whether the outputs are measurable or, if not, whether acceptable surrogate measures can be found	whether the effects of interventions are known	whether the activity is repetitive	Cybernetic vs. non-cybernetic features
Routine	Yes	Yes	Yes	Yes	Perfect cybernetic system and hence control is routinized.
Expert	Yes	Yes	Yes	No	Cybernetic control but with control entrusted to experts (i.e. personnel having prior experience in such activities)
Trial and error	Yes	Yes	No	No	Cybernetic, but the control methods are learnt through trial and error
Intuitive	Yes	No, but acceptable surrogate measures can be found	No	No	Non-Cybernetic. Management control is an art rather than a science.
Judgmental	Yes, or any ambiguities of objectives can be resolved	No	No	No	Non-cybernetic. Control becomes a matter of subjective judgements.
Political	No	No	No	No	Non-cybernetic. Here the control is always political, which depends on power structures, negotiation processes, distribution of resources, and compromising between conflicting interests and values.

Source: based on Hofstede (1981)

that is, through goal-related feedback and adjustment. ... These concepts - organizational order, strategy, and cybernetics - are based on a particular view of organizations. According to this view, management controls the organization from outside, setting the thermostat as it were, observing results, and resetting as necessary. Organisational order is thus seen as the creation of management, strategy and cybernetics as the tools it uses" (Dermer 1988, 25).

For Dermer and others sharing his perspective, control goes beyond this cybernetic model. Control can be non-cybernetic; organizations

> **Key point:**
> Cybernetic conception may be more limiting and obstructive than enlightening.

can self-govern and establish order through the underlying assumptions, principles, and rules guiding their beliefs and behaviors. Dermer argues that the cybernetic view of management control often obscures, rather than clarifies, the concept of management control. Therefore, there's a need to revise the cybernetic conceptualization of management control, particularly concerning 'multi-rationality' and 'pluralism' (see Dermer 1988; Dermer and Lucas 1986). The upcoming section of this chapter will delve deeper into these revisions, extensions, and critiques.

Hierarchical perspectives and structural functionalism in management control

> **Key point:**
> Hierarchical perspectives emphasize hierarchical authority distribution and functional goal division, addressing conflicts between hard and soft systems.

Aligned with the system theory's view of an organization as an open system, hierarchical perspectives emphasize (a) the distribution of authority and responsibility and (b) the functional division of organizational goals and activities. These perspectives view management control as the process of designing, achieving, and maintaining co-ordination and productive interconnections among organizational subsystems. This becomes crucial as organizational systems consist of interdependent subsystems with conflicting objectives and logics, such as hard (technical) and soft (socio-psychological) systems.

> **Key point:**
> Balancing conflicting sub-systemic objectives through functional division and hierarchical arrangement of subsystems is a critical element of management control.

Exploring contradictions between these conflicting subsystems have led to a series of studies that Burrell and Morgan termed "socio-technical system theories" and "theories of bureaucratic dysfunctions" (see Burrell and Morgan 1979; Hopper and Powell 1985). The crust of these studies is that organizational systems comprise interdependent subsystems with contradictory objectives, requiring compromise for optimal balance. Shareholder profit maximization, customer satisfaction, employee welfare, and other objectives must be balanced. This plurality in organizational objectives is often expressed in frameworks like Kaplan and Norton's balanced scorecards, which recognize financial, customer, internal, and learning and growth logics. Accordingly, the functional division and hierarchical ordering of organizational systems constitute the institutional basis of management control. In that sense, controlling involves systemic structuring of the organizational systems to achieve a particular set of functional purposes and imperatives and aligning them towards a set of higher-order principles such as return on investment, ecological justice, and social justice.

Underlying these perspectives is the concept of "functional imperatives". As Talcott Parson, a prominent system theorist, articulating these "imperatives" into his famous AGIL schema, puts it, "Any social system is subject to four independent functional imperatives or 'problems' which must be met adequately if equilibrium and/or continuing existence of the system is to be maintained" (Parsons and Smelser 2005, 16 [1959], see also Burrell and Morgan, 1979, 54).

1. **Adaptation (A):** establishing a viable and continuing fit between the system and its environment.
2. **Goal attainment (G):** defining the goals of the system; mobilizing and managing the resources and effort to attain goals.
3. **Integration (I):** establishing control; inhibiting deviancy from the expected system behavior; maintaining coordination between subsystems; avoiding serious disturbances.
4. **Latency or pattern maintenance (L):** Holding the effort, energy, and performance of the social actors and subsystems at expected levels through motivation and leadership.

These imperatives form the basis of "structural functionalism" that underpins much of the system theory-based understanding of management control. Following Burrell and Morgan (1979), structural-functionalism is a theoretical tradition that uses a biological analogy to explain sociological phenomena. Akin to biological beings, the concepts of holism, interrelationships between parts, structure, functions, and functional imperatives are deployed to understand and explain social phenomena such as management control. Accordingly, two key propositions are central to understanding management control:

Key point:
Structural functionalism underscores the key propositions of management control.

1. relationships among their various parts and with their ecological surrounding and
2. functional roles that parts perform within such relationships to maintain a productive totality.

Seminal works in performance management and management control, particularly by Simons (1995), Otley (1999), and Ferreira and Otley (2009), distinctly reflect structural functionalism. In this research domain, management control refers to the processes—whether intentional or unintentional, formal or informal, strategic or operational—implemented to regulate, sustain, and foster the growth of a social system, namely, the organization.

> **Key point:**
>
> Structural functionalism in management control literature recognizes the importance of structures, relationships, and processes directed toward externally imposed goals.

In this light, managers must configure the organization into a 'cohesive structure of units' encompassing not only divisions, departments, teams, and individuals but also conceptual elements of management control, operational control, and strategic planning. These elements are then unified through vertical and horizontal relationships established via the division of work and delegation of objectives, authorities, responsibilities, accountabilities, and information flows.

Consequently, the functional purpose of management control is to ensure the organization's continuity and growth. This continuity is upheld through the processes inherent in the organizational life involving accountants, other managers, employees, and regulators. According to Ferreira and Otley (2009), these processes encompass analysis, planning, measurement, control, rewarding, and facilitating organizational learning and change. Their collective focus is on sustaining and growing the organization by efficiently and effectively achieving goals and objectives—such as profits, customer satisfaction, employee well-being, and environmental friendliness—imposed by the external environment.

One of the most celebrated management control theorists, Robert Anthony (1965), posits the necessity for three interconnected organizational processes—operational control, management control, and strategic planning. Management accounting researchers have widely embraced this conceptual framework; for example, major textbooks on management control systems (e.g., Anthony et al. 2014; Merchant and Van der Stede 2007; Emmanuel et al. 2004) organize their content around these three categories. Popularised through such textbooks, this three-level framework offers a structured lens through which management accounting scholars and practitioners understand organizations as functional configurations of hierarchically arranged control and planning systems. The organizational life processes are then interpreted in relation to this hierarchical planning and control structure.

1. At the top of this hierarchy are the strategic processes, where long-term organizational directions, ambitions (mission, vision, corporate goals), policies, and strategies are formulated. These processes define the organization's relationship with its environment and stakeholders, long-term character, and ability to sustain structural continuity. These strategic processes are crucial due to the competitiveness and dynamism of the organizational environment.

Strategic processes address the challenge of "adaptation" (following Parson's AGIL schema of structural functionalism), establishing a viable relationship between the system and its external environment. Unlike the subconscious adaptation of organic systems, organizational adaptation is a conscious managerial process embedded in strategic planning, leadership, and change management.

2. Management control processes are in the middle layers of the control hierarchy, ensuring the implementation and achievement of strategic decisions. These systems serve two functional imperatives: goal attainment (defining relevant goals and mobilizing resources) and integration (maintaining coordination between operational units, inhibiting deviancy).

   Goal attainment involves defining systemic goals derived from strategic decisions, such as budgets, targets, benchmarks, and standards. Conversely, integration involves processes inhibiting deviancy and maintaining coordination between operational units. These efforts require conscious managerial intervention, facilitated by various technologies and calculative practices, including management accounting techniques like budgeting, standard costing, Balanced Scorecards, enterprise resource planning, and quality control.

3. At the bottom of the control hierarchy are operational, task, and tactical control systems, ensuring routine activities are carried out efficiently and effectively. Operational control systems handle the functional imperative of latency or pattern maintenance (L), focusing on programming and routinization of tasks to maintain predictable and controllable patterns of organizational activities. Examples include production and operational supervision, quality control, record keeping, internal checks, day-to-day staff meetings, and performance appraisals.

Key point:

How structural functionalism underpins the classical classifications of management control systems.

See Table 5.2 for a summary of how structural functionalism underpins classical understanding of management control systems.

Table 5.2: Parson's structural functionalism and classical theory of management control systems

Control function/ hierarchy	Functional imperatives addressed	Calculative practices through which the functional imperatives are met
Strategic planning	Adaptation (A): establishing relations between the system and its external environment	SWOT analysis, industry analysis, market analysis, value chain analysis, capital investment decisions, corporate planning.
Management control	Goal attainment (G): define the goals of the system and mobilise and manage resources and efforts. Integration (I): inhibiting deviancy and maintain coordination between different operational units, avoiding serious system disturbances	Budgeting, standard costing and variance analysis, financial statement analysis, balanced scorecards, transfer pricing, and performance management.
Operational control	Latency or pattern maintenance (L): programming and routinization of tasks; providing the necessary motivation for the people and units.	Production scheduling, inventory management, quality control, internal checks and balances, record keeping (of production, sales, expenditures, employee performance etc.).

Environmental perspectives on management control

Under the bandwagon of systems theory, the third perspective of management control is the environmental perspective, closely linked to cybernetic and hierarchical viewpoints discussed earlier. Environmental perspectives focus on how organizations navigate external pressures, adjusting their internal subsystems to adapt. The environment is perceived as a complex supra-system, enveloping organizations in intricate and dynamic relationships and influences.

Organizational environments are stratified into interdependent institutional settings and social actors. The dynamic interactions among these elements create a highly volatile system, presenting unpredictable changes that offer both challenges and opportunities for organizations. This environment is often described as a complex web of "external control". Pfeffer and Salancik (2003, 2-3) elaborate on this complexity and environmental contingency in their much-celebrated text, "The External Control of Organizations".

> The fact that organizations are dependent for survival and success on their environments does not, in itself, make their existence problematic. If stable supplies were assured from the sources of needed resources, there would be no problem. If the resources needed by the organization were continually available, even if outside their control, there would be no problem. Problems arise not merely because organizations are dependent on their environment, but because this environment is not dependable. Environments can change, new organizations enter and exit, and the supply of resources becomes more or less scarce. When environments change, organizations face the prospect either of not surviving or of changing their activities in response to these environmental factors.

Viewing the environment as a complex supra-system of organizational control, Buckley (1969) reinforces this perspective by describing the enterprise's environment as composed of "other equally groping, loose-limit, more or less flexible, illusion ridden, adaptive organizations". To address this complexity, managers often categorize the environment into distinct spheres where different stakeholders operate. The interests of these stakeholder categories are identified as "functional imperatives," prioritizing among them depending on the specific conditions of power and influence that they exert on the organization. Organizations then structure themselves functionally to address these imperatives. Figure 5.3 provides a conceptual schema illustrating the relationships between stakeholder interests and organizational internal configurations.

Key point:
Environment as complex supra-system of organizational control.

Analyzing Figure 5.3, starting from the outer circle, stakeholders are categorized into market and non-market domains. The market domain encompasses output, labor, factor, and capital markets, consisting of customers, employees, trade unions, suppliers, and investors. In contrast, the non-market domain includes political, civil, societal, and ecological dynamics and pressures.

Key point:
Connection between internal configurations and external environmental stakeholder pressures.

Organizations often structure their internal management in alignment with this external environment perspective. Functional divisions

Figure 5.3: Environment as a supra-system of external control

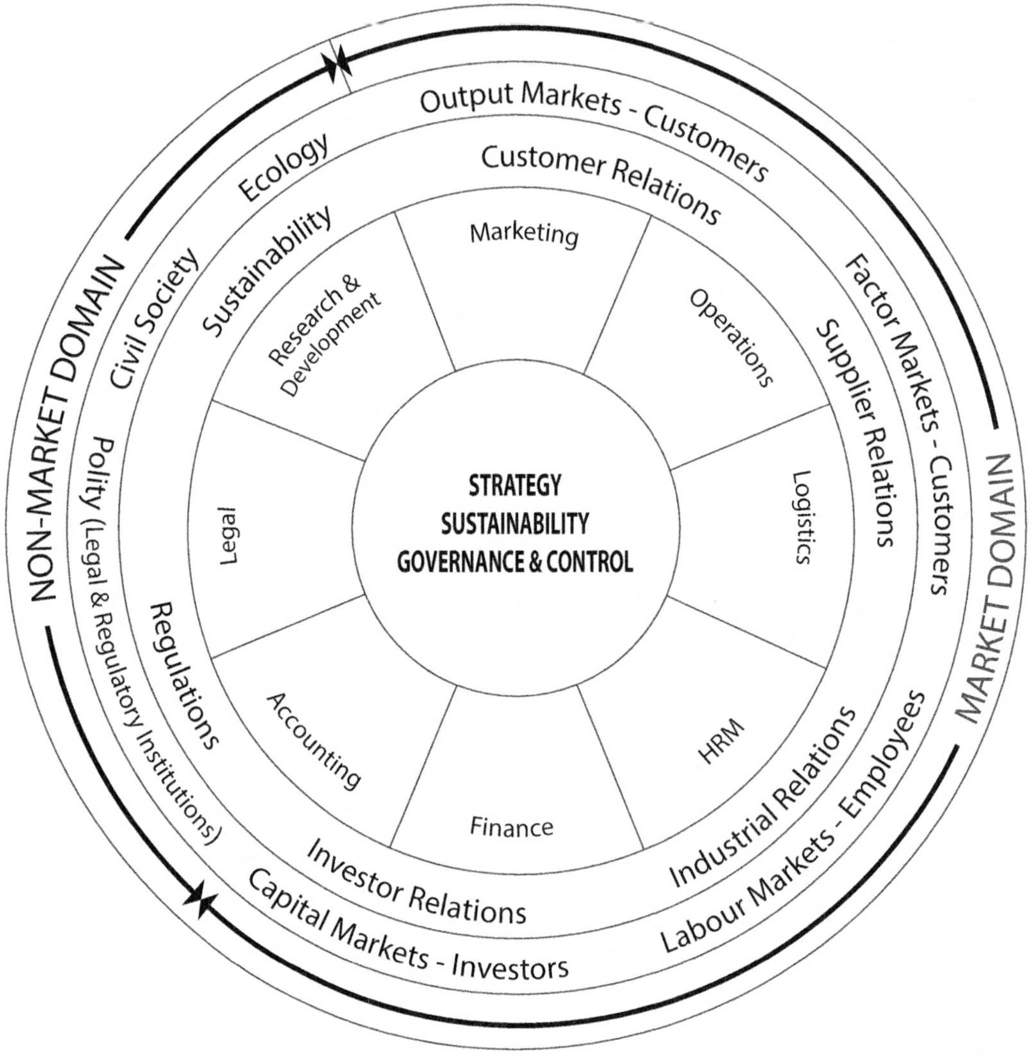

of organizational activities commonly exist, with specialized divisions managing stakeholder interests or functional imperatives imposed by stakeholders. These divisions, referred to as functional management areas (such as marketing, operations management, logistics, HRM, accounting, finance, legal, and research & development), interactively and interdependently handle customer relations, industrial relations, supplier relations, investor relations, public and state relations, as well as sustainability.

At the core, top management functions related to corporate strategy, sustainability policies, governance, and strategic control should integrate all these aspects to ensure the organization's survival and growth.

5.3 Strategic management control: levers of control

Recent advancements in strategic management control build upon the system theory-based concept of management control. Recognizing the inseparable link between management control and performance management, two notable developments aim to integrate management control with corporate strategy discussions.

1. **Strategic performance management system:** The first development is the strategic performance management system movement, spearheaded by Kaplan and Norton's Balanced Scorecard approach. As discussed in the previous chapter, their effort to strategize performance management was internally directed to 'link' operations with corporate strategies through 'cascading'. It involves pluralizing corporate objectives by 'balancing' across multiple dimensions of key performance indicators.
2. **Levers of control in strategic management:** The second development involves the strategic management control ideas popularized by Robert Simons' levers of control framework. This framework focuses on a broader spectrum of strategic dynamics and definitions that encompass the various ways strategies are defined and the boundaries within which they are deployed. This section delves into the fundamental principles of strategic management control embodied in Simons' Levers of Control (LOC) framework.

Key point:
Two streams of conceptual developments converging management control and strategy discourses.

Simons' conception of strategic contradictions

According to Simons (1995), the conventional "command and control" methods and principles of classical management control systems are inadequate for addressing strategic challenges arising in today's highly dynamic and competitive business environment:

> "management theorists and economists have ... paid relatively little attention to understanding how to imple-

ment and control strategies. ... Notwithstanding recent advances in theories of organization and strategy, the tenor of management control reaches back to the 1960s. A "command-and-control" rhetoric underlies phrases associated with traditional management control: top-down strategy setting, standardization and efficiency, results according to plan, no surprises, keeping things on track. ... But command-and-control techniques no longer suffice in competitive environments where creativity and employee initiative are critical to business success. Increasing competition, rapidly changing products and markets, new organizational forms, and the importance of knowledge as a competitive asset have created a new emphasis that is reflected in such phrases as market-driven strategy, customization, continuous improvement, meeting customer needs, and empowerment"(1995, p. 3).

Consequently, Simons promotes his notions of "levers of cotrol" by proposing that:

"A new theory of control that recognizes the need to balance competing demands is required. Inherent tensions must be controlled, tensions between freedom and constraint, between empowerment and accountability, between top-down direction and bottom-up creativity, between experimentation and efficiency. These tensions are not managed by choosing, for example, empowerment over accountability – increasingly, managers must have both in their organizations" (1995, p. 4).

As such, for Simons, the core managerial challenge for any organization is not to choose one force over another but to manage tensions between opposing forces by integrating them, creating a dynamic equilibrium within the organization. Hence, organizations face the strategic imperative of balancing systemic tensions like unlimited opportunities vs. limited organizational attention, intended vs. emergent strategies, and self-interest vs. the desire to contribute. These tensions broadly arise from the opposing dynamics of:

1. value creation (flexibility, innovation, change, entrepreneurship), on the one hand, and,

2. regulation and control (measurement, standardization, pattern maintenance, risk minimization, self-interest, and control), on the other hand.

In this context, Simons argues that the functional role of strategy formulation and control is to address the system imperative of balancing these tensions. This involves establishing managerial processes to ensure due attention to these tensions in both long and short-term decision-making processes and information flows. Simons introduces four interrelated approaches to strategy formulation and four distinct control apparatuses, which he terms "levers of control."

Key point:

Simons' strategic management control framework addresses systemic tensions between value creation and regulation/control.

Levers of control

Simon's framework revolves around the central concept of strategy. Drawing on Mintzberg's (1987) work, Simon defines strategy in four interconnected ways: strategies as plans, patterns of actions, competitive positions, and overarching perspectives. This allows him to link these different forms of strategy with four distinct 'levers of control' (LOC) that organizations should establish to address four strategically vital systemic imperatives (see Figure 5.4).

Key point:

Four definitions of strategy, four strategic imperatives to address, and four levers of control to deal with them.

According to Simons, LOC are specific control mechanisms or control subsystems that organizations should implement to oversee four key strategic imperatives: core values, risks to be avoided, strategic uncertainties, and critical performance variables. These strategic imperatives are managed through four LOC: belief systems, boundary systems, interactive control systems, and diagnostic control systems. As such, according to this framework, strategy formulation and control processes are ascribed to four distinct yet interconnected strategic functionalities.

1. Defining organizational core values, purposes, and directions: Organizations must consistently redefine their core values, purposes, and directions in response to evolving technologies, market dynamics, and cultural/political values. Strategy formulation thus becomes an ongoing exploration to align the organization with its external environment, emphasizing its social purposes and values. Simon, influenced by Mintzberg, terms this aspect of strategy as a 'perspective'. It represents a valuable perspective towards which the top management seeks the organization's collective commitment. To manage this, Simon proposes the use of belief systems, which consti-

Key point:

Belief systems define core values and purposes, inspiring members to explore new opportunities and learning.

Figure 5.4: Simons' Levers of Control Framework

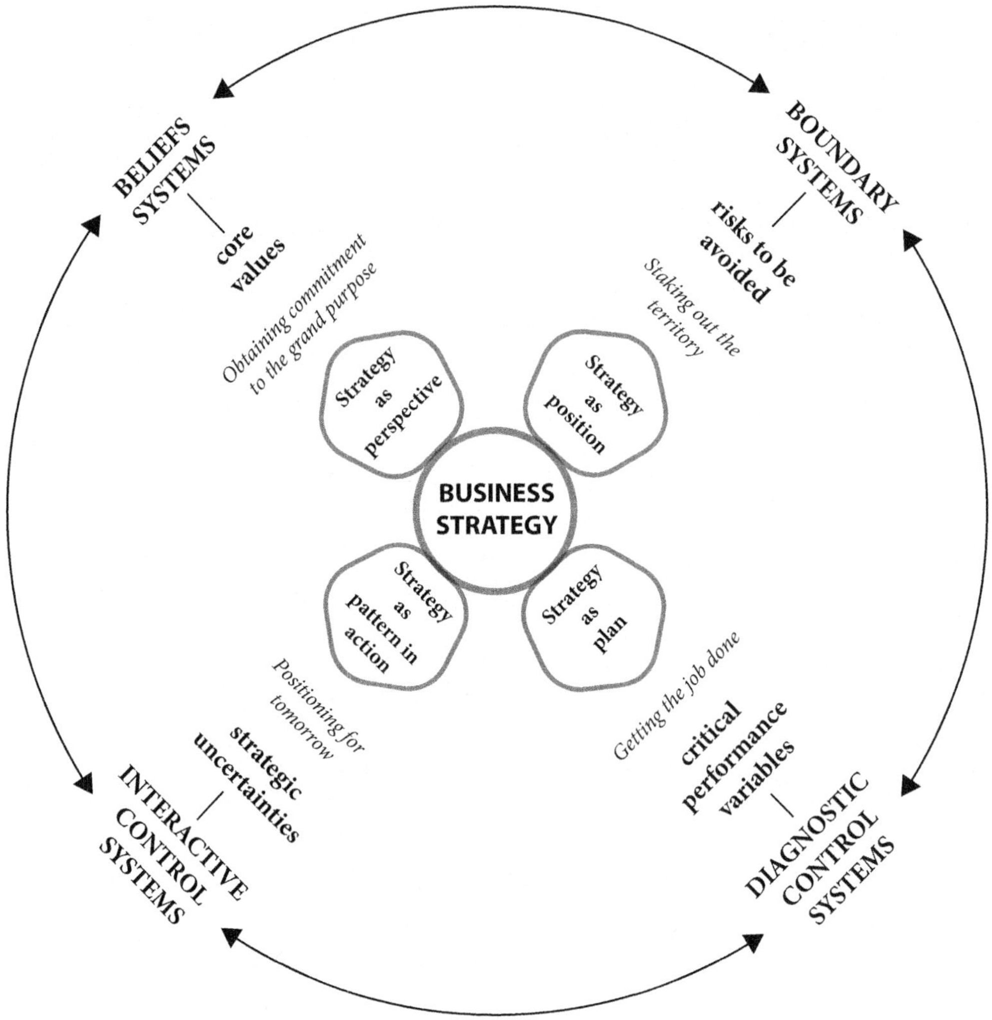

```
                    BELIEFS                  BOUNDARY
                    SYSTEMS                  SYSTEMS
                       |                        |
                    core                    risks to be
                    values                   avoided
              Obtaining commitment       Staking out the
              to the grand purpose          territory

                  Strategy              Strategy
                     as                    as
                 perspective            position

                       BUSINESS
                       STRATEGY

                  Strategy              Strategy
                     as                    as
                  pattern in              plan
                   action

              Positioning for           Getting the job done
                tomorrow
                    |                        |
                strategic                  critical
              uncertainties             performance
                                          variables
                INTERACTIVE               DIAGNOSTIC
                 CONTROL                   CONTROL
                 SYSTEMS                   SYSTEMS
```

Source: Simons' various publications.

tute explicit organizational definitions that senior managers communicate formally to articulate fundamental values, purpose, and direction. Belief systems often articulated through the organization's vision and mission, aim to inspire and guide members in discovering new ways to create value and expand the strategic domain.

2. **Mitigating risks through boundary systems:** Avoiding risks involves defining the acceptable scope of activities, a strategic imperative managed through boundary systems, the second control lever in Simons' framework. These systems counterbalance and regulate the inclination of belief systems to seek expansionary opportunities and expand the organization's strategic remit to possibly too risky domains of operations. Boundary systems establish parameters to regulate and restrict such expansionary tendencies fueled by beliefs in continuous growth.

   Boundary systems operate in two ways. Firstly, they set operational boundaries, framing strategic limits for business areas and opportunities the organization should avoid or not profit from. This approach emphasizes strategic positioning, ensuring the organization excels in competitive market segments where risks are justifiable based on returns, capacities, and resources. Equally important is avoiding positioning in risky domains where the firm cannot or should not operate.

   Secondly, boundary systems establish conduct boundaries by imposing codes of business conduct that outline how the organization and its employees should or should not conduct business. These codes draw from societal laws, the organization's belief system, and codes of conduct from industry and professional associations. Conduct boundaries prove particularly effective in times of high environmental uncertainty (i.e., risk) and low internal trust.

   Key point:

   Boundary systems restrict entrepreneurial behavior, safeguarding against strategic risks.

   In comparison, the belief system encourages corporate behavior that seeks opportunities, driving the firm to explore new ventures, business spaces, and entrepreneurial risks. Conversely, the boundary system acts as a restrictive and punitive mechanism, limiting such behavior to ensure entrepreneurial actions stay within necessary boundaries. In this sense, the boundary system forms a protective ring around the strategic space and behavior.

   Specialized staff, including accountants, lawyers, quality controllers, risk assessors, regulation compliance managers, health and safety specialists, internal auditors, and information system control experts, play a vital role in developing and implementing boundary systems. While business leaders, marketing, operational, and strategic managers focus on exploring new competitive and profitable opportunities and encouraging creative yet risky entrepreneurial behavior among organizational members, control specialists establish boundaries that define acceptable conduct for the business. According to Simons, collaborating, these two mechanisms—belief systems and boundary systems—generate forces of yin and yang: "The warm, positive, inspirational beliefs are a foil to dark, cold constraints. The result is a dynamic tension between commitment and punishment. Senior managers drive both processes".

3. **Managing performance and implementing strategies**: Managing critical performance variables and implementing intended strategies constitute a crucial aspect of organizational function. According to Simons, this imperative relies on "diagnostic control systems," the third lever of control. These systems, characterized as feedback mechanisms, are integral to ensuring predictable goal attainment and form the foundation of traditional management control. The term "management control" is often used interchangeably with "diagnostic control."

Key point:

Diagnostic control systems ensure predictable goal achievement through performance management and responsibility accounting.

Diagnostic control systems primarily involve processes and technologies that serve three essential control functions:

a. Definition of key performance dimensions, variables, and indicators used to conceptualize and measure the organization's intended strategic and operational outcomes. For instance, a company employing the balanced scorecard might define its strategic and operational goals across four key dimensions: financial, customer, internal processes, and innovation and learning.

b. Measurement of actual outcomes in these key performance dimensions, facilitating easy comparison with predefined standards, benchmarks, and objectives.

c. Deciding and implementing corrective actions to address deviations between actual and intended performance.

It's important to note that this lever of control specifically addresses the "intended strategy" or the strategy as a plan. Its functional role involves coordinating and monitoring the implementation of the intended strategy. Specialized planning and control staff, including accountants, sales planners, engineers, quality controllers, and human resource managers, play a vital role in devising, maintaining, and updating diagnostic control systems. They rely on processes to translate the intended strategy into a clear, measurable set of performance indicators.

The core activity of diagnostic controls lies in evaluating the actual performance of the organization, its sub-units, and individual members in light of these performance measures. This concept aligns with the earlier-discussed notion of cybernetic control, encompassing responsibility accounting and strategic performance management apparatuses such as the Balanced Scorecard, as discussed in the previous chapter.

4. Managing strategic uncertainties and adapting to competitive environments: Strategic uncertainties refer to environmental factors that could jeopardize or render the current strategy (i.e., intended strategy) ineffective. These uncertainties encompass shifts in fundamental production and delivery technologies, significant changes in competitive market conditions, and alterations in legal and regulatory contexts. The result of such uncertainties is the need for the firm to either abandon or modify its original strategy. Mintzberg's concept of emergent strategy does not signify the complete failure of the initially intended strategy but rather highlights the organization's ability to comprehend, respond to, and adapt to changing competitive conditions.

This adaptive capacity does not stem from providing precise answers to the strategic question, "What must we do well to achieve our intended strategy?" posed by top managers when defining critical performance variables. Instead, it involves asking the right questions about potential factors that could invalidate the current strategy. Thus, the pivotal question becomes, "What assumptions or shocks could derail the achievement of our vision for the future?" (Simons 1995, 95).

Key point:

Any control system can become interactive to the extent that it deals with strategic uncertainties.

According to Simons, the imperative of managing strategic uncertainties and adaptation is addressed by interactive control systems—the fourth lever of control. He emphasizes that an interactive control system is not a distinct type but rather any control system that becomes interactive based on how managers employ them. When used to activate the search, control systems become interactive. They can focus on strategic uncertainties, stimulate dialogue across the organization, provide frameworks for debate, and encourage information gathering beyond routine channels. Interactive control systems, therefore, serve as a mechanism for organizational learning, challenging existing intended strategies to develop emergent strategies that enhance the organization's ability to adapt to changing environmental conditions.

In essence, an interactive control system is a collection of processes and systems that evolve to facilitate an ongoing search for strategic uncertainties and emergent strategies. Any control system can be interactive by enabling emergent strategies to address strategic uncertainties, display sensitivity, and adapt to environmental changes. The emerging discourses of organizational resilience have now captured this aspect of control, the theme of the next chapter of this book.

In summary, Simons' LOC framework provides a system theory-based functional logic for managing organizational control and strategy. It views an organization as a social system striving to achieve dynamic equilibrium by addressing tensions arising from various functional imperatives, such as defining core values, managing risks, overseeing critical performance variables, and handling strategic uncertainties. The organizational control systems are organized into four interconnected subsystems or levers of control: belief systems, boundary systems, diagnostic control systems, and interactive control systems. When applied to strategy formulation and control, these levers of control represent four aspects of strategy: strategy as a perspective, a position, a plan, and a pattern in action.

This framework aligns with Parson's model of functional structuralism (the AGIL model) discussed earlier. Adaptation remains a fundamental functional imperative in Simons' LOC framework, integrated into the belief system and interactive control systems. These elements are directed toward fostering creativity, change, and dynamism necessary for system adaptation. Goal attainment and integration play critical roles in diagnostic control systems, while latency or pattern maintenance serves as the fundamental functional objective of boundary and diagnostic control systems.

Levers of control and integration of sustainability

Simon's LOC framework is highly adaptable and capable of encompassing diverse control dimensions and dynamics through its four levers. In a broader context, it offers comprehensive categories that can accommodate various control techniques and procedures. The LOC framework proves valuable as a managerial control model for viewing sustainability as a strategic challenge, necessitating overarching transformations in value systems, belief systems, interactive control systems, and diagnostic control systems. Arjaliès and Mundy (2013), for example, provide an analysis of how Simon's LOC framework can be used to analyze the manners in which sustainability issues permeate organizational control structures. They draw insights from data collected from France's largest listed companies, shedding light on how these companies integrate sustainability and corporate social responsibility (CSR) issues into their levers of control.

1. Belief Systems for Communicating CSR Core Values: LOC posits a belief system to encapsulate an organization's core values, inspiring stakeholders and soliciting their commitment. Arjaliès and Mundy's research on France's major listed companies (CAC40 members) reveal the use of formal and explicit statements, such as CSR strategic plans, organizational-wide conferences, "values' chart," mission statements, training sessions, and intranet, to convey the integration of CSR into organizations' core values.

2. Boundary Systems for Risk Management: Arjaliès and Mundy's findings highlight that companies refer to external laws, regulations, benchmarks, and sustainability and CSR reporting protocols when establishing the limits within which their actions and communications should operate. This involves formal and explicit statements outlining the appropriate and inappropriate considerations for CSR strategy, acceptable and prescribed behaviors, and strategic priorities. Boundary setting encompasses utilizing external documents to identify priorities, define acceptable behaviors, address inappropriate conduct, and navigate relationships, particularly across supply chains. Specific examples of external sources for such boundary setting include NRE, GRI, regulatory guidelines, ethics guidelines, codes of conduct, anti-bribery guidelines, guidelines on best or recommended practices, community best practices, and supplier venting.

Side note:

It is crucial to note that Simon's LOC differs from Kaplan and Norton's BSC in that it does not offer a specific set of tools or techniques for managing performance or controlling organizations. Instead, the LOC framework can be broadly viewed as one that helps managers comprehend, conceptualize, discuss, and justify how the various control elements that organizations dynamically innovate and adopt fit into a broader schema of strategizing that considers performance and compliance as fundamental control challenges enabling and constraining as the control functionalities (see Tessier and Otley 2012).

> **Key point:**
>
> Empirical examples showcase how the four key levers of control frame sustainability and CSR as control imperatives.

3. **Interactive Control Systems and Processes for Managing Strategic Uncertainties:** Integrating sustainability and CSR into organizational control involves revealing and debating emergent strategies and identifying opportunities for CSR-related innovation in the operational processes and practices. Regular and formal discussions between CSR teams, senior management, and operational managers prove popular for integrating CSR/sustainability imperatives and operational requirements. These discussions facilitate the exchange of best practices and innovations.

4. **Diagnostic Processes for Managing Critical Performance Variables:** While belief systems, boundary systems, and interactive control systems set strategic parameters, the diagnostic lever demands firms translate them into specific key performance variables. Arjaliès and Mundy's study emphasizes the role of environmental management systems (EMS), standardized sustainability reporting processes (e.g., GRI and Global Compact), and competitive benchmarking in continuous measurement, appraisal, monitoring, and corrective actions.

In a broad sense, Arjaliès and Mundy's study indicates that companies are actively making commendable efforts to incorporate sustainability into their control systems. This emphasizes the strategic importance of integrating sustainability into the core business strategy, and then regularly planning, monitoring, and controlling to ensure and enhance this integration. However, a closer examination of the data presented in their paper, with a critical-political mindset, reveals the challenges managers face in addressing sustainability within well-established control mechanisms that are primarily designed to prioritize capital accumulation.

> **Key point:**
>
> Similar to BSC and Porterian discourses on strategy, LOC reveals a 'managerial capture' of sustainability. Therefore, for a critical understanding, corporate sustainability efforts need to be recontextualized beyond the institutional control apparatuses of capital, which inherently prioritize capital accumulation over social and ecological justice issues.

Implicit in the data that Arjaliès and Mundy provide is that sustainability and corporate social responsibility (CSR) seem to have become crucial considerations primarily for mitigating potential profit losses stemming from non-compliance with regulatory issues. That means corporate sustainability endeavors are underpinned by a 'mitigative motive'. In contrast, even the positive innovations toward sustainability/CSR often originate from a 'profit motive': the belief that strategizing for sustainability can lead to increased profits by redefining markets. Similar to our discussion in the previous chapter on "reinventing the BSC in the age of ESG" and Porterian discourses on gaining competitive advantages through sustainability, in this French examples also, there appears to be a notable "managerial capture of sustainability." This refers to leveraging sustainability to enhance the capital accumulation processes of organizations without fundamentally transforming the ideological and political purposes for which such organizations and their managerial frameworks should exist.

Approaching Arjaliès and Mundy's empirical data with a critical-political perspective involves considering critical accounting scholars' broader political-economic understanding of sustainability, exemplified by works like Milne (1996). These critical accounting papers emphasize that genuine sustainability can only be achieved by acknowledging the politically strategic necessity of prioritizing social, political, and ecological justice issues over the capitalistic motives of accumulation.

It's important to note that frameworks like LOC and BSC are tailored for profit-seeking, capitalistic organizations and are fundamentally 'organizational-centric.' They analyze how the environment affects the organization, concentrating on economic value creation. The primary normative focus is the well-being and progress of the organization, with strategizing, including strategic integration of sustainability, centered on capitalizing on environmental dynamics for economic expansion. These frameworks are inward-looking and lack the analytical capacity to adopt an environmental-centric perspective, understanding how the firm's actions impact entities outside the organization. As Milne (1996) and others (e.g., Gray 2010; Gray and Bebbington 2001) vividly explain, achieving true sustainability demands an environmental-centric approach to accountability rather than narrow organizational-centric approaches that can only see sustainability as an instrument to expand further the fundamentally exploitative "capitalocene" (Haraway 2015).

Key point:

Strategy frameworks like LOC and BSC offer organizational-centric approaches to managing sustainability, limiting our capacity to achieve a truly environmental-centric perspective for a sustainable planet.

Expand your understanding:

Milne (1996), Gray (2019), and Gray and Bebbington (2001), among many others, present critical reviews of conventional management accounting, highlighting its incapacity to address sustainability issues. They stress the necessity of interdisciplinary approaches to progress toward sustainable forms of management accounting.

Chapter summary:

As a site of strategic action, organizational hierarchy encompasses three interrelated strategy themes: performance management, management control, and organizational resilience. While the previous chapter covered performance management, the current chapter delves into strategic control, with the upcoming chapter centering on organizational resilience.

Contradictions and conflicts serve as the fundamental conditions for various forms of control; controls become necessary due to the presence of conflicting conditions and contradictions. Consequently, the way we conceptualize contradictory situations forms the epistemological basis for understanding management control problems and designing/implementing management control systems.

Agency and systems theories are the prominent theoretical frameworks underpinning the classical understanding of management control. They offer distinct perspectives on the origins and resolution of management control problems. Agency theory, rooted in neoclassical economic doctrines, focuses on optimizing agency relationships within organizational hierarchies and transactions through contracts. Contracts, a key tool for agency theorists, establish a legal or institutional framework to regulate relationships and transactions between conflicting parties, aiming to minimize inefficiencies associated with agency problems and information asymmetry while maximizing returns for the principal.

In contrast, systems theory-based conceptions of management control address issues related to system contradictions and encompass multiple perspectives. These include a cybernetic perspective that emphasizes operational control's processual and programmatic aspects, a hierarchical perspective that emphasizes the division of work and hierarchical arrangement of things and people to enhance control, and an environmental perspective that emphasizes the dynamic interplay between the organization's internal configurations and external environmental pressures. Structural functionalism underlies systems theory-based conceptions of management control, providing a comprehensive framework for understanding and addressing control challenges.

Simons' LOC framework extends classical systems theory, recognizing contemporary strategic imperatives. This framework acknowledges the tension between value creation and regulation, expressed through four control levers:

1. Belief systems define strategy as a perspective by outlining core values and a grand purpose.
2. Boundary systems operationalize strategy as a position by determining risks and staking out the organization's territory.
3. Diagnostic control systems treat strategy as planning by

identifying critical performance variables.
4. Interactive control systems view strategy as patterns in action by adapting to changing future conditions and strategic uncertainties.

LOC conceptualizes organizations as social systems striving for dynamic equilibrium by integrating tensions from different functional imperatives. By implementing these levers, strategic control aims to balance value creation dynamics with regulation and control dynamics.

Referencing pertinent literature, such as Arjaliès and Mundy (2013), the chapter also discussed the adaptability of the LOC framework to integrate sustainability into strategic management and control. Sustainability necessitates comprehensive transformations in value systems, belief systems, interactive control systems, and diagnostic control systems. The findings indicate that companies are actively engaging in noteworthy efforts to incorporate sustainability into their control systems. This integration aims to position sustainability as a strategic imperative, requiring deliberate planning, continuous monitoring, and strategic control.

However, a critical political analysis of these studies reveals the managerial difficulties in addressing sustainability issues within already well-established control mechanisms designed to uphold capital accumulation objectives. It seems, more than anything else, sustainability and CSR have become critical considerations in mitigating the potential losses to corporate profits from not attending to the regulatory issues of compliance. Achieving true sustainability demands an environmental-centric approach to accountability rather than narrow organizational-centric approaches that tend to see sustainability as an instrument to expand further the fundamentally exploitative profit-centric control apparatuses.

Test your knowledge

1. Explain how conflicting or contradictory conditions necessitate and underpin control.
2. How does agency theory conceptualize the fundamental contradictions that necessitate management control? According to agency theory, what is the fundamental problem that man-

agement control is designed and implemented to mitigate?
3. Explain the role of the 'performance contract' in the agency-theory-based conception of management control.
4. According to systems theory conceptions of management control, what is the fundamental condition management control should try to mitigate?
5. List the three perspectives that the classical system-theory-based conception of management control takes, as discussed in this chapter.
6. List and explain the critical elements of a cybernetic control system.
7. The detector, comparator, and effector are the key fundamental functionalities upon which a cybernetic model operates. Briefly explain them using budgeting and standard costing as an illustration.
8. Explain the six types of control types that Hofstede's control typology identifies. What are the fundamental questions that Hofstede asks in differentiating these control types?
9. Briefly explain the focal points of attention that the hierarchical perspectives of management control concentrate on.
10. Briefly explain the four basic 'functional imperatives' that Talcott Parsons' AGIL framework outlines.
11. Explain how Parsons' structural functionalism underpins the classical theory of management control systems.
12. Briefly explain the notion of "external control of organizations," considering how the internal configurations of organizations reflect the environmental demands and pressures exerted on the organizations.
13. What is the fundamental contradiction that underpins Simon's LOC framework of strategic management control?
14. Briefly explain the four different definitions of strategy that Simon's LOC deploys.
15. What are the four key strategic control functionalities that Simon's LOC framework identifies?
16. What are the specific levers of control (or control systems) related to those control functionalities you mentioned in the question above?
17. Considering your answers to questions 14, 15, and 16, briefly explain how Simon relates different strategy definitions to fundamental strategic control functionalities and the control systems (or levers of control).

Explore further:

1. Choose an organization, preferably a large multinational corporation with diverse online reports (e.g., BHP Billiton), for an illustrative case study. Examine various published strategic statements, including the chairman's review, risk management statements, vision and mission statements, and integrated reports. Use publicly available secondary data to create a 'strategic profile of the company' employing the LOC framework. Specifically, craft a narrative about the company using the LOC framework's four key strategic control imperatives: core values, risks to be avoided, critical uncertainties, and critical performance variables. Consider the extent to which the company prioritizes 'sustainability-related issues' within these four control imperatives. In conclusion, reflect on the challenges of utilizing LOC as a framework for developing a strategic profile, particularly based on publicly available secondary data.
2. Read two papers:
   a. Beusch, P., Frisk, J. E., Rosén, M., and Dilla, W. (2022), "Management control for sustainability: Towards integrated systems," Management Accounting Research, Vol. 54, pp.1-14
   b. Bebbington, J. (2001), "Sustainable development: a review of the international development, business, and accounting literature," Accounting Forum, Vol. 25 No. 2, pp. 128-157.

   The first paper focuses on an organizational-centric view of sustainability, while the second offers a broader socio-ecological interpretation of sustainability. Write a review of the approaches discussed in the first paper in light of the broader socio-ecological understanding of sustainability provided in the second paper.

Develop your critical argumentation skills

1. Write an argumentative essay on the following theme.

   "Contradictions underpin management control, and the manner in which management control is conceptualized, designed, and implemented depends pretty much on the specific contradictory conditions that they try to resolve".

2. Write an argumentative essay on the following theme.

   "Strategizing management control involves establishing distinct but interrelated control systems to manage the strategic imperatives emanating from the contradictions between the dynamics of value creation, on the one hand, and dynamics of regulation and control, on the other".

3. Write an argumentative essay on the following theme.

   "Strategy frameworks such as LOC and BSC only provide rather organizational-centric approaches to manage sustainability and limit the human civilization's capacity to become truly environmental-centric in achieving a sustainable planet".

Mini case study

Dynamics of management control in Enron's rise and fall.

In an insightful Investopedia article, Tony Segal captures the gripping narrative of the Enron Corporation – a saga that saw a company ascend to staggering heights only to plummet precipitously, akin to a Disney cartoon character careening off a cliff after running on air. In the zenith of the year 2000, Enron's shares soared to an unprecedented pinnacle of $90.56, only to succumb to the depths of bankruptcy on December 2, 2001, with shares plummeting to a mere $0.26. This marked one of the most severe, if not the most egregious, corporate failures, impacting thousands of employees and sending shockwaves through Wall Street, precipitating a cascade of corporate collapses.

Numerous executives faced criminal charges, accused of a litany of offenses, including conspiracy, insider trading, and securities fraud. Ultimately, they were found guilty, alongside Enron's accounting firm, Arthur Andersen, which faced charges of obstructing justice.

Enron's genesis as an energy company materialized through a merger between Houston Natural Gas Co. and InterNorth Inc. As the energy market underwent deregulation, Enron swiftly diversified into the futures and derivatives market, establishing the Enron Finance Corporation in 1990. Over the subsequent decade, Enron earned a reputation for 'innovation' in financial derivatives and accounting practices.

A pivotal moment came in 1992 when Enron secured approval from the Securities and Exchange Commission (SEC) to transition its accounting methodology from historical cost accounting to mark-to-market (MTM). The company's foray into the electronic trading sphere culminated in the creation of Enron Online (EOL) in October 1999, a platform focusing on commodities where Enron became the counterparty in every transaction, either as a buyer or seller. This 'innovative' expansion garnered accolades from the business press, earning Enron the title of "America's Most Innovative Company" by Fortune for an impressive six consecutive years between 1996 and 2001.

By the fall of 2000, Enron began to buckle under its own weight, concealing its mounting issues through the use of mark-to-market accounting. Tony Segal succinctly articulates this pivotal moment, noting:

> "the company would build an asset, such as a power plant, and immediately claim the projected profit on its books, even though it hadn't made one dime from it. If the revenue from the power plant was less than the projected amount, instead of taking the loss, the company would then transfer the asset to an off-the-books corporation (a so-called special purpose vehicle), where the loss would go unreported. This type of accounting enabled Enron to write off unprofitable activities without hurting its bottom line".

The extensively debated case of corporate failure, commonly known as Enron's downfall, has undergone thorough scrutiny from various perspectives, including corporate governance, accounting regulations, and white-collar crimes. However, a crucial dimension often overlooked is the aspect of 'management control'.

REQUIRED:

Drawing upon pertinent conceptual frameworks of management control, such as Simons' Levers of Control, elucidate the management control implications entwined with Enron's rise and fall. In this analysis, give careful consideration to the following:

a. According to your chosen conceptual framework of management control, what are the key' control elements' necessitating scrutiny for understanding the company's evolution?
b. How would you characterize the company's evolution? Which strategic control elements have assumed precedence, potentially at the expense of pivotal elements?
c. How do you interpret the role of the audit firm (Arthur Andersen) in this case? Which specific control element were they expected to execute but regrettably failed to do?

By addressing these questions, you aim to unravel the intricate layers of Enron's demise, focusing on the management control dynamics that played a pivotal role in this high-profile corporate collapse.

References

Anthony, R., V. Govindarajan, F. Hartmann, K. Kraus, and G. Nilsson. 2014. Management control systems. European edition ed. Berkshire: McGraw-Hill Education.

Anthony, R. N. 1965. Planning and control systems: a framework for analysis. Massachusetts: Division of Research, Graduate School of Business Administration, Harvard University.

Arjaliès, D.-L., and J. Mundy. 2013. The use of management control systems to manage CSR strategy: A levers of control perspective. Management Accounting Research 24 (4):284-300.

Baecker, D. 2001. Why systems? Theory Culture Society 18 (1):59-74.

Baiman, S. 1990. Agency research in managerial accounting: a second look. Accounting, Organizations and Society 15 (4):341-371.

———. 2006. Contract theory analysis of management accounting issues. In Contemporary Issues in Management Accounting, edited by A. Bhimani. Oxford: Oxford University Press, 20-41.

Berry, A. J., J. Broadbent, and D. Otley. 2005. Management control: theories, issues, and performance. 2nd ed. London: Palgrave Macmillan.

Buckley, W. F. 1969. Modern systems research for the behavioral scientist. A sourcebook. Chicago: Aldine Publishing Co.

Burrell, G., and G. Morgan. 1979. Sociological paradigms and organisational analysis: elements of the sociology of corporate life. London: Heinemann.

Dermer, J. 1988. Control and organizational order. Accounting, Organizations and Society 13 (1):25-36.

Dermer, J. D., and R. G. Lucas. 1986. The illusion of managerial control. Accounting, Organizations and Society 11 (6):471-482.

Emmanuel, C., D. Otley, and K. Merchant. 2004. Accounting for management control. 2nd ed. ed. London: South-Western, Cengage Learning.

Fama, E. F. 1980. Agency problems and the theory of the firm. Journal of Political Economy 88 (2):288-307.

Fama, E. F., and M. C. Jensen. 1983. Separation of ownership and control. The Journal of Law & Economics 26 (2):301-325.

Ferreira, A., and D. Otley. 2009. The design and use of performance management systems: an extended framework for analysis. Management Accounting Research 20 (4):263-282.

Gray, R. 2010. Is accounting for sustainability actually accounting for sustainability...and how would we know? An exploration of narratives of organisations and the planet. Accounting, Organizations and Society 35 (1):47-62.

Gray, R., and J. Bebbington. 2001. Accounting for the environment: Second Edition: SAGE Publications.

Haraway, D. 2015. Anthropocene, capitalocene, plantationocene, chthulucene: making kin. Environmental Humanities 6 (1):159-165.

Hofstede, G. 1981. Management control of public and not-for-profit activities. Accounting, Organizations and Society 6 (3):193-211.

Hopper, T., and A. Powell. 1985. Making sense of research into the organizational and social aspects of management accounting: A review of its underlying assumptions. Journal of Management Studies 22 (5):429-465.

Merchant, K. A., and W. A. Van der Stede. 2007. Management control systems: performance measurement, evaluation and incentives. Essex: Financial Times/Prentice Hall.

Milne, M. J. 1996. On sustainability; the environment and management accounting. Management Accounting Research 7 (1):135-161.

Mintzberg, H. 1987. The strategy concept I: five Ps for strategy. California Management Review 30 (1):11-24.

Otley, D. 1999. Performance management: a framework for management control systems research. Management Accounting Research 10 (4):363-382.

Otley, D. T., and A. J. Berry. 1980. Control, organisation and accounting. Accounting, Organizations and Society 5 (2):231-244.

Parsons, T., and N. Smelser. 2005. Economy and society: a study in the integration of economic and social theory. London: Taylor & Francis.

Pfeffer, J., and G. R. Salancik. 2003. The external control of organizations: a resource dependence perspective. Stanford Stanford Business Books.

Simons, R. 1995. Levers of control: how managers use innovative control systems to drive strategic renewal. Massachusetts Harvard Business School Press.

Tessier, S., and D. Otley. 2012. A conceptual development of Simons' levers of control framework. Management Accounting Research 23 (3):171-185.

CHAPTER

6 Strategizing the hierarchy: organizational resilience

6.1 Introduction: from management control to organizational resilience

Especially in the wake of a series of financial crises, the global impact of the COVID-19 pandemic, and escalating political conflicts and wars leading to the looming threat of a second Cold War, discussions surrounding 'organizational resilience' have gained prominence in both the popular business press and academic spheres. There appears to be a noticeable shift in focus from strategic control to organizational resilience. The imperative is to embed resilience within the fabric of organizational structures, processes, capabilities, and human resources. Consequently, organizational resilience has become a pervasive theme, capturing the attention of management consultants and thought leaders.

Key point:

How organizational resilience has become a strategic imperative.

For instance, by subscribing to daily updates from McKinsey & Company, a global consulting giant, I've witnessed their substantial investment in resilience as a comprehensive consulting package. This trend is mirrored by other leading global consulting firms such as BCG, KPMG, Deloitte, PWC, and others. In essence, resilience has evolved into a multi-billion-dollar knowledge product positioned for further development and sale in the global consultancy market; consulting firms and thought leaders are actively vying for their share in this lucrative market, offering their versions of organizational resilience strategies.

This surge in resilience-oriented strategies has far-reaching implications for the landscape of management accounting. Unprecedented uncertainties and vulnerabilities pervade organizational environments, making uncontrollability and failure more commonplace. Traditional methods of control are proving less effective, compelling managers to explore alternatives beyond control and governance. Resilience emerges as a strategic imperative for management accounting, thus becoming a crucial topic for discussion in strategic management accounting classrooms. Consequently, it is imperative to critically evaluate discourses surrounding organizational resilience within the context of a strategic management accounting course, such as the one covered by this textbook.

Key point:

How this chapter fits into the overall structural logic of book.

Reminding you of the overall logic of this textbook, the chapters in this book are organized under three key themes: strategizing the market, strategizing the organizational hierarchy, and strategizing the labor process. This chapter falls under the theme of strategizing the organizational hierarchy. The preceding two chapters explored two of its sub-themes: strategic performance management and strategic management control. In this chapter, I delve into 'organizational resilience' as the third strategic theme under strategizing the organizational hierarchy. This is essentially an extension of the previous chapter's discussion on strategizing management control, focusing on how organizations can navigate adversities stemming from events and evolutions that elude their existing control systems.

In this context, at least for the purpose of this textbook, I consider organizational resilience as an extension of the theme of strategizing the organizational hierarchy but in relation to factors generally perceived as uncontrollable or beyond the scope of existing control systems. Essentially, organizational resilience becomes paramount when organizational controls prove insufficient and ineffective. Nevertheless, discussions on resilience revolve around configuring and reconfiguring organizational structures, processes, and capabilities to empower organizations to anticipate and 'bounce back' from crises, adversities, failures, and collapses – situations beyond immediate control (Giustiniano et al. 2018).

The chapter is structured as follows to cover the following main themes:

1. Understanding resilience across disciplines (Section 6.2): In this section, we delve into the multidisciplinary nature of resilience, examining its definitions and explanations in diverse fields such as psychology, sociology, engineering, and economics. By exploring these perspectives, we establish a comprehensive conceptual foundation, providing insights into the various dimensions and systemic components of resilience. This section aims to cultivate an appreciation for the diverse meanings and applications of resilience.

2. Consultocratic perspectives on organisational resilience (Section 6.3): This section explores organizational resilience through consultocratic discourses. This involves an examination of two interrelated consultocratic discourses on organizational resilience: expository narratives and consultocratic modeling approaches. By analyzing consultancy materials, we gain an understanding of how leading consulting firms and influential thought leaders promote organizational resilience as part of their consulting offerings. Through a careful review of this section, readers will gain insights into prominent management guru ideas from prominent figures in the field and the rhetorical/epistemic strategies they employ to advocate and popularize these ideas.

Key point:

Key themes and learning objectives

3. Academic discourses on organisational resilience (Section 6.4): This section delves into academic discussions surrounding organizational resilience to elucidate the fundamental conceptual/theoretical elements underpinning organizational resilience. The focus here is on how academic discourses conceptualize the inherent tensions and contradictions underpinning the necessity of resilience and how such contradictions lead to different forms or domains of organisational resilience. Accordingly, careful reading of this section will provide you with a broader understanding of fundamental concepts and principles underpinning organizational resilience discourses.

4. Conclusion and summary: Section 6.5 concludes the chapter by providing a concise summary of the key insights and findings discussed throughout the chapter. This concluding section serves as a wrap-up, offering a synthesized overview

of the diverse perspectives on resilience presented in the preceding sections.

6.2 Defining resilience: understanding the concept's diversity in applications

Resilience is not confined to organizational contexts; it is a widely adopted normative concept that extends across various academic and professional domains, including psychology, engineering, disaster management, organizational studies, and economics. Despite variations in its interpretations and applications within these fields, the fundamental idea revolves around an entity's ability to navigate and recover from adversity (see Giustiniano et al. 2018). Analyzing how resilience is utilized in diverse fields serves not only to grasp its intricate interdisciplinary nature but also to identify shared features applicable to defining and comprehending organizational resilience.

Key point:

Resilience is a multi-field concept centered on coping and rebounding from adversity.

In psychology, *'psychological resilience'* pertains to an individual's capacity to bounce back from adversity, trauma, or stress. It encompasses emotional fortitude, coping skills, and the ability to maintain mental and emotional well-being in challenging situations, facilitating a return to normalcy. The American Psychological Association defines resilience as "the process and outcome of successfully adapting to difficult or challenging life experiences, especially through mental, emotional, and behavioral flexibility and adjustment to external and internal demands." Notably, resilience is described here as both a process and an outcome, intricately linked.

Key point:

Psychological definitions of resilience emphasize the process and outcome of one's adaptation to difficult and challenging experiences.

In disaster management, *'social resilience'* refers to a community's or society's capacity to maintain stability and function effectively amidst disruptions, such as natural disasters, economic crises, or political upheavals. It involves community cohesion, adaptive governance, and effective disaster response. Broadly speaking, social resilience encompasses the collective ability of people and communities to handle external stresses and shocks. This includes specific processes and capacities a community or society implements to enhance preparedness, disaster response, and post-disaster recovery. Kwok et al. (2016) categorize these processes and capacities into two interconnected categories: structural and cognitive. Structural elements encompass resource capabilities and infrastructure, while cognitive dimensions involve individual and collective processes and capacities that boost social, cultural, and psychological preparedness to rebound from adversities.

Key point:

Social resilience involves specific processes and capacities for enhancing preparedness, disaster response, and post-disaster recovery within communities or societies.

The *engineering concept of resilience* is invaluable in comprehending both the general characteristics and specificities of a resilient techno-managerial system. In engineering, resilience denotes the capacity of a system, structure, or process to endure and recover from adverse conditions, shocks, or disturbances while maintaining its essential functions and performance (Ruault et al. 2012). This concept holds significant importance across various engineering disciplines, such as civil engineering, mechanical engineering, and electrical engineering. Similar to other disciplinary definitions discussed earlier, engineering definitions of resilience also center on the fundamental idea of withstanding and recovering from adversity.

Key point:
Engineering resilience emphasizes a set of system characteristics equally applicable to organizational systems.

However, engineering offers a more systemic approach to resilience, which can be particularly relevant when considering organizational systems with a techno-managerial focus. In techno-managerial terms, an engineering understanding of resilience underscores a set of system characteristics that are equally applicable to organizational systems. The following list outlines the essential parameters for a resilient organizational system (see Hollnagel 2010; Hollnagel et al. 2006; Ruault et al. 2012; Sundström and Hollnagel 2011).

1. Redundancy: Ensure backup components, subsystems, or resources are in place to take over in case of failure or disruption.
2. Robustness: Maintain system performance and functionality in the face of variations or uncertainties.
3. Risk assessment: Identify potential failure modes, analyze consequences, and develop strategies to mitigate or manage risks.
4. Adaptability: Design systems to adapt to changing conditions or recover quickly from disturbances.
5. Modular design: Design complex systems into smaller, interchangeable components, facilitating easier repair or replacement and reducing downtime in case of failure.
6. Material selection: Choose materials with high durability, corrosion resistance, and fatigue resistance for critical applications.
7. Predictive maintenance: Incorporate predictive maintenance practices using sensors and data analysis to anticipate component failures and prevent catastrophic breakdowns.
8. Contingency planning: Develop contingency plans and emergency procedures to guide responses during unexpected disruptions, minimizing damage and downtime.

Key point:
Parameters of a resilient techno-organizational system.

9. **System monitoring:** Rely on real-time system performance monitoring using sensors and data analysis to detect anomalies and deviations from expected behavior, enabling prompt corrective actions.
10. **Testing and simulation:** Employ various testing and simulation techniques to evaluate system resilience under different conditions, including worst-case scenarios, identifying weaknesses, and enhancing the system's ability to withstand adverse events.
11. **Sustainability:** Extend resilience to sustainability concerns, ensuring systems are designed to minimize environmental impacts and resource consumption, contributing to long-term resilience in a broader sense.

The economic policy discussions on resilience also offer valuable insights that shed light on the intricate nature of organizational resilience. At its core, resilience entails the ability to endure and recover from adverse experiences. *Economic resilience*, in particular, refers to an economy's capability—whether regional, national, or global—to withstand and rebound from external shocks, disruptions, or adverse events without enduring severe and enduring damage (Linkov et al. 2018). It serves as a metric for an economy's adaptability, absorptive capacity, and bounce-back ability in the face of challenges such as financial crises, natural disasters, pandemics, or shifts in market conditions. The application of economic resilience spans various levels, encompassing individual businesses, regions, or entire nations. Below are key components and factors contributing to economic resilience, as outlined by the OECD (see OECD 2016):

1. **Diversification:** Economies that diversify across industries, trade partners, and income sources tend to be more resilient. This strategy reduces dependence on a single sector or market, spreading risk and minimizing the impact of disruptions in one area.
2. **Robust infrastructure:** A well-maintained and strong infrastructure, covering transportation, communication, and utilities, is crucial for ensuring resilience. Infrastructure capable of withstanding natural disasters and supporting efficient business operations is a key asset.
3. **Financial stability:** A stable financial system supported by effective regulatory frameworks and prudent fiscal policies can mitigate the effects of financial crises and banking failures.

Strong monetary and fiscal policies can stabilize the economy during times of crisis.
4. **Social safety nets:** Adequate social safety nets, including unemployment benefits and healthcare, help individuals and families weather economic shocks and maintain consumer confidence.
5. **Innovation and technology:** Economies investing in research and development, innovation, and technology are better positioned to adapt to changing circumstances and remain competitive.
6. **Access to capital:** Easy access to credit and capital markets assists businesses and individuals in recovering more quickly from economic disruptions and investing in their future.
7. **Education and workforce development:** A well-educated and skilled workforce is essential for adapting to changing economic conditions and seizing emerging opportunities.
8. **Government resilience strategies:** Effective government policies and strategies, such as disaster preparedness plans and crisis response mechanisms, are crucial for mitigating the impact of shocks on an economy.
9. **Global trade and connectivity:** Engaging in global trade and maintaining strong international connections help an economy tap into a wider range of opportunities and resources, enhancing resilience.
10. **Risk management and contingency planning:** Businesses and governments can improve resilience by developing and implementing robust risk management and contingency plans to respond to unexpected events.

Key point:

Critical components and factors contributing to economic resilience.

While no economy can be entirely resistant to shocks, enhancing resilience through the factors mentioned can mitigate the severity and duration of economic disruptions, facilitating a faster recovery. Economic resilience is an ongoing process that necessitates collaboration among various stakeholders, including transnational organizations, governments, businesses, communities, and individuals (Linkov et al., 2018; OECD, 2016).

Both economic and engineering perspectives emphasize that resilience is a complex phenomenon requiring an integrative approach among global and local players in diverse fields. An exemplary acknowledgment of this institutional complexity is the OECD's New Approaches to Economic Challenges Initiative. The OECD collaborates

Key point:

OECD's definition and approach to economic resilience.

with the US Army Corps of Engineers (USACE) to implement a resilience approach outlined in Pillar I of the US National Security Strategy. Other partners in this initiative include the Institute for Applied Systems Analysis (IIASA), the National Institute of Standards and Technology (NIST), and the Joint Research Centre of the European Commission. In this collective endevor, resilience is defined as "the ability to withstand and recover rapidly from deliberate attacks, accidents, natural disasters, as well as unconventional stresses, shocks, and threats to our economy and democratic system" (Linkov et al. 2018, 133).

Our exploration so far highlights three critical aspects of the resilience concept, as summarized in Figure 6.1:

1. It involves facing and rebounding from adversities.
2. The ability to do so depends on the various capabilities and capacities possessed by a given economy, society, organization, community, or individual.
3. Resilience is not a static condition but a dynamic process encompassing preparation, prevention, shock absorption, recovery, and adaptation (Linkov et al., 2018).

Figure 6.1: Processual and capability parameters of resilience

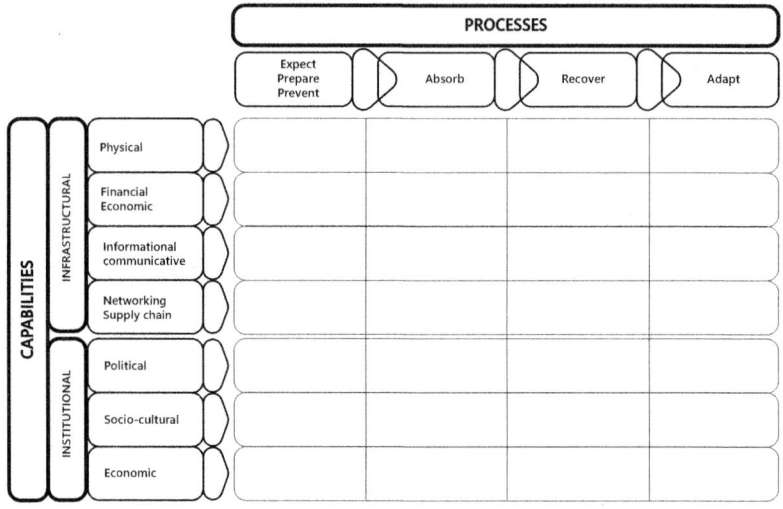

Upon reviewing Figure 6.1, we can refine our definition of resilience. It extends beyond mere recovery from crises and encompasses a blend of processes and capabilities. These include anticipating, preparing for, adapting to, preventing, absorbing, recovering from, and adapting to adversity. Resilience involves both infrastructural and institutional elements, spanning techno-physical, informational, economic, social, and environmental dimensions. It is important to note that the categorization of these capabilities may vary depending on specific circumstances. The key insight here is that resilience comprises both procedural and capability aspects. With this comprehensive understanding of resilience, the following section will delve into organizational and accounting discussions surrounding resilience.

Key point:
Resilience encompasses both procedural and capability dimensions.

6.3 Organizational resilience and management control: analyzing consultocratic discourses

While transnational organizations such as the OECD and World Bank adopt a broader global approach to resilience (see Linkov et al. 2018; OECD 2016; World Bank 2013, 2021b, 2021a), consultocratic discourses, prevalent in business management and accounting adopt a more focused 'leadership and corporate-centric' perspective. In these discussions, organizational resilience often takes the form of 'management consultancy packages' or a collection of 'guru ideas' (see Jupe and Funnell 2015; Kantola and Seeck 2011) marketed to corporate leaders and managers worldwide. The content bundled into these consultancy packages provides intriguing insights into how resilience is propagated in management consultancy and accountancy, particularly in how it influences concepts of strategy, control, governance, and sustainability. Therefore, an analysis of consultocratic discourses on resilience is crucial in a strategic management accounting course that aims to foster a critical understanding of how management accounting thought evolves and is shaped in this neoliberal era.

Key point:
Consultocratic discourses shape the conceptualization and dissemination of organizational resilience through a set of guru ideas.

In addition to various publications from consulting giants like McKinsey and the Boston Consulting Group, the popular business press (e.g., Harvard Business Review and MIT's Sloan Management Review) introduces a specific set of guru and consultocratic ideas on organizational resilience. Broadly, these ideas can be categorized into two interdependent, interlocking, and somewhat overlapping discursive categories: *expository narratives* and *consultocratic modeling*.

Key point:
Consultocratic discourses on resilience can be broadly categorized as (a) expository narrative and (b) consultocratic modeling.

Expository narratives on organizational resilience

Gary Hamel and Liisa Välikangas's (2003) well-known article in the Harvard Business Review stands as a classic example of expository narratives discussing organizational resilience. Much like similar pieces in popular business publications, their rhetoric is geared toward promoting a marketable concept of resilience within the consultancy market. These expository narratives employ persuasive language to establish guru-like ideas about organizational resilience. We can identify four characterizing elements of such discourses, which I will explain below.

1. Framing resilience as a consultocratic necessity
2. Identifying points of departure
3. Providing guidelines and prescriptions.
4. Building faith through corporate storytelling

Framing resilience as a consultocratic necessity:

Key point:

In consultocratic discourses, resilience is primarily depicted as a corporate character deficiency.

In contrast to discussions on resilience in transnational organizations like the UN, World Bank, and OECD, which portray resilience as a global systemic issue requiring broad global cooperation, the consultocratic narrative defines it as a 'consultocratic problem.' This approach characterizes resilience issues in terms of 'slumps' and 'downturns' in corporate performance, especially profits. These challenges are predominantly attributed to deficiencies in corporate character, hindering adaptability to turbulent organizational environments. Leadership styles, strategy, culture, team composition, individual personalities, and coping capabilities are often highlighted as key elements of organizational resilience.

Key point

the concept of the "resilience gap".

For instance, Hamel and Välikangas (2003) introduce the concept of a *"resilience gap,"* depicting a scenario where "The world is becoming turbulent faster than organizations are becoming resilient". Consequently, "corporate earnings are more erratic," and "even perennially successful companies are finding it more difficult to deliver consistently superior returns" (Hamel and Välikangas 2003, 1). While Hamel and Välikangas (2003) take a broad organizational approach, other gurus, based on their consultative expertise, may define the consultocratic problem with a specific focus. For example, it may be seen as a mental state that must be instilled among corporate employees to foster resilience (see Hougaard and Mohan 2020), or as team building through cultivating a shared mental model of teamwork (see Kirkman et al. 2019). In these consultocratic discourses, the issue of organizational resilience takes diverse forms but is consistently portrayed as an intra-organizational phenomenon related to corporate character and thought processes.

Identifying points of departure:

Expository narratives often highlight a necessity of departure from the current status of affairs or modes of doing things. These narratives present a series of essential declarations that communicate to corporate leaders what is flawed in their current modes of thinking and actions. For instance, according to Hamel and Välikangas (2003, p. 2), corporate leaders may possess a misguided understanding of resilience that requires correction.

> Strategic resilience is not about responding to a onetime crisis. It's not about rebounding from a setback. It's about continuously anticipating and adjusting to deep, secular trends that can permanently impair the earning power of a core business. It's about having the capacity to change before the case for change becomes desperately obvious.

Key point:
A critical element of consultocratic discourses on resilience involves pinpointing negativities that need consultocratic help to be corrected.

These departure points serve as the cornerstone of the consultocratic narrative, persuading corporate leaders that they need to make changes and seek the assistance of management gurus and consultants. This transformation of the concept of resilience into a consultocratic problem turns it into an organizational-focused managerial training issue that necessitates consultancy, as exemplified by Hougaard and Mohan (2020, pp. 1-2).

> As the CEO of a firm that brings mindfulness to companies to unlock new ways of thinking and working, let me share a bit about how the mind responds to crises, like the threat of a pandemic. ... When your mind gets stuck in this state, a chain reaction begins. Fear begins to narrow your field of vision, and it becomes harder to see the bigger picture and the positive, creative possibilities in front of you. As perspective shrinks, so too does our tendency to connect with others. Right now, the realities of how the coronavirus spreads can play into our worst

fears about others and increase our feelings of isolation, which only adds fuel to our worries.

Providing guidelines and prescriptions:

Addressing the specific consultative challenge highlighted earlier (refer to the previous point), they offer a set of normative prescriptions, scriptures, or commandments as to how corporate managers should think, rethink, act, react, and proact to build a resilient corporate strategy, structure, and persona, teams, individual employees. These guidelines are often presented as visionary insights from thought leaders with significant corporate and consultancy experience. This experience serves as the epistemic foundation that enables these narrators to assert themselves as gurus and their statements as doctrines.

Consequently, innovative ideas, new processes, or a series of actions are proposed to the consultative market, encouraging managers to adopt and implement them. Frequently, these explanatory discussions aim to guide corporate leaders in their thinking and actions. For instance, Hamel and Välikangas (2003), in contrast to the zero-defect concept in quality management (refer to Chapter 7 in this textbook), introduced the idea of *"zero-trauma"*.

Key point:

Hamel and Välikangas' idea of "zero-trauma" as a visionary basis for building organizational resilience.

Imagine a ratio where the numerator measures the magnitude and frequency of strategic transformation and the denominator reflects the time, expense, and emotional energy required to effect that transformation. Any company that hopes to stay relevant in a topsy-turvy world has no choice but to grow the numerator. The real trick is to steadily reduce the denominator at the same time. To thrive in turbulent times, companies must become as efficient at renewal as they are at producing today's products and services. Renewal must be the natural consequence of an organization's innate resilience.

The quest for resilience can't start with an inventory of best practices. Today's best practices are manifestly inadequate. Instead, it must begin with an aspiration: zero trauma. The goal is an organization that is constantly making its future rather than defending its past. The goal is a company where revolutionary change happens in lightning-quick, evolutionary steps—with no calamitous surprises, no convulsive reorganizations, no colossal write-offs, and no indiscriminate, across-the-board lay-offs. In a truly resilient organization, there is plenty of excitement, but there is no trauma.

Expository narratives on resilience often adopt a guru-like rhetoric. These narratives impart advice as if coming from "wise ones who have realized the Truth", echoing the sentiment found in the Bhagavad Gita (4:34). Despite acknowledging the current turbulent and unpredictable times, these consultocratic discourses paradoxically encourage readers and clients to approach resilience with a form of religious faith. Echoing religious inscriptions and commandments, these narratives suggest a specific approach to resilience that corporate leaders should follow faithfully towards ideal statuses such as "zero trauma", a sort of nirvana, or a heavenly peaceful, perfect end to achieve. They identify a set number of obstacles, sins, or karma to overcome, such as, for example, four reasons for strategy decay and three things to break through the hard carapace of denial, exemplified by Hamel and Välikangas (2003). They then offer a set of solutions to understand, appreciate, and faithfully follow; for example, conquering denial, valuing variety, liberating resources, and embracing paradox (Hamel and Välikangas 2003).

Although these narratives start by disapproving of a resilience quest based on a mere inventory of best practices, authors like Hamel and Välikangas (2003) ironically end up enlisting a similar set of doctrinal prescriptions that enumerate best practices. Hamel and Valikangas' "quest for resilience" thus lays down a particular emancipatory path that corporate leaders should faithfully follow to achieve the ultimate resiliency, the "zero-trauma". Table 6.1 outlines their creed for resilience. Think of the extent to which the elements therein manifest religious scripting.

Building faith through corporate storytelling:

Corporate storytelling plays a pivotal role in expressing the consultocratic wisdom of organizational resilience. Stories of both failure and success from prominent corporations are extensively utilized to persuade audiences that specific definitions, doctrines, advice, and prescriptions regarding what should and should not be done are valid. This validation is rooted in their being perceived as 'factual' and 'real', drawn from actual stories within the corporate world, often closely associated with industry experts. The article by Hamel and Välikan-

Side note:

While the concept of a guru has its origins in Hindu texts like the Bhagavad Gita, today, it can be broadly understood in the context of modern management discussions, often referred to as management gurus. These individuals play the roles of teachers, preachers, or thought leaders, asserting to possess knowledge that can guide individuals through challenges and illuminate their paths. In contemporary terms, they aim to address secular issues such as a lack of resilience (see Young 2014).

Key point:

Expository narratives on resilience employ guru-type rhetoric, aiming to guide individuals along a wise and emancipatory path that is expected to be faithfully embraced for perfect resilience.

Table 6.1: Hamel and Valikangas' "Quest for Resilience" – a creed towards "zero-trauma"

The aspiration to attain	Challenges to overcome	Commandments for leaders to follow
ZERO-TRAUMA The goal is a strategy that is forever morphing, forever conforming itself to emerging opportunities and incipient trends. The goal is an organization that is constantly making its future rather than defending its past. The goal is a company where revolutionary change happens in lightning-quick, evolutionary steps—with no calamitous surprises, no convulsive reorganizations, no colossal write-offs, and no indiscriminate, across-the-board layoffs. In a truly resilient organization, there is plenty of excitement, but there is no trauma (p.2).	**The Cognitive Challenge:** A company must become entirely free of denial, nostalgia, and arrogance. It must be deeply conscious of what's changing and perpetually willing to consider how those changes are likely to affect its current success (p.3).	**Conquer denial** To be resilient, an organization must dramatically reduce the time it takes to go from "that can't be true" to "we must face the world as it is." So what does it take to break through the hard carapace of denial? Three things. Senior managers must make a habit of visiting the places where change happens first. You have to filter out the filterers. Most likely, there are people in your organization who are plugged tightly in to the future and understand well the not-so-sanguine implications for your company's business model. You have to find these people. You have to make sure their views are not censored by the custodians of convention, and their access is not blocked by those who believe they are paid to protect you from unpleasant truths. You have to face up to the inevitability of strategy decay. Strategies decay for four reasons: (1) Over time, they get replicated; (2) good strategies also get supplanted by better strategies; (3) Strategies get exhausted as markets become saturated, customers get bored, or optimization programs reach the point of diminishing returns; (4) strategies get eviscerated.
	The Strategic Challenge: Resilience requires alternatives as well as awareness—the ability to create a plethora of new options as compelling alternatives to dying strategies (p.3).	**Value variety** The larger the variety of actions available to a system, the larger the variety of perturbations it is able to accommodate. Put simply, if the range of strategic alternatives your company is exploring is significantly narrower than the breadth of change in the environment, your business is going to be a victim of turbulence. Resilience depends on variety.

The Political Challenge	Liberate resources
An organization must be able to divert resources from yesterday's products and programs to tomorrow's. This doesn't mean funding flights of fancy; it means building an ability to support a broad portfolio of breakout experiments with the necessary capital and talent" (p.3).	As every manager knows, reallocating resources is an intensely political process. Resilience requires, however, that it become less so. On average, markets are better than hierarchies at getting the right resources behind the right opportunities at the right time. Unlike hierarchies, markets are apolitical and unsentimental; they don't care whose ox gets gored. The average company, though, operates more like a socialist state than an unfettered market. A hierarchy may be an effective mechanism for applying resources, but it is an imperfect device for allocating resources. Specifically, the market for capital and talent that exists within companies is a whole lot less efficient than the market for talent and capital that exists between companies.
The Ideological Challenge:	Embrace paradox
Few organizations question the doctrine of optimization. But optimizing a business model that is slowly becoming irrelevant can't secure a company's futur" (p.3).	The final barrier to resilience is ideological. The modern corporation is a shrine to a single, 100-year-old ideal—optimization. From scientific management" to "operations research" to "reengineering" to "enterprise resource planning" to "Six Sigma," the goal has never changed: Do more, better, faster, and cheaper. An accelerating pace of change demands an accelerating pace of strategic evolution, which can be achieved only if a company cares as much about resilience as it does about optimization. ... embrace the inherent paradox between the relentless pursuit of efficiency and the restless exploration of new strategic options. ... all those accountants and engineers, never great fans of paradox, can learn to love the heretics and the dreamers.

Source: Hamel and Välikangas (2003). The text inside the table consists of direct quotes from various pages to preserve the original rhetoric. These words belong to them, reflecting their intended message and belief in their doctrine , so you can see how guru-type rhetoric is constructed.

gas (2003), discussed earlier, offers numerous examples illustrating how corporate storytelling is employed to give their normative expository discourse an authentic and realistic perspective.

Routines, hermeneutics, and improvisation for organizational resilience

Examining organizational resilience through the lenses of routines, hermeneutics, and improvisation provides valuable insights. A noteworthy example illustrating a unique perspective on organizational resilience is found in Suarez and Montes's (2020) Harvard Business Review article, "Building Organisational Resilience." This article stems from a more comprehensive academic paper published in an Organizational Science journal (see Suarez and Montes 2019). They draw on their study of a mountaineering expedition tackling the challenging Kangshung face of Mount Everest. This experience informs their Harvard Business Review article, where they apply the insights gained to explain how a hospital dealt with the challenges of the COVID-19 pandemic.

Suarez and Montes introduce a unique perspective by emphasizing the importance of defining the "focal context" of the organization. Rather than broadly categorizing the context as high-velocity or turbulent, they define the "*focal context*" as a constructed temporary reality that encompasses both objective environmental traits and subjective perceptions of organizational members (Suarez & Montes, 2019, p. 574). Identifying the salient objective elements and understanding organizational members' perceptions at a specific moment become crucial elements of defining the "focal context."

In the light of their idea of "focal context", organizational resilience can be interpreted as how an organization perceives and responds to contextual adversities, primarily through three behavioral strategies: *routines, heuristics*, and *improvisation*.

Departures from routines as an element of resilience. Routines are the "scripted work processes" that regulate and stabilize the way organizational activities are carried out and performance outcomes are achieved. The "focal context" should be stable and predictable for them to be effective. Established routines can be ineffective and problematic when the "focal context" changes, and according to Suarez and Montes (2019, 2020), such changes can trigger minor, fragmental,

Key point:

Corporate storytelling serves as the primary epistemic strategy for legitimizing expository discourses on organizational resilience.

Key point:

The concept of "focal context."

or major non-routine responses in the form of heuristics or improvisation. Their analysis identifies four different 'triggers' of non-routing responses.

- Speed/Time: Existing routines may become too slow to meet new demands imposed by the changes in the "focal context".
- Resources: Changes in the "focal context" may impose new resource constraints, rendering established routines impractical.
- New Problems: The evolving "focal context" may introduce problems beyond the scope of existing routines.
- New Opportunities: Changes in the "focal context" may present new opportunities that existing routines cannot seize.

Key point:

How changes in "focal context" trigger for non-routine Responses

Suarez and Montes (2019, 2020) argue that changes in the focal context can trigger three different forms or extents of departures from existing routines.

a. **Minor departures** occur when the changes in the focal context have not challenged the key assumptions of normal operating procedures, and hence, the preexisting designs can still be used with minor modifications to the routines, often in terms of heuristic changes (see below).
b. **Fragmental departures** occur when the changes in the focal context have not challenged the key assumptions of normal operating procedures, but they have made the existing designs and routines no longer useful or valid. As such, the changes in the focal context trigger new heuristic adaptations and certain degrees of improvisations.
c. **Major routine breakdowns** occur when changes in the focal context are so great that the existing key system design assumptions do not hold anymore and, hence, preexisting designs and routines are no longer effective. This then demands new sensemaking and improvisations.

Heuristics as an element of resilience:

Heuristics represent responsive adaptations in routines to accommodate changes in the focal context. Manifesting as minor or fragmental departures, heuristics aim to make routines shorter and quicker. Described as "a strategy that ignores part of the information, with the goal of making decisions more quickly, frugally, and/or accurately

Key point:

Definition of heuristic as a resilience element.

than more complex methods" (Gigerenzer and Gaissmaier 2011, 454), heuristics contribute to organizational resilience, responding frugally to the changes in the "focal context".

Improvisation as an element of resilience

Improvisation as an element of resilience occurs when the focal context changes so much that the organization is now operating in uncharted territory with an extremely high degree of uncertainty. As such, the existing system assumptions no longer hold, and the decision-makers have to experiment to figure out what might work under the new conditions. Not even heuristics are sufficient to deal with the changes in the focal context. For example, during the COVID-19 pandemic, organizations had to partially and fully shut down their offices and improvise working at home. Universities reinvented their teaching and administration through online platforms such as Zoom and Microsoft Teams. Subsequently, through experimentation, reinventions, and fine-tuning, improvisation establishes new routines, for example, Zoom and Microsoft teams team technologies, which have become more or less permanent features of post-COVID organizational conduct.

Key point:

Improvisation as a resilience element.

While they both manifest consultocratic expositions on organizational resilience, there is a remarkable contrast between the two papers I took as examples to discuss here. Hamel and Välikangas' (2003) paper, manifesting more of a 'guru discourse' (see Young 2014), propagates the idea that organizational resilience needs a paradigmatic shift in the way corporate leaders think of and lead their organizations. In contrast, Suarez and Montes's (2019, 2020) work conceives the idea that organizational resilience can be incrementally built from existing routines and is a gradual evolutionary process. They postulate that established and new routines are important to building organizational resilience.

Consultocratic modeling of organizational resilience

In contrast to the rhetorical narratives presented in the expository discourses discussed earlier, consultocratic modeling approaches to organizational resilience place a greater emphasis on data integration and aggregation. Aggregated and integrated data are drawn to execute specific analytical tasks crucial for fortifying organizational resilience, including predictive analytics, real-time monitoring alerts, scenario analysis and planning, resource allocation optimization, regulatory compliance, and fostering a data-driven mindset throughout the organization.

Drawing insights from various consultancy papers (see Ahlawat et al. 2022; Diedrich et al. 2021; Görner et al. 2022; World Economic Forum and McKinsey & Company 2022; Deloitte 2022), we can pinpoint key features that characterize consultocratic modeling discourses on resilience. It is important to underscore the pivotal role of data analytics in these approaches.

1. Data-driven conception of crises and resilience.
2. Data-driven flagging of 'bigger issues' that underpin the necessity for being resilient
3. Modularizing organizational resilience into components as separate consulting packages in specific sub-fields of corporate management.
4. Highlighting doctrinal prescriptions of organizational resilience to program and codify corporate leadership, strategic thinking, decision-making, and conduct.

These elements are expounded upon in the following sections, shedding light on the distinctive features of the consultocratic modeling approach to organizational resilience.

Data-driven definition of crises and resilience

The process of resilience modeling begins by integrating and aggregating macroeconomic, financial market, and corporate data. This helps illustrate how the necessities and conditionalities of resilience are reflected in the data, with data analytics playing a crucial role. Tables, charts, and figures are generated to depict the unfolding crises, guiding top corporate managers on what they should be concerned about and how to prepare for future adversities through different scenarios based on key variables. Figure 6.2 provides an illustration of the generic outlook into which data aggregation and integration are directed with the aim of:

1. Identifying and explaining the resilience gap to direct the top leadership's attention to the necessity of incorporating resilience into their strategic priorities. This is usually done

Figure 6.2: Phases and capabilities of resilience – consultancy modelling

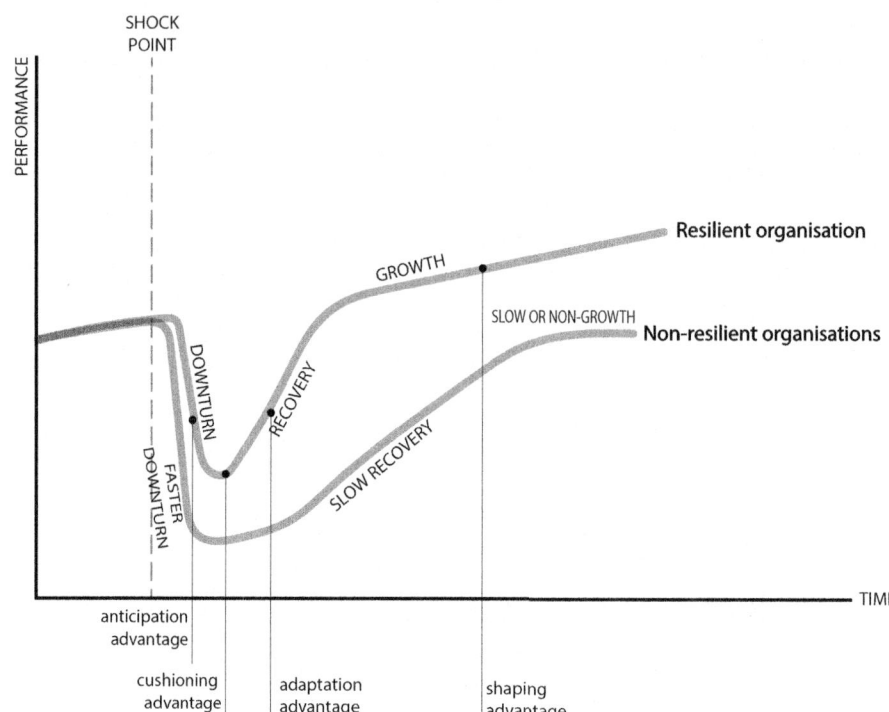

Key point

Data analytics are directed at identifying and explaining the resilience gap, path, and phases.

by showing the 'slumps' in the performance curve, where the performance is plotted against the time, showing the effect of a particular event or a trajectory such as COVID-19, Ukraine war, financial crisis, central bank's interest increases, disruptions in the EU GDP growth path, and global warming indexes, etc. The consultocratic idea here is that "datafication" (see Mayer-Schonberger & Cukier, 2013) of the crises is necessary to understand and signify the factuality and gravity of the crises and the transformation of corporate thinking and strategies they demand. Datafication will provide the statistical validity for the conceptual models to be built.

2. Identifying and explaining the resilience path vis à vis non-resilience path. This is done by comparing a faster recovery path (i.e., the path understood to be resilient) to a slower recovery path (i.e., the path understood to be non-resilient) taken by different scenarios or examples of strategic thinking and actions.

3. Identifying and explaining the resilience phases or stages. In relation to the resilience curve depicted in Figure 6.2, consultancy firms identify the resilience phases with different terminology, but they all resemble more or less the same idea. For example, McKinsey identifies three phases: downturn, recovery, and growth, together with strategic capabilities of response, foresight, and adaptation (see Ahlawat et al. 2022). For Boston Consultancy Group, resilience phases are anticipation, cushioning, adaptation, and shaping, and a resilient company would enjoy the following advantages over non-resilient companies (see Shmul et al. 2022).

    a. **Anticipation advantage**, as described by BCG consultants, refers to the edge that a resilient organization has over a non-resilient counterpart. This advantage arises from the organization's capacity to effectively anticipate and respond to crises. Having established contingency plans for unforeseen disruptions and actively scanning the environment for emerging crises are key components that prepare companies to weather such challenges. Other consultancy bodies and experts often refer to this capability as foresight, ultimately resulting in a less severe downturn.

    b. **Cushioning advantage** is another strength of resilient organizations compared to non-resilient ones. This advantage allows resilient organizations to 'bounce back' from shocks more quickly than their counterparts. According to BCG consultants, this cushioning advantage is built on creating financial and operational resource buffers, promoting diversity, ensuring operational modularity, achieving financial separation, and embedding the organization into broader socio-political infrastructure and support systems.

    c. **Adaptation advantage** stems from an organization's ability to adapt to new situations created by crises. BCG consultants emphasize that this depends on various factors, including the organization's integration into wider social and political institutional infrastructure, agility, capacity for experimentation, operational flexibility, and the ability to shift operational and market portfolios.

Key point:
Four types of resilience advantages: anticipation, cushioning, adaptation, and shaping.

d. **Shaping advantage** is the benefit that a company enjoys by strategically positioning itself to bounce back from adversity faster than others. Consequently, this positions the organization to shape new post-crisis realities, embrace fresh perspectives, and redefine the industry.

Data-driven flagging of 'bigger issues' that underpin the necessity for being resilient

Consultancy firms are one of the key epistemic pillars of creating corporate knowledge of strategic management. Talking and listening to corporate leaders play a critical role in the construction, popularisation, and legitimation of such consultocratic knowledge. Corporate surveys being the key epistemic instruments in this regard, consultancy firms are now producing a continuous stream of data analytics that periodically update the macroeconomic, political, and technological issues that underpin the necessities of being resilient. They highlight the external factors (or "geopolitical threats" as labeled by Deloitte) that should be at the forefront of their resilience strategies. Such corporate surveys help consultancy firms and corporations identify specific modular elements of resilience they should prioritize. A good example is the surveys carried out by Deloitte, where they prioritize the following resilience issues according to a survey question: "Rank the scenarios from the most impactful at the top to the least impactful at the bottom".

Key point:

Data-driven prioritization of resilience issues.

- Data security
- Cyber security
- Extreme weather
- Geopolitical
- Reputational
- Terrorism
- Natural disaster
- Economic/Financial

Systemic and modular elements of organizational resilience

Consultocratic discourses conceptualize organizational resilience as comprising a specific set of interconnected modules or system elements. While various consulting firms employ different terminology to articulate their consulting concepts and modules, a substantial conceptual isomorphism is evident. In essence, despite variations in wording and slight differences in explanations, they all posit the existence of fundamental building blocks, institutional elements, or modules that collectively form organizational resilience. Deloitte refers to these foundational elements as "the five capitals of organizational resilience": people, reputational, operational, financial, and environmental resilience (see Deloitte 2022).

Conversely, McKinsey identifies "levers of resilience," which are categorized into six organizational modular elements: financial, operational, digital and technological, brand reputation and climate, business model and innovation capabilities, and organizational resilience. According to McKinsey consultants, these levers provide resilience capabilities such as foresight, adaptation, and resilient growth (see Ahlawat et al. 2022). In either case, consultocratic discourses aim to modularize organizational elements into more refined resilience modules or packages that consulting firms can offer to their clients, depending on the specific functional expertise embraced and marketed by consultancy firms (or their competing divisions).

Key point:

Different ways in which modular elements of organizational resilience are conceptualized.

For the purpose of developing a generic understanding of how organizational resilience is modularized, I will draw your attention to some of the most commonly discussed resilience modules by many consultancy firms, each presented in distinct ways.

Financial resilience

Financial resilience refers to an organization's capacity to maintain its financial health and stability in the face of various economic, operational, and external disruptions. Financial resilience is often discussed as an ongoing process that requires proactive management and continuous monitoring of an organization's financial health. Consultancy discourses often emphasize and prescribe the following elements to ensure financial resilience.

Key point:

Financial resilience is a crucial module of organizational resilience.

- **Financial planning and management** to allocate resources strategically, control costs, and maintain healthy operational and financial leverage.
- **Diversification of revenue streams**: Relying on a single source of income can make an entity vulnerable to changes in that particular market. Diversification of revenue streams can enhance financial resilience by spreading risks across different sectors or products.

- **Cash flow management:** Maintaining positive cash flow is essential for financial resilience. Organizations must ensure they have enough liquid assets to cover short-term obligations, such as paying bills, salaries, and other immediate expenses.
- **Financial risk management:** Identifying, assessing, and mitigating market and currency fluctuations risks is crucial for financial resilience.
- **Debt management:** Managing debt levels and obligations is vital for financial resilience. Excessive debt can strain an entity's financial resources, making it challenging to navigate economic downturns.
- **Insurance and risk transfer:** Having appropriate insurance coverage and utilizing risk transfer mechanisms can help protect an entity from unforeseen events and financial losses.
- **Investor communication:** Maintaining transparent and effective communication with investors is crucial during challenging financial times. Open communication can help build trust and support in the capital markets.
- **Regulatory compliance:** Adhering to relevant financial regulations and compliance standards is essential for financial resilience. Non-compliance can result in legal issues and financial penalties.

key point:

Critical elements of financial resilience.

Operational resilience

Consultocratic discourses define operational resilience as a critical aspect of organizational resilience. It involves an organization's ability to anticipate, prepare for, respond to, and recover from disruptions to its normal business operations. The operational resilience module is a specific component within the broader organizational resilience strategy, focusing on ensuring the continued functioning of key business processes despite various challenges. According to Deloitte's consultants, operational resilience refers to "the way an organization uses its non-financial resources to withstand, absorb, recover from, adapt to, or regenerate from the impacts caused by shocks and stresses affecting its products and services, data, technology, cyber security, facilities, and supply and demand" (Deloitte 2022, 11).

Key point:

Operational resilience defined.

Examining various consultocratic materials on operational resilience reveals key elements contributing to an organization's operational resilience.

- **Risk assessment and identification:** Identify and assess potential risks and threats to the organization's operations, considering both internal and external factors that could disrupt business processes.
- **Business impact analysis (BIA):** Conduct a thorough analysis of the potential impact of disruptions on critical business processes, understanding dependencies between different processes, systems, and resources.
- **Scenario planning:** Develop and test various scenarios to simulate potential disruptions, aiding organizations in evaluating preparedness and identifying areas for improvement.
- **Preventive measures:** Implement measures to prevent or minimize the impact of disruptions, such as redundancy in critical systems, cybersecurity measures, and other risk mitigation strategies.
- **Response planning:** Develop detailed response plans outlining steps to be taken during a disruption, including communication plans, resource allocation, and coordination of activities to minimize downtime.
- **Resilience testing:** Regularly test the effectiveness of operational resilience measures through simulations and drills, identifying weaknesses in response plans and refining them for better effectiveness.
- **Communication and coordination:** Establish effective communication channels and coordination mechanisms internally and externally, which are crucial for disseminating information during a disruption and ensuring a cohesive response.
- **Continuous improvement:** Regularly review and update the operational resilience module based on lessons learned from real incidents or simulation exercises. Continuous improvement is essential for staying ahead of evolving threats and challenges.
- **Regulatory compliance:** Ensure that the organization's operational resilience practices align with relevant regulatory requirements. Compliance with industry standards and regulations is often crucial to a robust operational resilience framework.
- **Supplier and partner resilience:** Assess and enhance the resilience of key suppliers and partners since disruptions in their operations can have a cascading effect on the organization.

Key point:

Critical elements of operational resilience.

Consultocratic modeling of resilience conceives the operational resilience module as an integral part of the broader organizational resilience strategy, encompassing not only purely functional aspects but also certain financial, strategic, and reputational resilience elements (see below). One key point to emphasize is that consultocratic classifications of resilience modules overlap to certain degrees.

Structural resilience

I am using the term "structural resilience" here to encapsulate the modularization that consultancy firms describe variably as "people resilience," "resilience culture," "resilience leadership," "resilience teams," and so forth. Broadly speaking, this facet of organizational resilience aims to encompass the human, relational, communicative, and accountability elements that render organizational structures and systems agile, flexible, responsive, accountable, and adaptive to adversities and crises. Under this modular label, Deloitte emphasizes the necessity of establishing the right cultural norms, conduct, and behaviors to foster creativity and engineer growth (see Deloitte 2022). Similarly, McKinsey consultants underscore structural and behavioral elements related to strategy and workforce planning, people and talent, as well as the organization's structures and processes of accountability, responsibility, communication, and governance. Nevertheless, after reviewing various consultocratic discourses, the following can be listed as the key attributes of structural resilience.

Key point:

Structural resilience captures the human, relational, communicative, and accountability elements that make organizational structures and systems agile, flexible, responsive, and adaptive to adversities and crises.

1. Leadership and governance:

   - Clear leadership: Effective leadership is crucial for guiding the organization through disruptions. Leaders should be able to make informed decisions, communicate effectively, and inspire confidence amid adversities and crises.
   - Governance Structure: A robust governance structure ensures that decision-making processes are well-defined and aligned with the organization's objectives. It helps in the efficient allocation of resources during disruptions.

2. Adaptive structural capacity:

   - Flexibility and agility: Build a flexible organizational structure that can adapt quickly to changing circumstances. This may involve cross-training employees, adopting agile methodologies, and fostering a culture of innovation.

- Scenario planning: Anticipate different scenarios and develop strategies for each. This allows the organization to be better prepared for a range of potential disruptions.

3. Information management:

- Communication systems: Establish robust and trustworthy communication channels to facilitate the rapid exchange of information during disruptions. This includes both internal and external communication strategies.

4. Human capital:

- Talent management: Foster a culture that values and develops employees. This includes training programs, mentorship, and succession planning to ensure a skilled and adaptable workforce.
- Employee well-being: Consider the physical and mental well-being of employees. Resilient organizations prioritize employee health and provide support during challenging times.

5. Learning and continuous improvement:

- Post-incident analysis: Conduct thorough reviews and analyses after disruptions to identify areas for improvement. Use these insights to continuously refine and enhance resilience strategies.
- Organizational learning: Foster a culture of continuous learning and improvement. Encourage employees at all levels to share insights and contribute to the organization's overall resilience.

Key point:

Critical elements of structural resilience

Digital and technology resilience

Consultants often discuss digital and technology resilience as an organization's ability to handle disruptions or threats in the digital environment. It means being able to withstand, respond to, and recover from challenges like cyberattacks, system failures, and data breaches. Here are important aspects of digital and technology resilience:

1. Secularity measures:

- Use strong cybersecurity measures to protect digital assets and sensitive information.

- Regularly update and patch software to fix vulnerabilities.
- Conduct security audits and risk assessments to find potential weaknesses.

2. Data protection and privacy:

- Set up protocols for secure data storage, transmission, and processing.
- Follow data protection regulations and privacy laws.
- Use encryption and access controls to safeguard sensitive data.
- Business Continuity Planning:
- Create and update a comprehensive business continuity plan for technology systems.
- Identify critical digital assets and processes and prioritize their protection and recovery.
- Conduct regular drills to test the plan's effectiveness.

3. Redundancy and backups:

- Implement redundancy in critical systems to ensure continuity in case of failures.
- Regularly back up data and systems and ensure quick restoration.
- Use cloud services for data storage and backup to enhance redundancy.

4. Incident response and recovery:

- Form an incident response team to quickly detect, respond to, and recover from security incidents.
- Define clear procedures for reporting and addressing technology-related incidents.
- Conduct post-incident reviews to learn from events and improve future responses.

5. Employee training and awareness:

- Train employees on cybersecurity best practices and potential technology risks.
- Cultivate a culture of security awareness and responsibility among staff.
- Regularly update training to address emerging threats and technologies.

Key point:

Critical elements of digital and technology resilience.

6. Regulatory compliance:
   - Stay informed about laws and regulations related to technology and data protection.
   - Ensure technology systems comply with industry standards and legal requirements.

7. Adaptability and innovation:
   - Foster a culture of adaptability and innovation to tackle evolving technological challenges.
   - Continuously assess and update technology infrastructure with new security measures and technologies.
   - Collaboration and Information Sharing:
   - Collaborate with industry peers and organizations to share threat intelligence and best practices.
   - Participate in information-sharing initiatives to stay informed about emerging threats.

8. Monitoring and analytics:
   - Implement real-time monitoring of digital systems for unusual activities or security breaches.
   - Use analytics and artificial intelligence to identify patterns and potential security threats.

Reputational and environmental resilience in consultancy discourse

In consultocratic discourses, reputational and environmental resilience are often intertwined, but they represent distinct yet interconnected aspects of organizational resilience. McKinsey consultants, for instance, group these dimensions under "brand reputation and climate resilience," encompassing elements like stakeholder management, communications, brand reputation, and ESG alignment (see Ahlawat et al. 2022). On the other hand, Deloitte categorizes them as two "capitals of organizational resilience."

Deloitte defines reputational resilience as the organization's ability to respond to external perceptions, examine self-limiting behaviors, build brand capital, and maintain trust and dependability during crises. Meanwhile, environmental resilience is described as the "way in which an organization works to achieve homeostasis with the natural world, making strategic choices that are both good for the environment and sustainable for the organization" (Deloitte 2022, 11).

Key point:
Consultancy firms have different emphases on reputational and environmental resilience.

Let us consider them separately.

Reputational resilience:

Reputational resilience refers to an organization's ability to withstand and recover from challenges or crises that may impact its reputation. A positive reputation is a valuable asset for any organization, influencing customer trust, investor confidence, and employee morale. Reputational resilience involves strategies and practices that help an organization maintain or rebuild its reputation in the face of adversity. Reading through multiple consultocratic discourses, the following can be identified as the key components of reputational resilience:

> **Key point:**
>
> Reputational resilience defined.

1. **Crisis communication:** Effective communication strategies are vital for addressing and managing crises transparently and in a timely manner.
2. **Stakeholder engagement:** Building strong relationships with key stakeholders contributes to a positive reputation and provides support during challenging times.
3. **Ethical practices:** Upholding ethical standards in business operations is crucial for maintaining trust and resilience.
4. **Proactive reputation management:** Regularly monitoring public perception and addressing potential issues before escalation helps prevent reputational damage.

Environmental resilience:

On the other hand, encapsulating themes of sustainability, environmental resilience refers to an organization's ability to adapt to and mitigate the impacts of environmental challenges, such as climate change, natural disasters, or resource scarcity. Organizations that prioritize environmental resilience aim to reduce their ecological footprint and enhance their ability to operate sustainably. Key components of environmental resilience include:

> **Key point:**
>
> Environmental resilience defined.

1. **Sustainable practices:** Implementing environmentally friendly and sustainable business practices, such as reducing waste, conserving energy, and using renewable resources, contributes to environmental resilience.
2. **Adaptation strategies:** Anticipating and adapting to changes in the environment, whether due to climate change or other factors, is essential. This may involve adjusting supply chains, diversifying sourcing, or investing in new technologies.

3. **Regulatory compliance:** Staying compliant with environmental regulations and proactively seeking ways to exceed minimum requirements demonstrates a commitment to environmental responsibility.
4. **Stakeholder collaboration:** Working with environmental organizations, government agencies, and other stakeholders can help organizations address environmental challenges collectively and enhance their overall resilience.

Key point:
Critical elements of environmental resilience.

In summary, reputational resilience focuses on an organization's ability to manage and recover from challenges that impact its reputation, while environmental resilience involves strategies to adapt to and mitigate the environmental impacts of its operations. In effect, one can even consider environmental resilience so fundamental that the organization's ability/inability to deal with environmental and sustainability issues can have a strong positive/negative impact on the reputation. Both are critical for an organization's long-term success and sustainability in a rapidly changing global landscape.

Doctrinal prescriptions in consultocratic organizational resilience discourses

Consultocratic models often conclude with specific doctrinal and prescriptive elements. Consulting experts advocate for what they consider to be the ideal mindset and actions for "truly resilient" organizations and leaders, often branding these as "paradigm-shifting" strategies. These doctrinal prescriptions are presented as proven concepts and practices derived from successful consultocratic experiences and corporate achievements.

For instance, McKinsey consultants, in a white paper titled "A Defining Moment: How Europe's CEOs Can Build Resilience to Grow in Today's Economic Maelstrom" " (see Ahlawat et al. 2022, 4), offer the following advice to corporate leaders:

- Do not follow the old rules;
- prepare for the crises, but at the same time, prepare to exit them;
- Use scenarios rather than forecasting;
- Develop a resilience agenda that addresses burning short-term issues as well as longer-term challenges;
- Ensure resilience is measured so progress can be tracked and return on resilience investment can be maximised;

- Focus on resilient growth by reviewing their competitive position and finding strategic opportunities amid the crises.

Similarly, Deloitte, based on a survey of corporate leaders, outlines their doctrinal prescriptions in their "Deloitte's Global Resilience Report: Towards True Organisational Resilience" (Deloitte 2022):

- Accelerate journey to organizational resilience: organizations should expedite their path to resilience.
- Strategic priority: make organizational resilience a strategic priority by appointing a chief resilience officer.
- Incorporate geopolitical threats: address geopolitical threats within the resilience framework.
- Welcome regulatory roles: embrace the involvement of regulators in resilience efforts.
- ESG risk consideration: give greater attention to environmental, social, and governance risks.
- Proactive management of reputational risks: manage reputational risks proactively.
- Leverage digitalization: enhance resilience through digitalization.
- Overcoming resilience barriers: identify and overcome obstacles to achieving greater resilience.

Key point:

Doctrinal prescriptions form a significant part of the consultocratic frameworks of organizational resilience.

These examples illustrate what I call "doctrinal prescriptions," consistent features of consultocratic discourses. They are integral to the consultocratic concept of organizational resilience, suggesting that adherence to such prescriptions is key to "true organizational resilience".

6.4 Academic discourses on organizational resilience

So far, our discussion has centered on consultocratic discourses that outline how organizational resilience is conceptualized and packaged into a set of consultancy products. As future professional accountants, it is crucial for you to approach these ideas with a critical mindset. In the preceding sections, you should have grasped that these discourses are targeted at practitioners, aiming to promote consultocratic ideas, programs, or packages that can be effectively implemented in organizational settings when faced with challenging conditions requiring resilience at various levels and functional fields.

This subsection will briefly examine the key features of academic discourses on organizational resilience. There is a rapidly expanding body of academic literature on this subject, and a comprehensive review is beyond the scope of this chapter. Therefore, my focus here will be on elucidating the key features through selected examples of academic work, providing a broader conceptual and theoretical understanding of organizational resilience.

In contrast to the consultocratic discourses discussed earlier, academic discourses focus on offering a conceptual and theoretical analysis of the conditions under which organizational resilience emerges and the forms it takes. They do not aim to prescribe doctrines but rather explore how and why organizations, including consulting firms, might adopt different approaches or systems of organizational resilience and which approaches would be most suitable in various contingent situations.

Key point:
Differentiating academic vs consultocratic discourses on organizational resilience.

To arrive at their conclusions, academic discourses integrate appropriate theoretical and conceptual frameworks (such as systems theory, contingency theory, institutional theory, etc.), prior academic literature on specific resilience issues, and empirical data from illustrative cases or representative samples. Often, they develop broader conceptual schemas that other researchers, corporate managers, and consultants can use to explore, understand, and address specific resilience issues they encounter.

Within the scope of this book, and especially to confine the discussion to the most fundamental conceptual elements of resilience, I will concentrate on two interrelated themes highlighted by academic discourses:

1. Resilience's underlying contradictions and
2. Different domains of resilience that address these contradictions.

Exploring the underpinning contradictions of resilience

One of the focal points in academic research on organizational resilience revolves around exploring and conceptualizing the contradictory conditions that organizations must navigate to achieve different modes of organizational resilience. Drawing from classical organizational theory, scholars examining organizational resilience often assert that "the existence of tensions and contradictions between different instances constitutes resilience" (Giustiniano et al. 2018, 78). In this context, resilience is seen as the outcome of dialectics between various contradictory conditions, which Giustiniano et al. (2018, p. 119) describe as a dialectical synthesis—a unity of oppositions—between two opposite "templates" of responding to external challenges and stressors: reactivity and adaptivity.

1. Reactivity, in this context, refers to the capacity to bounce back or recover from challenges after they occur. This form of action involves responding to adversity or disruptions as they unfold, focusing on managing and mitigating the immediate impact of stressors. Qualities such as coping, hardiness, grit, recovery, redundancy, post-traumatic growth, and healing are associated with reactivity as a resilience template. Overall, the term "reactivity" seems to connote survival skills in adversity—the ability not to succumb and perish in difficult situations.

2. On the other hand, adaptivity involves proactively preparing for and anticipating challenges, enabling individuals or systems to adjust and thrive in the face of ongoing stressors or changes. While it often stems from and is closely connected to reactivity, this form of action is forward-thinking and strategic. It encompasses the capacity to learn from experiences, make necessary adjustments, and build skills to navigate future uncertainties. Qualities such as agility, anticipation, prevention, flexibility, improvisation, and maneuverability are associated with adaptivity as a resilience template.

Key point:

Resilience emerges as a dialectical synthesis of reactivity and adaptivity, emphasizing the integration of these opposing templates of actions to achieve a balanced and effective response to challenges.

Key point:

Other instances of how the fundamentality of contradictions in the conception of resilience is emphasized.

In a similar vein, Frigotto et al. (2022) position the concept of resilience within the paradoxical demands of stability and change. Striving to reconcile these conflicting needs, they propose a model reminiscent of Giustiniano et al.'s (2018) aforementioned conceptions. This model suggests that resilience can manifest in absorptive, adaptive, and transformative forms. Conversely, Denyer (2017) broadens the understanding of resilience contradictions by blending defensive and progressive contradictions on one axis and consistency and flexibility on the other.

Relating contradictions to different domains of resilience strategies

Academic discussions on organizational resilience often adopt a topological approach, emphasizing spatial relationships and connections among contradictory elements. Essentially, these discussions attempt to pinpoint potential areas, regions, or domains of action and reaction by treating relevant contradictions as 'variables' or 'continuums.'

Illustratively, in Figure 6.3 (Panel A), Giustiniano et al. (2018) delineate a continuum of reactivity and adaptivity, identifying three potential templates for resilience actions and reactions:

1. Adaptive resilience (Template 1): template of resilience populated by purposing (i.e., focusing on long-term purposes), planning, protecting and perfecting.
2. Reactive resilience (Template 2): a template of resilience that encompasses rethinking, responding, relating, and resolving.
3. Organizational resilience (Template 3): the ideal type template of resilience constituting a synthesis of adaptive and reactive elements mentioned above.

Key point:
How adaptive vs reactive dichotomies are used to construct domains of resilience.

Within this topological framework, adaptivity and reactivity emerge as fundamental contradictions that organizations must navigate when facing adversities. Entities can position themselves within the domain of reactivity, adaptivity, or the third domain created by their synthesis. Thus, Giustiniano et al. (2018) posit' organizational resilience' (Template 3) as an 'ideal type,' encapsulating both reactive and adaptive qualities in addressing challenges.

Similarly, Frigotto et al. (2022) intricately map the potential domain of resilience by examining the dichotomous continuity and variability between change and stability (see Figure 6.3 Panel B). By categorizing each dimension into low, medium, and high scales, they identify three significant domains of resilience: absorptive, adaptive, and transformative. Beyond these meaningful domains exist the extreme possibilities of either non-resilient survival or unrecognizably dynamic change. Yet again, the key conceptual proposition to note here is how contradictions/tensions are related as spatial connections to identify and explain possible domains of resilience.

Key point:
Forms of resilience are identified in the dichtomous continuum of stability and change orientations.

Figure 6.3: Tensions and domains of organisational resilience

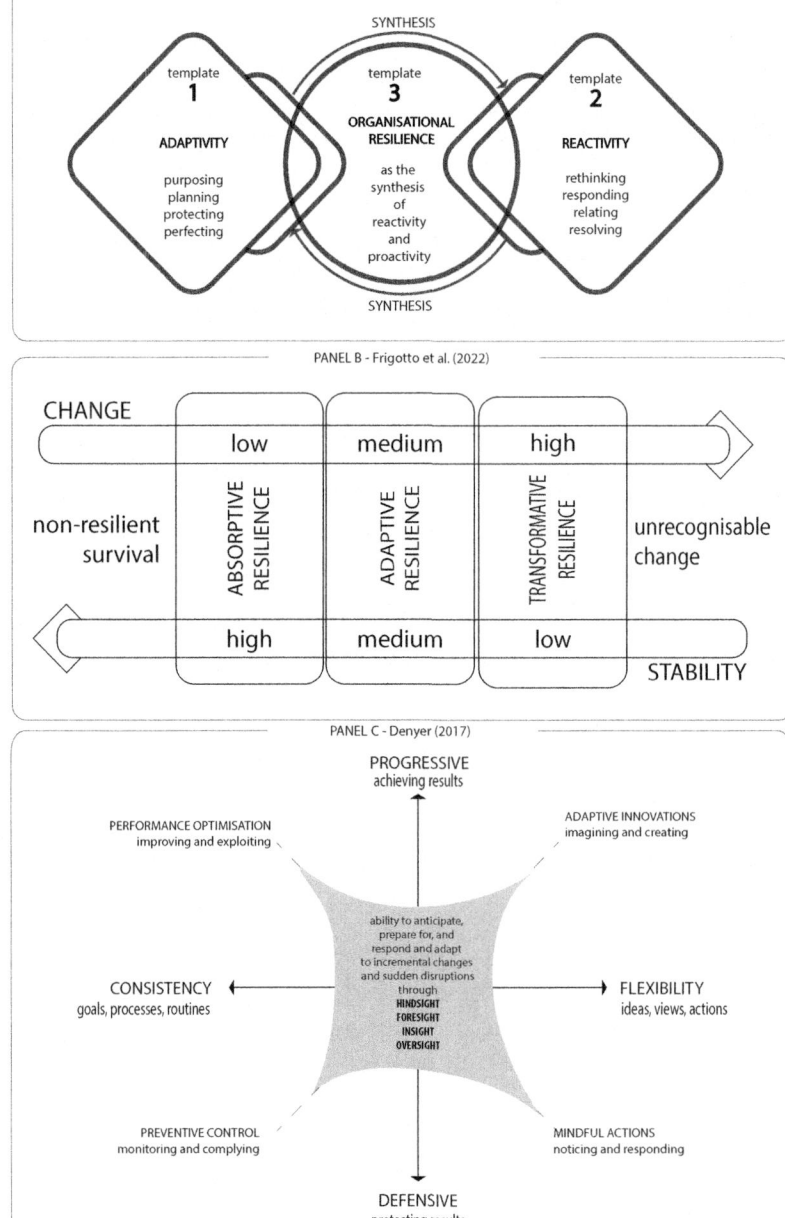

Source: Frigotto et al. (2022), Giustiniano et al. (2018), Denyer (2017).

Figure 6.3, Panel C, illustrates how Denyer (2017) postulates his domains of organizational resilience by plotting two dichotomous conditionalities of: (a) defensive vs. progressive and (b) consistency vs. flexibility. This arrangement yields four distinct domains of resilient actions and reactions:

1. **Preventive control** characterized by monitoring and compliance.
2. **Performance optimization** characterized by improving and exploiting.
3. **Adaptive innovation** characterized by imagining and creating.
4. **Mindful actions** characterized by noticing and responding.

Similar to Guistiniano et al.'s resilience model mentioned earlier, Denyer considers organizational resilience as a synthesis of these forms (located in the middle region of Figure 6.3, Panel C). This domain consolidates dichotomous divisions of actions and reactions, formulating organizational resilience as the "ability to anticipate, prepare for, and respond and adapt to incremental changes and sudden disruptions" (Denyer 2017, 16). Manifesting a somewhat Guru-like rhetoric discussed in previous sections, Denyer materializes this "ability" through four interrelated elements, which he aptly terms "4sihgts":

Key point:
Denyer's organizational resilience topology.

1. **Hindsight:** Learn the right lessons from your experiences.
2. **Foresight:** Anticipate, predict, and prepare for the future.
3. **Insight:** Interpret and respond to present conditions.
4. **Oversight:** Monitor, review, and assess changes.

Chapter summary

This chapter focused on organizational resilience as the third key aspect in structuring the organizational hierarchy. In the preceding chapters, we delved into the first two elements: strategic performance management and strategic management control.

The concept of resilience is versatile, finding application across various disciplines, each emphasizing different aspects based on their scope. Despite these disciplinary variations, a consistent thread is the understanding of resilience in the context of dealing with adversities. At its core, resilience encompasses an entity's capacity, capabilities, and processes to anticipate, prepare for, face, and recover from adversities. We explored how this fundamental concept manifests differently in diverse fields, from psychology to economics, spanning individual to global levels.

Transitioning from resilience to organizational resilience, this chapter examines two primary perspectives: consultocratic and academic. First, consultocratic discourses unfold within two main themes: expository narratives and modeling of organizational resilience. Expository narratives aim to construct consultocratic "guru ideas" through corporate storytelling, while modeling approaches seek data-driven conceptual frameworks for organizational resilience. Both approaches offer doctrinal guidelines for achieving resilience in distinct ways.

Academic discourses on organizational resilience elucidate the contradictions and tensions underlying this concept. They highlight the dichotomous connections and balancing acts required between stability and change, adaptivity and reactivity, defensive and progressive strategies, and consistency versus flexibility. Interactive spaces between dichotomies create different domains or modes of resilience.

Summarizing our discussion in this chapter, organizational resilience comprises four interconnected elements, emphasized by both consultocratic and academic perspectives. First, *contextual elements* encompass the dynamics and events that necessitate resilience, making entities vulnerable to failures. Anticipating and understanding these dynamics is crucial for organizational resilience.

Second, *processual elements* involve the specific processes and phases an entity must undergo to become resilient. Consultocratic and academic discourses explore these processes in various ways, with many terminologies: response, absorption, recovery, adaptation, anticipation, improvisation, cushioning, performance optimization, adaptive innovation, preventive control, hindsight, foresight, insight, and oversight.

Third, organizational resilience is often discussed in terms of *modular elements*, such as people, reputation, operations, finance, environment, and structure. These elements compartmentalize the totality of organizational resilience into sub-elements.

Finally, organizational resilience is explained in terms of *behavioral elements,* encompassing individual, collective, and systemic attributes necessary for an entity to become resilient. Doctrinal guidelines from consulting gurus and academics often outline these behavioral elements, specifying the do's and don'ts or musts and must-nots of organizational resilience.

Test your knowledge

1. Provide brief descriptions or definitions of the following types of resilience.

    a. Psychological resilience
    b. Social resilience
    c. Engineering resilience
    d. Economic resilience

2. Identify the core concepts of resilience included in the types of resilience you defined in the question above.
3. Explain how processual and capability dimensions constitute resilience.
4. Differentiate between the approaches that organizations like the OECD and World Bank take on resilience and the approaches taken by corporations and their consultants.
5. List the two approaches that characterize consultocratic discourses of organizational resilience that this chapter discussed.
6. List and briefly describe the four characterizing elements of expository narrative discourses of organizational resilience.
7. Listed here is a set of resilience-related concepts propagated in expository narrative discourses on organizational resilience. Briefly explain them.

    a. Resilience gap
    b. Zero-trauma
    c. Cognitive challenge
    d. Strategic challenge
    e. Political challenge
    f. Conquering denial
    g. Valuing variety
    h. Liberating resources
    i. Embracing paradox

8. Referring to Suarez & Montes (2020),
    a. Briefly describe the concept of "focal context" and how it is relevant in conceptualizing organizational resilience.

b. Explain how changes in the "focal context" trigger departures from routines as an element of organizational resilience.
c. Considering your answers to the above two sub-questions, explain the role of routines, hermeneutics, and improvisation in organizational resilience.

9. List the characterizing features of the "consultocratic modeling approach" to organizational resilience.
10. Using appropriate illustrations, explain the following phases and advantages of being resilient.

    a. Anticipation advantage
    b. Cushioning advantage
    c. Adaptation advantage
    d. Shaping advantage

11. List the critical "geopolitical threats" or "big issues" that consulting firms have identified as driving dynamics of organizational resilience strategies.
12. Consultancy firms identify modular elements of organizational resilience with different labels and terminologies, such as "five capitals of organizational resilience" and "levers of organizational resilience." Identify such key modular elements and provide a brief description of each of them.
13. Consultocratic modeling discourses on organizational resilience often end up with certain "doctrinal prescriptions." With some examples from the consultancy firms, explain how they constitute consultocratic discourses of organizational resilience.
14. Briefly explain how paradoxical contradictions underpin academic discourses of organizational resilience.
15. Briefly explain the different domains of organizational resilience strategies as identified by the following authors.

    a. Giustiniano et al. (2018)
    b. Frigotto et al. (2022)
    c. Denyer (2017)

Explore further

1. Visit the British Standards Institute (BSI) pages on organizational resilience, focusing on two crucial areas: the BSI Organizational Resilience Framework and the BSI Organizational Resilience Index. Identify the key elements and variables these frameworks and indices use to conceptualize and measure organizational resilience.

2. Engage in the ongoing policy debate concerning the necessity of requiring large corporations and public interest entities (PIEs) to produce an annual resilience report. Initially proposed in Sir Donald Brydon's independent review on audit quality and effectiveness, this recommendation has been addressed in the UK government's white paper titled "Restoring trust in audit and corporate governance: Government response to the consultation on strengthening the UK's audit, corporate reporting, and corporate governance systems" by the Department for Business, Energy, and Industrial Strategy. Subsequently, various discussion papers on this topic have been released by accountancy professional bodies and the Big Four accounting firms.

   Analyze these reports and papers to elucidate how an annual resilience report would assist large corporations in enhancing their long-term sustainability and bolstering stakeholder confidence in the face of diverse resilience risks.

Develop your critical argumentation skills

1. Write an argumentative essay on the following theme.

   The fact that resilience has become a strategic imperative conversely implies that uncontrollability has become the norm of the day.

2. Write an argumentative essay on the following theme.

   Organizational-centric approaches of resilience propagated by consultocratic discourses have limited value in building resilience against the geopolitical threats.

3. Write an argumentative essay on the following theme.

   In the light of the global sustainability agenda and the necessity of being resilient against global geopolitical threats, management accounting needs to expand its epistemic scope beyond its traditional remit of costing, decision-making, performance management, and management control.

References

Ahlawat, H., A. Raggl, H. Hatami, M. d. M. Martinez, A. Natale, and T. Poppensieker. 2022. A defining moment: how Europe's CEOs can build resilience to grow in today's economic maelstrom. McKinsey Quarrterly, 1-10.

Deloitte. 2022. Toward true organizational resilience: Deloitte's Global Resilience Report: Deloitte.

Denyer, D. 2017. Organizational resilience: a summary of academic evidence, business insights and new thinking.

Diedrich, D., N. Northcote, T. Röder, and K. Sauer-Sidor. 2021. Strategic resilience during the COVID-19 crisis.

Frigotto, M. L., M. Young, and R. Pinheiro. 2022. Resilience in organizations and societies: the state of the art and three organizing principles for moving forward. In Towards Resilient Organizations and Societies: A Cross-Sectoral and Multi-Disciplinary Perspective, edited by R. Pinheiro, M. L. Frigotto and M. Young. Cham, Switzerland: Palgrave Mcmillan, 3-40.

Gigerenzer, G., and W. Gaissmaier. 2011. Heuristic Decision Making. Annual Review of Psychology 62 (1):451-482.

Giustiniano, L., S. R. Clegg, M. P. e. Cunha, and A. Rego. 2018. Elgar Introduction to theories of organizational resilience: Edward Elgar Publishing.

Görner, S., A. Govindarajan, E. Greenberg, J. Kelleher, I. Kristensen, L. Liu, A. Padhi, A. Panas, and Z. Silverman. 2022. Something's coming: How US companies can build resilience, survive a downturn, and thrive in the next cycle. In McKinsey & Company, Risk and Resilience Practice.

Hamel, G., and L. Välikangas. 2003. The quest for resilience. Harvard Business Review 2003 (September):1-12.

Hollnagel, E. 2010. Resilience engineering in practice: a guidebook. Farnham, Surrey, England;Burlington, VT;: Ashgate.

Hollnagel, E., D. D. Woods, and N. Leveson. 2006. Resilience engineering: concepts and precepts. Aldershot, England;Burlington, VT;: Ashgate.

Hougaard, J. C., and M. Mohan. 2020. Build your resilience in the face of a crisis. Harvard Business Review 2020 (March):1-5.

Jupe, R., and W. Funnell. 2015. Neoliberalism, consultants and the privatisation of public policy formulation: the case of Britain's rail industry. Critical Perspectives on Accounting 29:65-85.

Kantola, A., and H. Seeck. 2011. Dissemination of management into politics: Michael Porter and the political uses of management consulting. Management Learning 42 (1):25-47.

Kirkman, B., A. C. Stoverink, S. Mistry, and B. Rosen. 2019. The 4 things resilent teams do. Harvard Business Review 2019 (July):1-5.

Kwok, A. H., E. E. H. Doyle, J. Becker, D. Johnston, and D. Paton. 2016. What is 'social resilience'? Perspectives of disaster researchers, emergency management practitioners, and policymakers in New Zealand. International Journal of Disaster Risk Reduction 19:197-211.

Linkov, I., B. D. Trump, K. Poinsatte-Jones, P. Love, W. Hynes, and G. Ramos. 2018. Resilience at OECD: current state and future directions. IEEE Engineering Management Review 46 (4):128-135.

OECD. 2016. OECD G20 policy paper on economic resilience and structural policies. Geneva: OECD.

Ruault, J.-R., F. Vanderhaegen, and D. Luzeaux. 2012. Sociotechnical systems resilience. INCOSE International Symposium 22 (1):339-354.

Shmul, Y., M. Reeves, and S. Levin. 2022. Building a mutually reinforcing system of organizational and personal resilience: BCG Henderson Institute.

Suarez, F. F., and J. S. Montes. 2019. An integrative perspective of organizational responses: routines, heuristics, and improvisations in a mount everest expedition. Organization Science 30 (3):573-599.

———. 2020. Building organizational resilience. Harvard Business Review, 1-7.

Sundström, G., and E. Hollnagel. 2011. Governance and control of financial systems: a resilience engineering perspective. Burlington, VT; Farnham, Surrey: Ashgate.

World Bank. 2013. Building resilience : integrating climate and disaster risk into development. Washington: World Bank.

———. 2021a. Integrating resilience attributes into operations: a note for practitioners. Washington: World Bank.

———. 2021b. Resilience rating system: a methodology for building and tracking resilience to climate change. Washington: World Bank.

World Economic Forum, and McKinsey & Company. 2022. Resilience for sustainable, inclusive growth: white paper: World Economic Forum.

Young, A. M. 2014. Prophets, gurus, and pundits : rhetorical styles and public engagement. Carbondale, UNITED STATES: Southern Illinois University Press.

CHAPTER 7

Strategizing the point of production: quality costing and management

7.1 Introduction

Once again, I commence a new chapter by revisiting the overarching structural logic of this book: strategies are enabled and enacted in three interconnected arenas of strategic actions – markets, organizational hierarchies, and the point of production. After delving into various strategic themes related to the market and organizational hierarchy in the preceding chapters, we now focus on the point of production, where labor processes are strategized.

The point of production encompasses the labor processes, the complex web of techno-managerial and political relations and processes through which the 'surplus value' is created by manufacturing goods and services (see Braverman 1998 [1974]; Burawoy 1979). While markets serve as the sites for appropriating and realizing 'surplus value', the point of production is the site in which 'surplus value' is created through the efficient and effective management of labor processes. As such, strategizing the point of production entails the configuration and reconfiguration of labor processes both within and beyond the organization's production floors. This continuous endeavor is aimed at ensuring that these labor processes can consistently produce goods and services to meet the demands of the market while aligning with the broader sustainability goals of the contemporary world.

Reminder:

How the current chapter fits into the overall structural logic of the book.

As mentioned in previous chapters, three pivotal strategic imperatives are intricately linked to formulating labor processes: quality, flexibility, and costs. This chapter focuses on quality costing as a strategic imperative, while upcoming chapters will address flexibility and cost. Recognizing the extensive nature of quality management as a managerial subdiscipline—too vast to be comprehensively covered within the confines of a book like this—this chapter primarily delves into the costing aspects of quality management. It also includes discussions on the pertinent managerial, institutional, and political facets that underlie quality costing.

Key point:

Value for money and survival zone concepts to explain the strategic significance of quality costing.

The strategic connection and importance of quality can be discussed in many ways. However, it would be best to refresh your mind on the concepts of *"value for money"* and *"survival zone"* discussed in Chapter 3. The idea of value for money (i.e., value divided by the cost of a product to the customer) is often understood in strategic marketing discourses as the ultimate criteria for making a purchase decision. The perceived quality of a product is the enumerating core of the value element in this formula, which also determines the particular manner in which the firm would 'position' its products in the mind of the customer. Hence, quality constitutes a critical element of the firm's market strategy, which the point of production must produce at an acceptable cost, denominating the value for money. Strategizing with quality involves conceptualizing and realizing this intricate connection between quality and cost both at the point of production and the market, hence the importance of 'quality costing'. This intricate strategic connection is further emphasized by the target costing and value engineering concept of "survival zone" (Cooper and Slagmulder 1997), where a third variable – functionality – is brought into consideration to complicate the quality-cost connection.

The chapter is structured around three main themes and corresponding learning objectives.

1. **Exploring and appreciating the plurality and complexity of product quality:** In section 7.2, the learning objective is to delve into multiple definitions and perspectives of quality. The section ultimately provides a specific operational definition crucial for elucidating the costing dynamics of quality management.
2. **Articulating constitutive elements of the total quality cost function:** Building upon the definitions explored in section 7.2, section 7.3 articulates the constitutive elements of a total quality cost and explains how they are related to the level of

quality that a company would pursue as a strategic decision. Reading this section will enhance your understanding of the quality cost categories.
3. **Understanding the paradigmatic nature of quality costing:** Section 7.4 delves into how a firm would determine the optimum quality level, emphasizing its paradigmatic nature. It explains quality costing under three paradigms: traditional, zero-defects, and continuous improvement. Upon completing this section, readers should be able to elucidate how paradigmatic assumptions about quality cost behavior influence a firm's decision on the level of quality it should pursue.
4. **Understanding design and calculative elements of a quality costing system:** Section 7.5 focuses on key elements of designing a quality costing system. This part of the chapter aims to guide readers through specific calculative procedures and processes related to quality costing.
5. **Quality-centric organizational transformations:** In section 7.6, you will explore how quality discourses, especially the Japanization movement, resulted in ideological, structural, and processual transformations in Western organizations.
6. **Conclusion and further exploration:** Finally, section 7.7 concludes the chapter with a summary, followed by chapter-end revision, further exploration, and critical argumentative exercises.

Key point:
Learning objectives and the structure.

7.2 Defining quality: multiplicity of perspectives and an operational definition

The concept of quality is inherently multifaceted, encompassing a spectrum of perspectives that vary across disciplines, industries, and individual experiences. Quality is not a monolithic entity but rather a nuanced and dynamic phenomenon subject to diverse interpretations. From a consumer standpoint, for example, quality may be considered by the reliability, durability, and performance of a product or service. In contrast, manufacturers may prioritize aspects such as precision, consistency, and adherence to standards in their pursuit of quality. Moreover, cultural and societal contexts play a crucial role in shaping perceptions of quality, with different communities valuing different attributes. The multiplicity of perspectives regarding quality reflects the complex interplay of subjective preferences, objective criteria, and contextual factors that contribute to a rich and

Key point
Different approaches to define quality can be identified.

evolving understanding of what constitutes excellence in various domains. Recognizing and navigating this diversity is essential before we launch into more pragmatic, programmatic, and calculative elements of quality management and costing. Reading through various quality management books and papers, at least six main approaches to defining quality can be identified. We should first elaborate on them briefly before pinpointing the operational definition of quality that we use to understand quality cost behavior.

Product-based approach

In this approach, the definition of quality centers around specific attributes or characteristics inherent to that product, especially emphasizing the tangible features and measurable properties of the product itself. Key elements of the product-based approach to defining quality include:

- **Conformance to specifications:** One of the primary criteria for assessing quality in a product-based approach is its conformance to established specifications and standards. This involves evaluating whether the product meets the requirements and criteria set forth during its design and development phases. For example, whether the product meets the size, volume, and ingredient requirements set forth by the industry standards.
- **Performance:** The performance of a product is a critical factor in determining its quality. This involves assessing how well the product carries out its intended functions and whether it meets or exceeds the performance expectations defined for it. For example, a buyer of a high-end digital camera would consider performance attributes such as resolution, sensor size, optical quality, aperture range, burst speed, low-light performance, size and weight, wireless connectivity, 4K/6K/8K video capabilities, and so forth.
- **Reliability:** The reliability of a product refers to its ability to consistently perform its intended functions without failure over a specified period. A reliable product is one that customers can depend on to work as expected under normal operating conditions. For example, Sony boasts that its high-end cameras can outperform Cannon's high-end cameras in terms of high-resolution video recording without overheating and shutting down.

- Durability: Durability focuses on the longevity and resistance to wear and tear of a product. A high-quality product is expected to have a longer lifespan and be able to withstand the rigors of regular use without significant deterioration in performance or appearance.
- Aesthetics: A product's visual and sensory appeal also plays a role in the product-based approach to quality. Aesthetics include aspects such as design, color, texture, and overall appearance, which can influence customers' perceptions of a product's quality.
- Extra features and functionalities: Closely related to the performance dimension mentioned above, the inclusion of extra features that enhance the overall functionality of a product is a crucial factor in assessing its quality. Products with advanced features that enhance user experience and provide additional utility are often considered of higher quality.
- Usability and user experience: A quality product should be user-friendly and easy to use. Usability considerations include factors such as intuitive design, clear instructions, and accessibility, all of which contribute to a positive user experience.

Key point:
The product-based definition of quality centers around the product's inherent attributes.

Manufacturing-based approach

A manufacturing-based approach to product quality emphasizes conformance to manufacturing standards, encompassing not only the standards on final product attributes but also the standards pertaining to the manufacturing processes. This approach is based on the engineering doctrine that the quality of the final product is intricately linked to the methods and processes employed during manufacturing. Here are key elements associated with a manufacturing-based approach to product quality:

- Process control: Rigorous control of manufacturing processes is a cornerstone of this approach. It involves closely monitoring and managing each step of production to minimize variations and deviations from established standards. Process control helps prevent defects and ensures consistency in product quality.
- Quality assurance systems: Implementing robust quality assurance systems is crucial. This includes the development and adherence to stringent quality standards, inspection procedures, and testing protocols. These systems are designed

to catch and address any issues before they impact the final product.
- **Continuous improvement:** Embracing a philosophy of continuous improvement is fundamental to maintaining and enhancing product quality. Manufacturers strive to identify areas for optimization, efficiency gains, and quality enhancements through regular assessments and feedback loops. This iterative process contributes to long-term excellence.
- **Employee training and engagement:** The skills and commitment of the workforce play a significant role in achieving high product quality. Manufacturers invest in training programs to ensure that employees understand the importance of their roles in maintaining quality standards. Engaged and knowledgeable employees are more likely to contribute to a culture of quality.
- **Supplier quality management:** A manufacturing-based approach extends beyond the factory floor to include the entire supply chain. Ensuring that raw materials and components meet specified quality standards is crucial for preventing defects and maintaining consistency in the final product.
- **Root cause analysis:** When quality issues arise, a manufacturing-based approach involves conducting a thorough root cause analysis. Identifying the underlying factors contributing to defects allows manufacturers to implement corrective actions and prevent similar issues in the future.
- **Data-driven decision-making:** Leveraging data and analytics is essential for making informed decisions about product quality. Monitoring key performance indicators and using data to identify trends or potential issues enables manufacturers to proactively address challenges and optimize processes.

In summary, a manufacturing-based approach to product quality emphasizes proactive measures, systematic control, and continuous improvement throughout the production process. By integrating these principles, manufacturers aim to deliver consistent, high-quality products that meet or exceed customer expectations.

Key point:

Manufacturing-based definitions emphasize the conformance to manufacturing process and product standards.

User-based approach

The user-based approach to product quality places a primary emphasis on the product's capacity to meet the needs and expectations of end-users. In this approach, the perspective of the customer is central to the evaluation and improvement of product quality. Here are some key elements of the user-based approach:

- **Customer satisfaction:** The ultimate goal is to ensure customer satisfaction. This involves understanding customer preferences, desires, and requirements and aligning the product features and performance with these expectations.
- **User experience:** A critical component of the user-based approach is enhancing the overall user experience. This includes factors such as ease of use, user interface design, and the emotional response elicited from users during product interactions.
- **Feedback and reviews:** Continuous feedback from users is essential. Monitoring user reviews, conducting surveys, and actively seeking input allow organizations to identify strengths and weaknesses in their products and make informed decisions for improvement.
- **Customization and personalization:** Recognizing the diverse needs of users, a user-based approach often involves providing customization options or personalization features. This allows users to tailor the product to better suit their individual preferences.
- **Usability testing:** Regular usability testing is employed to evaluate how easily users can interact with a product. By observing users in real-world scenarios, organizations can identify areas of friction and address usability issues promptly.
- **Agile development:** The user-based approach often aligns with agile development methodologies, emphasizing iterative development and quick responses to changing user needs. This ensures that the product evolves based on real-time user feedback.
- **Post-launch support:** Quality is not just about the product at launch but extends into the post-launch phase. Providing efficient customer support and addressing issues promptly contribute to a positive user experience and long-term customer satisfaction.

Key point

The user-based approach emphasizes the product's capacity to satisfy the end user's needs and expectations.

- Data-driven decision making: Analytics and data play a crucial role in the user-based approach. Analyzing user behavior, preferences, and usage patterns provides valuable insights that can guide decision-making for product enhancements and updates.

In essence, the user-based approach to product quality places the user at the center of the development process, emphasizing a customer-centric mindset that strives to exceed user expectations and deliver a product that not only meets functional requirements but also delights and engages its users.

Value-based approach

Extending the user-based approach discussed above, this approach examines how customers correlate a product's performance and attributes (discussed in the product-based approach) with the cost of owning and using that product. The foundation for evaluating quality is the price-performance ratio, a measure of how well a product performs relative to its price. A superior product in this context excels at meeting or surpassing customer expectations while maintaining competitive pricing. Consumers typically seek products that strike the optimal balance between affordability and functionality.

Key point:

Value-based definitions correlate the product attributes that create value with the product price.

In this framework, low-priced products may not necessarily imply poor quality if they deliver satisfactory performance for the cost incurred. Conversely, high-priced items are expected to provide exceptional features and durability to justify their premium. Striking the right balance between price and performance is crucial for businesses looking to meet customer expectations and gain a competitive edge in the market.

Ultimately, defining product quality based on the price-performance ratio underscores the significance of considering the overall value proposition according to which the product is positioned in the customer's mind. At this point, it would be helpful to revisit Chapter 3's discussion on segmentation, targeting, and positioning, especially Figure 3.5.

In the neoclassical economic theory of consumer behavior, this value-based approach aligns with the doctrine that, for a customer to make a buying decision, the marginal utility gained by a unit of spending on a product (i.e., marginal utility divided by the price of the product) should be equal to or greater than that of the other alternative products available.

Transcendental approach

Taking us to a philosophical realm of defining quality, this approach holds the idea that quality is something beyond definition and is neither a property of matter nor solely a construct of the mind. It is rooted in the philosophy of Robert M. Pirsig, particularly in his influential work "Zen and the Art of Motorcycle Maintenance" (Pirsig 2011 (1974)). Pirsig introduces the concept of Quality as a fundamental and elusive aspect of reality that goes beyond conventional understanding. According to Pirsig, Quality is not something that can be easily defined or categorized. It is not merely a subjective judgment or an objective property of the physical world. Instead, Quality is posited as a dynamic and holistic synthesis of the classical duality between subject and object, mind and matter. Here's a breakdown of the key elements of this doctrine:

- **Quality transcends dualism:** Pirsig challenges the traditional dualism between mind and matter, suggesting that Quality is not limited to the subjective realm of the mind or the objective realm of matter. It transcends these dualities, serving as a bridge between them.
- **Dynamic synthesis:** Quality is seen as a dynamic synthesis that emerges from the interaction between the observer (subject, the consumer, user etc.) and the observed (object, the product). It is not fixed or static but is a process that unfolds in the subject's act of experiencing or engaging with the object.
- **Ineffability:** Quality is considered ineffable, meaning that it cannot be adequately expressed or captured through language or conventional definitions. Attempts to define Quality may limit its essence, as it eludes rigid conceptualization.
- **Integral to experience:** Pirsig argues that Quality is not an abstract concept but is integral to our lived experiences. It permeates all aspects of life, influencing our perceptions, judgments, and interactions with the world.
- **Harmony and balance:** Quality is associated with a sense of harmony and balance. It is found in the seamless integration of elements, whether in a work of art, a technological innovation, or a philosophical idea.

Key point:

The transcendental approach takes a philosophical view on product quality to understand it as a dynamic and holistic synthesis of the duality between subject and object, mind and matter.

In summary, transcendentalism proposes that quality is a transcendent and dynamic synthesis that goes beyond the limitations of dualistic thinking. It is a pervasive aspect of reality that connects the subjective and objective realms, and its nature is best apprehended through direct experience rather than through rigid definitions. Pirsig's exploration of Quality encourages a more holistic and open-minded approach to understanding the nature of reality and the values we ascribe to it.

Social constructivist approach

The social constructivist approach to defining product quality emphasizes the role of social and cultural factors in shaping perceptions of what constitutes a high-quality product. Unlike product or manufacturing-based approaches that focus primarily on objective measures such as technical specifications or functional performance, social constructivism recognizes that quality is a socially constructed concept influenced by contextual and subjective elements.

Key point:

The social constructivist approach considers the role of broader cultural-political and contextual elements in defining quality.

In this perspective, product quality is not an inherent attribute of the product itself but rather a product of the meanings and values assigned to it by socio-cultural and political processes, including advertisement and media promotions of a product or brand. Social constructivists argue that people's understanding of quality is shaped by their cultural background, experiences, and the social context in which they interact with the product. Key aspects of the social constructivist approach to defining product quality include:

- **Subjectivity and perception:** Quality is seen as a subjective and context-dependent concept. Individuals and communities may have diverse perspectives on what constitutes a high-quality product based on their unique experiences and social backgrounds, including social classes and categories they manifest.
- **Cultural influence:** Cultural norms, values, and traditions play a significant role in shaping perceptions of quality. Products that align with or challenge cultural expectations may be evaluated differently in terms of quality.
- **Social interactions:** Quality assessments are influenced by social interactions and discourses. People often rely on social networks, reviews, and word-of-mouth to form opinions about a product's quality.

- Consumer involvement: The level of consumer involvement in the product, including participation in the design or customization process, can impact how individuals perceive its quality.
- Dynamic nature: Quality is not a fixed attribute but evolves over time. Changes in societal values, technological advancements, and cultural shifts can redefine what is considered a high-quality product.

In conclusion, like the transcendental approach discussed above, the social constructivist approach challenges the notion of a universal and objective definition of product quality. Instead, it highlights the importance of considering the social, cultural, and subjective class dimensions that contribute to the multifaceted nature of quality assessments. This approach encourages a more holistic understanding of product quality that considers the diverse perspectives and influences that shape people's perceptions.

An operational definition of quality for quality costing

Our discussion so far provides a rather divergent understanding of quality, expanding into multiple perspectives. Such a pluralistic understanding helps us to see the broader context within which quality needs to be conceptualized and appreciated in its techno-managerial, cognitive, and socio-cultural plurality. However, accounting endeavors of quality costing need a much narrower definition of quality, especially to see how quality costs would change according to the level of quality achieved. For that, quality is defined by the following formula, which encapsulates the idea that quality is the probability of not producing defective products.

$$Quality = 1 - Defective\ Rate$$
$$q = 1 - d$$

This is, in effect, a system-oriented definition, and it is measurable. It defines not the quality of a particular product but of the production system: the capacity of the system, or the trust we can place in the system, to produce quality products or, inversely, not to produce defective products. For example, a defective rate of 5% means that the system has a probabilistic quality measure of 95%. The ideal idea of Six Sigma captures this probabilistic definition of quality.

The term Six Sigma refers to a statistical concept that measures how

Key point:

For the purpose of quality costing, an operational definition of quality is necessary as

$q = 1-d$.

far a process deviates from perfection. The goal of Six Sigma is to reduce process variation and defects to a level where they occur at a rate of no more than 3.4 defects per million opportunities (DPMO). The term "Sigma" represents the standard deviation of a process. In a Six Sigma process, the process variation is limited to six standard deviations from the mean of the process. This level of performance corresponds to a defect rate of 3.4 defects per million opportunities. Here is a breakdown of the sigma levels and corresponding defect rates:

- Six Sigma (6σ): 3.4 defects per million opportunities
- Five Sigma (5σ): 233 defects per million opportunities
- Four Sigma (4σ): 6,210 defects per million opportunities
- Three Sigma (3σ): 66,807 defects per million opportunities
- Two Sigma (2σ): 308,537 defects per million opportunities
- One Sigma (1σ): 691,462 defects per million opportunities

As I will further elaborate in the forthcoming sections, this definition of quality is the basis upon which we understand and plot the variability of quality cost elements. Q=1-d will be the independent variable upon which we mathematically explain the dependent variability of quality costs.

7.3 Quality costs

The above operational definition of quality, in turn, provides the basis for identifying and defining the elements of quality costs. Two inversely related fundamental possibilities are embedded in the quality formula mentioned above. It is in relation to these possibilities that quality costs are identified.

First is the possibility of producing defective products (d). When the system produces defective products, resulting costs can be broadly interpreted as the quality cost of non-compliance or the cost of being defective or bad. In quality costing systems, items included in this category are sub-categorized under two headings: internal failure costs (IFC) and external failure costs (EFC)

Key point

Four main categories of quality cost.

Second is its inverse, the possibility of producing good products (q). Costs incurred to ensure and enhance this possibility can broadly be interpreted as the quality cost of compliance or being good. Items included in this cost category are sub-categorized into two headings in quality costing systems: prevention costs (PC) and appraisal costs

(AC). The sum totality of all these costs items constitutes the total quality costs. See Figure 7.1 for an illustration of this constitution of the total quality cost.

Prevention costs

Prevention costs are expenses incurred to prevent defects or errors from occurring in the first place. These costs are positively related to the level of quality, manifesting a positively sloped cost curve. Generally, more investments in the preventive elements of the quality control system are needed to lower the probability of defects in the system (i.e., to enhance the probability of producing quality products). Examples of prevention costs include:

- Training programs for employees to enhance their quality control skills.
- Quality planning and design processes.
- Quality assurance activities, such as pre-production inspections and audits.
- Implementation of process improvements and quality management systems.
- Supplier verification and vetting for selection.
- Raw materials quality inspections.

Appraisal costs

Appraisal costs are associated with evaluating and assessing products, components, or processes to ensure they meet quality standards. Like prevention costs, these are also positively related to the level of quality, as these are needed to lower the possibility of getting a defective product through the system to the customer. Generally, more investments are needed in appraisal costs to lower the probability that defective products pass through the system. Examples of appraisal costs include:

Examples:

- Quality inspection and testing.
- Ongoing quality audits and supplier evaluations.
- Calibration of measuring equipment.
- Costs associated with quality control activities.

Internal failure costs

Definition: Internal failure costs are incurred when defects or errors are detected before the product or service is delivered to the customer. While such internal detections reduce further costs to be incurred by non-detection, internal failures do include considerable costs, for example:

- Scrap and rework of defective products.
- Costs related to retesting and reinspection.
- Downtime and disruption in production.
- Cost of waste and reprocessing.

These costs are negatively related to the level of quality, meaning that a higher q value in the quality formula we mentioned above (i.e., q = 1-d) lowers the internal failure costs.

External failure costs

Definition: External failure costs arise when defects or errors are identified by customers after the product or service has been delivered. This is the most dangerous and vulnerable failure cost element as it can have unpredictable costs, reputational consequences, and damages. Some examples of identifiable external failure costs include:

- Customer complaints and returns.
- Warranty claims and repairs.
- Legal costs associated with product recalls or liability issues.

Similar to internal failure costs, these costs are negatively related to the level of quality.

7.4 Quality paradigms

A paradigm refers to a generally accepted set of beliefs and assumptions that guide the way individuals or a society perceive, understand, and approach a particular subject or problem. Paradigms influence the way people interpret information, form hypotheses, conduct research, and make decisions. Thomas Kuhn, a philosopher of science, introduced the concept of "paradigm shift" to describe a fundamental change in the basic assumptions and practices within a scientific discipline. A paradigm shift often occurs when new evidence or perspectives emerge, challenging the existing paradigm and leading to reevaluating and transforming the accepted beliefs.

Key point

A paradigm refers to a distinct set of underlying assumptions and beliefs that frame how one thinks and acts upon a particular subject or problem.

In the context of quality management and costing, three paradigms have emerged, each reflecting shifts in underlying assumptions about how quality costs vary in relation to the desired level of quality and the perceived "optimum" quality level:

1. Traditional quality paradigm
2. Zero-defect and continuous improvement quality paradigms.

Traditional quality paradigm

In line with various managerial problem-solving scenarios, such as economic order quantity in inventory management, quality managers have traditionally applied the neoclassical economic logic of optimization. This approach aims to determine the optimal quality level by inverting the profit maximization logic into cost minimization. It involves an analytical process to identify the quality level at which total quality cost is minimized.

Key point

Decision variables and criteria of a quality paradigm.

Analytically, the initial step in creating such a quality optimization model is to conceptualize and graph how quality cost relates to the level of quality, enabling decision-makers to choose the level of quality based on the associated cost. Quality, defined as q = 1 - d, serves as the decision variable in this framework.

The total quality cost is defined to encompass two key elements: the cost of conformance and the cost of non-conformance, further divided into their subelements of internal failure costs, external failure costs, appraisal costs, and prevention costs.

As previously noted, non-compliance or failure costs (i.e., the sum total of IFC and EFC) are negatively related to the level of quality. Reminding that quality is operationally defined as *q = 1 − d*, a quality level of zero implies a situation where d = 100%, meaning everything the system produces is defective, and the cost of such failure can be immeasurably high. In Figure 7.1, this is illustrated by the fact that the non-conformance cost curve (i.e., IFC + EFC) does not touch the y-axis when Q = 0 but points towards infinity. On the contrary, a perfect quality level of 1 (i.e., d = 0) means that nothing the system produces is defective, resulting in zero internal and external failure costs.

The cost of compliance, on the other hand, is assumed to be positively related to the level of quality. The traditional assumption is that the more you spend on appraisal and prevention measures of quality control, the more you will achieve in reducing the defects that the system produces. In Figure 7.1, the conformance cost curve (i.e., PC + AC) manifests this positive relationship.

The quality optimization logic in this paradigm operates by determining the quality level at which the total quality cost is minimized. Being the sum total of conformance and non-conformance costs (i.e., (PC + AC) + (EFC + IFC)), the total quality cost manifests its minimum where its two inversely related components intersect, designating the corresponding level of quality on the x-axis as the optimum.

Key Point:

The traditional quality cost paradigm views a lower level of quality as the optimum rather than embracing zero-defect as the standard.

To reinforce your understanding, this model's decision variable is the quality level, and the decision criterion is the total quality cost; the decision logic is cost minimization. The optimum level of quality is decided as the level at which the total quality cost is minimized. Any point other than Q_{opt} in Figure 7.1 is considered non-optimal because the total cost at any of them will be higher than that of Q_{opt}

Figure 7.1: Traditional quality paradigm

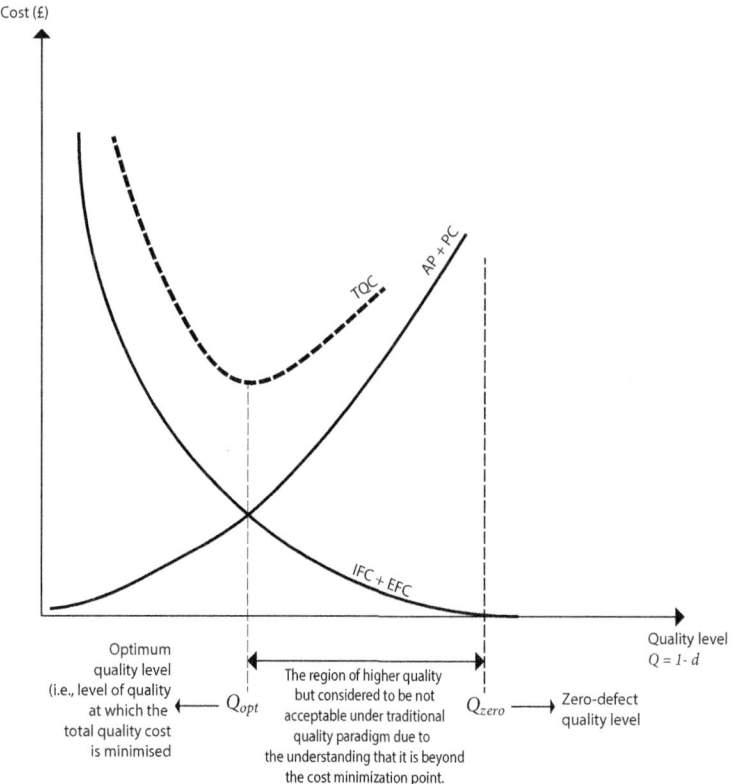

By implication, a quality level higher than Q_{opt} is to be rejected on the basis that it is 'too costly' compared to what it should be according to the neoclassical economic logic of profit maximization/cost minimization. In essence, the traditional paradigm of quality costing is neoclassically economic. It provides an economically logical basis for managers not to opt for a higher level of quality, which, nevertheless, can dangerously lead to unethical and even illegal situations, as evidenced by the now notoriously famous Ford Pinto case.

The Ford Pinto case is a well-known example often cited in business ethics and product liability discussions. In the 1970s, Ford produced the Pinto, a subcompact car, which gained notoriety due to how the company dealt with a quality issue. The key issue was the decision-making process involving a cost-benefit analysis of whether to address a potential safety flaw in the design of the car's fuel system. The Pinto had a design flaw that resulted in a series of deadly accidents where the fuel tanks would ignite, causing fires and serious injuries or fatalities. The design flaw was known to Ford management during the development and testing stage of the car, but it was decided to proceed with the defect based on a cost-benefit analysis, which estimated that the cost of correcting the defect was approximately $137.5 million compared to $49.5 million in consequential costs of letting the car go to the market with the defect. Key figures of the company's cost-benefit analysis were as follows:

Key point:
The Ford Pinto case is an illustration of the problem with the traditional quality paradigm.

Cost estimation for potential punitive damages due to the defective fuel tank

Cost component	Number of items	Cost per item	Total cost per item
180 burn deaths @ $200,000 per death	180	200,000	36,000,000
180 serious burn injuries @ $67,000 per injury	180	67,000	12,060,000
2100 burned vehicles @ $700 per vehicle	2,100	700	1,470,000
Total cost			49,530,000

Cost savings of not attending to correct the defect.

Components	number of items	cost per item	total cost per item
11 million cars @ $11 per car	11,000,000	11	121,000,000
1.5 million light trucks @ $11 per truck	1,500,000	11	16,500,000
Total savings of not attending to the defect			137,500,000

How Ford arrived at the $200,000 cost per death used in its cost-benefit analysis.

Component	Cost
Future productivity losses	
Direct	132000
Indirect	41300
Medical costs	
Hospital	700
Other	425
Property damage	1500
Insurance administration	4700
Legal and court	3000
Employer losses	1000
Victim's pain and suffering	10000
Funeral	900
Assets (lost consumption)	5000
Miscellaneous	200
Total per fatality	200725

Side note:

For a good synopsis and discussion on the Ford Pinto case, read Hoffman, W. M (2014), "The Ford Pinto," in W. Michael Hoffman, Robert E. Frederick, and Mark S. Schwartz (Editors), Business Ethics: Readings and Cases in Corporate Morality, pp. 139-144.

From 1971 to 1978, Ford faced approximately fifty lawsuits related to rear-end collisions involving the Pinto. In the Richard Grimshaw case, the jury not only awarded over $3 million in compensatory damages to the Pinto crash victims but also issued a groundbreaking $125 million in punitive damages against Ford. However, the judge later reduced the punitive damages to $3.5 million. In 1978, Ford was obligated to recall all 1971-76 Pintos for fuel-tank modifications.

This classic example highlights the dangers and ethical concerns associated with determining the level of quality solely through a cost-minimization logic within the traditional quality management paradigm.

Nevertheless, the Ford Pinto case served as a catalyst for changes in the automotive industry and beyond, leading to a paradigm shift towards a zero-defect quality approach. Companies began to recognize that quality and safety decisions should be based on criteria beyond the cost-minimization logic, considering ethical, legal, and reputational implications.

Zero-defect and continuous improvement quality paradigms

Shifting from the traditional to a 'zero-defect' quality goal involves a paradigmatic acknowledgment and acceptance that the optimum quality level should always be nothing else but zero defects. This paradigmatic shift can be explained from two interrelated angles:

1. Post-WWII discourses of quality management (especially Japanese) leading to total quality management (TQM)
2. Analytical revision to the traditional quality costing paradigm

Post-WWII discourses

Key Point:

Two ways of explaining zero-defect and continuous quality paradigms.

The history of the zero-defect quality paradigm can be traced back to the mid-20th century, with its development influenced by several key figures and movements in the field of quality management. One of the prominent figures associated with this paradigm is the Japanese industrial engineer and statistician Genichi Taguchi. However, the concept has roots in various quality improvement philosophies and practices pioneered by leading quality gurus such as Walter Shewhart and W. Edwards Deming. Shewhart, often considered the father of statistical quality control, introduced the concept of statistical process control in the 1920s. Deming, who worked with Shewhart, later became a key figure in the quality management movement and played a crucial role in Japan's post-World War II reconstruction and quality revolution.

After World War II, Japan faced the challenge of rebuilding its economy. Deming and other quality experts, including Joseph Juran, were invited to Japan to share their knowledge of statistical quality control and management principles. This period laid the foundation for the Japanese quality revolution.

Taguchi further developed the concept of zero defects in the 1950s and 1960s. Taguchi's approach was based on the idea that variation in the manufacturing process leads to product defects and that quality management should focus on reducing this variation. He introduced robust design and robust optimization methods to minimize the impact of variations on product performance.

The concept of zero defects became a key component of the total quality management (TQM) movement that emerged in the 1970s and 1980s. TQM emphasized a holistic approach to quality, involving all members of an organization in a continuous effort to improve processes and products.

Quality circles were a classic invention in the promotion of this TQM ideology. Quality circles are a concept and practice in management and organizational development that originated in Japan. The idea was popularized by Kaoru Ishikawa in the 1960s as part of the total quality management (TQM) philosophy. Quality circles involve a group of employees who voluntarily come together to identify, analyze, and solve quality-related problems. Quality circles, in effect, manifest cultural or 'soft' aspects of moving toward a zero-defect quality paradigm.

Key Point:

Japanese quality management discourses were instrumental in the evolution of zero-defect and continuous improvement paradigms.

The principles of zero defects also align with the lean manufacturing philosophy, which originated from the Toyota Production System. Lean Manufacturing aims to eliminate waste, including defects, from the production process.

The zero-defect quality paradigm reflects a shift from traditional quality control methods to a proactive approach that focuses on preventing defects rather than detecting and correcting them after production. This shift has profoundly impacted various industries and continues to influence modern quality management practices.

Revisiting the Cost Optimization Model

While industrial engineers and statisticians were exploring the engineering possibilities of reducing defects to zero through six-sigma quality management programs and associated total quality management practices, academics and accountants revisited the cost optimization model discussed earlier, paradigmatically changing the fundamental assumptions upon which it was built.

Rethinking the traditional cost optimization logic into a zero-defect paradigm involved revising the fundamental assumptions behind the way in which appraisal and preventive costs of quality would behave over the level of quality. The new assertion was that, with continuous improvements, the cost of conformance (i.e., the sum of prevention and appraisal costs) would be at its maximum when the production system reached the zero-defect level of quality. This is because, once it reaches that stage, there would be no need to incur any more preventive and appraisal costs.

This means that, as illustrated in Figure 7.2, the conformance cost curve (i.e., AC + PC) will not continue upward beyond the zero-defect level, and the total quality cost will be minimized only when the production system reaches the zero-defect point, making zero-defect, at least theoretically, the only optimal quality level, even if one adopts a cost minimization logic.

Figure 7.2: Zero-defect and continuous improvement quality paradigms

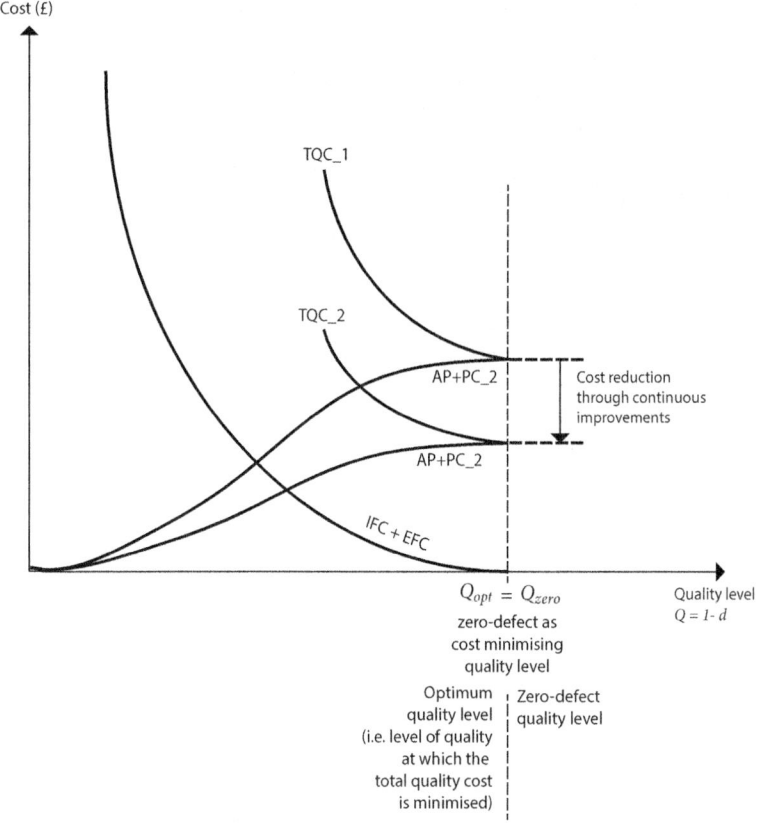

It is important to note that, even in this refined cost optimization model that validates the potential and necessity of zero-defect, the model's decision variable remains the quality level, the decision criterion is still the total quality cost, and the decision logic continues to be cost minimization. However, a paradigmatic shift in the underlying assumption regarding how costs behave across different quality levels

Key Point:

How the logic of cost minimization was adapted to justify the possibility and necessity of achieving a zero-defect quality level.

has enabled managers to reconceptualize zero-defect as the only conceivable optimality.

The concept and practice of continuous improvement further reinforce this zero-defect paradigm by emphasizing the notion that, in the long run, the firm should be capable of consistently reducing these costs (as depicted by the downward shifts in quality cost curves in Figure 7.2). This implies the theoretical possibility of achieving zero defects with no quality costs (i.e., AC, PC, IFC, and EFC) being incurred. Quality gurus argue in this context that, through various continuous improvements to production processes (e.g., the renowned *5S quality control practices*), quality management should be so ingrained in every activity that everyone in the firm performs it, thereby making everyone a quality manager. This eliminates the need for separate acts of prevention and appraisal activities independent of the routine activities already carried out by individuals as part of their normal functionalities. This philosophy is often encapsulated by the TQM slogan that quality is ubiquitous and everyone's responsibility.

Side note:

The 5S quality control practice constitutes seri (sort), seiton (set in order), seiso (shine), seiketsu (standardize), and sitsuke (sustain) and was originally implemented by manufacturing enterprises in Japan. It was then introduced to the various sector in the West as one of the total quality management techniques (Ishijima et al. 2016).

7.5 Quality costing system

As discussed earlier, quality management involves two conflicting forms of actions and outcomes. First, there is an outcome that companies strive to mitigate: failures, which are analytically categorized for managerial purposes into external and internal failures. Despite concerted efforts to avoid these undesirable outcomes, they inevitably occur, incurring costly consequences—some of which are quantifiable in financial terms, while others are not. The process of costing for quality entails attempts to estimate these costs using appropriate accounting methods, techniques, and processes. Essentially, it involves the financial estimation of the consequential costs resulting from non-conformance to quality standards.

Secondly, companies must implement a series of activities and processes to prevent the negative consequences mentioned above. As mentioned earlier, these activities are categorized as appraisal and preventive for managerial purposes and, like any other organizational activities, come with associated resource costs. Quality costing requires accurately capturing and estimating the resource costs involved in carrying out these preventive and appraisal activities and processes.

Consequently, a quality costing system is a structured framework a company establishes to capture, record, process, analyze, report, and manage the costs associated with conformance activities and non-conformance outcomes. In developing such a structured framework, consideration must be given to the following system elements (see Dale and Plunkett 2017):

1. Scope of the quality costing system.
2. Techniques and methods.
3. Reporting and assessments.

Key Point:
Critical elements of a quality costing system.

Defining the scope of a quality costing system

One of the crucial aspects of an effective quality costing system lies in clearly delineating its scope, particularly in terms of whether it will encompass the entire organization, specific departments or projects, a particular product line, a specific product, or a particular process. When designing a quality costing system, consideration should also be given to the timeframe for its implementation, whether it is a short-term initiative or a long-term, permanent element of the organization's accounting and quality management.

Defining the scope of the system facilitates the identification of specific stakeholders associated with the quality costing system. This includes determining from whom, to whom, by whom, and in what ways quality costing data and information are to be collected, reported, and utilized.

Costing techniques and methods

Recognizing that activity-based costing is now considered the most advanced and accurate costing technique, its applicability to quality costing has been well acknowledged and recognized (see Giannetti 2013; Ittner 1996, 1999). The fundamental logic of activity-based costing is that cost objects demand activities, and those activities consume resources, thereby generating costs (Kaplan and Anderson 2007). Consequently, identifying and calculating the costs of activities associated with conformance and non-conformance are at the core of an activity-based quality costing system.

Ideally, the process of designing quality costing systems begins by identifying activity centers responsible for specific conformance or non-conformance-related activities. This involves a meticulous analysis of the entire value chain, starting from supplier-related processes and activities to after-sales activities and processes. The goal is to identify how conformance and non-conformance-related activities are organized and executed. For instance, an after-sales service center handling customer complaints, returns, and repairs is a critical activity center where external failure-related activities are located. Examples of internal failure processing include a machine repair workshop and a scrap processing process. A quality management training center represents preventive activities, while activities conducted by a specific quality inspection department or a supervisor serve as examples of appraisal.

Within the context of these activity centers, costing involves the following steps:

1. Identifying and defining key activities of relevant activity centers.
2. Measuring the volumes and quantities associated with these activities.
3. Establishing cost driver rates for the identified activities.
4. Multiplying the cost driver rates by the activity volumes to determine the total activity costs for each category.
5. Aggregating the relevant activity center cost items to arrive at higher-level quality cost categories.

Key Point:

Critical steps in calculating quality cost using activity-based costing.

These five elements constitute the analytical and computational hierarchy of quality costing. Let us take an example to explain how this computation hierarchy works. This example pertains to a specific activity center that represents only a portion of the activities associated with internal failure costs. This center exclusively handles scraps of a particular variant of the product produced by the company, and several other similar centers operate for other product variants. Furthermore, there are additional incident-handling departments related to other elements of the production systems, such as machine breakdowns, raw-material handling and acceptance sampling, processing employee injuries, and so forth. The aggregation of all these activity costs constitutes the total internal failure cost calculation. Figure 7.3 illustrates this hierarchical arrangement of quality costing.

The activities at the scrap processing center are identified and categorized into four sequential steps:
- Scrap Collection,
- Scrap Classification into non-reworkable and reworkable, and based on that classification,

- Scrap Disposal,
- Transferring to the rework department.

Activity volumes are measured based on the number of scrap items processed in this sequence. The table below exemplifies how the costs of this activity center are calculated.

Cost Centre: Scrap Handling Centre 2 - Department Z						
Manager:						
Accounting Period: February 20xx						
Activity	Volume		Activity driver rate			Activity cost for the period.
Scrap collection (units)	120		£5		per unit	£600
Scrap classification (units)	120		£12		per unit	£1,440
Disposal units)	80	66.67%	120		per unit	£9,600
Transfer to rework department (units)	40	33.33%	20		per unit	£800
Total activity center cost						£12,440

Figure 7.3: Activity-based hierarchy of quality cost calculations

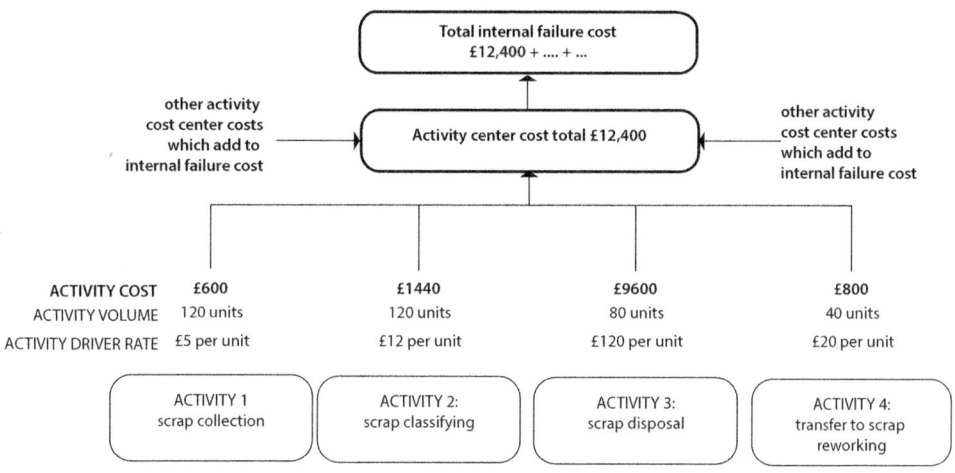

Figure 7.3 offers only a partial illustration of the total cost calculation. This calculative logic and process must be iterated in numerous activity cost centers across the organization. The integration and aggregation of these calculations form the higher-quality cost categories and subcategories for comparison, assessment, judgment, and decision-making.

Reporting and assessments of quality costs and performance

When reporting and assessing quality cost performance, it is crucial to consider the following elements:

1. Meaningful aggregation and classification: Ensure a meaningful aggregation and classification of costs into four key quality cost categories—internal failure and external failure costs (non-conformance) and appraisal and prevention costs (conformance). This enables managers to assess how costs incurred in appraisal and prevention have impacted internal and external failure costs.
2. Presentation of cost information: Present cost information in a way that highlights its relative significance, allowing managers to understand whether cost variations correspond to operational volume and capacities. Achieve this by expressing each quality cost category item as a percentage of sales.
3. Comparability of cost information: Comparatively present cost information, for example, comparing the actual cost information with:

    a. budgeted values to reveal cost variances (see Table 7.1 for a simplified example).
    b. the figures from previous years to facilitate periodic comparisons and comprehension of cost trajectories (refer to Table 7.2 for a simplified example).
    c. competitive benchmarks.

Key point:

Different forms of quality cost reporting.

Periodic comparisons and trend identification can be highly valuable in assessing the efficacy of costs of conformance. This assessment involves determining whether the cost of conformance has contributed to a reduction in costs of non-conformance. In essence, for preventive and appraisal activities to be effective, they should result in a decrease in both internal and external failure costs. Therefore, comparing conformance costs with the cost of non-conformance can reveal the following scenarios, as depicted in Figure 7.4:

1. Increase in conformance costs with a reduction in non-conformance costs:

    This favorable outcome indicates that the company has achieved a higher level of system quality, thereby reducing de-

Table 7.1: An example of quality cost variance analysis

Cost Category	Cost Item	2023 actual	2023 Budgeted	variance (bugeted - actual)	
Internal Failure Costs	Rework and Scrap	450	400	-50	ADVERSE
	Machine repairs and reset costs due to defective operations	350	300	-50	ADVERSE
	Product Design Changes Due to Defects	180	150	-30	ADVERSE
	Product Disposal	120	100	-20	ADVERSE
	Cancellation costs	60	50	-10	ADVERSE
		1160	1000	-160	ADVERSE
External Failure Costs	Cost of customer Returns	380	400	20	FAVORABLE
	warranty payments	400	500	100	FAVORABLE
	Product Liability Claims	280	220	-60	ADVERSE
	Field Service and Support	140	150	10	FAVORABLE
	Product Recalls	100	80	-20	ADVERSE
	Penalties and Fines	40	25	-15	ADVERSE
		1340	1375	35	FAVORABLE
Appraisal Costs	Inspection and Testing	580	620	40	FAVORABLE
	Quality Audits	220	220	0	FAVORABLE
	Quality Evaluation of raw materials	130	140	10	FAVORABLE
	Calibration of Measurement Equipment	80	75	-5	ADVERSE
	Product Performance Testing	110	120	10	FAVORABLE
		1120	1175	55	FAVORABLE
Prevention Costs	Employee Training on Quality	320	350	30	FAVORABLE
	Quality Management System Development	230	300	70	FAVORABLE
	Process Improvement Programs	200	250	50	FAVORABLE
	Design Reviews and Testing	150	160	10	FAVORABLE
	Quality Planning	100	110	10	FAVORABLE
		1000	1170	170	FAVORABLE

fects. Essentially, the company has invested more in preventive and appraisal activities, decreasing internal and external failure. It is ideal if the cost savings from reduced failure costs surpass the increment in conformance costs, resulting in a net positive cash flow effect in quality cost management.

2. Increase in conformance costs with an increase in non-conformance costs:

This undesirable scenario signals a fundamental issue with

Table 7.2: An example of a periodic comparison of quality costs

Cost Category	Cost Item	2022 actual	2023 actual	Increase/ decrease
Internal Failure Costs	Rework and Scrap	500	450	-50
	Machine repairs and reset costs due to defective operations	300	350	50
	Product Design Changes Due to Defects	200	180	-20
	Product Disposal	100	120	20
	Cancellation costs	50	60	10
		1150	1160	10
External Failure Costs	Cost of customer Returns	400	380	-20
	warranty payments	600	400	-200
	Product Liability Claims	250	280	30
	Field Service and Support	150	140	-10
	Product Recalls	120	100	-20
	Penalties and Fines	30	40	10
		1550	1340	-210
Appraisal Costs	Inspection and Testing	600	580	-20
	Quality Audits	200	220	20
	Quality Evaluation of raw materials	150	130	-20
	Calibration of Measurement Equipment	70	80	10
	Product Performance Testing	120	110	-10
		1140	1120	-20
Prevention Costs	Employee Training on Quality	300	320	20
	Quality Management System Development	250	230	-20
	Process Improvement Programs	180	200	20
	Design Reviews and Testing	130	150	20
	Quality Planning	90	100	10
		950	1000	50

preventive and appraisal activities. A thorough review of quality management activities is necessary to understand why they fail to achieve their intended outcomes of reducing internal and external failures.

3. Decrease in conformance cost with an increase in internal and external failure costs:

    This outcome is also suboptimal, as failure costs have risen. It suggests that the company may have scaled back on its preventive and appraisal activities, increasing internal and external failure costs.

4. Decrease in conformance cost with a decrease in non-conformance costs:

    This represents the most ideal scenario, where the company has achieved a lower defective rate cost-effectively, shifting the conformance cost curve downwards. If sustained over time, this trajectory signifies "continuous improvement" and "total quality management."

Key point:

Various scenarios for cost-based assessments of the effectiveness of quality management.

Figure 7.4: Assessing the cost efficacy of appraisal and preventive activities

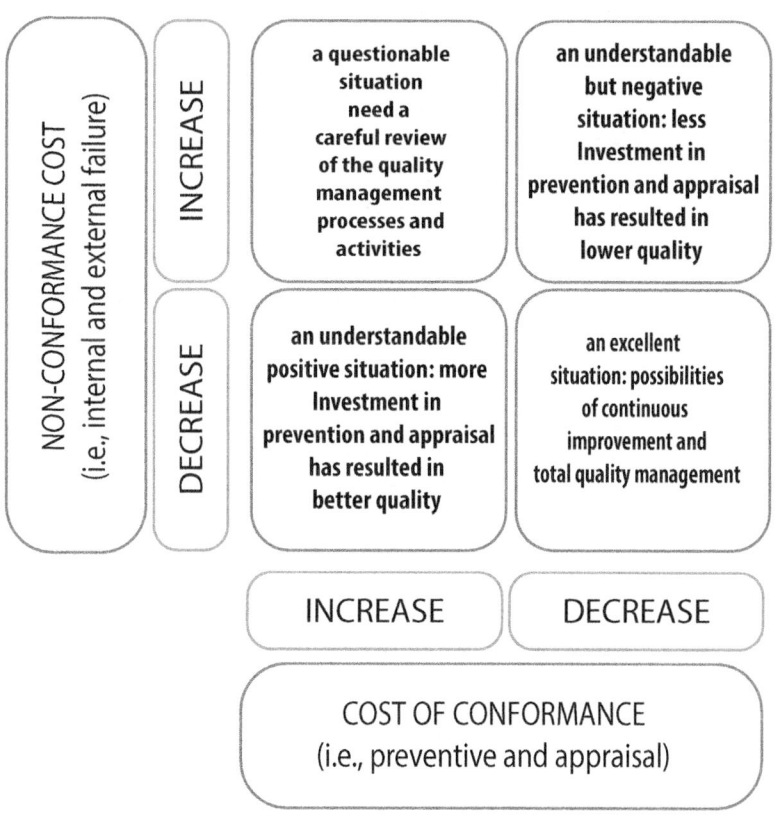

7.6 Quality-centric organizational transformations

Western companies needed to undergo certain ideological and structural transformations to align their organizational structures and practices with quality-driven post-Fordist organizational principles when prioritizing quality as a strategic imperative, especially as a strategy for facing the Japanese competition. This transformation introduced novel managerial elements in two interrelated spheres of management:

1. Introducting quality as a philosophical element of corporate leadership.
2. Japanization of organizational processes to internalize quality management as an operational reality.

Introducing quality as a philosophical element of corporate leadership

At the top managerial level, a commitment to quality has emerged as a prominent discourse. This commitment is evident in the integration of quality as a strategic imperative into the communicative frameworks of corporate strategy, including the vision statement, mission statement, and other strategic declarations made by top management. In conjunction with concepts such as innovation, creativity, flexibility, and cost efficiency, quality has begun to feature prominently in corporate discourses, reshaping organizational purpose and strategic leadership.

Key point:

Quality-centric transformations of corporate leadership.

The credibility of top management is now contingent on their dedication to quality and their ability to articulate its significance in the corporate strategy. This extends beyond product attributes and the company's ability to meet customer needs; it also encompasses how they organize and coordinate organizational units to achieve quality. Top management commitment must transcend mere rhetorical expressions and incorporate relational and structural elements.

Top management is expected to proactively introduce quality improvement agendas, typically achieved through substantial investments in specific quality improvement projects. External consultants are often enlisted for their expertise in this endeavor. To oversee these projects, cross-functional steering committees comprising senior management are established. These committees bear the responsibility for designing and implementing corporate quality improvement policies and projects, determining the applicable procedures, and monitoring outcomes (Hill 1991). They subsequently establish, monitor, and supervise middle and lower-level quality management arrangements, such as departmental or divisional quality management committees and quality circles.

Japanization of organizational processes

In the 1980s and 1990s, Japan emerged as a pivotal reference point in Western managerial reformations. Japanese firms' quality, variety, flexibility, and cost efficiency exerted significant competitive pressure on Western companies. According to Oliver and Wilkinson's (1992) survey on the Japanisation of British industry, a vast majority of companies underwent extensive managerial reforms for 'defensive' reasons—boosting competitiveness and reducing costs—to effectively face growing competition from Japanese and other East Asian competitors.

While Japanese firms presented challenges and threats, they were also viewed as opportunities—a wellspring of wisdom to reform Western firms genuinely, enhancing their flexibility and enabling the provision of high-quality products and varieties at a lower cost. Japanisation represents the historical episode of importing Japanese organizational practices to reform Western firms, aiming to enhance their flexibility, cost efficiency, quality, and variety.

In a broader sense, the Japanisation of Western management involves institutionalizing the three strategic or critical success factors mentioned earlier (i.e., quality, flexibility, and cost). It entails institutionalizing a specific set of managerial practices and ideologies for them to become ingrained assumptions and collective practices guiding organizational decisions for the benefit of the organization and its customers. These ideologies and practices came in the form of both 'hard' or 'soft' management technologies and are directed towards achieving quality, flexibility, and cost efficiency. 'Hard' technologies involve engineering elements, such as statistical process control techniques, technologies for set-up time reduction, mechanical and digital redesign of manufacturing, and cellular design of manufacture through flexible machines (see next chapter). 'Soft' technologies emphasize behavioral and cultural elements, examples being quality circles, operator responsibility for quality, and *kanban* material control.

Japanisation, in this sense, is the specific managerial movement witnessed in the 1980s and 1990s that strategized the factory floor. In this context, strategizing means reforming production processes to cater to the strategic success factors of quality, flexibility, and cost efficiency. This is achieved through a set of managerial practices that integrate the firm's capacity to address these three issues, some of which will be discussed in the forthcoming chapters. The terms 'lean manufacturing', 'total quality management', and 'just-in-time manufacturing' are often used interchangeably in literature to denote various managerial techniques, processes, and philosophies introduced by Japanese firms, particularly Toyota.

Key point:

Quality-centric transformations through Japanization.

In an overall sense, as outlined by Monden and colleagues (see Monden 1994; Monden and Hamada 1991; Monden and Sakurai 1998), Japanese manufacturing aims to increase profit in a 'slow-growing economy.' In such an environment, where market growth is minimal, competition intensifies, and sales increments can only be achieved by offering higher quality products at lower costs than competitors. Profit increases are primarily sought through 'cost reduction by eliminating waste.' Toyota's managerial revolution stemmed from innovations focused on cost reduction through waste elimination. Managerial terminologies associated with Japanese management, such as JIT, *kanban*, TQM, quality circles, '*jidoka*,' and '*shojinka*,' all contribute to this cost reduction by waste elimination. Figure 7.5 summarizes the main elements of Toyota's production system, a landmark in what we now recognize as Japanese management. While a brief description of key elements is included in the figure, readers are strongly advised to explore other sources, particularly Monden (1994), for a comprehensive techno-managerial discussion of Toyota's production and control system.

Chapter summary

The central focus of this chapter was quality costing. Before delving into the specifics of quality costing processes and techniques, it began by examining various perspectives on defining quality. The chapter explored product-based, manufacturing-based, user-based, value-based, transcendental, and social constructivist approaches to defining quality. Subsequently, an operational definition of quality is presented as the foundation for defining quality costs and elucidating the behaviors of quality costs across different levels of quality. This operational definition posits quality as the inverse of the defective rate.

Figure 7.5: An overview of Japanese quality-centric management

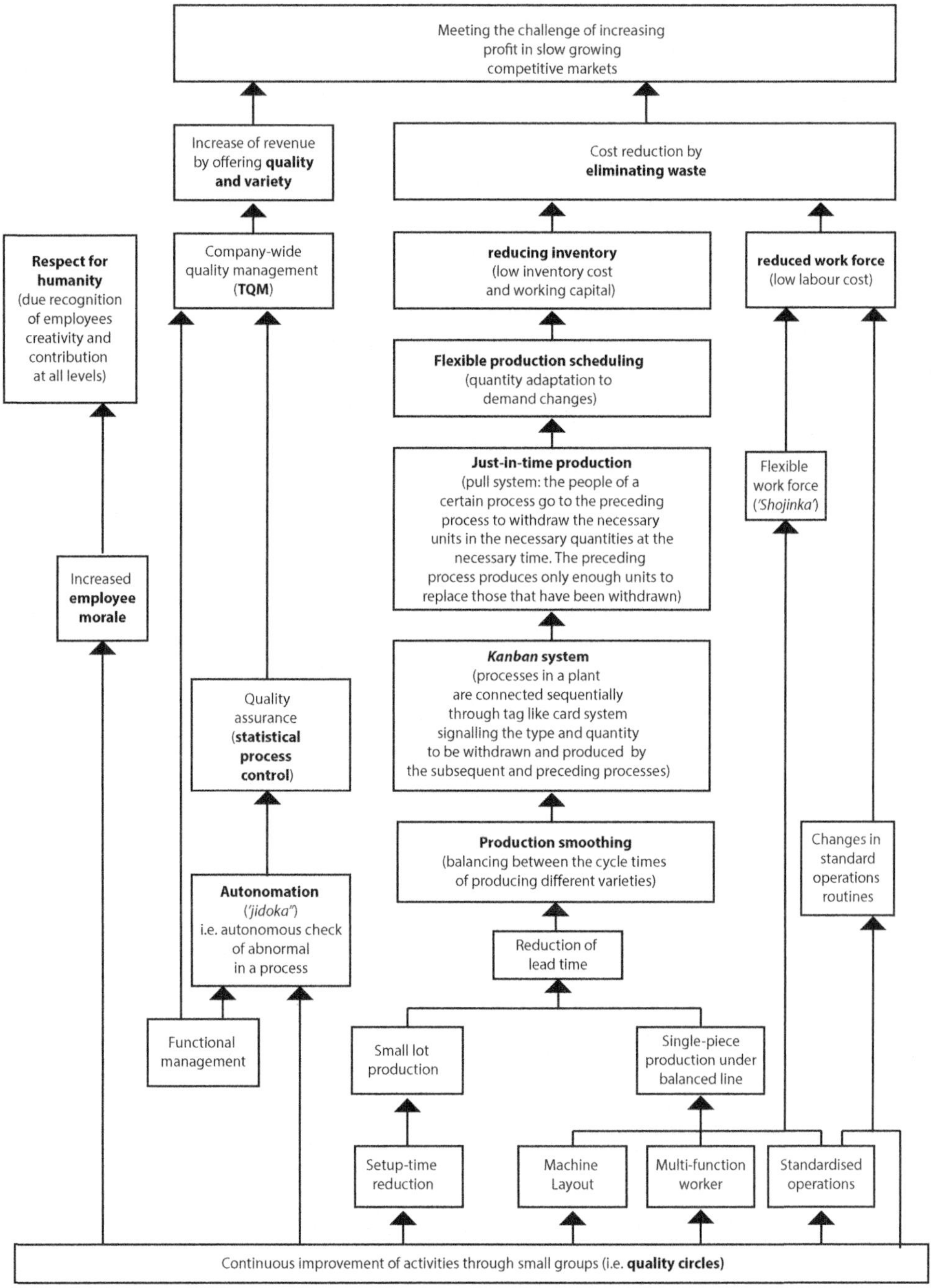

Source: adapted from (Monden 1994, 4).

In its second theme, the chapter explained the constitutive elements of the total quality cost function. Two opposingly interrelated quality cost elements constituted the total quality cost: cost of conformance and cost of non-conformance, which could be further extended into their constitutive elements of appraisal cost and prevention costs, on the one hand, and internal failure cost and external failure cost, on the other hand. These two cost categories were inversely related to each other, relating to the level of quality that a firm should have pursued. The level of quality was defined by the formula $q = 1-d$.

The third key theme of the chapter was quality cost paradigms, where the traditional quality paradigm was compared with the zero-defect and continuous improvement quality paradigms. In all these paradigms, the decision variable was the level of quality (defined as $q = 1-d$) to be decided based on total quality cost as the decision criteria, with the neoclassical economic logic of cost minimization. However, highlighting the problematic nature of the traditional quality costing paradigm, underpinning assumptions of zero-defect and continuous improvement paradigms explained how managers could appreciate the necessities and possibilities of achieving a zero-defect quality level.

Fourthly, the chapter delved into techno-managerial and calculative elements of quality costing. The possibility of using activity-based costing in ascertaining quality costs was discussed, followed by different forms of quality cost reports that could be used to assess the efficacy of a firm's quality management activities.

Finally, the chapter also explained how quality discourses, especially the Japanization movement, resulted in ideological, structural, and processual transformations in Western organizations.

Test your knowledge

1. Briefly describe how quality can be defined differently using the following approaches.
   a. Product-based
   b. Manufacturing-based
   c. User-based
   d. Value-based
   e. Transcendental
   f. Social constructivist

2. Provide an operational definition of quality based on which the quality cost behavior can be explained.
3. Explain what you meant by six-sigma quality level.
4. Briefly explain the total quality function and its sub-elements.
5. Briefly explain how those quality cost elements would vary according to the level of quality.
6. Briefly explain the decision variable, decision criteria, and the decision logic embedded in the quality costing paradigm.
7. With appropriate diagrams to help you, explain how the optimum quality level is conceptualized in:

    a. Traditional quality paradigm
    b. Zero-defect and continuous improvement paradigm

8. Briefly explain the role of Japanese quality discourses in propagating zero-defect and continuous quality paradigms.
9. List the key elements that one should consider in designing a quality costing system.
10. Glasgow Manufacturing Limited produces two different variants of a product in one of its manufacturing facilities. As a pilot project element of designing a quality costing system, the accountant extracted the following information from its cost accounting system for a specific workshop where much of the work for returned items takes place.

	Product A	Product B
Units produced	220,000	380,000
Warranty-related repairs (number of repairs)	2,100	1,400
Scrapped units (number of units)	3,600	1,200
Inspection (hours)	3,850	2,100
Quality training (hours)	120	120

Total period costs related to:	£
Warranty repairing	260,000
Scrapping and disposal	180,000
Inspecting	90,000
Quality training	60,000

Calculate the quality cost per unit attributable to each product from this repair center.

11. Using the following information, prepare a quality cost report and comment on the quality costing performance outcomes.

quality cost item	2022 Quarter 1 actual £	2022 Quarter 2 actual £	2022 Quarter 2 Budgeted £
SALES	20,000,000	25,000,000	25,000,000
Quality engineering	200,000	260,000	250,000
Scrap	32,000	29,000	30,000
Product recalls	50,000	55,000	50,000
Returns and allowances because of quality problems	30,000	29,000	30,000
Costs of sales data re-entered because of keying errors	10,000	12,000	8,000
Supervision of in-process inspection	150,000	200,000	200,000
Quality circles	90,000	90,000	100,000
Component inspection and testing	65,000	75,000	80,000
Quality training	125,000	150,000	160,000
Reinspection of reworked product	35,000	25,000	30,000
Product liability	25,000	15,000	14,000
Internal audit assessing the effectiveness of the quality system	50,000	60,000	50,000
Disposal of defective product	20,000	26,000	25,000
Downtime attributable to quality problems	56,000	30,000	40,000
Quality reporting	12,000	12,000	12,000
Proofreading	4,000	4,500	4,000
Correction of typing errors	2,500	2,500	2,000
In-process inspection	66,000	76,000	80,000
Process controls	65,000	75,000	80,000
Pilot studies	50,000	60,000	50,000
TOTAL	1,137,500	1,286,000	1,295,000

12. Briefly explain how quality-centric management discourses impacted organizational transformations in the West.

Explore further

1. Read the following three papers to enhance your understanding of quality costing.

    Ittner, C. D. (1999). Activity-based costing concepts for quality improvement. European Management Journal, 17(5), 492-500. https://doi.org/https://doi.org/10.1016/S0263-2373(99)00035-3

    Ittner, C. D. (1996). Exploratory Evidence on the Behavior of Quality Costs. Operations Research, 44(1), 114-130. http://www.jstor.org/stable/171909

    Giannetti, R. (2013). Quality costing. In F. Mitchell, H. Nørreklit, & M. Jakobsen (Eds.), The Routledge Companion to cost management. (pp. 296-319). Routledge.

2. To explore the connection between quality management, value engineering, and strategy, read Chapter 3's materials on target costing and Cooper, R., & Slagmulder, R. (1997). Target costing and value engineering. Productivity Press.

Develop your critical argumentation skills

1. Making reference to relevant quality paradigm concepts, critically evaluate the following statement by Phillip B. Crosby, a well-known quality guru: "There is absolutely no reason for having errors or defects in any product or service."
2. Drawing on the Ford Pinto case or other relevant cases in quality management, elucidate the pivotal role that legal frameworks and external environmental pressures play in compelling corporations to prioritize quality and safety.

References

Braverman, H. 1998 [1974]. Labor and monopoly capital: the degradation of work in the twentieth century. 25th anniversary ed. ed. New York: Monthly Review Press.

Burawoy, M. 1979. Manufacturing consent: changes in the labour process under monopoly capitalism. Chicago; London: University of Chicago Press.

Cooper, R., and R. Slagmulder. 1997. Target costing and value engineering. Portland: Productivity Press.

Dale, B. G., and J. Plunkett, J. 2017. Quality costing. London: Routledge.

Giannetti, R. 2013. Quality costing. In The Routledge companion to cost management., edited by F. Mitchell, H. Nørreklit and M. Jakobsen. Abingdon, Oxon: Routledge, 296-319.

Hill, S. 1991. How do you manage a flexible firm? the total quality model. Work Employment Society 5 (3):397-415.

Hoffman, W. M (2014), "The Ford Pinto", in W. Michael Hoffman, Robert E. Frederick, and Mark S. Schwartz (editors), Business ethics: readings and cases in corporate morality, pp. 139-144

Ishijima, H., E. Eliakimu, and J. M. Mshana. 2016. The "5S" approach to improve a working environment can reduce waiting time: Findings from hospitals in Northern Tanzania. *The TQM Journal* 28 (4):664-680.

Ittner, C. D. 1996. Exploratory Evidence on the Behavior of Quality Costs. Operations Research 44 (1):114-130.

———. 1999. Activity-based costing concepts for quality improvement. European Management Journal 17 (5):492-500.

Kaplan, R. S., and S. R. Anderson. 2007. Time-Driven Activity-Based Costing: A Simpler and More Powerful Path to Higher Profits: Harvard Business Review Press.

Monden, Y. 1994. Toyota production system: an integrated approach to just-in-time. 2nd ed. London: Chapman & Hall.

Monden, Y., and K. Hamada. 1991. Target costing and kaizen costing in Japanese automobile companies. Journal of Management Accounting Research 3 (Fall):16-34.

Monden, Y., and M. Sakurai. 1998. Japanese management *a*ccounting. London: Taylor & Francis.

Oliver, N., and B. Wilkinson. 1992. The Japanization of British industry: new developments in the 1990s. [2nd ed] ed: Blackwell.

Pirsig, R. M. 2011 (1974). Zen and the art of motorcycle maintenance: 40th Anniversary Edition. London: Vintage Books.

CHAPTER

8

Strategizing the point of production: **manufacturing flexibility**

8.1 Introduction

This chapter delves into the crucial concept of manufacturing flexibility, the second element within the overarching theme of strategizing the point of production. Quality and cost, covered in previous and upcoming chapters, respectively, constitute the other two pivotal elements.

In today's organizational landscape, flexibility has gained immense importance, especially in navigating the challenges of neoliberalized, globalized, digitalized, and virtualized markets. Mainstream management discourses assert that an organization's competitiveness in such a dynamic market hinges on its adeptness at flexibly responding to changes dictated by market forces. Flexibility has consistently been highlighted as crucial for competitive success (see Adler et al. 1999; Kanter 1990).

Beyond mainstream management discourse, even critical sociological analyses frequently employ the term 'flexible' to describe post-modern, post-Fordist shifts in production systems. Examples include flexible manufacturing, flexible specialization, and flexible accumulation (see Gertler 1988; Harvey 1990). Essentially, flexibility is a key concept associated with the changes observed in neoliberal transformations within production systems. While the term 'flexibility' may have varied interpretations, this chapter focuses not on providing an all-encompassing definition but on elucidating how different facets of flexibility manifest in post-Fordist production systems as a strategic imperative, emphasizing the distinct role played by management accounting.

To guide our exploration, the chapter is structured around the following themes and learning objectives:

1. Section 8.2 delves into the broader meaning of flexibility, its neoliberal political rationale, and how this rationale underpins the necessities and modes of strategizing the point of production.
2. Flexibility is not a singular concept. It is a complex phenomenon that captures a multitude of techno-managerial as well as political-institutional elements within and outwith organizations. Sections 8.3 to 8.7 explore this multiplicity of the notion of flexibility by articulating flexible consumption, flexible machines, flexible labor, flexible specialization, and flexible accumulation. In these discussions, throughout the chapter, you will appreciate not only the techno-managerial developments pertaining to flexible manufacturing systems but also the economic dynamics underpinning their evolutions. You will also understand how management accounting implicates techno-managerial and political conditions of flexible manufacturing.

Key point:

Chapter structure and learning objectives.

8.2 Neoliberal political rationale of flexibility

From our discussion in the previous chapters, we can derive two key propositions concerning neoliberal organizations, forming the foundation for the discussion of manufacturing flexibility in this chapter. Firstly, contemporary neoliberalized, globalized, digitalized, and virtualized organizations and management prioritize market dynamics to the extent that the market is viewed as the catalyst for all changes. The market has evolved into a fundamental reference point guiding the rationalization of managerial actions, turning management into the practical and rhetorical endeavor of establishing a dynamic and sustainable link between market dynamics and the activities and processes taking place within and between organizations.

Implicit in this market-centric connection is the notion that a company must exhibit flexibility in its structure, processes, and relationships to swiftly adapt to market changes. The conceptual parameters defining this market connection are encapsulated in ideas such as competitive advantage, competitive strategy, strategic pricing, target costing, strategic performance management systems, strategic management control, and organizational resilience. They all encapsulate the managerial doctrines and practices that connect the point of production with the market dynamics through strategically reinventing organizational hierarchy.

The second proposition posits that neoliberal organizations function as *biopolitical* arenas where life is set into circulation. Departing from the disciplinary confinement of bodies in specific time-space locations, characteristic of liberal modernist organizations as discussed in previous chapters and elsewhere (see Alawattage and Wickramasinghe 2019, 2022), neoliberal organizations autonomously transform themselves into sites in which life is reproduced as an entrepreneurial self (see Cooper 2015; Munro 2012). This reproduction aligns productive laborers with the economic model of neoliberal capital through concepts like human capital and entrepreneurship. Consequently, the emphasis shifts towards circulating lives by instilling self-control and entrepreneurial ambitions rather than controlling them within specific time-space confinements of production. As this chapter will further elaborate later, entrepreneurialization and the immaterialization of labor are critical in this neoliberal transformation of organizations into biopolitical entities.

One of the core ideas connecting both of these neoliberal propositions is the concept of flexibility. It has become a versatile concept operating differently in different spaces, ranging from how organizations dynamically position themselves in the market, responding to changing competitive conditions, to how they reconfigure their organizational hierarchies and systems to be agile and resilient to changing environmental dynamics. It extends to reinventing the manner in which machinery and labor are synchronized at the point of production, enabling the labor process to dynamically adjust to the techno-managerial and political-economic changes that dominate production. The idea of flexibility is, in effect, a placeholder concept whose shape and constitution take different forms contingently in relation to the context in which it is operationalized. It has a biopolitical meaning in the realm of macro politics, encapsulating notions such as "flexible accumulation" (see Harvey 1990; Hirst and Zeitlin 1991). At the same time, it has micro-organizational and techno-managerial meanings encapsulating "*anatomico-political*" ideas such as "flexible labor" and "flex-

Key point:

Two neoliberal propositions that signify flexibility.

A side note:

I am using the term 'anatomico-political' to encapsulate the power dynamics associated with understanding and controlling the human body, especially in terms of synchronizing it with the productive machinery to enhance the controllability of the body and, as a consequence, improve its economic efficiency. On the other hand, 'Biopolitical' extends the reach of power to the level of the population. It involves managing and regulating life processes as totalities, such as populations and economies.

Key point:

Multiplicity of realms in which flexibility is deployed differently but interrelatedly.

ible machines." A multitude of ideas of flexibility extends from macro to micro, from the market to the point of production, from biopolitical to anatomico-political, and from political-economic to techno-managerial. So, its meaning must be derived from the particular locational necessity for which it is deployed. To that end, I can list a set of conceptual elements with which the flexible meaning of flexibility and its strategic implications can be explored.

1. Flexible consumption
2. Flexible machines
3. Flexible labor
4. Flexible manufacturing systems
5. Flexible specialization and integration
6. Flexible accumulation.

Each of these flexibility concepts manifests in a particular realm, where flexibility is deployed differently but interrelatedly, forming a hierarchy of flexibility. The idea of flexibility should be considered simultaneously through the meanings these specific realms attribute to it and the biopolitical totality they collectively construct.

8.3 Flexible consumption

In earlier chapters, particularly Chapters 2 and 3, we explored the emerging competitive landscape characterized by neoliberalism, globalization, digitalization, and virtualization of markets, hierarchies, and networks. These conditions have given rise to segmented and fragmented markets, where distinctions among buyers hold greater importance than their similarities. This shift departs from the concept of 'monopoly capitalism,' a term coined by political economists like Braverman (1998 [1974]) to describe the Fordist mass production regime.

Key point:

Flexible consumption synthesizes customers' desires to be treated differently with the firms' strategic willingness and capacity to do so.

Gone are the days when the market was seen as a homogeneous group that could be satisfied by offering a standardized product. There is now a growing recognition that the 'one-size-fits-all' strategy is no longer viable in a highly competitive, fragmented, and segmented market. Consequently, as we discussed in Chapter 3, the cornerstone of marketing strategies in this new landscape is STP marketing – market segmentation, targeting, and positioning. The competitive dynamics have transformed into a 'war of positioning,' where producers and consumers, as well as competing producers, engage in battles across different market segments with distinct marketing mixes.

The neoliberal concept of 'flexibility' is integral to these competitive conditions, manifesting as 'flexible consumption' in the market. This term embodies two strategic intentions emanating from both customers and producers. From the customers' perspective, it signifies the power to demand variety and differences within a specific segment, rejecting the notion of a standardized product. From the producers' viewpoint, it reflects firms' capacity, albeit reluctant at times, to cater to the diverse demands of buyers.

It is important to note that the term 'flexible consumption' is often narrowly used in business press and consulting circles, primarily focusing on high-tech companies offering customizable services or consumption-as-a-service models. Terminologies used to define these initiatives include, for example, software-as-a-service (SaaS), platform-as-a-service (Paas), and infrastructure-as-a-service (IaaS), or in general, XaaS, where X can be anything provided as a service (see Deloitte 2018). In contrast, I use the term more broadly, sociologically, to describe the competitive conditionality where innovative offerings of variety and difference, such as various XaaS models, become crucial.

In this broader sense, the notion of 'flexible consumption' captures not just the fact or the possibility that consumers now consume variety and difference flexibly but also the producers' keenness and capacity to offer the variety and difference that customers demand. From the producers' perspective, considering it as a strategy, flexible consumption encompasses the strategic understanding, necessity, readiness, and capacity of the firm to offer flexibility to consumers. As a strategy and managerial mentality, 'flexible consumption' drives firms to develop the organizational capacity needed, grounded in two interlocking elements:

Key point: As a strategy, flexible consumption depends on two types of capacities.

1. Operational Capacity
2. Informational Capacity

Operational capacity for flexible consumption

The operational capacity of a firm to offer variety and differences according to the market dynamics depends on how it reconfigures its operational processes and business model. As we will further explain in the forthcoming sections, this depends on how firms bring in and mobilize fundamental elements of flexible manufacturing: flexible machines, flexible labor, flexible manufacturing systems, and flexible

Key point:

Critical elements of operational capabilities for flexible consumption.

specialization and integration. As consulting firms like Deloitte advocate, reconfiguring a firm toward a flexible consumption business model involves shifting from a sequential value chain model (where the customer is served at the end) to a customer-centric circular model of interconnections in which every element of the value creation system is directed towards the customer to create a short cycle time of service offerings. Deloitte's idea of business process reengineering towards an XaaS model is visualized in Figure 8.1.

Figure 8.1: From traditional to flexible manufacturing business model

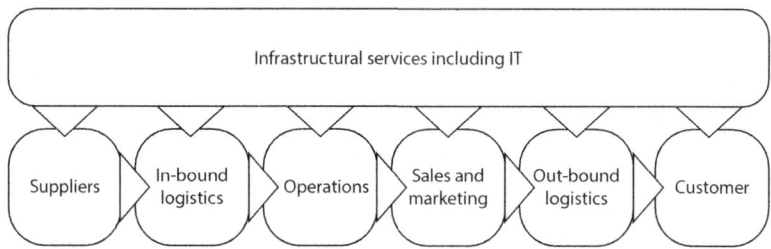

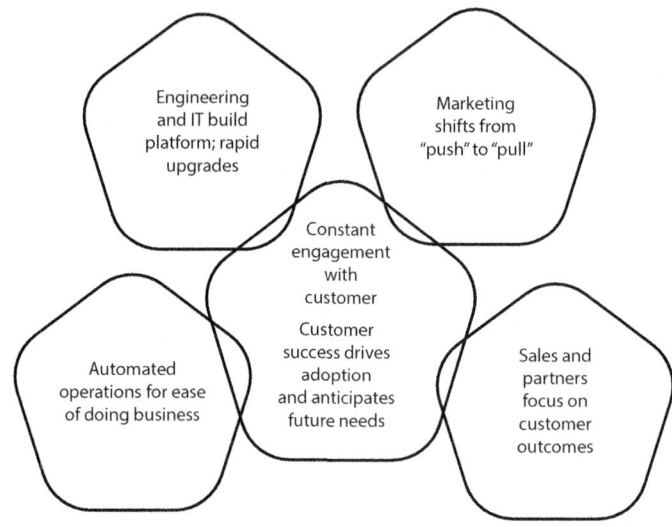

Source: based on Deloitte (2018, 4)

Informational capacity for flexible consumption

A flexible consumption regime relies on robust informational capabilities across markets, firms, and consumers to establish and sustain an effective communication network among the various components of flexible production. As we will see later (especially in the discussion on flexible manufacturing systems and flexible specialization and integration), the capacity to produce flexibly cannot be reached by individual firms on their own. It is by no means firm-specific. Instead, it demands a high degree of interfirm (as well as intrafirm) coordination, spanning across industries and other regulatory and cultural fields.

The rapid evolution of information technology, including the 'Internet of Things (IoT)' in recent decades, has greatly facilitated this coordination. For instance, supply chain management platforms and software play a crucial role in integrating different aspects of this network, such as demand planning, import/export management, inventory and warehouse management, and transportation management with delivery tracking. This integration is essentially what is referred to as 'abstract cooperation,' a concept addressed by Hardt and Negri (2000), wherein 'communicative labor' maintains connections between decentralized organizations, production systems, and sites.

In the era of flexible consumption, the focus of management accounting information needs to shift towards this new form of cooperation—abstract cooperation. This involves abstracting otherwise distant and decentralized organizational entities and consumers from their local contexts, placing them in integrated 'informational spaces', and facilitating the connection of various human and non-human elements involved in flexible manufacturing.

Key point:
Informational capacity to achieve flexible consumption goes beyond the firm, demanding "abstract cooperation" among a multitude of elements associated with flexible consumption.

8.4 Flexible machines

A firm's ability to implement flexible consumption as a strategy relies on various elements, with flexible machines among the most crucial. Broadly defined, flexible machines can alter what they produce with minimal cost and time involvement. This flexibility in production is no longer cost-prohibitive, and additional investments are minimized. At the pinnacle of the technological spectrum, notable examples include:

- Universal Robots UR5: The UR5 robotic arm is designed for flexibility, capable of handling a range of tasks in manufacturing, including welding, pick-and-place, and assembly. Its

adaptability lies in its ability to be easily reprogrammed for different applications without the need for specialized expertise.
- 3D Printers with Multi-Material Capabilities: Modern 3D printers equipped with multi-material capabilities showcase flexibility in manufacturing. These printers can produce intricate designs using various materials, allowing for the creation of diverse products with a single machine.
- Medical Robots for Surgery: Surgical robots, such as the da Vinci Surgical System, demonstrate flexibility in the healthcare sector. These robots can be adapted for different types of surgeries, providing surgeons with enhanced precision and control.

Key point:

Some examples of flexible machines.

One of the best and most easily understood examples at the lower end of the technical spectrum is the printing/copying machine or multifunction device (MFD). These machines can alter what they print and copy at almost no cost and with minimal time involved in resetting the machine. To better understand, one can contrast these machines with the older printing press models that required cleaning, typesetting, plate redoing, reinking, and other steps to undertake a new printing or copying job. This process in a modern-day printing/copying machine is just replacing the original on the copier or sending another print command from the computer.

A specific management accounting logic in these machines' functionality facilitates flexible manufacturing. These machines influence the financial calculations and rationalization of the economic production quantity (EPQ). As you have learned in your intermediary management accounting courses, the EPQ calculation involves a particular optimization logic aiming to minimize the total of inventory holding costs and production setup costs.

As depicted in Figure 8.2, the optimal production size occurs when the total cost is minimized, precisely at the intersection of holding cost and setup cost. The setup cost represents the expense associated with resetting the machine for a new production batch, essentially the cost incurred for flexing the machine for another production run.

Figure 8.2 illustrates a scenario of traditional mass production where the setup cost is relatively high (depicted by curve SC1) for each possible order size. Consequently, due to this higher setup cost, the economic order quantity remains elevated (EPQ1 in Figure 8.2). On the

Figure 8.2: How flexible machines reduce EPQ

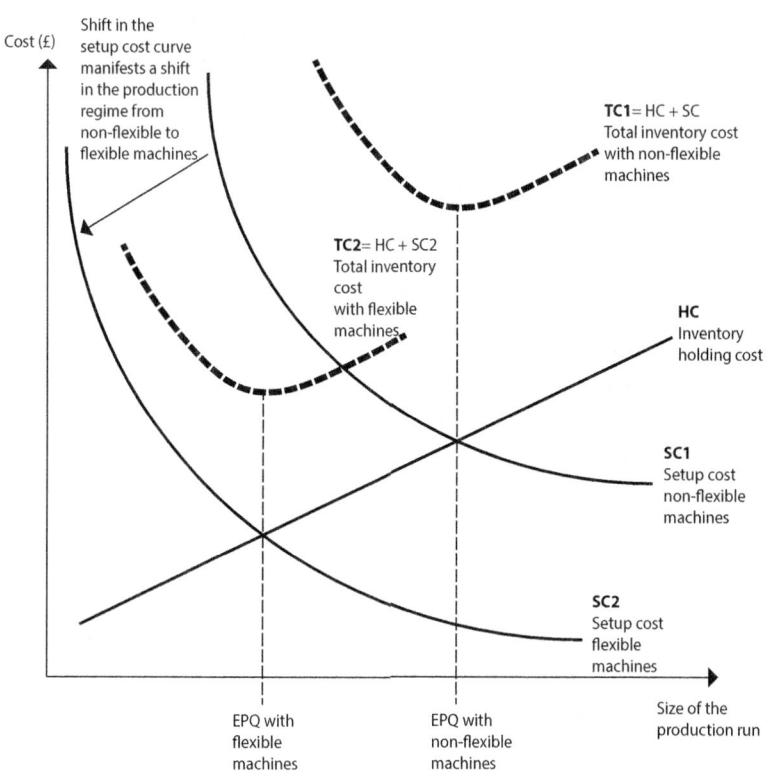

other hand, setup cost curve SC2 represents a situation involving flexible machines, where the setup cost is comparatively low for all possible batch quantities. The downward shift in the setup cost signifies the transition in production technology from non-flexible to flexible machines.

With this reduced setup cost, the EPQ decreases to EPQ2, enabling economically viable smaller batch sizes. Consequently, when the setup cost approaches its absolute minimum, nearing zero, the EPQ reaches an optimal state for perfect mass-customized production – a scenario where producing even a single unit remains economically optimal.

In addition to reducing the EPQ, flexible machines will also significantly impact the longevity of fixed capital. They eliminate the necessity to scrap and replace existing fixed machines (i.e., fixed capital) when a company needs to update its market offerings. Flexible machines can

Key point:

How flexible machines affect optimization logic of production batch size.

be reprogrammed at minimal cost, extending their technical lifespan. Consequently, the payback period for the investment in flexible machines can be extended, covering multiple product lifecycles.

8.5 Flexible labor

The third component of flexible manufacturing is flexible labor. In a broader context, flexible labor refers to forms of labor that can be easily transferred across various jobs, different skill categories, diverse production locations, different time slots, and even removed when no longer deemed necessary. Unlike the relatively fixed nature of permanent labor, flexible labor can be adjusted according to the changing labor requirements imposed by flexible consumption and adaptable machines. Two forms of labor flexibilization are pertinent here: skill flexibility and time flexibility.

Skill flexibility of labor

The essence of skill or functional flexibility is to enable firms to quickly change the division of labor without incurring additional costs and to shift workers between tasks, positions, and workplaces (Standing 2011). Since the Industrial Revolution, the division of work has not been solely attributable to the qualities and skills of the labor force itself. Instead, it often originates from the techno-managerial apparatuses of the production system. Machinery itself frequently triggers changes in the division of work. The invention and reinvention of flexible machines have thus reconstructed the division of work and the type of labor it demands, especially immaterialized labor.

Hardt and Negri (2000, 2017), in their influential work, particularly in "Empire" and "Multitude," argue that skill flexibility in these neoliberal times occurs within the "immaterialization of labor."

Immaterial labor exemplifies an 'implosion' between labor and capital, with labor now assuming many tasks formerly carried out by the agents of the capital, the management. During the early phases of capitalism and modernism, laboring activities were radically heterogeneous. Tailoring and weaving, for instance, involved incommensurable concrete actions, rendering each tailor and weaver distinct in terms of their production capabilities.

However, in computer-aided manufacturing and service production systems with flexible machines, this heterogeneity of labor is diminishing. The labor of computerized tailoring and computerized weaving now entails precisely the same concrete practices — namely, the manipulation of symbols and information. In a more pragmatic and programmatic sense, this involves selecting options from drop-down menus and checking boxes on a computer screen. Workers make choices within the technical parameters of the flexible manufacturing system so that the machine can produce the desired output. This represents a form of the immaterialization of labor, where labor increasingly engages in what is termed "symbolic-analytical labor" of problem-identifying and problem-solving (Hardt and Negri 2000, 292).

Kep point:

Symbolic-analytical labor as immaterialized labor as a form of flexible labor.

The second form of the immaterialization of labor is "communicative labor": labor engraved and enacted in computerized information networks, where the laborer's role has now primarily shifted to information processing and communication. Consequently, the labor process has predominantly become informational and communicative. In postmodern organizations, laborers are involved in producing information for "abstract cooperation", which involves maintaining connections between deterritorialized organizations, production systems, and sites. They direct production systems and the remaining material labor, dispersed across geographically distant sites, to produce goods and services according to signals from the markets.

Key point:

Communicative labor as immaterialized flexible labor.

In contrast to the old vertical industrial and corporate model, production now tends to be organized in horizontal network enterprises (Hardt and Negri 2000, 296) – outsourced, dispersed, and deterritorialized systems coordinated through communicative labor. This becomes evident when examining the global ordering of production, with communicative and symbolic labor concentrated at communication and design centers in the developed West, while the remaining deskilled material labor elements of production are distributed across still modernist and Taylorist factories in peripheral countries such as China, Vietnam, Indonesia, Bangladesh, and India. "Abstract cooperation" between them is ensured through quasi-market information networks organized in the form of franchises, supply chains, joint ventures, platform organizations, etc.

The third form of immaterialization is "affective labor", which is expressed through kin work and caring labor (Hardt 1999). As organizations increasingly evolve into biopolitical sites—environments where life itself is put into circulation in the form of, for example, entrepreneurial human capital—they must transform into spaces of care and love. Thus, organizations should not merely be sites for material production but places where lives are spent meaningfully, safely, and healthily, free from any form of harassment or discrimination. Achieving this necessitates the institutionalization of various social, cultural, family, and welfare considerations within the organizational structures, processes, and practices. For instance, aspects like physical and mental well-being, the welfare of organizational members, health and safety, equity and justice, customer care, and various other "caring dimensions" should be formally acknowledged as integral structural elements of organizations. Often re-organized into support teams, labor thus performs "affective labor" for each other, providing motivational, emotional, inspirational, cognitive, and educational support.

> **Key point:**
>
> Affective labor as immaterialized flexible labor.

In production systems employing flexible machines, as labor is immaterialized into symbolic-analytical, communicative, and affective forms, labor can effortlessly be shifted from one flexible machine to another. This is because most of these machines require similar symbolic-analytical and communicative actions. The 'physicality' that was traditionally associated with labor is now executed by machines and robot arms. Moreover, as labor now encompasses communication with machines and interactions with other co-workers through these machines, altering the division of labor and transitioning labor to new jobs, skill categories, positions, and locations has become considerably more manageable.

Time flexibility of labor

Time flexibility, on the other hand, refers to the enhanced discretion of management in temporally deploying labor. This involves labor flexibility across different timeframes, including the extension of 'normal' work hours (e.g., overtime) in contexts like 24-hour machine shops and offices with shift workers receiving standard wage rates regardless of their shift. In a broader sense, this entails augmenting managerial discretion for hiring, firing, transferring, and determining work schedules without significantly impacting labor costs. This dimension is more political than techno-managerial and involves substantial changes in the landscape and dynamics of industrial relations within and beyond organizational boundaries. Some critical political movements and trends influencing the time flexibility of labor include:

> **Key point:**
>
> Labor flexibility is political.

1. The discursive establishment of the economic policy idea that easing labor termination is essential for job creation. Transnational organizations like the IMF, World Bank, and OECD have promoted this neoliberal economic ideology, often tying it to conditions in their loan and aid packages to countries. The argument often centers on the necessity of relaxing employment protection laws to attract foreign direct investment (see Standing 2011, 31-32).
2. The global trend of outsourcing labor contracts, with companies subcontracting a significant portion of their labor while retaining core knowledge workers responsible for symbolic-analytical and communicative aspects of labor (i.e., immaterial labor). This outsourcing is prevalent in developing countries with abundant and inexpensive labor and autocratic political systems facilitating coercive labor controls.
3. Simultaneously, companies are increasingly relying on temporary labor rather than establishing a robust, long-term permanent workforce. This shift is even observed in Japan, where lifetime employment was once a defining characteristic. Temporary labor offers cost advantages, including lower wages, avoidance of experience-rated pay, reduced entitlement to enterprise benefits, and lower overall risk. Hiring someone temporarily avoids committing to a long-term relationship that might later be regretted (Standing 2011, 32).
4. The growth of project-based hiring of employees, with work often organized as short- or medium-term projects. Employment contracts have adapted to this project-based organization of work.
5. These neoliberal changes in employment practices are facilitated by the diminishing influence of trade unions as a political institution in society. The proportion of unionized labor has significantly decreased in recent decades. With limited resistance from unionized labor, employers are supported by right-wing governments advocating aggressive neoliberal reforms and right-wing media outlets promoting neoliberal ideologies to introduce more flexible labor contracts, such as 'zero-hour contracts.'

Key point

Global political movements that underpin flexibilization of labor.

Considering skill-based and time-based aspects together, flexibilization encompasses both techno-managerial and political dimensions. Unlike flexible machines, the flexible labor component of flexible manufacturing has profound political consequences that can intersect with social justice issues related to sustainable development, including concerns about modern slavery, despotic labor control regimes, job insecurity, retirement benefits, and pension shortages. These sustainability issues will be further discussed in Chapter 10.

8.6 Flexible manufacturing systems

The flexible manufacturing system (FMS) is the techno-managerial organization of the above three elements – flexible consumption, flexible machines, and flexible labor – to form a distinct mode of production. Flexible consumption constitutes its strategic intention, while flexible machines and flexible labor provide the resources, competence, and capacity to realize flexible manufacturing. An FMS is formed by combining several flexible machines into an integrated system, usually linked and coordinated by computers. Such an aggregation of flexible machines is often called a manufacturing cell. An FMS can either be a small manufacturing cell or a large cluster of manufacturing cells that form an 'assembly highway' (see Miller and O'Leary 1994).

Key point:

An FMS integrates flexible machines and flexible labor to achieve flexible consumption.

The normative end of FMS is flexible consumption – offering customers the opportunity to meet their differing and changing needs. In operational terms, this normativity is often captured by the concept of 'mass customization', which is the ability of the production system to customize its product offerings to meet differences and changes in demand patterns but with the same or a higher degree of production and cost efficiency that a mass production facility can offer. In essence, an FMS should transform a mass production facility into a better one with the capacity to produce 'heterogeneity' rather than 'homogeneity'. This is, in fact, a techno-managerial challenge because it demands that the same or a higher degree of 'economies' are achieved but with a smaller scale of production in terms of volume. In other words, the FMS is designed to integrate the flexibility of 'job shops' and the efficiency of 'mass production systems'.

Traditionally, before the FMS era, small quantities of different products were produced in 'job shops' where multipurpose machines and multi-skilled labor were occupied. However, relatively long set-up times, large work-in-progress inventories, and delays in meeting customer demands were too common in job-shop environments, resulting in a relatively higher average cost of production. Conventionally, such inefficiencies were attributed to the lack of 'economies of scale', and scale of production volume was considered to be the primary driver of efficiency. On the other hand, producing large batches of identical products using specialized machines and labor in a high throughput plant layout created massive economies of scale and much lower average costs. However, such mass production systems were not flexible enough to cater to the different and changing demand patterns. In essence, flexibility and efficiency were conventionally taken as the polar opposites of production programming.

The FMS is indeed a negation of this opposition between flexibility and efficiency. With the advances in several fields of engineering and computer technology, the FMS makes efficient mass production of flexibility and difference possible with flexible labor, flexible multipurpose machines with fast tool-changing capabilities, automated material handling systems, computer-aided design and manufacturing, and digital communication networks that connect every aspect of production and distribution (Maleki 1991). How the FMS integrates job shops and mass production systems is summarized in Table 8.1.

Key point:

FMS as a synthesis of job shops and mass production systems

Different notions of flexibility in FMS

As detailed in Table 8.1, an FMS combines the efficiency characteristic of mass production systems with the differentiating capacity inherent in a job shop system, thereby providing the capability to offer variety and differentiation. This amalgamation is made feasible through the deployment of flexible machines and a flexible labor regime, embodying both techno-managerial and political-economic conditions requisite for a flexible manufacturing system. Within a FMS, various forms of flexibility are facilitated, and operational management literature (e.g., Maleki 1991) typically categorizes them into three main groups:

Basic or element flexibilities

- Machine flexibility: This pertains to how easily a machine can handle various/different jobs and operations.
- Labor flexibility: This involves the ease with which labor can be relocated and substituted across different jobs/operations within the system.
- Material handling flexibility: This addresses how easily different parts and materials can be handled and processed by various machines and tools in the system to enable varieties

Table 8.1: Flexible manufacturing integrating job shops and mass production systems

Comparative dimension	Job shop production	Mass production	Flexible manufacturing systems
Strategic focus and intention	Quality, product variety, differentiation	Cost efficiency, speed of delivery, and production	Flexibility, quality, and customization but with cost and time efficiency
Core competence sought	Capacity to meet varieties in demand.	Capacity to produce a standardized product at a lower cost at high speed.	Customizability with lower cost and high-speed production and delivery
Nature of the fixed capital	Multipurpose machines capable of producing varieties but with a high setup cost and time as they need major retooling for varying the products.	Specialized machines needing massive reinvestments to produce varieties.	Flexible machines capable of producing varieties with no major retooling; hence setup cost and time are very minimal.
Nature of the working capital			
Labor	Skilled jack of the all-trade sort of	Deskilled, specialized in a single task/job	Flexible immaterial labor mainly performs symbolic-analytical and communicative elements with automated machines.
Inventories	Large work-in-progress inventories	Large parts and raw material inventories	Just-in-time.

Source: Alawattage and Wickramasinghe (2019, 175)

in the outputs.
- Operation flexibility: This focuses on how easily alternative operation sequences can be employed for processing a product or part.

System flexibilities

- Volume flexibility: This refers to the system's capability to operate profitably at different production volumes.
- Expansion flexibility: This denotes the ability to incrementally expand the system.
- Routing flexibility: This concerns the availability of alternative processing paths that throughput can effectively follow through a system.

- Process flexibility: This considers the number of different parts/product types that a system can produce without incurring any re-setup.
- Product flexibility: This relates to the number of different parts/product types that a system can produce with minor re-setup.

Key point:
Different forms of flexibilities in an FMS.

Aggregate flexibilities

- Program flexibility: This refers to the ability of a system to run for reasonably long periods without external intervention.
- Production flexibility: This addresses the system's ability to produce a new product design without major investment in capital equipment.
- Market flexibility: This pertains to the ability of a system to efficiently adapt to changing market conditions.

Accounting in FMS

Various calculative practices, broadly identified as emerging management accounting techniques and concepts, including, for example, activity-based costing and enterprise resource planning, are critical in enabling flexible manufacturing regimes. Such accounting techniques and concepts have now been effectively integrated into multi-platform real-time and online data management, analytics, machine learning, and intelligent software systems that can handle various aspects of flexible manufacturing, ranging from market and demand analysis to supply chain integration. Embedded in various software and analytical platforms, how management accounting operates in FMS is quite complex and, in effect, 'black-boxed'. Such systems are either 'vendor-built' (e.g., SAP) or can be 'in-house proprietary systems'. In either case, they are rather complex, multi-dimensional data management systems that carry out a multitude of accounting activities. When coupled with Industry 4.0 'smart technologies', such 'black-boxed' accounting has now become what we can call 'smart-accounting'. As contemporary 'Industry 4.0 technologies' are at the core of this technological essence of accounting in FMS, it would be a good idea to briefly introduce this concept here, especially to understand how they implicate the management accounting functionalities of flexible manufacturing.

Key point:
Industry 4.0 technologies are at the heart of how management accounting is performed in FMS.

Industry 4.0 technologies and 'smart accounting' in FMS

Industry 4.0, also known as the fourth industrial revolution, refers to the ongoing transformation of traditional manufacturing and industrial practices through the integration of modern smart technology. This concept builds upon the previous industrial revolutions:

1. First Industrial Revolution: Mechanization with the use of water and steam power.
2. Second Industrial Revolution: Introduction of electricity and assembly line mass production.
3. Third Industrial Revolution: Adoption of computers and automation.

Industry 4.0 represents a fusion of digital, physical, and biological systems. It incorporates advanced technologies to enhance automation, communication, monitoring, and data exchange in manufacturing environments. Key components and technologies associated with Industry 4.0 include (see Javaid et al. 2022; PwC 2016):

- Internet of Things (IoT): Connecting physical devices and systems to the internet, enabling them to collect and exchange data.
- Location detection technologies: Tracing the exact locations of people and things so that the flows of things and people can be effectively traced, monitored, and controlled.
- Advanced human-machine interfaces: Automated system interfaces through cameras, body scanners, and augmented wearables such as smartwatches and shoes augmented with various scanners.
- Big Data and Analytics: Utilizing large sets of data with advanced algorithms to gain insights, optimize processes, and make informed decisions.
- Artificial Intelligence (AI) and Machine Learning: Employing intelligent algorithms to analyze data, predict patterns, and make autonomous decisions.
- Cloud Computing: Storing and accessing data and applications over the internet, providing scalability and accessibility.
- Cyber-Physical Systems (CPS): Integrating computational algorithms into physical processes, creating systems that monitor and control physical processes.
- Additive Manufacturing (3D Printing): Building objects layer

by layer based on digital models, allowing for more flexible and customized production.
- Augmented Reality (AR) and Virtual Reality (VR): Enhancing human-machine interactions and providing real-time information in a virtual environment.
- Autonomous Systems: Implementing robots and machines that can operate independently with minimal human intervention.
- Authentication and fraud detection technologies.
- Mobile devices, including smartphones, that are now part of the above elements

According to PwC (2016), these Industry 4.0 technologies enable data and analytics as a core capability and lead to three critical elements underpinning the creation of 'smart industries.'

Key point:
Industry 4.0 technologies enhance the core competencies of data and analytics.

1. Digitisation and integration of vertical and horizontal value chains.
2. Digitization of product and service offerings.
3. Digital business models and customer access

Javaid et al. (2022) provide a more comprehensive understanding of how Industry 4.0 technologies enable smart accounting in FMS. Following them, we can think of four critical dimensions of Industry 4.0 smart accounting in FMA.

1. Enabling a smart factory through the *Internet of Things and robotics*. Various 'smart technologies' help machines capture, process, and communicate real-time information and become automated self-moving machines. The factory floor thus becomes a highly flexible system of production. ERP systems and their various modular elements, such as line-balancing, production scheduling, etc., constitute the management accounting functionality embedded and automated through smart technologies.
2. Enabling *integrated logistics* to create automated warehouses through smart technologies. Accounting functionalities such as inventory management are now integrated into software and digital platforms that process real-time data and analytics.
3. Enabling a *tracking system* across the supply chain from suppliers to customers through factory floors and warehouses.

Key point:

Critical dimensions of Industry 4.0 technological revolution of accounting in flexible manufacturing.

Smart technologies such as barcode and QR code scanners, image recognition technologies, automatic weight processing technologies, global positioning technologies (GPS), etc., are critical in establishing effective tracking systems.

4. Data analytics, artificial intelligence, machine learning technologies, etc., to create *data-driven management and decision-making.* Such technologies help data-driven decision-making and management by creating visual and real-time feedback information, cost and time benchmarks, compliance criteria, operational algorithms, etc. While cybernetic elements of such decision-making can now be fully automated through algorithms, exceptional conditionalities needing human managerial interventions can be effectively flagged by the systems.

Figure 8.3 illustrates these critical elements of accounting in flexible manufacturing.

Figure 8.3: How Industry 4.0 technologies enable accounting in flexible manufacturing

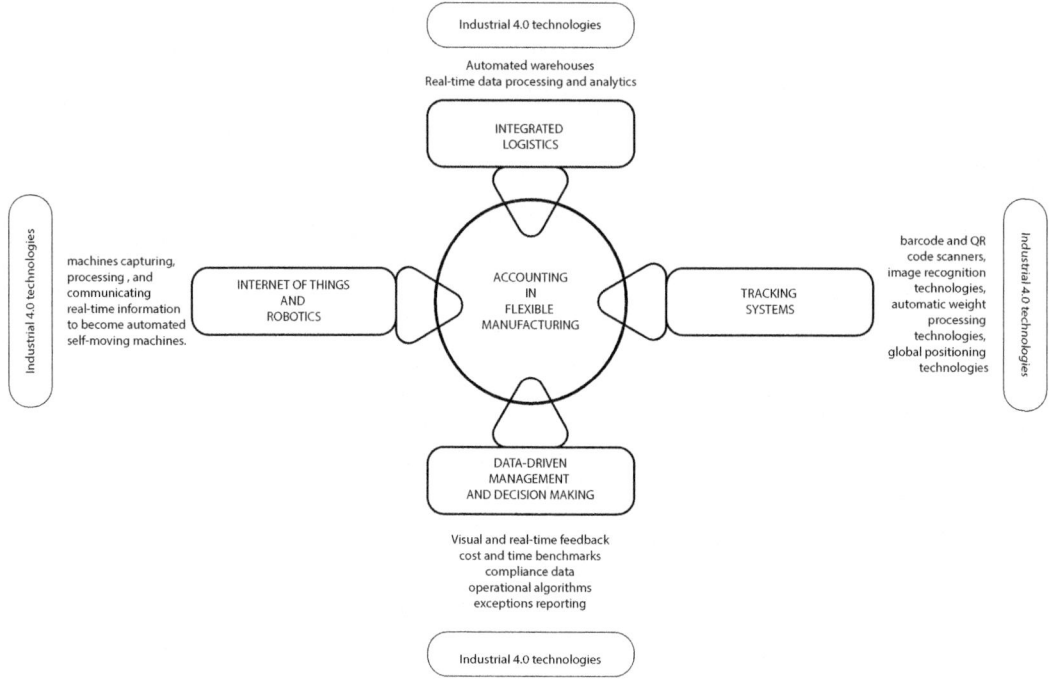

Source: adapted from Javaid et al. (2022, 52)

Synthesizing the discussion so far, the accounting functionalities of Industry 4.0 technologies related to the following capabilities that they enable:

1. Their capacity to analyze changing patterns in customer demands and preferences and identify the strategic imperatives (e.g., new product attributes) emanating from such changes.
2. Their capacity to offer financial insights into the value of differentiating 'tasks' or 'activities' that flexible machines and flexible labor carry out. In these new production environments, machines and labor cannot be meaningfully differentiated based solely on their location (i.e., cost centers), as was the case in traditional absorption costing and budgeting environments. Their value no longer emanates solely from their 'cost center location,' and the volume of output their cost center location collectively produces. Instead, their value stems from specific 'differentiating' activities they carry out. This means flexible manufacturing demands managerial attention to the particular activities that machines and labor perform. ABC terminology captures this in terms of 'activity cost drivers' and 'activity cost pools.' Proponents and adopters of ABC often argue that it provides a better calculation of the 'true' cost by capturing variations in the activities that flexible machines and flexible labor undertake. Industry 4.0 technologies enable organizations to integrate such detailed 'activity analysis' as they are performed by digitalizing, integrating, and automating activity-based costing within larger accounting systems and platforms such as ERP.
3. Their capacity to enhance communication between different elements of the FMS and, thereby, integrate the elements into a holistic system. In this regard, the provision of 'real-time information' is an essential condition that traditional budgeting and standard costing systems cannot achieve. Various computer-based and networked accounting software technologies (e.g., ERP and other supply chain management software) can achieve this essential real-time information condition (see Wagner et al. 2011).
4. Their capacity to make detailed comparisons between units, machines, individuals, and activity levels, comparing their own performances with competitors. As Miller and O'Leary (1994) explain with empirical data from their Caterpillar case

Key point:

How technology enhance 'capacities' to account in flexible manufacturing.

study, flexible manufacturing sometimes demands instilling a person-to-person sense of competition, where individuals and their tasks are directly compared with counterparts in competing firms. The calculative practices of competitor cost analysis are deployed to make this detailed comparison possible (Miller and O'Leary 1994, 23).

8.7 Flexible specialization and integration

Flexible specialization, as discussed by Piore and Sabel (1984) and Hirst and Zeitlin (1991), extends the concept of flexibility beyond the organizational boundaries of flexible manufacturing to the levels of industrial regulation and development. The argument posits that achieving organizational or production system-level flexibilities necessitates a broader set of politico-institutional arrangements. Therefore, the focus shifts to the political-institutional mechanisms that establish the necessary integration beyond organizations to meet the flexibility demands of postmodern organizations.

Key point:

Flexible manufacturing demands political strategies beyond the boundaries of the organization.

In contrast to interpretations that primarily concentrate on the techno-managerial aspects of change, the idea of flexible specialization directs attention to the politics beyond the organizational level that enable flexible manufacturing. According to Hirst and Zeitlin (1991), the distinction between such techno-managerial interpretations and the concept of flexible specialization lies in their perspectives on productive systems. Techno-managerial interpretations view productive systems as integrated and coherent totalities, while the theory of flexible specialization identifies complex and variable connections between technology, institutions, and politics. Techno-managerial interpretations perceive industrial change as a mechanical outcome of impersonal processes, whereas flexible specialization emphasizes contingency and the potential for strategic choice driven by politics.

Hirst and Zeitlin (1991, p. 10) argue that techno-managerial conceptions of industrial change (including post-Fordism) pay "little attention to the wide range of forms and hybrids of flexibly-specialized production and their social and institutional conditions". This implies that while techno-managerial explanations rely on firm-initiated reactions to the collapse of mass markets, flexible specialization contends that the strategic shift towards flexible manufacturing is "not merely the firm but inter-firm and collective regional and national patterns are crucial in the balancing of competition and co-operation necessary for their more progressive institutionalization" (ibid).

Piore and Sabel (1984) also posit that flexible specialization is not confined within the boundaries of individual organizations but is a result of micro-regulations of innovative activities across industries. They suggest that it involves "finding a compatible institutional answer to the problems of instigating and coordinating innovation, [because] competition of a wrong kind undermines the necessary coordination; misdirected coordination undermines competition" (Piore and Sabel 1984, 264-265). In other words, proponents of the flexible specialization hypothesis recognize the importance of inter-firm coordination through institutional mechanisms operating beyond individual organizational settings or markets. The transition from mass production to flexible manufacturing thus required an extra-organizational reconciliation of these apparently antagonistic principles of competition and coordination to facilitate financially viable innovations and ensure flexibility. According to Piore and Sabel (1984, pp. 265-268), this reconciliation took place in three different settings:

Key point:

Flexible manufacturing depends on extra-organizational reconciliation of antagonistic principles of competition and coordination.

1. Regional conglomerations: In the context of specialized industrial districts, regional conglomerations consist of a core comprising more-or-less equal enterprises interconnected through a complex web of competition and coordination. These conglomerations were established as 'strategic initiatives' aimed at enhancing both industry and national competitiveness. A notable illustration is Michael Porter's (1998) concept of 'industrial clusters,' which he advocated as a novel strategic arrangement for boosting national competitiveness. According to Porter:

   > Clusters encompass an array of linked industries and other entities important to competition. They include, for example, suppliers of specialized inputs such as components, machinery, and services, and providers of specialized infrastructure. Clusters also often extend downstream to channels and customers and laterally to manufacturers of complementary products and to companies in industries related by skills, technologies, or common inputs. Finally, many clusters include governmental and other institutions – such as universities, standards-setting agencies, think tanks, vocational training providers, and trade

associations – that provide specialized training, education, information, research, and technical support.

2. **Federated enterprises:** As exemplified by the pre-war Japanese *zaibatsu* and the more loosely structured post-war federations of Japanese enterprises, Federated enterprises played a pivotal role in steering Japan's industrial development toward flexible specialization. Miyajima (1994) identifies six corporate groups of this type in Japan. Among them, Mitsu, Mitsubishi, and Sumitomo originated as pre-war zaibatsu and were organized as corporate groups in the early 1950s. On the other hand, Fuyo, Sanwa, and Daiichi, which were originally large banks before the war, coalesced into corporate groups in the late 1960s.

Key point:

Three forms of industrial institutional arrangements to facilitate flexible manufacturing.

The distinctive features of these federated enterprises or corporate groups included cross-shareholding, a principal bank system, intermediary roles for trading companies, presidents' clubs, cooperative investments among member companies, and the sharing of financial, marketing, and technological expertise among member corporations. However, as noted by Piore and Sabel (1984, 267), these groups lack the same level of integration found in mass-production corporations. Member firms are not arranged hierarchically, but their collective identity is more pronounced compared to firms in regional conglomerates or industrial clusters.

3. **Solar firms and workshop factories** exemplify a form of coordination in innovative activities described as "firms with a solar-system model of orbiting suppliers and its close cousin, the workshop factory" (Piore and Sabel, 1984, p. 267). In contrast to the subordinate linkages found in divisions of a multi-divisional mass producer, the connection between suppliers and the factory is collaborative. In this model, the solar firm relies on subcontractors not merely as subordinates but as partners, seeking their input to address design and production challenges. The example Piore and Sabel provide is the Boeing Company, which produces neither the engines nor much of the avionic equipment for its airplanes.

In essence, the flexible specialization thesis extends the evolution of flexible manufacturing beyond organizational boundaries to the sphere of inter-firm coordination and competition. It emphasizes the significance of micro-regulatory institutional arrangements between firms and industries to reconcile competition and coordination—a necessary structural condition for the development of flexible manufacturing regimes.

8.8 Flexible accumulation

The concept of flexible accumulation further extends the idea of flexibility beyond its organizational and industrial boundaries to encompass the global dynamics of capital and labor. Here, the focus is on the "new capitalism" arising from micro-organizational changes in production systems, relationships, and technologies. Political economists employ various terms to characterize this new form of capitalism, such as the "post-industrial paradigm" (Halal 1986), "disorganized capitalism" (Lash and Urry 1987), and "just-in-time capitalism" (Swyngedouw 1986). In essence, the concept of flexible accumulation consolidates the techno-managerial discussions in previous sections and situates them within the broader framework of transformed capitalism. Swyngedouw (1986), for instance, elucidates this transformation in terms of shifts in production processes, labor, industrial space, state, and ideology. Harvey (1989) interprets "flexible accumulation" as a transformation in the patterns of international trade, business accumulation, profit rates, exchange rates, capacity utilization, property boom, and the structure of labor markets. Regardless of the terminology used, these scholars link flexible manufacturing to the macro dynamics of global capitalism. In this broader sense, flexible accumulation refers to post-Fordist capitalism, where the flexibilization of both capital and labor is central to the accumulation process. Flexible accumulation offers a specific theoretical framework explaining how the circulation of labor and capital through flexibilization became more critical than disciplinary confinement.

Key point:

The concept of flexible accumulation situates flexible manufacturing in the broader political economy context of 'new capitalisms'.

To identify elements of neoliberalization (i.e., integrating lives into circulation through biopolitics) within this transformation, it is crucial to scrutinize the changes in labor markets under the flexible accumulation regime. A modern Fordist production regime is characterized by a large blue-collar, unskilled workforce, often with long-term employment contracts and job security ensured through union negotiations with employers. The majority of the labor force is concentrated on factory floors, constituting the "core group" in the "primary labor market." Flexible accumulation refers to a different global order

Key point:

Flexible conditions of labor control are achieved through the circulation and peripheralization of labor.

of production. As depicted in Figure 8.4 and explained below, during the flexible accumulation regime, this core is diluted and dispersed to the periphery through various forms of labor contracts and labor market innovations, minimizing the core element of labor. Flexible conditions of labor control are achieved through the circulation and peripheralization of labor.

Figure 8.4: Circulation and peripheralization of labor to enable flexible manufacturing

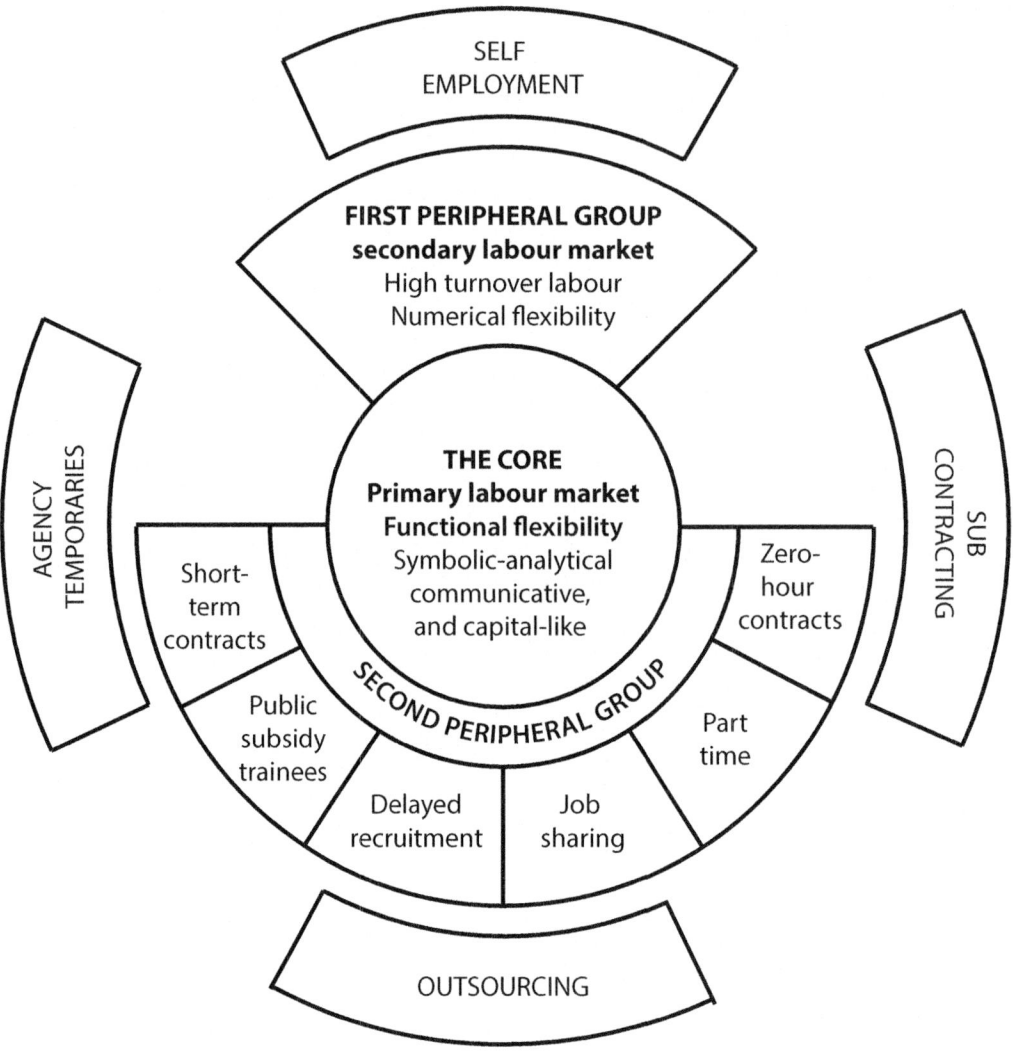

Source: adapted from Harvey (1990, 151)

The global reorganization of production illustrated in Figure 8.4 facilitated flexibilization, enacting and enabling different forms of labor flexibilities at the core and peripheries. At the core, which is primarily located in the Western centers, 'functional flexibility' is achieved through techno-managerial consolidation of capital-like symbolic-analytical and communicative labor. The core refers to the steadily shrinking group of employees primarily involved in what strategic management experts identify as dealing with strategic or core competencies (Prahalad and Hamel 1990). This group, often comprising top and middle management, plays a pivotal role in determining the company's strategic intent, shaping its vision and mission, and establishing collaborations through diverse partnerships and networks. These networks serve as conduits for the distribution of a significant portion of production and distribution activities, enabling the creation of the first and second peripheries to which non-core activities are distributed. For instance, Prahalad and Hamel (1990, p. 80) attribute NEC's business success to its organizational restructuring around the concept of 'core competencies':

Key point:

In the flexible accumulation regimes of global production, the 'core competencies' are concentrated in the centers of global capitalism.

> NEC articulated a strategic intent to exploit the convergence of computing and communications, what it called 'C&C' ... adopted an appropriate 'strategic architecture' ... [which] constituted a 'C&C Committee' of top managers to oversee the development of core products and core competencies ... put in place coordination groups and committees that cut across the interests of individual businesses ... determined that semiconductors would be the company's most important 'core product' ... entered into myriad strategic alliances – over 100 as of 1987 – aimed at building competencies rapidly and at low cost ... almost all the collaborative arrangements in the semiconductor-component field were oriented towards technology access. As they entered collaborative arrangements, NEC's operating managers understood the rationale for these alliances and the goal of internalizing partner skills. NEC's director of research summed up its competence acquisition during the 1970s and 1980s this way: "From an investment standpoint, it was much quicker and cheaper to use foreign technology. There wasn't a need for us to develop new ideas."

By nature, their roles are communicative and symbolic-analytical (i.e., immaterial labor), often aligning with the category of capital, specifically intellectual or knowledge capital, rather than traditional labor. They function more like dealers, networkers, collaborators, co-

> **Key point:**
>
> The core labor market constitutes a privileged capital-like managerial labor.

ordinators, and ultimately strategists aiming to capitalize on 'opportunities' brought to them by others. For this reason, akin to owners of capital (despite not having a financial stake in the business), they lay claim to a portion of profits through various forms of corporate performance-based compensation schemes rather than individual performance assessments. These employees hold full-time permanent positions and are central to the organization's long-term future, enjoying job security, promotion prospects, and opportunities for re-skilling, along with relatively generous pension, insurance, and fringe benefit rights. Nevertheless, this core is expected to remain adaptable, flexible, and, if necessary, geographically mobile (Harvey, 1989, p. 150).

While this core is increasingly acquiring the dominating features and capabilities of capital, the rest of the workforce is 'strategically' drawn to the periphery through "myriad strategic alliances" (see the above quote from Prahalad and Hamel (1990, 80)). As Harvey (1989, 150) explains, this peripheralization involves creating two rather different sub-groups:

> **Side note:**
>
> Here, the term "numerical flexibility" refers to the firm's ability to easily adjust the size of its workforce—expanding or contracting—without incurring significant costs associated with hiring and firing.

> The first consists of full-time employees with skills that are readily available in the labour market, such as clerical, secretarial, routine and lesser skilled manual work. With less access to career opportunities, this group tends to be characterized by high labour turnover which makes work force reductions relatively easy by natural wastage. The second peripheral group provides even greater *numerical flexibility* and includes part-timers, casuals, fixed term contract staff, temporaries, sub-contractors and public subsidy trainees, with even less job security than the first peripheral group.

> **Key point:**
>
> The first and second peripheral labor market segments constitute precarious labor.

The "appropriate strategic architecture" (see the above quote from Prahalad and Hamel 1990, 80) that makes this peripheralization possible includes letting various hitherto internal functionalities of the corporation go out. Experts who were previously managing support and service functions (e.g., security, labor contracting, research and development, training and development, process design, advertising, and even accounting and finance) would be 'encouraged' to set up their own enterprises and be self-employed in providing those support services as outsourcing companies. Different corporate functionalities are thus loosened from the core and are placed in quasi-market arrangements, facilitating the flexible labor and circulation of both labor and capital. As Guy Standing (2011) argues, and as Figure 8.4 illustrates, precariat classes of labor are constructed at the first and second peripheral segments.

Chapter summary

Flexibility was discussed as a multi-faceted and multi-level phenomenon with a broader set of techno-managerial and cultural-political implications. On its first strategic front, organizations confront flexibility in terms of 'flexible consumption'—a managerial acknowledgment of the imperative for competitive companies to provide customers with a greater choice in terms of product variety and customization. Flexible consumption needs to be comprehended as both a strategy and a managerial philosophy. Consequently, flexible consumption demands and compels firms to develop organizational capacity to deliver it. This capacity relies on two interlocking and interrelated elements. The first is the capacity to produce flexibly, and the second is the information capacity across markets and firms to construct and maintain an effective network of communication between various elements of producing flexibly. These capacities are achieved through flexible machines, flexible labor, and their organization into flexible manufacturing systems.

Flexible manufacturing systems realize the strategic intention of flexible consumption by bringing together flexible machines and flexible labor through various technologies that we can broadly conceptualize in terms of Industry 4.0 technologies. Collectively, they techno-managerially enable basic or element flexibilities, system flexibilities, and aggregate flexibilities, which are the different forms of flexibilities critical in achieving the strategic intentions of flexible consumption. In a multitude of ways, Industry 4.0 technologies make flexible manufacturing possible on a large scale by enhancing the data and analytical competencies across factory floors, warehouses, supply chains, and managerial hierarchies. Internet of things and robotics, integrated logistics with automated warehouses, digital and real-time tracking systems, and data-driven decision-making and management are critical dimensions of flexible manufacturing enabled by various Industry 4.0 technologies. Management accounting functionalities are now integrated and 'black-boxed' into platforms and software systems created through such technologies.

However, achieving flexibility is a strategic action that transcends organizational boundaries, necessitating extra-organizational and inter-organizational coordination across various agencies to form strategic alliances between firms, such as regional conglomerations, federated enterprises, and solar firms, and workshop factories. The concept of flexible specialization captures this extra-organizational element of industrial arrangements pertaining to flexible manufacturing.

The concept of flexible accumulation takes the notion of flexibility a step further into the global dynamics of capital and labor. Here, the focus is on the "new capitalism" that micro-organizational changes in production systems, relations, and technologies have brought about. Political economists use various terms to characterize this new form of capitalism, including the post-industrial paradigm, disorganized capitalism, just-in-time capitalism, and so on. In essence, flexible accumulation encompasses everything discussed in other sections—flexible consumption, flexible machines, flexible labor, flexible manufacturing systems, and flexible specialization—placing them within the broader schema of transformed capitalism.

After all, flexibility is a techno-managerial as well as political phenomenon enabled and enacted through a multitude of elements: flexible consumption, flexible machines, flexible labor, flexible manufacturing systems, flexible specialization, and flexible accumulation. Table 8.2 summarizes their ordering and interconnection.

Table 8.2: The hierarchy of flexibility concepts

Flexibility concept	Realm of operation and scope of analysis
Flexible consumption	Market/consumer and consumer-firm connection
Flexible machines	Fixed capital – firm level, technological
Flexible labor	Labor – firm level, techno-managerial and political
Flexible manufacturing systems	Firm-level – techno-managerial
Flexible specialization and integration	Industry/meso level – inter-firm coordination
Flexible accumulation	The total capitalist system, labor markets, capital markets, core-periphery distribution of labor and capital.

Test your knowledge

1. Briefly explain why flexibility should be considered a strategic imperative alongside quality and cost management.
2. List the six key concepts associated with flexible manufacturing.
3. Explain flexible consumption, paying special attention to how it synthesizes the strategic intentions of buyers and producers in a competitive market.
4. List and explain the two forms of capacities that a producer needs to build to operationalize flexible consumption as a strategic intention.
5. Differentiate between the traditional business model and the flexible manufacturing business model.
6. What is meant by a flexible machine? Explain using appropriate examples.
7. Using classical economic optimization logic pertaining to production batch size, explain the management accounting logic of flexible machines.
8. Explain the notion of flexible labor, paying attention to the skill and time aspects of flexibilization.
9. Drawing on Hardt and Negri's notions of the immaterialization of labor, explain how the nature of labor is transformed in high-tech production systems with digitally connected flexible machines. Pay special attention to the following concepts:

    a. Symbolic-analytical labor.
    b. Communicative labor.
    c. Affective labor.

10. List and explain some critical political-economic dynamics underpinning the time flexibilization of labor.
11. What is an FMS? Briefly explain.
12. Explain how an FMS synthesizes traditional job shop production systems and mass production systems.
13. With suitable examples of subcategories, briefly describe the following types of flexibilities associated with an FMS:

    a. Basic or element flexibilities.
    b. System flexibilities.
    c. Aggregate flexibilities.

14. Explain what is meant by Industry 4.0.
15. List key technologies that constitute Industry 4.0.
16. Explain how Industry 4.0 technologies enable flexible manufacturing.
17. Explain how Industry 4.0 technologies complicate management accounting functionalities in a flexible manufacturing environment.
18. Briefly explain the theory of flexible specialization.
19. What are the different types of industrial arrangements that facilitate the evolution of flexible specialization?
20. Explain the concept of flexible accumulation.
21. In relation to the concept of flexible accumulation, explain the following:

    a. The core.
    b. First peripheral group.
    c. Second peripheral group.

Explore further

1. There are numerous online consultocratic discourses on flexible manufacturing, encompassing promotional materials from consulting firms and software vendors such as SAP. Identify the key organizational actors involved, such as Big Four accounting firms, major consulting firms, and leading software and platform vendors. These sources offer valuable insights into the evolution of Industry 4.0 technologies and their impact on reshaping the industrial landscape. Select a few prominent materials as a sample for review.

    Utilizing sociological and theoretical concepts introduced in this chapter, particularly the theory of flexible accumulation, compose an essay titled "Industry 4.0 Capitalism."

2. Using the materials reviewed for task 1, elucidate how technology providers, as highlighted, consider the notion of sustainability in their efforts to advance "Industry 4.0 Capitalism."

Develop your critical argumentation skills

1. Write an argumentative essay on the theme:

   "While techno-managerial innovations at the point of production play a critical role, there are equally important political-economic and regulatory dynamics that underpin the possibilities of achieving flexible manufacturing."
2. Craft an argumentative essay on the theme:

   "In ever-evolving regimes of flexible manufacturing, the management accounting functionalities become 'black-boxed' into highly complicated software and analytical platforms, yet their functionalities matter more than ever."
3. Develop an argumentative essay on the theme:

   "Regimes of flexible manufacturing, politically characterized by flexible accumulation, point to a global order of production where the tyrannies of labor control are peripheralized to the Third World while a privileged class of labor is created at the centers of contemporary capitalism."

References

Adler, P. S., B. Goldoftas, and D. I. Levine. 1999. Flexibility versus efficiency? A case study of model changeovers in the Toyota production system. Organization Science 10 (1):43-68.

Alawattage, C., and D. Wickramasinghe. 2019. Strategizing management accounting: liberal origins and neoliberal trends. London: Routledge.

———. 2022. Strategising management accounting: liberal origins and neoliberal trends. Accounting, Auditing & Accountability Journal 35 (2):518-546.

Braverman, H. 1998 [1974]. Labor and monopoly capital: the degradation of work in the twentieth century. 25th anniversary ed. New York: Monthly Review Press.

Cooper, C. 2015. Entrepreneurs of the self: the development of management control since 1976. Accounting, Organizations and Society 47:14-24.

Deloitte. 2018. The shift to flexible consumption: how to make an "as a service" business model work. Deloite Insight.

Gertler, M. S. 1988. The limits of flexibility: comments on the post-Fordist vision of production and its geography. Transactions of the Institute of British Geographers 13 (4):419-432.

Halal, W. E. 1986. The new capitalism. New York; Chichester: Wiley.

Hardt, M. 1999. Affective labour. Boundary 2 26 (2):89-100.

Hardt, M., and A. Negri. 2000. Empire. Cambridge, Mass.; London: Harvard University Press.

———. 2017. Assembly: Oxford University Press.

Harvey, D. 1989. The condition of postmodernity: an enquiry into the origins of cultural change. Oxford: Basil Blackwell.

———. 1990. Flexible accumulation through urbanization reflections on "post-modernism" in the American city. Perspecta 26:251-272.

Hirst, P., and J. Zeitlin. 1991. Flexible specialization versus post-Fordism: theory, evidence and policy implications. Economy and Society 20 (1):5 - 9.

Javaid, M., A. Haleem, R. P. Singh, and R. Suman. 2022. Enabling flexible manufacturing system (FMS) through the applications of industry 4.0 technologies. Internet of Things and Cyber-Physical Systems 2:49-62.

Kanter, R. M. 1990. When giants learn to dance: Free Press.

Lash, S., and J. Urry. 1987. The end of organized capitalism. Cambridge: Polity.

Maleki, R. A. 1991. Flexible manufacturing systems: the technology and management. Englewood Cliffs, N.J.: Prentice Hall.

Miller, P., and T. O'Leary. 1994. Accounting, "economic citizenship" and the spatial reordering of manufacture. Accounting, Organizations and Society 19 (1):15-43.

Miyajima, H. 1994. The transformation of zaibatsu to postwar corporate groups—from hierarchically integrated groups to horizontally integrated groups. Journal of the Japanese and International Economies 8 (3):293-328.

Munro, I. 2012. The management of circulations: biopolitical variations after Foucault. International Journal of Management Reviews 14 (3):345-362.

Piore, M. J., and C. F. Sabel. 1984. The second industrial divide: possibilities for prosperity. New York, N.Y.: Basic Books.

Porter, M. E. 1998. Clusters and the new economics of competition. Harvard Business Review 1998 (November-December):77-90.

Prahalad, C. K., and G. Hamel. 1990. The core competence of the corporation. Harvard Business Review 1990 (May-June):79-90.

PwC. 2016. Industry 4.0: Building the digital enterprise: 2016 Global Industry 4.0 survey. www.pwc.com/industry40: PWC.

Standing, G. 2011. The precariat: the new dangerous class. London: Bloomsbury Academic.

Swyngedouw, E. 1986. The socio-spatial implications of innovations in industrial organisation: JIT manufacturing and regional production milieus. In Working Paper, No.20, Johns Hopkins European Center For Regional Planning and Research.

Wagner, E. L., J. Moll, and S. Newell. 2011. Accounting logics, reconfiguration of ERP systems and the emergence of new accounting practices: A sociomaterial perspective. Management Accounting Research 22 (3):181-197.

CHAPTER

9

Strategizing the point of production: **strategic cost management**

9.1 Introduction

After exploring a range of strategic themes that delineate how strategies are enabled and enacted in sites of strategic actions – the market, organizational hierarchy, and the point of production – we have now come to almost the end of this textbook. Two key strategic themes remain: cost management and sustainability. Earlier chapters delved into a comprehensive list of strategic themes, including market positioning, pricing, performance management, management control, organizational resilience, quality, and flexibility. All these themes are intricately interconnected and interdependent, enabling firms to navigate the strategic challenges of neoliberalized, globalized, digitalized, and virtualized competitive landscapes.

Strategic themes of cost management and sustainability climax this interdependency and interconnectivity; they are the ultimate strategy themes into which everything else can be encapsulated. In terms of strategic cost management – the subject matter of this chapter – this encapsulation is operational and processual, manifesting how a firm would reconfigure its vertical and horizontal ordering of economic relationships to ensure that it produces strategically advantageous value propositions for its stakeholders. Sustainability – the subject matter of the next chapter – manifests this encapsulation by explaining how such vertical and horizontal ordering of value creation enhances or disturbs the ecological and socio-political orders that have a bearing on everyone's collective future existence and well-being on this planet.

As sites where strategies are enabled and enacted, the market, organizational hierarchy, and point of production are not mutually exclusive. How a firm interconnects these sites through its decisions and actions within and across them enables and enacts strategies, creating competitive advantages. For example, decisions and actions pertaining to the marketing mix variables predominantly concern how a firm should position itself in the market vis-à-vis its competitors. However, these decisions and actions are also related to how such decisions are made and actions are organized within the organizational hierarchy. Additionally, they are connected to how a value chain is designed and implemented to produce and deliver the value proposition that constitutes the positioning strategy.

Similarly, strategic performance management, strategic control, and organizational resilience are predominantly hierarchy-related issues. Nevertheless, they must also address how the performances of individuals, teams, and larger administrative units are managed, controlled, and made resilient to market vulnerabilities at the point of production. Quality and flexibility primarily concern how value-creation processes at the points of production are designed and managed, but they are always in relation to the market dynamics that the performance management and control apparatuses of the hierarchy can communicate to the points of production.

Key point:

How cost management links to the other strategic themes covered in the book.

Cost management encapsulates and underpins this triadic interdependency between the market, hierarchy, and the points of production much more vigorously, as costs are an inherent occurrence in all of them. Even though, schematically, I have located strategic cost management in the domain of the point of production; its presence is much more pervasive. Therefore, the elements to be discussed under the theme of strategic cost management encapsulate themes already covered in the previous chapters. Strategic cost management invites us to revisit them to see how cost underpins everything else's possibilities of being strategic.

This chapter delves into the overarching theme of strategic cost management, structured as follows:

1. Section 9.2 serves as a prelude to strategic cost management. It examines the traditional approach to cost management, focusing on the role of responsibility accounting, which includes standard costing and budgeting. This section will en-

able you to understand the structures and methods of traditional cost management and to recognize their strategic limitations.
2. Section 9.3 delves into the realm of strategic cost management. It contrasts the concept of strategic cost management as a holistic program with its role as a surveillant assemblage. This section aims to highlight the complexities in perceiving strategic cost management as a unified framework.
3. Section 9.4 focuses on activity-based costing and management (ABC/M), a cornerstone of strategic cost management. You will explore the strategic implications of ABC/M, particularly its impact on manufacturing flexibility, quality management, continuous improvement, and strategic market positioning.
4. Section 9.5 revisits target costing, initially discussed in Chapter 3, but from a strategic cost management perspective. This section offers a refresher on Chapter 3's content and demonstrates how target costing functions within strategic cost management.
5. Section 9.6 provides an overview of lean manufacturing, emphasizing its role as the techno-philosophical foundation for various strategic cost management concepts and methods.
6. Section 9.7 examines enterprise resource planning (ERP), introducing its historical context and the key modular elements of contemporary ERP systems.
7. Section 9.8 explores throughput accounting (TA) and the theory of constraints (TOC). This section focuses on capacity optimization as a critical aspect of cost management.
8. Section 9.9 concludes the chapter with a comprehensive summary.

Key point:
Chapter structure and learning objectives.

9.2 From costing to cost management: the traditional approach

Since wealth accumulation became synonymous with capital accumulation at the inception of capitalism, notions of cost and cost management were formalized into accounting, embodying the calculative apparatuses of capital. Accounting facilitated the periodic calculation of the rate at which wealth is accumulated in the form of capital, recognizing that profit represents the rate at which capital accumulates within a specific accounting period. A double-entry bookkeeping sys-

Key point:
How costing became integral to capitalist enterprises.

tem, incorporating a capital account wherein the net difference between revenue and costs in a given accounting period is recorded, laid the foundational calculative groundwork for this process. Since then, cost calculations or costing have become indispensable to the operation of any capitalistic organization, as they are crucial for periodic profit assessments.

Key point:

Lack of cost management in mercantile capitalism.

However, the possibility of cost management emerged only later with the advent of factories during industrial capitalism. Before that, in the mercantile phase or form of capitalism, capitalists would purchase goods from farmers, craftsmen, and guild masters, selling them in the output markets for a profit. Their ability to 'negotiate' in these markets was the fundamental competitive condition that determined their costs and revenue. Costs primarily consisted of prices established in the factor markets (i.e., prices paid to source the goods-for-sale as well as services such as transport, warehousing, etc.). Cost management was the capitalists' and their agents' capacity to negotiate a cheaper price, either 'diplomatically' or 'coercively,' leveraging whatever powers they possessed, as seen in the case of colonial trade. Such negotiations were often reinforced by despotic forms of labor controls available to the capitalists at that time to expedite the work associated with such trading.

Key point:

The invention of the factory as a historical condition in cost management.

During this mercantile phase, capitalists did not 'own' the 'processes of production' but merely purchased the output of processes owned and traditionally managed by farmers, craftsmen, and guild masters. Consequently, capitalists had little or no control over the cost and volume of production to meet the demands of the output markets in which they sold what they bought. The solution to this problem was the factory, where capitalists began acquiring labor instead of the product the labor produced and controlled the labor itself to manufacture goods they sold in output markets at the required costs and volume.

For Marxist accounting researchers such as Hopper and Armstrong (1991), this shift was driven by the historical necessity of subordinating labor to the interests of capital. Meanwhile, for Johnson and Kaplan (1987a, 1987b), it represented the invention of a hierarchical system of production where transaction costs could be minimized compared to those in the market. According to Foucauldian accounting researchers (see Hopper and Macintosh 1993), the factory became a 'disciplinary institution' where labor was synchronized with productive machinery through principles and techniques disciplining the body, mind, and time.

Standardization as a basis of traditional cost management

From this 'disciplinary' perspective, what emerged during that period wasn't merely the physical site known as the 'factory'. Inextricably linked to this pivotal spatial innovation was a more potent 'discipline,' now recognized as manufacturing or industrial engineering. In this context, a 'discipline' denotes a distinct body of knowledge (such as medicine, industrial engineering, etc.) established and institutionalized as a 'science' that is independent of, and alternative to, the knowledge embedded in craftsmanship, tradition, religious dogma, and the workers' cultural knowledge of their work and existence. A discipline encapsulates 'scientific' principles, strategies, techniques, and practices involving normalization/standardization, surveillance, hierarchical examination, and regulation. Initially, the "Scientific Management Movement," pioneered by Frederick W. Taylor and others, embodied a 'disciplinary' approach to cost management through the "rationalization of work," which encompassed "standardization" (see Alawattage and Wickramasinghe 2019, 35).

Key point:

Cost management's disciplinary roots.

From its early beginnings, one of the most critical elements of cost management has been the idea of standardization and standards. Initially emerging through the scientific management practices of motion and time studies, standardization refers to the process of prescribing, for each job, the 'standard method' and 'performance levels' in terms of time and quantities. Once standard time and quantities are determined, they can be coupled with standard prices and rates of payments to arrive at cost standards. Cost standards thus represent the monetary value of job processes and outcomes when they are carried out at the best efficiency levels established by management. They embody the ideal conditions of production to be achieved; standard costs are those ideal conditions of production expressed in accounting terms.

Standard costing and variance analysis thus became the bedrock of traditional cost management. Organized within accountability structures and relations of 'responsibility accounting,' as discussed in Chapter 4, standard costing can provide a distributed system of cost management where actual costs are compared with standard costs to identify cost variances, holding responsibility center managers responsible and accountable for such variances. In a responsibility accounting system of cost management, standard costs provide the basis for preparing budgets. Budgets serve as the foundation upon which costs are authenticated, and performances are assessed across various cost centers distributed vertically and horizontally across the organization.

Understanding the connection between standard costing and budgeting is essential because their integration forms a comprehensive and organization-wide profit planning and control system. The link between the two is established by the fact that they share five common principles (Boyns 1998, 265):

Key point:

The connection between budgeting and standard costing.

- The establishment of predetermined standards or targets of performance.
- The measurement of actual performance.
- The comparison of actual performance with predetermined standards.
- The disclosure of variances between actual and standard performance and the reasons for such variances.
- The suggestion of corrective actions if necessary.

Coupling standardization with budgeting

However, it should be noted that, though interrelated, they are not absolutely interdependent. Standard costing systems can operate without budgeting in any given organization and vice versa. Nevertheless, their usefulness could be limited in either of these isolated applications. On the other hand, one can be supplementary and value-adding to the other. Therefore, integrating the two can result in a better system of profit planning and control. Their integration is sought because their best applications are in different areas, and their approaches are different. Listed below are such differences.

- Standard costing's historical roots are linked to the scientific management movement discussed above, whereas budgeting has historically longer roots, connecting it to the practices of the state bureaucracy.
- Standard costing is generally applied in manufacturing activities, i.e., to 'standard cost centers,' where output can be measured, and input required to produce each unit of output

can be specified. Typically, non-manufacturing activities are often not incorporated within standard costing. On the other hand, budgeting can also be applied to non-manufacturing activities. Though budgeting can also be singularly applied to manufacturing activities, it would benefit much if coupled with standard costing.
- Budgets relate to an entire activity or operation. A standard, on the other hand, presents the same information on a unit basis. Hence, standard costing often provides the basis upon which budgeted figures can be calculated.
- Budgeting represents a top-down approach. That means the preparation of budgets starts with estimates and forecasts on aggregated figures such as sales, profits, and production targets and then goes down to elementary budgets such as material purchase budgets and labor usage budgets, etc. Standard costing, on the other hand, employs a bottom-up approach: it starts with predetermined standards pertaining to individual units and goes on to calculate aggregates on the basis of actual volumes.
- Budgeting provides figures on future targets, i.e., management expectations for the budget period. On the other hand, standard costing provides 'figures that should have been' pertaining to the realized level of performance for that period.
- Budgeting is more on management's planning and delegation functions, while standard costing is more on the controlling function.

Key point:
Differences between budgeting and standard costing and how their integration provides a comprehensive system of cost management.

These differences and common principles imply that there are both unique and shared domains of operations for budgeting and standard costing. Figure 9.1 illustrates these domains and also the link between them. Not only that, it also outlines an integrative ideal system of profit planning and control.

Processual elements of traditional cost management and profit planning

We can now delve into Figure 9.1 to elucidate how traditional cost management operates within a responsibility accounting system of standard costing and budgeting.

1. Within the realm of standard costing, there are established standards for output and input of materials, labor, and pro-

332 | Strategic Management Accounting: a critical exploration

Figure 9.1: Standard costing and budgeting as cost management and profit planning

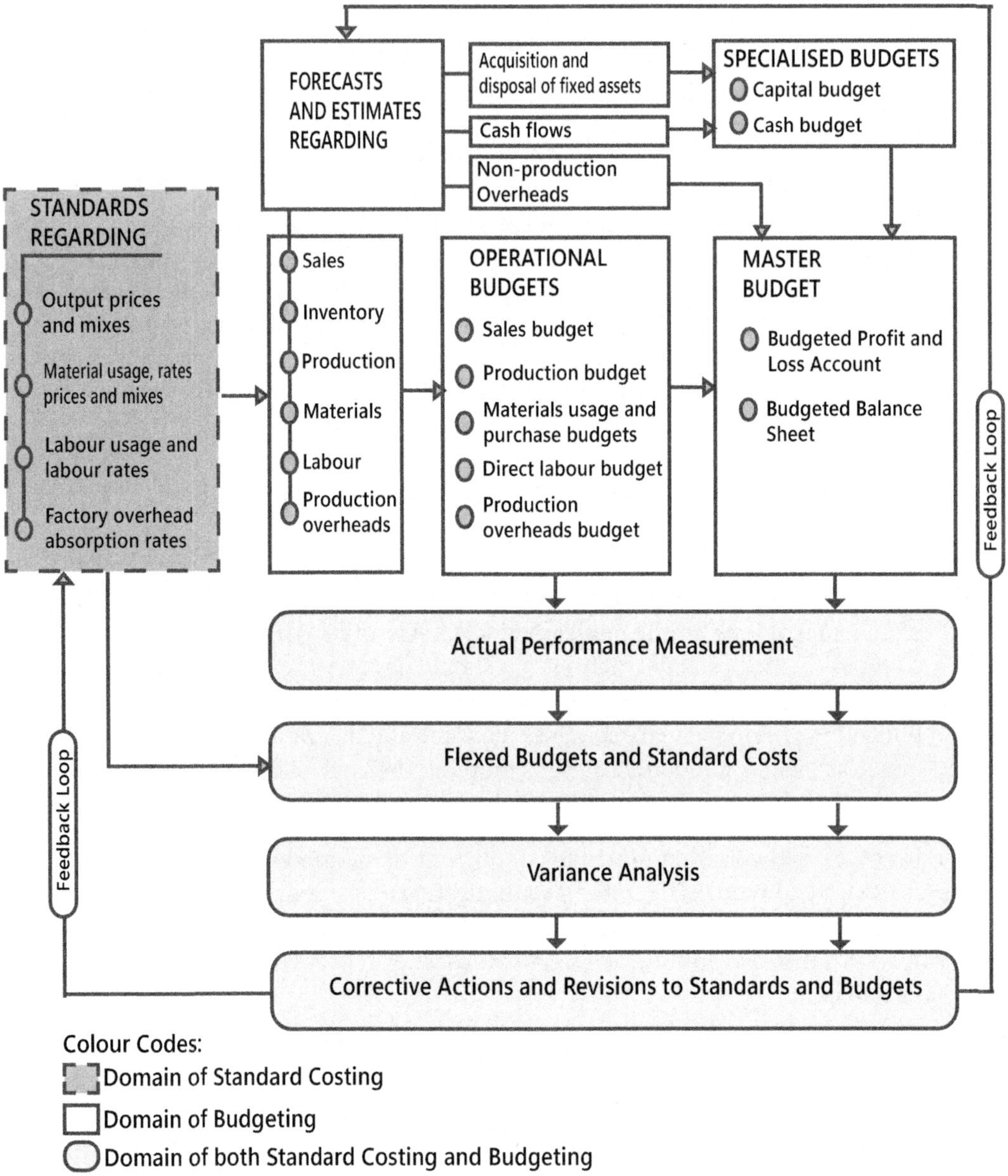

STANDARDS REGARDING
- Output prices and mixes
- Material usage, rates prices and mixes
- Labour usage and labour rates
- Factory overhead absorption rates

FORECASTS AND ESTIMATES REGARDING
- Acquisition and disposal of fixed assets
- Cash flows
- Non-production Overheads
- Sales
- Inventory
- Production
- Materials
- Labour
- Production overheads

SPECIALISED BUDGETS
- Capital budget
- Cash budget

OPERATIONAL BUDGETS
- Sales budget
- Production budget
- Materials usage and purchase budgets
- Direct labour budget
- Production overheads budget

MASTER BUDGET
- Budgeted Profit and Loss Account
- Budgeted Balance Sheet

Actual Performance Measurement

Flexed Budgets and Standard Costs

Variance Analysis

Corrective Actions and Revisions to Standards and Budgets

Colour Codes:
- Domain of Standard Costing
- Domain of Budgeting
- Domain of both Standard Costing and Budgeting

duction overheads. These standards typically encompass standard prices/rates of input and output, standard mixes of output and input, and standard usage of input (e.g., labor hours per unit of output, material consumption per unit of output, etc.,). These standards are usually set during the design stage of products and manufacturing processes and are often revised based on subsequent manufacturing and selling experiences. Non-accounting functions such as Operations Management, Research and development, and Marketing provide essential information to establish these standards.

2. Within the purview of budgeting, there are periodic forecasts and estimates related to aggregate levels of operations for the company and its major subdivisions. These include forecasts and targets for sales, production, and inventory levels, among others. These forecasts are often derived from corporate planning or strategic planning exercises for the entire company and operational programs for its major subdivisions. Long-term planning exercises determine strategic goals, such as market share and sales, which are translated into annual (and even quarterly and monthly) sales targets, forming the basis for other estimates like production and purchases.

3. Operational budgets within the budgeting domain represent targets for major operational aspects such as sales, production, material usage, material purchase, direct labor usage, and production overheads. These budgets, expressed in quantitative and/or monetary terms for a budget period, are derived by combining standards with budgetary estimates.

4. In the realm of budgeting, there are forecasts and estimates concerning 'non-operational' aspects of the business, including acquisitions and disposals of fixed assets, cash flows, and non-production overheads. These estimates are sourced from various functional departments. Cash flow estimates, for example, relate directly to sales and purchases and debt collection and credit settlement policies.

5. These forecasts and estimates provide information for specialized budgets, namely the capital budget (containing approved capital expenditure plans) and the cash budget (showing the budgeted cash position of the firm on a monthly timeline). These specialized budgets, along with operational budgets and estimates on non-production overheads, are

Key point:

The budget-based process of traditional cost management.

summarized in the master budget, which includes the budgeted profit and loss account and the balance sheet.
6. The budgets so prepared provide a managerial framework guiding day-to-day managerial actions and decisions, with specific objectives for managers at various divisions, departments, and levels. Managers are delegated the authority and responsibility to ensure these budgetary objectives are met. However, at the end of the budget period, actual performance may deviate from expectations, necessitating examining any variances and analyzing specific reasons for them.
7. Variance analysis, the intersection of standard costing and budgeting, requires 'flexing' the budgeted figures to reflect actual performance levels. This involves updating the 'static budget' using elementary standards—standard prices/rates, labor, and material usage standards, etc.—with actual volumes. In this context, variances represent the differences between 'flexed' and actual budget figures.
8. Variance analysis provides a hierarchical structure to understand the reasons for the difference between budgeted profit and actual profit. Profit variance is initially explained by sales and cost variances, which are then analyzed into elementary categories: material cost, labor cost, and overhead. Total cost variances for each cost element are further analyzed into their causes, such as price and quantity variances.

9.3 Strategic cost management

The traditional cost management regime, as previously discussed, was deemed "irrelevant" " (see Johnson and Kaplan 1987a) in light of the new competitive conditions ushered in by the "strategic turn". Various critiques were raised against traditional cost management systems, underscoring their inadequacy in addressing the challenges posed by the evolving competitive landscape.

For instance, the "beyond budgeting movement" in mainstream accounting research contended that conventional budgets exhibited excessive rigidity and inflexibility. They were criticized for overly fixating on predetermined targets, employing a time-consuming annual planning cycle, placing disproportionate emphasis on inputs rather than outcomes, and fostering internal competition for resource allocations within organizations (see Hope and Fraser 1997, 2000, 2001, 2003a, 2003b).

Similarly, in connection with the traditional budgeting system's inability to adapt to the dynamism and complexity of the new competitive conditions outlined in Chapter 1, many argued that responsibility accounting lacked a sufficiently strategic orientation. A thorough examination of diverse consultocratic discourses advocating for a strategic approach to cost management reveals the following fundamental issues with the traditional approach, which, they believe, must be corrected to achieve the requirements of a strategic approach to cost management as follows.

- Focus on historical data: Traditional budgeting relies heavily on historical data and past performance as a basis for future projections. In dynamic industries, historical data may not accurately reflect future conditions. Strategic cost management should emphasize forward-looking approaches that consider future trends, innovations, and disruptions.
- Lack of alignment with strategy: Traditional cost management systems may not be directly aligned with an organization's strategic goals. In contrast, contemporary competitive conditions require a close alignment between cost management practices and overall business strategy. Companies need to allocate resources in a way that supports their strategic objectives.
- Inability to capture non-financial metrics: Traditional cost management systems often focus solely on financial metrics, overlooking non-financial aspects that are increasingly important in today's business environment. Factors such as customer satisfaction, innovation, and employee engagement are crucial for long-term success and cannot be adequately addressed by financial metrics alone.
- Globalization and complex supply chains: Many businesses operate in a global context with complex supply chains. Traditional cost management systems may struggle to capture and account for the intricacies of global operations, making it challenging to manage costs effectively. Strategic cost management recognizes the need to account for global factors and complexity.
- Technology and automation: The rapid advancement of technology has changed the way businesses operate. Traditional cost management systems may not fully leverage technology and automation to streamline processes and reduce costs.

Key point:

Non-strategic characteristics of traditional cost management and desires of strategic cost management.

Strategic cost management embraces technology to enhance efficiency and competitiveness.
- **Customer-centric focus:** In contemporary business environments, there is a growing emphasis on customer satisfaction and value creation. Traditional cost management may not sufficiently address the need to align costs with customer value. Strategic cost management emphasizes understanding customer needs and aligning costs accordingly.
- **Lean and agile principles:** Modern business practices often adopt lean and agile principles to improve efficiency and responsiveness. Traditional budgeting and standard costing may be too bureaucratic and hinder the implementation of lean and agile practices that are essential in a competitive landscape.

In summary, the shift towards a strategic approach to cost management is driven by the need for flexibility, alignment with strategic goals, consideration of non-financial metrics, adaptation to technological advancements, and responsiveness to dynamic market conditions. Traditional budgeting and standard costing may fall short of addressing these requirements, making them less relevant in today's competitive business environment. These ideas basically encapsulate what we already discussed in the previous chapters. This was one of the reasons for me to emphasize at the beginning of this chapter that strategic cost management is a theme that demands us to revisit all the themes we covered in this book.

Strategic cost management as a holistic program and surveillant assemblage

Key point:

Concepts of holism and assemblage: two theoretical dispositions to explain strategic cost management.

A strategic cost management system endowed with such qualities and capabilities would not adhere to a highly structured hierarchical model, contrasting with traditional responsibility accounting systems discussed earlier. Instead, it would manifest as a diverse and dynamic amalgamation of technologies, techniques, processes, and practices. It would be paradoxically oriented towards often contradictory strategic imperatives such as accurate costing, control, regulation, return on investment, multi-dimensional performance evaluation, strategic positioning, quality, flexibility, innovation, continuous improvement, customer satisfaction, sustainability, resilience, and more. Acknowledging the multiplicity and complexity inherent in contemporary neoliberal cost management practices, Alawattage and Wickramasinghe

(2019) characterize strategic cost management as both a "surveillant assemblage" and a "holistic program."

Theoretically, these two terms represent contradictory dispositions, manifesting paradoxically distinct understandings of cost management. Nevertheless, they coexist to signify the paradoxical nature inherent in contemporary cost management technologies and practices.

The concept of cost management as a holistic program reflects the aspiration for unity and essence. Its operation is characterized by convergence—the intention to bring disparate elements together to form a comprehensive unity capable of generating synergistic value. Within this holistic framework, strategy is perceived as the force that engenders this unity. As discussed in the preceding chapters, there exist various discourses on costing, cost management, performance management, management control, organizational resilience, and more. These discourses endeavor to harness the concept of strategy as a unifying principle in organizational decision-making and actions.

Such discourses signify efforts to reconcile otherwise diverse and sometimes contradictory elements and intentions. For instance, Porterian and Kaplanian discourses regarding strategy, performance, and cost management encapsulate ideas of holism. According to Kaplan and colleagues, an effective strategy should amalgamate financial, customer, internal process, and learning and growth perspectives when operationalized in a framework of balanced scorecards and activity-based management (ABM). This amalgamation forms a holistic management program rooted in analysis, costing, and management of 'activities'.

Key point:

Holism in strategic cost management.

Similarly, Porterian ideas of strategy, as discussed in Chapter 2, strive to create a holistic approach to strategy-making through a unified conceptual framework. This framework integrates market strategies and actions with the value chain, utilizing strategic choices of differentiation and cost leadership based on analyses of industry structure, value chain, and competitors' profiles.

Therefore, when viewing various cost management practices such as ABC/M, target costing and value engineering, ERP supply chain management, throughput accounting, etc., as part of a holistic program, the objective is to understand how they come together to form a synergetic totality. The aim is to comprehend how these techniques and methods collectively form a cohesive whole that can be conceptualized as strategic cost management. Holism requires us to construct a comprehensive picture of strategic cost management, akin to assembling a jigsaw puzzle, where various costing techniques and methods neatly fit as pieces to constitute the larger picture.

The disposition of holism, however, can appear illusory when considering the evolving and increasingly diverse nature of cost management technologies and practices. The unity and essence of these technologies become elusive as they take on a multitude of forms and directions. While strategy discourses and their advocates strive to integrate systems, practices, and technologies into a holistic framework of strategy and strategic thinking, the outcome of their endeavors often deviates from the intended unity, resulting in a multiplicity. In this context, understanding strategic cost management (or any other strategic phenomenon) as an assemblage proves useful.

Key point:

The idea of assemblage to understand strategic cost management.

The theoretical construct of assemblage is from Deleuze and Guattari (1987, 1994). A quote from Nail (2017, 22) provides a well-articulated and insightful description of what we can take from Deleuze and Guattari's idea of an assemblage.

> In contrast to organic unities, for Deleuze and Guattari, assemblages are more like machines, defined solely by their external relations of composition, mixture, and aggregation. In other words, an assemblage is a multiplicity, neither a part nor a whole. If the elements of an assemblage are defined only by their external relations, then it is possible that they can be added, subtracted, and recombined with one another ad infinitum without ever creating or destroying an organic unity. This is what Deleuze and Guattari paradoxically call a "fragmentary whole" (What is Philosophy? 16). The elements of the assemblage are "not pieces of a jigsaw puzzle," they say, but like a "dry-stone wall, and everything holds together only along diverging lines" (What is Philosophy? 23). Each new mixture produces a new kind of assemblage, always free to recombine again and change its nature.

Assemblages thus consist of a multiplicity of heterogeneous objects. From this theoretical perspective, strategic cost management embodies this heterogeneity by combining and recombining technologies, techniques, concepts, and practices, forming a "fragmented whole." Technologies, techniques, concepts, and practices are continuously added, subtracted, and recombined within this "fragmented whole," rendering it consistently fragmented and perpetually open to recombination, thereby changing its nature. These additions, subtractions, recombinations, and fragmentation occur as events. For instance, the addition of activity-based costing and the subtraction of absorption costing from the assemblage of cost management unfold as a series of events.

Therefore, when considering strategic cost management as an assemblage, it is essential to perceive and comprehend the elements of strategic cost management as a series of 'events' that construct its heterogeneity and fragmentation. This contrasts with viewing them as jigsaw puzzle pieces contributing to a holism. An event, within the context of Deleuze's theory of assemblage, is a significant happening or occurrence that disrupts the stability of an assemblage. Events introduce novelty and unpredictability, causing the assemblage to undergo transformation. Events are not predetermined or pre-existing; rather, they emerge from the immanent processes within the assemblage itself. Deleuze and Guattari emphasize the non-linear and open-ended nature of events in the context of assemblages. Events do not follow a predetermined script or teleological trajectory but introduce new possibilities and potentialities. The transformative impact of an event can lead to the reconfiguration or reorganization of the elements within the assemblage (see Patton 1997). The subsequent sections of this chapter delve into this perspective by elucidating the 'eventuality' of various techniques and practices that are now recognized as elements of strategic cost management. Tracing something's eventuality involves considering something as an event and tracing its connections to its preceding and proceeding events.

Key point:

The necessity of seeing elements of strategic cost management as events.

The concept of surveillance plays a central role in elucidating the eventualities of cost management techniques and practices. Strategic cost management operationalizes heterogeneous and fragmented surveillance when seen as "surveilent assemblages" (Haggerty and Ericson 2000). This occurs not necessarily in a hierarchical manner akin to Foucault's panopticon or George Orwell's 'Big Brother,' but rather through the making and recording of discrete observations across rhizomatically distributed spaces and centers of calculations.

Key point:

The concept of surveillance in 'surveillant assemblages.'

Contemporary forms of surveillance, which form the technical core of strategic cost management, amalgamate computers with optics—combining brains and eyes for surveillance. Distributed and networked computers are employed for recording and analyzing, while optics, such as cameras and barcode/QR code readers, are utilized for observation. This combination's collective impact constitutes surveillance in the diverse and fragmented spaces of production and control. Surveillance unveils the otherwise imperceptible, making them visible and subjecting them to control.

Integrated with various Industry 4.0 technologies, as discussed in the previous chapter, a plethora of cost management techniques, concepts, and frameworks collectively form this surveillant assemblage. However, to maintain the chapter's focus, we will delve into the following key elements:

1. ABC/M: This serves as a foundational step towards strategic cost management.
2. Target costing: This consolidates strategic cost management efforts.
3. **Lean manufacturing:** manufacturing philosophy and system that encapsulates strategic cost management.
4. ERP: software infrastructure of managing contemporary organizations.
5. Throughput accounting and theory of constraints: maximizing capacity utilization

9.4 Foundational steps toward strategic cost management: ABC/M

Side note:

Reading Chapter 1's 'epistemic and contextual factors' behind the strategic turn would be a good idea at this point.

Founded on their consultocratic engagements and popularized through the powerful "actor-networks" associated with them (Cooper et al. 2017; Jones and Dugdale 2002), Norton and Kaplan's ABC considerably influenced the evolution of cost management's strategic outlook. To thoroughly understand the 'eventuality' of ABC, one should read Jones and Dugdale's (2002) excellent paper. As they reveal, the eventuality of ABC is strongly connected to a particular 'epistemic context' that emerged around Harvard University Business School and Computer-Aided Manufacturing International (CAM-I). These epistemic actor networks were attempting to address the problem of eroding competitiveness in US firms, especially in comparison to

Japanese firms, who were making superior use of advanced manufacturing technologies—with just-in-time (JIT) and total quality management (TQM) being recognized as central to Japanese success (see, Jones and Dugdale 2002, 126).

Most importantly, there was an understanding that the long-run, large-batch, long-term production in which the USA had previously excelled might now be obsolete in the face of emerging 'flexible manufacturing' and 'segmented market positioning' regimes (see Armstrong 2002; Jones and Dugdale 2002, and also see chapters 3 and 8 of this textbook). ABC was an event written into these preceding eventualities of addressing the problem of US competitiveness. It was directed toward the necessity of aligning cost accounting with advanced manufacturing technologies, flexible manufacturing, and segmented market positioning that industrial engineers and strategic managers were promoting in US firms in response to the Japanese Challenge.

Key point:
ABC's preceeding eventuality.

Traditional absorption costing, often viewed as a hindrance to integrating advanced manufacturing technologies and implementing competitiveness initiatives driven by flexible manufacturing, has come under scrutiny. It has been criticized for distorting the concept of 'true cost,' potentially misguiding managers with inaccurate pricing, flawed marketing strategies, and a skewed perception of competitiveness.

ABC emerged as a remedy to address these shortcomings in traditional methods of allocating overhead expenses in product pricing and profitability assessments. Kaplan and colleagues argued persuasively that ABC could allocate overheads more 'accurately' by considering 'real cost drivers' instead of relying on 'arbitrary overhead absorption bases.' The introduction of a 'cost hierarchy' marked the beginning of this approach, categorizing activities into four levels: unit, batch, product-sustaining, and facility-sustaining. The objective was to attribute the first three types directly to the product, reserving the last for allocation at the plant level.

This shift redefined many costs traditionally labeled as 'overheads' (and, hence, to be absorbed based on arbitrary factors like labor hours) into directly attributable and variable costs. Technical procedures for implementing ABC were established and popularized through Harvard Business School publications, accompanied by case studies to facilitate teaching in classrooms.

The implementation of ABC was greatly facilitated by the rapid development of information technologies, especially in networking, real-time data processing, and expert-system integration with transaction processing systems. These advancements were incorporated into accounting and ERP packages. Consequently, many companies adopted ERP systems with integrated ABC modules (Jones and Dugdale, 2002).

Numerous texts, including a series by Kaplan and Cooper and case studies published by Harvard Business School, delve into the technicalities of implementing ABC. The creation of such packages and knowledge bases, coupled with consultancy services for their implementation, evolved into a multi-billion-dollar business, creating a market for further development of epistemic products associated with ABC/M.

Key point:

Beginning and the evolution of ABC.

As a product costing method, ABC is a concept that is far from complex. As extensively elucidated in various textbooks, case studies, and exam practice questions that you should have encountered in prior management accounting courses, its fundamental process involves:

1. Reorganizing cost hierarchy as activity-related. This is done by recognizing how different activities embedded in cost categories are hierarchically related to the cost object.

    a. **Unit-level costs:** These costs fluctuate with each unit of production or service and are directly linked to the production of a single unit of a product or service delivery. They align with variable costs, even within traditional absorption costing systems.

    b. **Batch-level costs:** Incurred for a specific batch of products or services; these costs arise from activities performed for a group or batch of units rather than for each individual unit. Examples encompass machine setup costs, quality control inspections, and production scheduling. These costs are incurred each time a new batch is produced or a set number of units are processed.

    c. **Product-sustaining costs:** Incurred to support specific products or product lines, these costs are associated with activities necessary for the production and maintenance of a particular product or product line. They are not directly tied to the number of units produced but rather

to the existence of a specific product. Examples include product design, engineering, and marketing expenses specific to a particular product.
    d. Facility-sustaining costs: Supporting the overall operation of the entire facility or business, these costs are not tied to individual products, batches, or units. They are often considered fixed and do not vary with the volume of production or the number of products. Examples include rent, facility management, and general administrative expenses.
2. Identifying specific activities that drive different cost categories: Particular emphasis is placed on activities associated with batch-level, product-sustaining, and facility-sustaining costs. This key differentiation from traditional absorption costing underscores the notion that activities represent the true cost incidents, driving costs. Therefore, to enhance cost accuracy, costs need to be traced to the cost object based on the underlying activities, with activities as the linking pin between overhead costs and the cost object.
3. Determining activity cost driver rates: The 'activity cost driver rate' should be established for each cost driver activity. This rate forms the basis for tracing the activity costs to the cost objects. It is computed by dividing the total periodic cost of the activity pool by the activity volume for that period.
4. Tracing unit cost: The final step involves tracing unit cost based on the established activity cost driver rates, ensuring a more accurate representation of costs associated with the production or service delivery process.

Key point:
ABC's processual elements.

ABC's strategic significance

ABC marked a strategically significant shift from traditional absorption methods, with implications across multiple dimensions. This transition yields two closely interconnected effects:
1. Cost controllability effect.
2. Strategic effect.

ABC's controllability effect

In a system where overhead was absorbed based on direct labor cost, the managerial challenge of controlling overheads was simplified to

Side note:

'Black box' is a metaphor introduced by Latour to elucidate science in action. Borrowed from cybernetics, it designates an operational context where intricate technical instructions are enclosed in a black box. This box operates based on input and output instructions, obviating the necessity to comprehend its internal operational logic.

managing direct labor spent on production, assuming that it was the primary driver of overheads. The conventional cost allocation system operated to disclose how overhead facilities were consumed by labor hours and machine hours. Instead of revealing the true "drivers" of overhead, it "black-boxed" them while making the direct labor process visible for managerial controls. Consequently, wages, working hours, and production rates of direct laborers became the visible and controllable bases for cost management (Armstrong 2002). Conventional absorption costing made the factory labor process visible and controllable from a distance but obscured the nature of overheads.

This approach meant that staff departments such as HR, Marketing, and Accounting were exempt from accounting surveillance. These "staff costs" were deemed "fixed," making them immune to performance measurements and controls. The fixed nature of these costs resulted from a lack of meaningful costing techniques linking staff costs to cost objects (i.e., products and product lines). Additionally, staff costs were considered fixed due to a "hierarchical privilege" protecting staff from top management controls.

Without a thorough articulation of the issue, accountants asserted that staff costs were not determined by the "number of output units" (traditionally understood basis for cost variability and controllability). Consequently, these costs were directly placed into the income statement, often implying they were "uncontrollable" and beyond managerial scrutiny. Armstrong (2002, 100) observed, "Employment in the staff department, on the other hand, remained relatively secure, depending on the abilities of its representatives to convince the rest of the management team of the importance of the services which it provided". This protection concealed the real activities of staff functions and left their cost implications unaccounted for. Standard costing mechanisms imposed accountability on production workers but raised the question of "who controls the controllers?"

However, the competitive pressures of neoliberal markets and the strategic necessity of achieving cost efficiency throughout the firm prompted an exploration into previously uncharted territories, including staff functions. ABC provided the basis for this exploration, opening up their "activities" as the basis for understanding cost variability and controllability (Armstrong 2002).

Accordingly, with ABC, cost management has now come to cost not only products and services (which have been the only 'cost objects' in a conventional sense) but also all functional entities, including people, their knowledge and intellect, customers, market segments, relationships, environmental factors, and many more often based on reconstituting them as 'activities' that consumes resources (whose financial value being the cost). New categories were identified as cost pools and activity pools, interconnected through cost drivers. These interconnections became the basis for 'cost driver rates' through which staff time and activities can now be attributable to cost objects (Innes et al. 2000). This allows the managers to calculate "true costs" and set the "correct prices" of cost objects so that they can be "strategically positioned" in the competitive markets.

Activities that people carry out have become visible through activity cost analysis, providing opportunities for capital to maximize the efficacy of the labor time it purchases from blue-collar workers and management. The managerial labor process, once a black box under traditional cost accounting regimes, is now open to perpetual scrutiny by capital (see Armstrong 2002). This revelation has prompted the staff function to undergo constant reassessment of its validity in terms of its "value-added" criteria. The new managerial doctrine of justification has emerged: all staff costs must be justified based on their contribution to the value enhancement of the cost objects ultimately positioned in the market. Otherwise, the services provided by certain staff functions must be deemed redundant. Other rhetoric and practices, including business process re-engineering, total quality management, and lean manufacturing have facilitated this shift. On this point, Armstrong (2002, 102) made a vivid observation:

Key point:
ABC opened up the black box of staff functions' overheads.

> In its prescription of multi-functional committees as means of implementation..., ABC promised the production function a major say in determining the services of which it bore the cost. As part of the same deal, the scrutiny of staff departments through which its activities were to be established could be used to reveal any which were 'non-value added', ...thus creating respectable front for the productivist suspicion that quite a lot of staff activity is of no value at all. It is no accident that the some of the most successful applications of ABC have been initiated by operational managers ...and also no ac-

cident that some applications have resulted in job losses in the staff departments... In summary, ABC ... proposed that staff department should be subjected to regimes of accountability similar to those already experienced by manufacturing.

ABC effectively began dismantling the shelter provided for staff functions, employing the traditional rhetoric of "fixed costs." This process gained momentum when Kaplan and Cooper expanded ABC to ABM. Critiques of ABC's narrow focus on overhead reallocation prompted Kaplan and Cooper to underscore that their project wasn't solely about ABC; it encompassed ABM, offering a broader perspective on cost management rather than just cost accounting (see Armstrong 2002; Drennan and Kelly 2002; Jones and Dugdale 2002). ABM extended ABC's "vertical or cost assignment view" into a "horizontal or process view" of cost management (see Figure 9.2). Therefore, it wasn't merely a task of cost accounting; industrial engineers, operations managers, and process managers needed to contribute significantly, as argued by Kaplan and Cooper.

Beyond calculating 'true' costs, activity-based management mandated that managers focus on the "strategic use of resources and time." This involved analyzing activities and cost drivers, eliminating unnecessary costs, and continuously revising work processes to enhance competitiveness throughout the entire value chain. Consequently, functional managers were no longer viewed solely as "cost centers" but as "self-entrepreneurial consumers" of corporate resources—individuals engaged in value creation or consumption for value creation. They were required to justify their resource and time consumption, transforming their roles into entrepreneurial acts to minimize costs and create value for the subsequent element in the value chain—now perceived as "internal customers." This transformation altered the organizational hierarchy into a social integration and surveillance system, achieved by redesigning organizational processes to identify internal customers as well as external customers.

ABC's strategic effect

As discussed previously, the control effect of ABC lies in its ability to unveil previously opaque staff functions for managerial scrutiny regarding their contribution to overall product costs. On the other hand, its strategic impact arises from its capacity to integrate with

Figure 9.2: From ABC to ABM

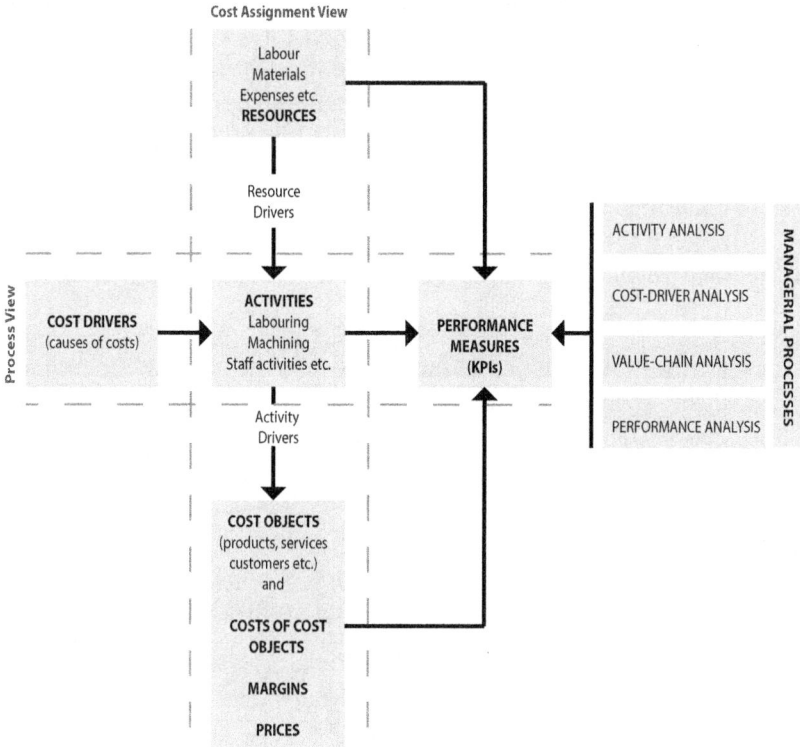

Source: Adapted from (Miller 1996, 236).

other elements of strategizing, including strategic market positioning, manufacturing flexibility, quality management, and continuous improvement. This integration primarily occurs when it is employed as a technique for 'cost and activity analysis' rather than merely as a method of product costing. Here are some examples of how ABC has the potential to exert a strategic effect.

Key point:

The strategic effect of ABC emanates from its capacity to integrate with other strategic processes.

Contribution to flexibility:

As mentioned earlier, a key conceptual transformation brought about by ABC is the reorganization of the cost hierarchy into output unit-level activities, batch-level activities, product-sustaining activities, and facility-sustaining activities. This reclassification of costs, through the process of ABC, transforms certain costs previously considered fixed in the traditional approach into variable costs.

From a decision-making perspective, consider the determination of the break-even production volume of a product or the volume of a product necessary to achieve a target profit. ABC's reclassification of costs often results in a downward shift in the fixed cost curve, as some fixed costs are now considered variable costs on an activity basis. Given that the break-even point equals fixed cost divided by contribution per unit, the firm now has a lower fixed-cost threshold to recover, resulting in a lower required production volume to break even and reach a target profit or return on investment. Therefore, ABC should lead to flexible manufacturing where smaller production volumes must be justified.

Key point:

ABC provides a calculative basis to justify small-volume production.

Furthermore, as discussed in the previous chapter, manufacturing flexibility involves labor, machine, and system flexibilities. The foundation of such flexibilities lies in the techno-managerial capabilities to re-engineer activity processes by adding, deleting, redesigning, and recombining activities. ABC not only necessitates a detailed activity analysis but also costs every activity in determining their cost driver rate, providing a better understanding of how those activities consume resources (including time). In that sense, ABC provides an accounting basis for flexibility.

Contribution to quality and continuous improvement:

Popular discourses on strategy and cost management often commend ABC for its integration into quality management and continuous improvement programs. A notable example is how activity analysis and costing are related to concepts, processes, and practices of target costing, as discussed in Chapter 3. The 'target costing triangle' (see Figure 3.7 in Chapter 3) emphasizes the necessity of making strategic connections between customers, designers, and suppliers through life-cycle costing, value engineering, and inter-organizational costing. Underlying all these is ABC (Cooper and Slagmulder 1997).

Contribution to strategic market positioning:

Popular strategy discourses often consider ABC and activity analysis as fundamental elements of operationalizing Porterian generic strategies. Here is a summary of such explanations.

- **Cost Leadership:** Organizations can focus on efficiency improvements and cost reduction in areas by identifying and managing activities that contribute significantly to costs.

ABC helps identify non-value-added activities and eliminate or reduce them, contributing to overall cost-reduction efforts.
- Differentiation: ABC can assist in understanding the costs associated with differentiating activities. By accurately assigning costs to various product features or service attributes, organizations can make informed decisions about which features contribute most to differentiation and allocate resources accordingly. Understanding the cost structure through ABC allows organizations to invest in and emphasize the activities that contribute to differentiation while managing costs effectively.
- Focus: ABC can aid organizations pursuing a focus strategy by providing insights into the costs associated with serving a specific market segment or niche. It helps allocate resources to activities crucial for success in the chosen focus area. By understanding the costs involved in serving a specific market segment, organizations can efficiently tailor their strategies to meet that segment's unique needs.

Key point:
How ABC aligns with generic strategies.

9.5 Consolidating strategic cost management through target costing

Target costing stands out as a crucial pillar in strategic cost management. Its significance lies in its ability to synthesize various facets of cost management, encompassing the strategic imperatives elucidated throughout this book. At its core, target costing emphasizes market positioning and endeavors to craft a compelling value proposition by intertwining the triadic dimensions of cost, quality, and functionality. These three elements are pivotal in shaping the overall strategy.

The approach underscores the importance of integrating three critical frontiers of quality management and continuous improvement: the customer, supplier, and product designers. This integration is achieved through market-driven, product-level, and component-level target costing. Moreover, target costing establishes connections with value engineering, life-cycle costing, and inter-organizational costing, weaving them into the broader fabric of the cost management process.

In Chapter 3, we delved into the essence of target costing. A revisit to that chapter is recommended for a comprehensive understanding. However, the following points merit particular attention to provide a quick refresher and reinforce the key dimensions of cost management.

1. Target costing is grounded in lean manufacturing principles (see section 9.6). Doctrinal aspects of target costing are derived from lean manufacturing principles. Cooper and Slagmulder (1997, 3) explain that at the heart of the lean enterprise is the belief that single-piece flow is more efficient than batch-and-queue. Removing all queues and inefficiencies associated with batch-and-queue systems enables lean enterprises to have faster reflexes, enjoy economies of scale at lower production volumes, and be inherently more efficient than their mass producer counterparts. They can produce products with higher quality and functionality faster at lower costs. Lean manufacturing needs to concentrate on three fundamental strategic imperatives of a particular product: quality, cost, and functionality.

2. Lean manufacturing is based on waste minimization, and inventories are considered waste because they involve non-value-added assets and activities. However, perfect quality is necessary for a manufacturing system to run on just-in-time. Without the buffer inventories inherent in batch-and-queue systems to substitute defective components, raw materials, or work-in-process, just-in-time production processes must halt when a defect is encountered until its cause is identified and corrected. System quality (i.e., 1-d, if you recall the operational definition we used in Chapter 7, the probability of manufacturing non-defective elements in the system) needs to be near perfect to mitigate the costs associated with stoppages of production processes. This is why quality is a critical element in lean manufacturing, and target costing considers it one of its fundamental conditional requirements to achieve.

3. Lean manufacturing embodies a different logic of competition than mass production. When applied to mass production conditions, generic strategies of differentiation and cost leadership can mean carving out non-confrontational competitive space, leaving competitors out for a sustainable period based on a superior cost or differentiation advantage that they cannot easily imitate. Competition among lean manufacturers assumes that no such advantage can be sustained, and hence, the competition is always confrontational: firms

should compete on product functionalities continuously. This is why functionality and continuous improvement are considered critical elements of target costing.

4. The lean manufacturing basis of target costing is encapsulated in its "survival zone" concept defined by the maxima and minima of quality, functionality, and price (cost). We have already discussed this in Chapter 3. See Figure 9.3 below, which is indeed Figure 3.6 repeated here for easy reference. The survival zone defines the competitive arena in which the firm should be able to operate in terms of the quality, functionality, and price it offers to the customers. This is a rather dynamic and volatile region that keeps changing in line with the level of continuous improvements and innovations that competitive firms can achieve. Figure 9.3: survival zone – how lean manufacturing doctrines are encapsulated in target costing.

Figure 9.3: Survival zone – how lean manufacturing doctrines are encapsulated in target costing

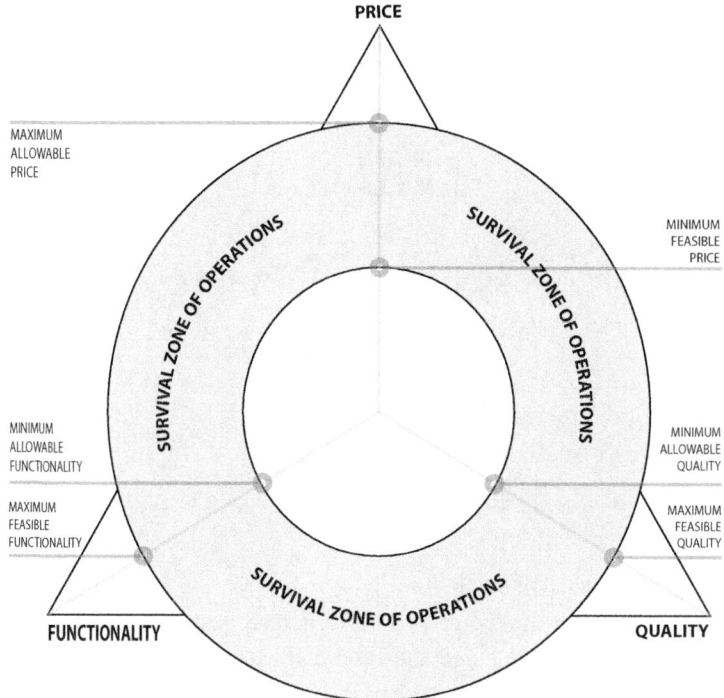

Source: adapted from Cooper and Slagmulder (1997, 9)

5. As a cost management system, target costing integrates three frontiers of decision-makers: the market (customers and competitors), internal product designers, and suppliers who design, produce, and supply the components to be used in the final product. The idea of the "target costing triangle" encapsulates these three frontiers and the different types of costings that target costing encompasses. This has been already discussed in Chapter 3. However, the target costing triangle is re-illustrated in Figure 9.4 for easy reference.

Figure 9.4: Target costing triangle – integrating three frontiers of decision-makers

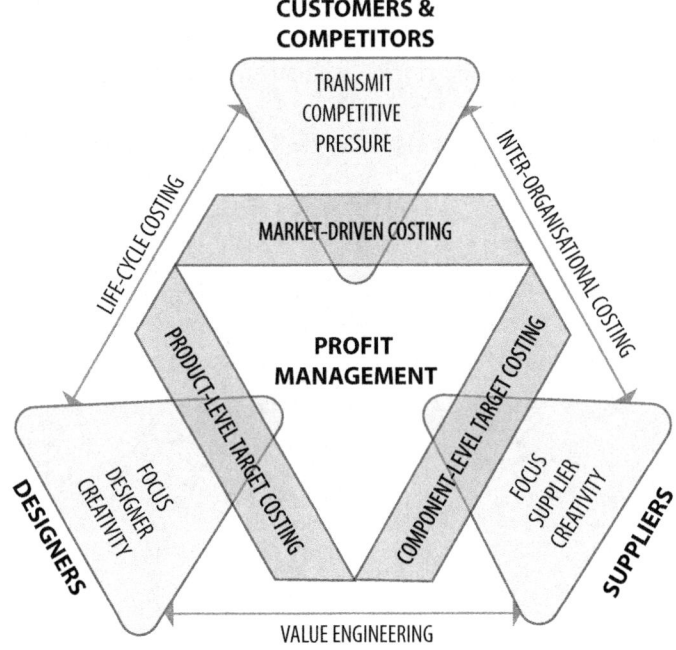

Source: Adapted from Cooper and Slagmulder (1997, p. 5)

6. At the market front, market-driven costing is mobilized to transmit competitive pressure by ascertaining the competitive market price and then the competitive cost at which the product should be produced. Guided by the survival zone concept mentioned above, a target price is determined in relation to the level of quality and the functionalities that the firm should incorporate into the product to face the com-

petition effectively. To this end, four key analyses should be carried out:

a. Technology analysis to determine the technology roadmap in the field,
b. Product requirement analysis to determine the minimum level of quality functionalities that should be technically incorporated into the product,
c. Market and competitor analysis to determine the level of quality and functionality that is needed to face the competition.
d. Financial analysis to determine the target profit and target cost. This should be facilitated by appropriate costing methods, such as ABC.

7. At the designer front, product-level target costing is mobilized to focus designer creativity on the market competition and supplier integration into the product and process design. Lifecycle costing operates as the key costing methodology that helps designers link the product and processes with the market requirements. Value engineering, on the other hand, connects designers with suppliers.

8. At the supplier front, component-level target costing is mobilized to focus on and enhance supplier creativity. As mentioned in Chapter 3, the focus here is on ensuring that specific components delivered by contracted suppliers meet quality requirements at specified target costs. Inter-organizational costing (e.g., open-book accounting and ERP systems across the supply chain) establishes operational and accounting connections between suppliers and the firm.

9. Considering all these, target costing can be defined as a structured, comprehensive processual approach to profit management, "*determining the lifecycle cost at which a proposed product with specified functionality and quality must be produced to generate the desired level of profitability over its life cycle when sold at its anticipated selling price*" (Cooper and Slagmulder 1997, 10).

10. Finally, target costing constitutes a meticulous process that incorporates a multitude of analyses on a continuous basis, making them a permanent feature of organizational management in a lean manufacturing setting. Figure 9.5 illustrates

Key point:
Critical elements of a target costing system.

the target costing process, which we have discussed in detail in Chapter 3.

Figure 9.5: Target costing process

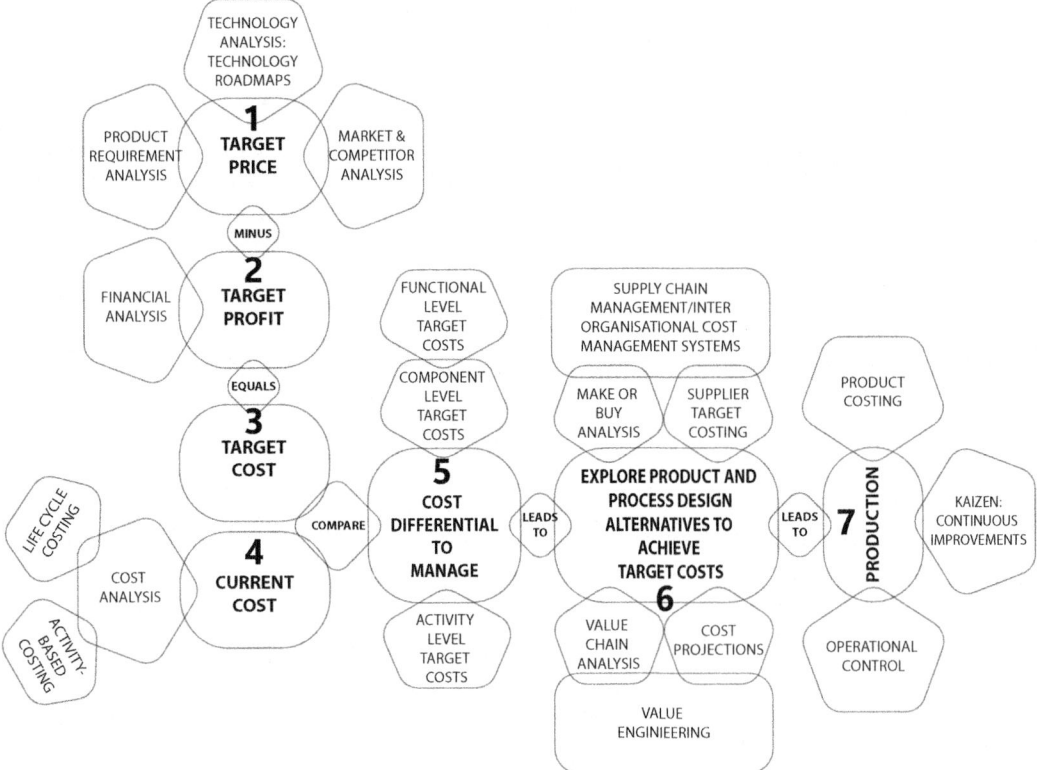

9.6 Lean manufacturing: manufacturing philosophy that encapsulates strategic cost management

Originating from Japanese manufacturing principles, particularly Toyota's production system (Monden 1994; Monden and Hamada 1991; Monden and Sakurai 1998), lean manufacturing is a production philosophy and management approach dedicated to minimizing waste while maximizing efficiency and value for the customer through quality and flexibility. The essence of strategic cost management is embedded within the concept of lean manufacturing. As previously discussed, target costing aligns with lean manufacturing, and the notions of flexibility and quality costing discussed earlier also directly correlate with lean manufacturing principles.

Given the extensive discussions and popularity of lean manufacturing in various management and industrial engineering fields, its fundamental elements have been examined from different perspectives. However, as highlighted in Chapter 7 regarding quality-centric organizational transformations, the core idea revolves around continuously improving workflows to facilitate small lot and single-piece production with reduced lead times (see Monden 1994). This philosophy gives rise to distinctive features characterizing a lean manufacturing system. Drawing from Monden's (1994) explanation of Toyota's manufacturing system, summarized in Figure 9.6 (a repetition of Figure 7.4), key elements can be identified:

1. Value: Determined based on competitive conditions, emphasizing price, quality, and product functionalities. The system aims to enhance capabilities for producing and delivering this value, ensuring continuous adjustments and improvements in response to changing competitive conditions.
2. Reduction of lead time: Achieved through small lot and single-piece production, necessitating setup time reduction and various manufacturing system flexibilities, including flexible machines, flexible labor, process standardization, and effective process layout for line production balancing and loading.
3. Production smoothing: Balancing cycle times for producing varieties.
4. Kanban system: Sequentially connecting production processes and stations through a tag-like card system, signaling the type and quantity to be withdrawn and produced by subsequent and preceding processes.
5. Pull system of production: Employing just-in-time production and inventory systems, where individuals of a certain process withdraw necessary units from the preceding process at the required time, with the preceding process producing only enough units to replace those withdrawn.
6. Flexible manufacturing scheduling: Adapting quantity to meet changes in demand.
7. Waste elimination: Focusing on eliminating all possible waste, identified in popular discourses as seven key sources:

Key point:

Critical elements of lean manufacturing.

356 | Strategic Management Accounting: a critical exploration

Figure 9.6: Toyota's lean manufacturing system

```
                    ┌─────────────────────────────────────┐
                    │ Meeting the challenge of increasing │
                    │       profit in slow growing        │
                    │         competitive markets         │
                    └─────────────────────────────────────┘
                           ↑                    ↑
            ┌──────────────────────┐   ┌──────────────────┐
            │ Increase of revenue  │   │ Cost reduction by│
            │  by offering quality │   │ eliminating waste│
            │     and variety      │   │                  │
            └──────────────────────┘   └──────────────────┘
```

(Diagram: Toyota's lean manufacturing system, showing hierarchical relationships between:

- **Respect for humanity** (due recognition of employees creativity and contribution at all levels)
- **Increased employee morale**
- **Company-wide quality management (TQM)**
- **reducing inventory** (low inventory cost and working capital)
- **reduced work force** (low labour cost)
- **Flexible production scheduling** (quantity adaptation to demand changes)
- **Just-in-time production** (pull system: the people of a certain process go to the preceding process to withdraw the necessary units in the necessary quantities at the necessary time. The preceding process produces only enough units to replace those that have been withdrawn)
- **Flexible work force** (*'Shojinka'*)
- **Quality assurance (statistical process control)**
- ***Kanban* system** (processes in a plant are connected sequentially through tag like card system signalling the type and quantity to be withdrawn and produced by the subsequent and preceding processes)
- **Production smoothing** (balancing between the cycle times of producing different varieties)
- **Changes in standard operations routines**
- **Autonomation** (*'jidoka'*) i.e. autonomous check of abnormal in a process
- **Reduction of lead time**
- **Functional management**
- **Small lot production**
- **Single-piece production under balanced line**
- **Setup-time reduction**
- **Machine Layout**
- **Multi-function worker**
- **Standardised operations**
- Continuous improvement of activities through small groups (i.e. **quality circles**))

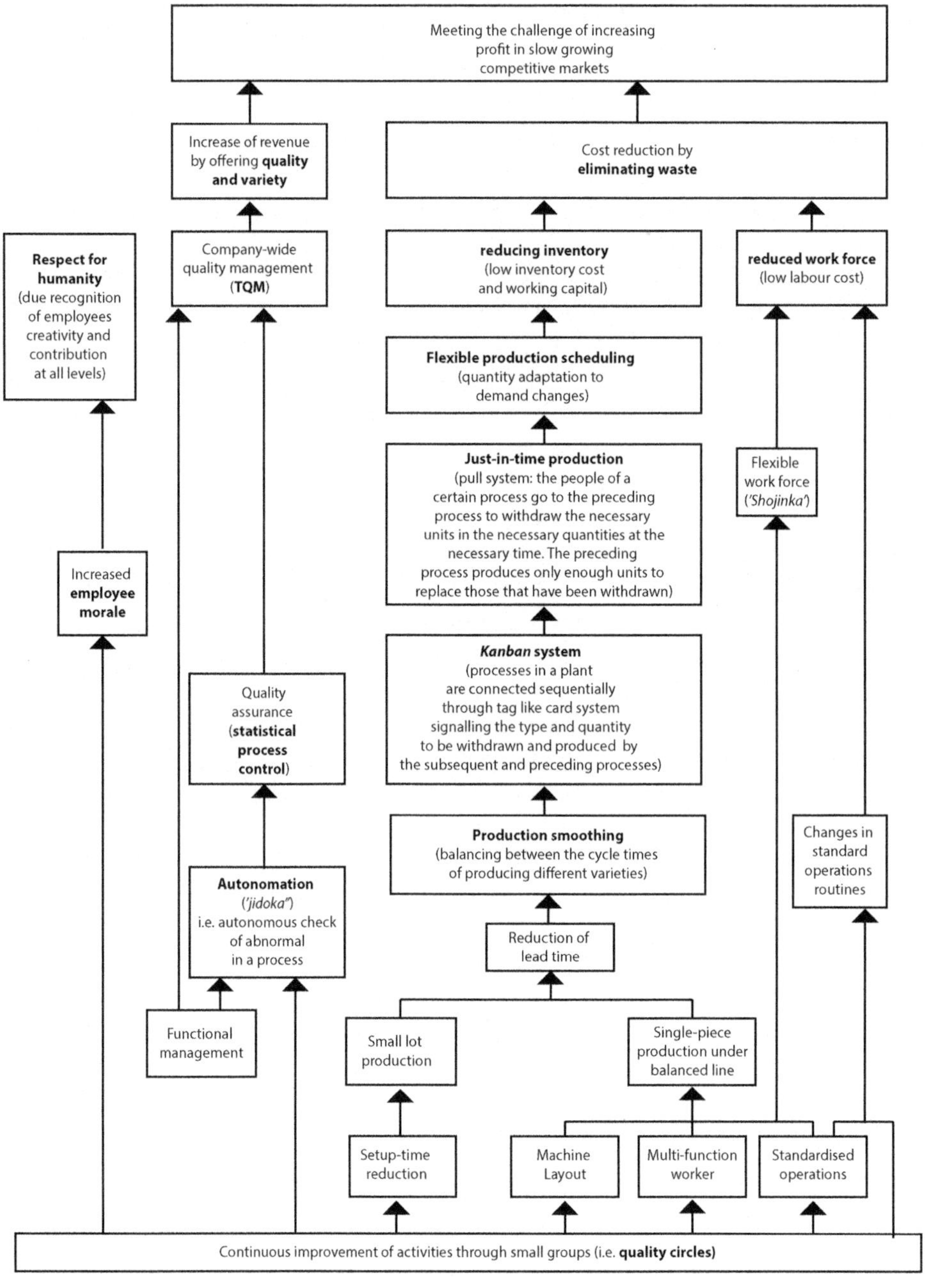

Source: adapted from (Monden 1994, 4).

- Transport,
- Inventory,
- Motion,
- Waiting,
- Overproduction,
- Overprocessing,
- Defects

8. **Near-perfect quality:** Lean manufacturing, especially just-in-time production systems without 'buffer stocks' to accommodate defects and errors, necessitates zero-defect quality conditions. Therefore, total quality management is a central element of lean manufacturing, encompassing not only hard system elements like statistical process controls and autonomation ("jidoka," i.e., autonomous checks for abnormalities in a process) but also soft system aspects such as quality circles operating under the principle of 'respect for humanity.'

9.7 ERP: software infrastructure of managing contemporary organizations

So far, discussions in this chapter and previous chapters have emphasized the importance of planning and coordinating activities throughout the entire value chain, from suppliers to customers. ERP systems play a crucial role in this aspect, enhancing a company's operational, cost management, and strategic capabilities. ERP systems are integrated software solutions designed to streamline and optimize business processes across various departments, providing real-time visibility and control over key aspects of the organization. With the advent of Industry 4.0 technologies, ERP systems have evolved to become internet and cloud-based. ERP systems can be developed in-house or by vendors; the latter is becoming increasingly popular, especially among small and medium-sized companies. To illustrate the growth of the vendor-based ERP system market, consider the sales of the largest ERP vendor, Germon SAP, which have grown from less than $500 million in 1992 to approximately $3.3 billion in 2023.

Before reaching their current state, ERP systems underwent significant technical evolution, starting as rudimentary inventory management systems before the 1970s. Initially, they were linked to accounting calculations of 'derived demand' or 'dependent demands', which refer to the demand for components or raw materials in production

Key point:

The origin of ERP systems can be traced back to inventory management calculations.

systems. The final products that a company produces and sells represent the 'independent demand', while the raw materials and components needed for these products constitute the dependent or derived demand. A key calculation in inventory management is estimating the purchase requirements, timing, and inventory levels of such components, enabling production planning to meet customer needs on time. Figure 9.7 provides a simple example of the calculative logic behind material requirement planning.

Figure 9.7: Material requirements planning – accounting logic

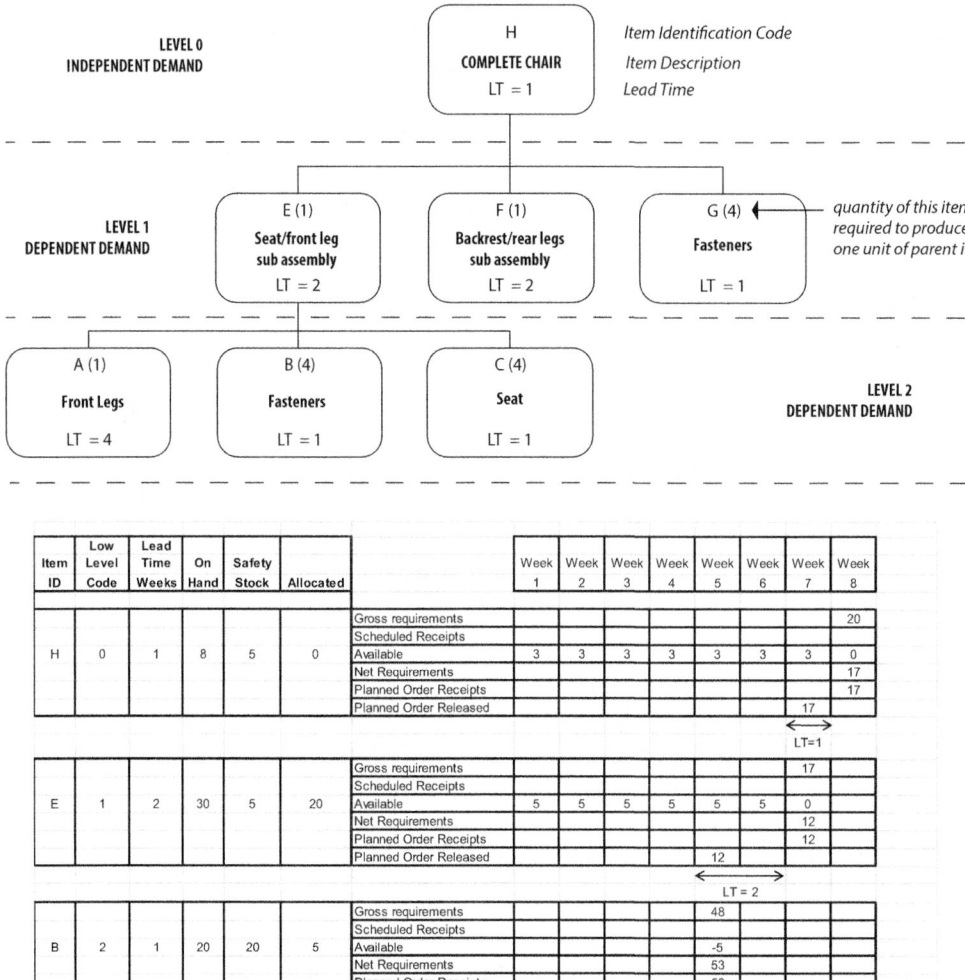

The illustration above presents only a partial calculation for the final product and two of its components. Imagine the complexity of calculations when a company manufactures numerous products, each with hundreds of components. This complexity increases with the need to determine economic order quantities. The digitalization of such inventory management marked the onset of the evolution of ERP, beginning with Material Requirements Planning I (MRP-I). The 1970s saw the emergence of MRP-I, initially operating on the bulky and costly IBM7094 and later on IBM's 360s and 370s series. During this era, the concept of a "database" was unheard of, and software tools were rudimentary compared to today's standards. In 1978, SAP introduced a more integrated version of its software, the SAP R/2 system, leveraging the then-available mainframe computer technology. This system allowed for interactivity between modules and included additional features such as order tracking (Jacobs and Weston 2007, 359).

In the 1980s, MRP evolved into Manufacturing Resource Planning (MRP-II). This period was also marked by a quality management revolution and a shift towards lean and flexible manufacturing. Advances in computer and networking technologies led to the development of integrated software systems that supported quality management and lean manufacturing information needs. Consequently, material requirement planning extended beyond inventory management to manufacturing planning, encompassing flexible manufacturing and quality management necessities, such as flexible production scheduling and line balancing, detailed cost reporting, enhanced shop floor reporting, and process control information. MRP-II systems were those enhanced systems that evolved to cater to these quality management and lean production necessities of the 1980s Japanized factories.

Key point:

MRP-I and MRP-II as predecessors of ERP systems.

However, a significant challenge arose with these evolving computer-based information systems: information fragmentation. As Davenport (1998) points out, large companies generate vast amounts of data, typically scattered across numerous individual systems. This fragmentation leads to high costs in data management and hinders efficient communication between different business functions, impacting manufacturing productivity and decision-making.

Contemporary ERP systems have evolved to address this fragmentation, offering all the functionalities of MRP-II systems but with more

Key point:

Data fragmentation is the key issue that ERP systems emerged to address.

efficiency and integration, thanks to Industry 4.0 technologies. At the heart of an ERP system is a unified database that serves various business functions globally, streamlining data collection and dissemination (Davenport 1998, 123). This integration is exemplified in Figure 9.8, which shows the modular architecture of an ERP system.

Figure 9.8: ERP architecture

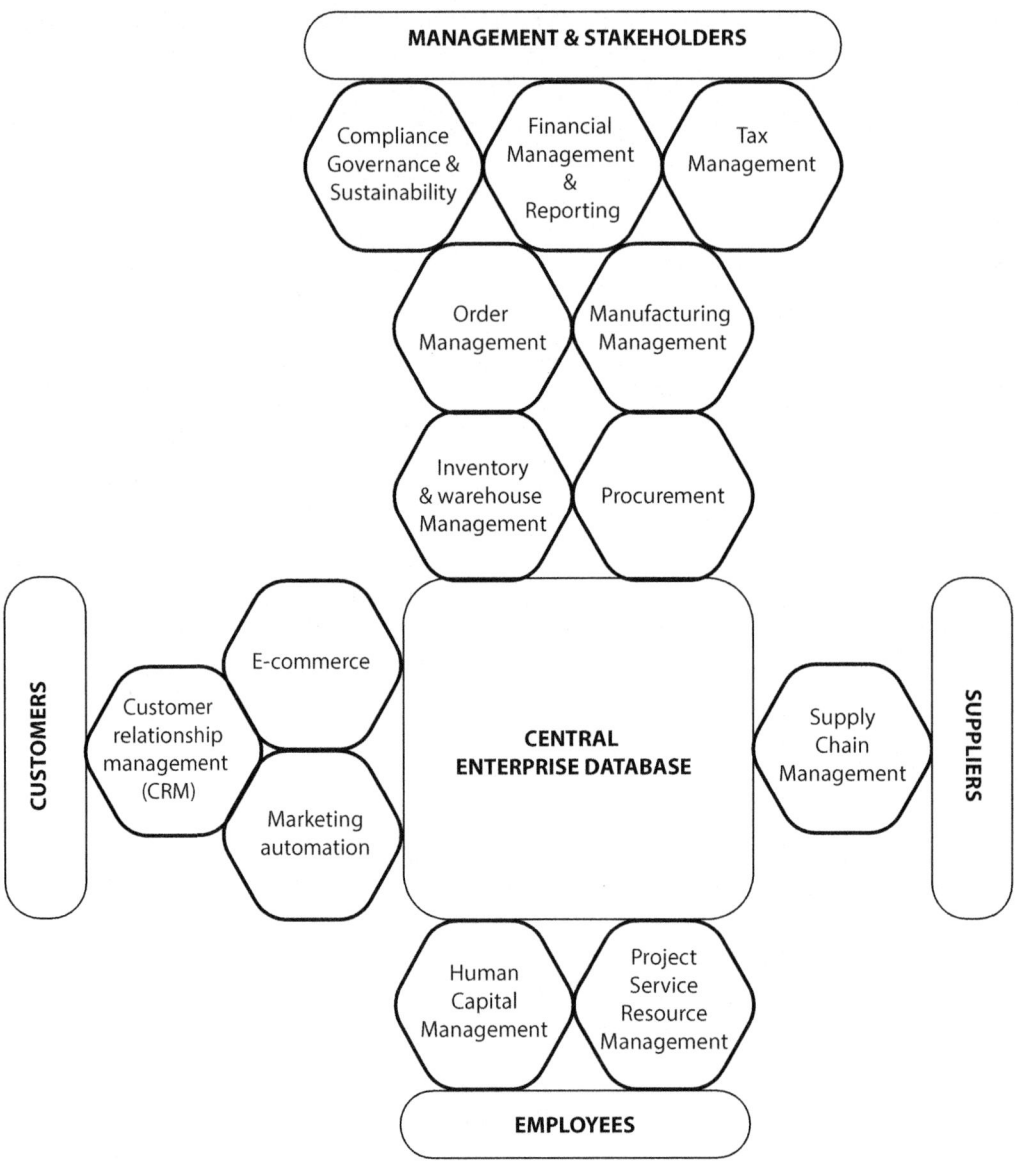

In conclusion, ERP systems are crucial in bolstering cost management and strategic capabilities. These systems enhance organizational efficiency by integrating processes, automating tasks, and offering real-time insights. Consequently, they enable organizations to make informed decisions, reduce costs, and strategically position themselves for sustained success in a dynamic business landscape. However, it's important to acknowledge the substantial risks associated with ERP implementations. To underscore this point, it is fitting to refer to the cautionary words of Davenport (1998, 122-123):

Key point:

A cautionary word on ERP implementation.

> An enterprise system, by its very nature, imposes its own logic on a company's strategy, organization, and culture. … It pushes a company toward full integration even when a certain degree of business unit segregation may be in its best interests. And it pushes a company toward generic processes even when customized processes may be a source of competitive advantage. If a company rushes to install an enterprise system without first having a clear understanding of the business implications, the dream of integration can quickly turn into a nightmare. The logic of the system may conflict with the logic of the business, and either the implementation will fail, wasting vast sums of money and causing a great deal of disruption, or the system will weaken important sources of competitive advantage, hobbling the company. [...] It is certainly true that enterprise systems can deliver great rewards, but the risks they carry are equally great. When considering and implementing an enterprise system, managers need to be careful that their enthusiasm about the benefits does not blind them to the hazards.

9.8 Throughput accounting and theory of constraints

Capacity optimization has long been a critical element in cost management decisions. Traditionally associated with economic modeling, capacity optimization decision-making is now evolving with recent developments in cost management practices, introducing new optimization logics. These advancements have not only ushered in fresh ideas and practices but have also provided alternative theoretical explanations for integrating cost management into novel scenarios of capacity optimization. To exemplify this, we will examine two interrelated developments: the Theory of Constraints (TOC) and Throughput Accounting (TA).

Theory of Constraints first emerged in the bestselling novel by Goldratt and Cox (1984). The novel narrates the story of a fictional manager striving to save his manufacturing plant. Guided by a professor, the manager learns to identify the plant itself as the bottleneck, recognizing it as the sole limited resource in his operation. He is encouraged to pinpoint the specific nature of this bottleneck and to explore ways to enhance the plant's throughput. This realization led him to understand that bottlenecks can be overcome by focusing on improved throughput, an approach now known as throughput accounting. Therefore, TOC and TA are intrinsically linked, enabling corporate managers to maximize performance by effectively leveraging this relationship.

The story of TOC and its associated TA calculations revolves around decision-making in the face of managerial constraints aimed at optimizing production plans. TOC provides a structured, step-by-step decision-making process to tackle issues arising from capacity constraints. As illustrated in Figure 9.9, this process comprises: (1) identifying the system's constraint; (2) devising a strategy to exploit this constraint; (3) subordinating and synchronizing all other elements to this constraint; (4) enhancing the constraint's performance; and (5) returning to the first step and repeating the cycle.

In fact, what TOC provides is a framework for continuously reevaluating shop-floor configurations. When capacity is insufficient for production demands, a constraint exists. Optimizing production around these constraints is a key aspect of cost management, involving an ongoing cycle of calculations, observations, comparisons, and decision-making. The process begins by identifying the constraint, which involves comparing the available capacity with production and sales requirements. The next step is brainstorming ways to leverage this constraint. Managers might ponder several crucial questions: Is optimizing the product mix necessary? Are we fully utilizing the facility's maximum capacity? Is achieving this consistently feasible? To tackle these questions, it's advised to first calculate the "throughput" (revenue minus the cost of purchased materials and services) and ascertain the throughput per bottleneck unit. It is key to establish buffer stocks ahead of the bottleneck and exploit them when the facility is

Figure 9.9: TOC and TA in action

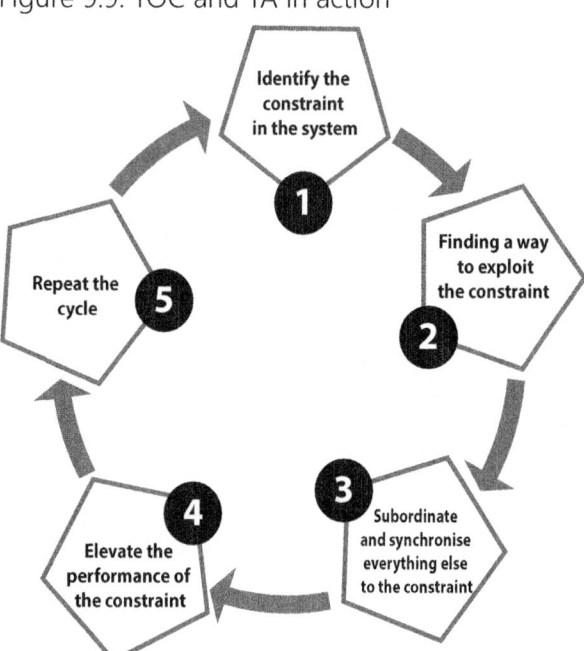

prepared. By maximizing throughput, you'll enhance your contribution. However, this requires meticulous coordination with non-bottleneck operations to ensure the bottleneck is utilized to its fullest while prioritizing non-bottleneck facilities less, as they can be utilized later once the bottleneck has been addressed. This coordination is facilitated by a scheduling technique known as DBR (Drum-Buffer-Rope), ensuring non-bottleneck operations commence only after bottleneck needs are met. Once a bottleneck is resolved, the process reverts to the initial step, seeking new constraints to exploit using the same principles and methods. This approach aids in reducing costs and maximizing profits through optimized throughput, embodying cost management via constraint management.

Certain accounting calculations are fundamental to throughput accounting:
- *Throughput Contribution in £* = Sales Revenue - Direct Material Costs
- *Throughput Accounting Ratio (TPAR)* = Return per Factory Hour/Cost per Factory Hour
- *Return per Factory Hour* = Throughput £ per Unit / Time per Unit
- *Cost per Factory Hour* = Total Factory Cost / Total Time Available

Let's examine an example of calculating these throughput accounting measures.

Theory of constraints and throughput accounting: an example

A company produces three products using three different machines. The following information is available for a period:

Product	X	Y	Z	Total
Sales price per unit (£)	32	22	18	
Material cost per unit (£)	20	12	12	
Machine hours required per unit:				
Machine 1	6	2	1	
Machine 2	9	3	1.5	
Machine 3	3	10	5	
Estimated sales demand	200	200	200	
Required machine hours				
Machine 1	1200	400	200	1800
Machine 2	1800	600	300	2700
Machine 3	600	200	100	900

Machine capacity is limited to 1600 hours for each machine, and the total factory cost for the period is £3,200.

First, calculate the machine utilization ratio to determine the most constrained resource:

	M1	M2	M3
Required machine hours	1800	2700	900
Available machine hours	1600	1600	1600
Machine utilisation ratio	113%	169%	56%
Bottleneck	2nd	1st	3rd

The table above shows that Machine 2 is the most constrained resource or the first bottleneck. Use this to calculate the relevant throughput accounting ratios:

	X	Y	Z
Sales price per unit (£)	32	22	18
Material cost per unit (£)	20	12	12
Throughput contribution per unit (£)	12	10	6
Required Machine 2 (bottleneck) hours per unit	9	3	1.5
Throughput contribution per bottleneck hour (£)	1.33	3.33	4.00
Ranking	3rd	2nd	1st

Factory cost per machine hour = Total Factory Cost/Total Machine Hours.

Given that the total factory cost is £3,200 and total machine hours for M2 are 1,600, the factory cost per machine hour = £3,200/1,600 = £2.

Calculate the Throughput Accounting Ratio (TPAR) as follows:

	X	Y	Z
(a) Throughput contribution per bottleneck hour (£)	1.33	3.33	4.00
(b) Factory cost per machine hour (£)	2.00	2.00	2.00
(C) TPAR ratio = (a)/(b)	0.67	1.67	2.00
Ranking	3	2	1

This indicates that product Z should be prioritized in utilizing machine hours over products X and Y. Accordingly, the optimized production schedule under Machine 2 as the first constraint will be:

Product	Quantity	Hours per unit	Machine 2 Hours used	Hours available
				1600
Z	200	1.5	300	1300
Y	200	3	600	700
X	78	9	700	0

To enhance capacity, the focus should first be on Machine 2. Once its capacity is increased and it is no longer a bottleneck, this calculation should be repeated to determine the new optimum production schedule under the new bottleneck.

TOC and TA have challenged traditional overhead absorption costing. Proponents, Goldratt and Fox viewed traditional cost accounting as an "enemy," criticizing its treatment of most facility or capacity costs as "fixed," which implies limited managerial discretion. Contrarily, TOC focuses on identifying bottleneck versus non-bottleneck facilities and preparing buffer stock to maximize bottleneck capacities, aiming to bypass constraints on sales and profitability. TOC advocates also argue that ABC doesn't align with Goldratt and Fox's objectives. However, their critique of ABC hasn't gained wide acceptance in management accounting literature, as ABC/M is recognized for its long-term cost calculation perspective, whereas TOC and TA prioritize short-term profitability (Dugdale 2013). Despite this conflict, TOC and TA have garnered some popularity. They can be integrated with linear programming and MRP packages, even when multiple constraints exist (Dugdale 2013). Concerning Goldratt and Fox's stance on ABC, some have recently explored integrating ABC with TOC to leverage both methods' strengths (Kee and Schmidt 2000), though TOC proponents remain skeptical. This rivalry requires careful handling from a cost management perspective, as both approaches have significant merits. TOC stands out for its simplicity and pragmatism, while ABC/M, with its global recognition and widespread use in various organizational settings, is hard to overlook.

Chapter summary

This chapter delved into strategic cost management, a broad topic encompassing and underpinning each key theme addressed in this textbook, ranging from market positioning to manufacturing flexibility and quality. Initially, the chapter explained how management accounting thought evolved from costing to cost management within a traditional cost management paradigm. In this paradigm, standard costing and budgeting played pivotal roles in a system commonly referred to as responsibility accounting. Although existing since the Industrial Revolution, transformations in competitive conditions associated with the 'strategic turn' have problematized the relevance of responsibility accounting. This necessitates new strategic approaches to cost management.

Strategic approaches to cost management encompass a broad spectrum of techniques, methods, concepts, frameworks, and philosophies. Given the diverse nature of strategic cost management, it can be interpreted and understood in two distinct ways: as a holistic program or as a surveillant assemblage. Viewing cost management as a holistic program underscores a desire for unity and essence. This approach is characterized by convergence—the drive to amalgamate different elements into a cohesive whole that can generate synergistic value. In this holistic context, strategy is seen as the catalyst for this unity. Kaplanian and Porterian discourses of strategy manifest attempts to see strategy and cost management as a holistic program.

Conversely, strategic cost management functions as a surveillant assemblage, illustrating how it embodies heterogeneity through the amalgamation and reconfiguration of various technologies, techniques, concepts, and practices, thereby forming a 'fragmented whole.' This 'fragmented whole' is dynamic, with technologies, techniques, concepts, and practices being consistently added, removed, and rearranged. Such continuous modification ensures that it remains perpetually fragmented and endlessly adaptable, thus evolving in nature. These processes of addition, removal, recombination, and fragmentation occur as distinct events. This chapter explores this concept by shedding light on the 'eventuality' of various techniques and practices, now integral to strategic cost management.

The chapter discussed five techno-managerial and accounting frameworks as critical elements of strategic cost management. Initially, it examined activity-based costing and management as foundational to strategic cost management. This section highlighted the strategic impact of activity-based costing, emphasizing its role in enhancing cost controllability, strategic positioning, flexibility, and quality management.

Subsequently, the focus shifted to the key aspects of target costing within a strategic cost management system. Emphasis was placed on how target costing integrates various lean manufacturing philosophies and principles. The concepts of the survival zone, target costing triangle, market-driven costing, and product- and component-level target costing were revisited. This discussion aimed to demonstrate how a combination of multiple costing techniques contributes to market positioning in terms of price, quality, and functionality.

The third topic addressed lean manufacturing as the foundational manufacturing philosophy underpinning strategic cost management. Key elements of lean manufacturing were outlined, illustrating their significance in reinforcing the strategic imperatives of cost management, manufacturing flexibility, and quality management.

Next, the evolution from material requirements planning to enterprise resource planning (ERP), including manufacturing requirements planning, was explored. The basic principles of material requirements planning were clarified, followed by an enumeration of the key modular components of ERP.

Lastly, the chapter delved into the theory of constraints and throughput accounting. This section elucidated their role in cost management, particularly in relation to optimizing capacity utilization.

Test your knowledge

1. Discuss the historical significance of factories in the development of cost management.
2. Analyze the impact of Scientific Management on early cost management practices.
3. Describe the role of standardization in cost management within the context of scientific management.
4. Examine the connection between standard costing and budgeting in traditional responsibility accounting.
5. Outline the procedural elements of cost management in traditional responsibility accounting.
6. Identify and summarize the main issues of traditional responsibility accounting as a cost management system.
7. Define strategic cost management as a 'holistic program' and discuss potential issues with this perspective.
8. Use Deleuze and Guattari's theories to explain the concept of an assemblage and its relevance to the evolution of strategic cost management.
9. Elucidate the 'epistemic context' behind Kaplan and colleagues' work on activity-based costing and management.
10. Detail the essential steps in the activity-based costing process.
11. Categorize the four hierarchical levels of costs in activity-based costing.
12. Discuss how activity-based costing and management affect:
    a. Cost controllability.
    b. Strategic market positioning.
    c. Quality management.
    d. Manufacturing flexibility.

13. Describe how lean manufacturing principles influence target costing.
14. Explain key concepts of target costing in a strategic cost management context:
    a. Survival zone.
    b. Target costing triangle.
    c. Market-driven costing.
    d. Component-level target costing.
    e. Product-level target costing.
    f. Value engineering.
    g. Life-cycle costing.
    h. Inter-organizational costing.
    i. Target costing process.
15. Outline the principal elements of lean manufacturing as a strategic cost management philosophy.
16. Provide a brief explanation of material requirements planning and manufacturing requirements planning as precursors to enterprise resource planning.
17. Compare the core techno-managerial challenges addressed by material requirements planning, manufacturing requirements planning, and enterprise resource planning.
18. Enumerate and describe the essential components of an enterprise resource planning system.
19. Identify and discuss the primary techno-managerial issue targeted by the theory of constraints and throughput accounting.
20. Detail the fundamental steps in throughput accounting.
21. List and describe the key accounting measures and ratios in throughput accounting.

Explore further

1. Conduct a search for academic articles on the "Beyond Budgeting Movement" and compile a scholarly critique of the traditional budgeting approach in cost management. Based on the literature, identify the primary shortcomings of traditional budgeting and outline potential solutions. Evaluate how these solutions address broader strategic issues in cost management.

2. Research leading enterprise resource planning (ERP) software vendors online and gather their promotional materials. Create a list of the ERP modules they offer. For each module, examine the specific strategic advantages they provide to an organization.
3. Investigate the core elements of Industry 4.0, including technologies such as the Internet of Things (IoT), Artificial Intelligence (AI), Big Data, Cloud Computing, and Advanced Robotics. Analyze how these technologies impact strategic cost management, focusing on improvements in cost prediction accuracy, real-time cost monitoring, and dynamic cost optimization strategies.

Develop your critical argumentation skills

1. Write an argumentative essay on the following theme.

    Strategic cost management is a surveillant assemblage rather than a holistic program. Hence, its evolution better be explored and understood as eventualities that produce heterogeneity rather than an overarching singular logic of cost management as in traditional cost management paradigms.

2. Write an argumentative essay on the following theme.

    Enterprise resource planning software and platforms provide companies with immense functional, hierarchical, and geographical integration capabilities. However, by its very nature, an enterprise system imposes its own logic on a company's strategy, organization, and culture. It pushes a company toward full integration even when a certain degree of business unit segregation may be in its best interests.

3. Lean manufacturing has increasingly been recognized as a pivotal element in strategic cost management, particularly within the manufacturing sector. In light of this, write an argumentative essay discussing how lean manufacturing principles underpin a manufacturing philosophy that effectively supports strategic cost management.

References

Alawattage, C., and D. Wickramasinghe. 2019. Strategizing management accounting: liberal origins and neoliberal trends. London: Routledge.

Armstrong, P. 2002. The costs of activity-based management. Accounting, Organizations and Society 27 (1-2):99-120.

Boyns, T. 1998. Budgets and budgetary control in British businesses to c.1945. Accounting, Business & Financial History 8 (3):261-301.

Cooper, D. J., M. Ezzamel, and S. Q. Qu. 2017. Popularizing a management accounting idea: the case of the balanced scorecard. Contemporary Accounting Research 34 (2):991-1025.

Cooper, R., and R. Slagmulder. 1997. Target costing and value engineering. Portland: Productivity Press.

Davenport, T. H. 1998. Putting the enterprise into the enterprise system. Harvard Business Review 1998 (July-August):121-131.

Deleuze, G., and F. Guattari. 1987. A thousand plateaus: capitalism and schizophrenia: University of Minnesota Press.

———. 1994. What is philosophy? London: Verso.

Drennan, L., and M. Kelly. 2002. Assessing an activity-based costing project. Critical Perspectives on Accounting 13 (3):311-331.

Dugdale, D. 2013. The theory of constraints. In The Routledge Companion to Cost Management, edited by F. Mitchell, H. Norreklit and M. Jakobsen. London: Routledge, 145-162.

Goldratt, E. M., and J. Cox. 1984. The goal: excellence in manufacturing. New York: North River Press.

Hope, J., and R. Fraser. 1997. Beyond budgeting breaking through the barrier to the 'third wave'. Management Accounting 75 (11):20-23.

———. 2000. Beyond budgeting. Strategic finance 82 (4):30-35.

———. 2001. Beyond budgeting: questions and answers. Dorset.

———. 2003a. Beyond Budgeting: how managers can break free from the annual performance trap: Harvard Business School Press.

———. 2003b. Who needs budgets? Harvard Business Review 81 (2):108–115.

Hopper, T., and P. Armstrong. 1991. Cost accounting, controlling labour and the rise of conglomerates. Accounting, Organizations and Society 16 (5-6):405-438.

Hopper, T., and N. Macintosh. 1993. Management accounting as disciplinary practice: the case of ITT under Harold Geneen. Management Accounting Research 4 (3):181-216.

Jacobs, R. F., and T. J. Weston, F.C. 2007. Enterprise resource planning (ERP)—A brief history. Journal of Operations Management 25 (2):357-363.

Johnson, H. T., and R. S. Kaplan. 1987a. Relevance lost: the rise and fall of management accounting. Boston, Mass.: Harvard Business School Press.

———. 1987b. The rise and fall of management accounting. Management Accounting 68 (7):22-29.

Jones, C. T., and D. Dugdale. 2002. The ABC bandwagon and the juggernaut of modernity. Accounting, Organizations and Society 27 (1-2):121-163.

Kee, R., and C. Schmidt. 2000. A comparative analysis of utilizing activity-based costing and the theory of constraints for making product-mix decisions. International Journal of Production Economics 63 (1):1-17.

Miller, J. A. 1996. Implementing activity-based management in daily operations: John Wiley & Sons.

Monden, Y. 1994. Toyota production system: an integrated approach to just-in-time. 2nd ed. ed. London: Chapman & Hall.

Monden, Y., and K. Hamada. 1991. Target costing and kaizen costing in Japanese automobile companies. Journal of Management Accounting Research 3 (Fall):16-34.

Monden, Y., and M. Sakurai. 1998. Japanese management accounting. London: Taylor & Francis.

Nail, T. 2017. What is an Assemblage? SubStance 46 (1):21-37.

Patton, P. 1997. The world seen from within: Deleuze and the philosophy of events. Theory & event 1 (1).

CHAPTER

10 Strategizing sustainability

10.1 Introduction

Having explored various themes related to strategizing in the market, organizational hierarchy, and the point of production, we now reach our final chapter. This chapter will explore the relationship between sustainability and strategic management accounting concepts and practices. In previous chapters, we selectively examined how sustainability influences specific management accounting practices, including Kaplan and colleagues' balanced scorecards, Porter's value chain analysis, and target costing as a pricing technique. Aiming to provide an integrative perspective on how sustainability interacts with management accounting practices, this chapter has a dual focus: (a) examining how the global sustainability agenda has been integrated into frameworks of corporate strategy formulation and (b) assessing the extent and ways these efforts embody the broader sustainability concept as understood by the UN and other key sustainability advocates. In this assessment, I will draw on critical accounting scholarship on sustainability accounting.

For many years, and still to a significant extent, social and environmental issues were considered 'externalities' in neoclassical economic and accounting analyses of organizational practices and outcomes. Traditional accounting and economics, driven by firm-centric, entity, and monetary measurement concepts, long overlooked the social and environmental impacts, as these were not directly related to the firm's cost, revenue, and profit functions. However, this oversight has faced severe criticism in academic and policy circles since the mid-1970s, especially following the Brundtland Commission's 1987 report on the global environment and development. Despite criticisms like Daly's (1993, 267) assertion that "sustainable growth when applied to the economy is a bad oxymoron – self-contradictory as prose, and un-evocative as poetry", there has been a growing global awareness and commitment to sustainability. Sustainability now challenges us to reconsider and redesign our decision-making processes, daily operations, and accountabilities within and beyond organizations.

Management accounting is not exempt from this shift. Like many other academic and professional fields, it has been urged to adapt its ideologies, techniques, and practices towards fostering a sustainable world. This chapter evaluates the extent to which management accounting thought has embraced this challenge. In doing so, the chapter is organized as follows:

Key point:

Chapter structure and learning objectives.

1. Section 10.2 defines and discusses the concept of sustainability and its four interrelated dimensions: economic, social, political, and ecological. You will develop a broader understanding of the fundamental contradictions within which the notion of sustainability should be located.
2. Section 10.3 examines the neoliberal logic of sustainability, starting with Fridman's and others' resistance to the nascent sustainability agenda framed as corporate social responsibility at that time. In this section, you will develop a critical understanding of the neoclassical economic logic that views corporate engagement in sustainability as economically irrational and provide a biopolitical perspective on the evolution of this "oxymoron."
3. Section 10.4 discusses how management accounting has responded to the sustainability agenda, offering a conceptual schema for understanding this response and analyzing sustainability's incorporation into corporate discourses: corporate accountability in response to sustainability, strategizing sustainability, envisioning sustainability, and sustainability as a strategic positioning postulate. Reading this section will provide you with an overall schema to explore how corporations integrate ideas of sustainability in their own way to suit

their business context and strategy approaches.
4. Section 10.5 explores the operational aspects of management accounting's response to sustainability, focusing on sustainability in capital investment decisions, value chain analysis, competitive positioning, sustainability-balanced scorecards, and cost accounting techniques like activity-based costing (ABC), life-cycle costing, and whole life costing for managing sustainability-related costs. Here, you will revisit and extend some of the discussion in previous chapters to further enhance how specific management accounting practices struggle to engage with sustainability.
5. Finally, the chapter concludes with a summary and an overarching critical comment.

10.2 Political and politics of sustainability: fundamental contradictions

Given the highly contested and debated nature of 'sustainability', it is perhaps best, to begin with the Brundtland Commission's definition of sustainability. This definition is pivotal as it arguably serves as the most influential reference point and marks the commencement of contemporary debates on sustainable development. The commission defines sustainable development as the development that meets *"the needs of the present without compromising the ability of future generations to meet their own needs"* (United Nations World Commission on Environment and Development 1987, 8). This definition immediately highlights the generational conflict between present and future interests: it suggests that our current exploitation of the globe's finite resources could lead to a future where the planet becomes, in the worst case, uninhabitable, or at least, where the standard of living is not as favorable as it is today. This early definition has sparked a significant debate over what sustainability should encompass, how it should be approached, and the feasibility of achieving sustainability within a capitalist political-economic framework (Bebbington 2001; Gladwin et al. 1995; Gray 2010; Thomson 2007). Despite the varying viewpoints, there is a broad consensus that sustainability involves preserving and maintaining a crucial and finite environment, entailing some degree of social justice obligation – intergenerationally and intragenerationally (Gray 2010, 53).

Key point:

UNWCED definition of sustainable development.

In exploring the diverse interpretations of sustainability, it is essential to consider the political contradictions inherent in the concept and identify political means to address them. For a critical understanding of the global sustainability agenda, it is helpful to consider the theoretical distinction made by Chantal Mouffe, a prominent political theorist in agonistic democracy, between '*the political*' and '*politics*'. Mouffe (1993, 1999, 2000, 2005, 2013) defines "the political" as the fundamental antagonisms and conflicts that underlie human civilizations. It is an inherent aspect of human societies, arising from the reality that any social order is established on the exclusion of certain possibilities in favor of others. This dimension is marked by divergent interests and the inevitability of conflict and confrontations, not only between different social or political groups but also among more fundamental structural categories. Four fundamental structural categories can be identified for conceptualizing the political nature of sustainability, as shown in Figure 10.1: economy, polity, society, and ecology.

Key point:

Moffue's differentiation between 'the political' and 'politics'.

Conversely, "politics" refers to the set of institutional arrangements and practices through which an order is created, organizing human coexistence in the context of conflictuality provided by 'the political'. Politics is about how power is exercised to reconcile conflicting interests and ensure the coexistence of diverse groups within a society. It involves constructing political identities and establishing a certain order, often through democratic institutions and negotiations. For instance, the United Nations Sustainable Development Goals (UN SDGs) exemplify a global institutional arrangement that tries to recognize and address the fundamental contradictions between the economy, polity, society, and ecology in how we manage these domains.

Mouffe posits that understanding the distinctions between these two terms is vital for democratic politics. She stresses the importance of acknowledging and managing inevitable conflicts and antagonisms in any society rather than attempting to eliminate them, which she deems impossible. Now, let us consider the four fundamental structural categories and the institutional logics underpinning each of these categories.

Figure 10.1: Sustainability's Political Contradictions

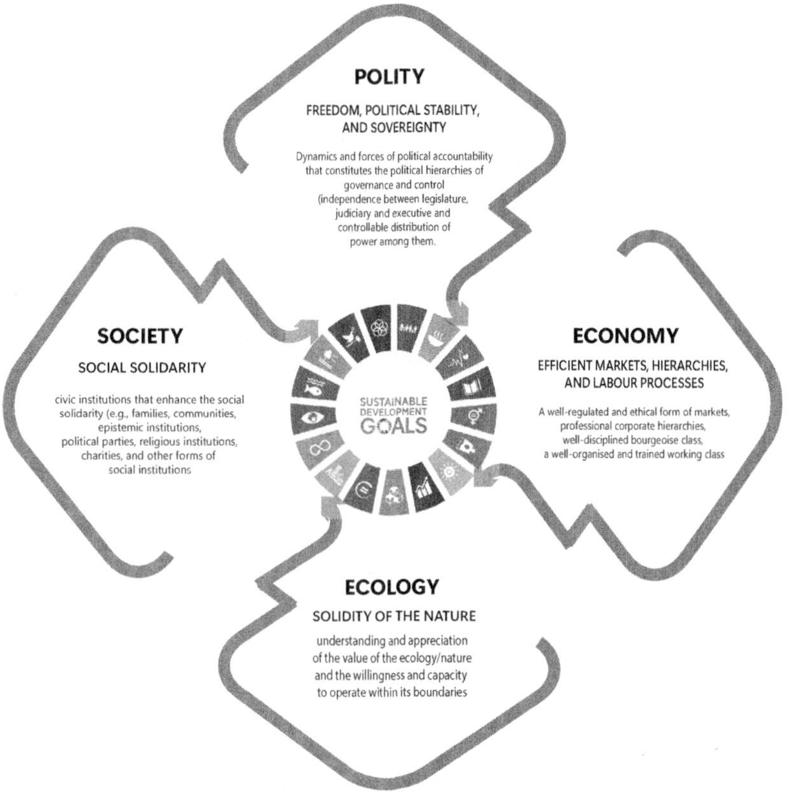

POLITY
FREEDOM, POLITICAL STABILITY, AND SOVEREIGNTY

Dynamics and forces of political accountability that constitutes the political hierarchies of governance and control (independence between legislature, judiciary and executive and controllable distribution of power among them.

SOCIETY
SOCIAL SOLIDARITY

civic institutions that enhance the social solidarity (e.g., families, communities, epistemic institutions, political parties, religious institutions, charities, and other forms of social institutions

ECONOMY
EFFICIENT MARKETS, HIERARCHIES, AND LABOUR PROCESSES

A well-regulated and ethical form of markets, professional corporate hierarchies, well-disciplined bourgeoise class, a well-organised and trained working class

ECOLOGY
SOLIDITY OF THE NATURE

understanding and appreciation of the value of the ecology/nature and the willingness and capacity to operate within its boundaries

SUSTAINABLE DEVELOPMENT GOALS

1. The economy manifests the manner in which nation-states, their global alliances, and regional economies are organized to fulfill the economic needs of consumption, production, exchange, savings, and investments. It comprises three key structural elements: markets, organizational hierarchies, and labor processes. These are the sites in which strategies are enabled and enacted, as discussed in the previous chapters. The primary driver of the economy is efficiency, particularly in a capitalistic system. This concept is linked to various indicators related to the rate of accumulation of 'socialized capital' (i.e., capital that is tradeable in capital markets). At the company level, efficiency is often measured by accounting metrics like return on investment and other related indicators. At the macroeconomic scale, efficiency encompasses the challenges of ensuring adequate economic growth to address issues

such as unemployment, poverty, economic insecurity, and the capacity to sustain a growing global population. Concerning sustainability, the economy involves technological and organizational advancements to ensure the production of income and resources for both present and future generations. However, a central aspect of sustainability is that economic efficiency and progress should not compromise the fundamental principles of politics, society, and ecology, i.e., ideals of political, social, and ecological justice. Sustainability requires not only economically efficient but also well-regulated and ethically operated markets, hierarchies, and labor processes. This entails a disciplined and ethical bourgeoisie (i.e., capitalist class), professional and ethical corporate management, and a well-trained, well-content, and motivated workforce.

Key point:

Four fundamental contradictions that underpin sustainability.

2. **Polity** is the manner in which the political state or the political system is organized to handle differences in political ideologies and other related cultural-political-economic contradictions. It embodies the dynamics of political accountability, illustrating the governance hierarchy through the independent legislative, judicial, and executive branches. From an orthodox Marxist viewpoint, it encompasses the political mechanisms controlling the class struggles between labor and capital. Post-Marxist perspectives expand this to include a contested terrain where not only class conflicts but also other political contradictions like race, ethnicity, elitism, regionalism, national identities, and cultural diversities emerge. In pre-modern societies, polity centered on affirming the sovereign power of monarchs ('God save the king/queen'), while modern democratic societies prioritize individual freedom alongside the independence and sovereignty of nation-states. Sustainable development hinges on these political doctrines of freedom and independence. The deterioration of these principles, as seen in recent neoliberal economic dominance, can lead to 'unsustainability,' manifesting as civil unrest, corruption, despotism, and civil and international wars. Despite its frequent omission in corporate and accounting discourses, polity is crucial for sustainability, especially considering it is a vision for a new global political order.

3. **The society** comprises civic institutions that bolster social solidarity, including families, communities, media, political parties, religious institutions, charities, and other social for-

mations where people unite to pursue diverse socio-cultural goals. It embodies the eco-justice aspect of sustainability, focusing on socio-political issues like social justice, fairness, cultural diversity, equality, indigenous rights, and more. This concept involves not only equitable distribution of developmental benefits among the present generation (intra-generational equity) but also between current and future generations (inter-generational equity). Additionally, it encompasses cultural and social struggles against the "increasing destruction of the world's diverse ecosystems, languages, and cultures by the globalizing and ethnocentric forces of [predominately] Western consumer culture." (www.ecojusticseduncation.com)

4. **Ecology**, often termed 'the planet', forms the natural foundation on which all else relies. It represents natural capital—also known as environmental or ecological capital—which encompasses the essential natural resources (energy and matter) and processes organizations utilize to produce goods and deliver services. This includes waste-absorbing sinks (such as forests and oceans), resources (renewable ones like timber, grain, fish, and water, and non-renewable ones like fossil fuels), and life-sustaining processes like climate regulation and the carbon cycle. According to the Forum for the Future, these elements are critical for maintaining ecological balance (see https://www.forumforthefuture.org/the-five-capitals). The accounting literature often ties ecological aspects to the eco-efficiency dimension of sustainability, focusing on minimizing environmental footprints and ensuring that economic, political, and social activities do not compromise ecological integrity and solidity. Gray et al. (1996) highlight that understanding eco-efficiency requires considering two additional concepts: biodiversity (inclusive of human and other species) and the planet's carrying capacity along with its stock of natural capital. Ideally, eco-efficiency implies conducting economic activities without depleting biodiversity or the planet's natural resource stock. Gray et al. (1996, 3) capture the notion of eco-efficiency as follows:

> "At minimum, a sustainable business is one which leaves the environment no worse off at the end of each accounting period than it was at the beginning

of that accounting period. For a full sustainability, the sustainable business would also re-dress some of the excess of current un-sustainability and consider the intra-generational inequalities. It is perfectly clear that few, if any, businesses, especially in the developed economies, come anywhere near to anything that looks remotely like sustainability".

Bebbington (2001, 137) contends that eco-efficiency aligns with the UNWCED's definition of sustainability mentioned earlier. While eco-efficiency is necessary for sustainable development, it alone is not enough. For instance, an environmentally neutral development scenario that results in a highly unequal distribution of benefits, failing to meet the needs of all people, would not fulfill the criteria for sustainable development. This scenario highlights the importance of the concept of eco-justice.

These four dimensions reflect key socio-political contradictions that have emerged from how Western societies and others worldwide have structured their political economies since the advent of modernity and the scientific revolution. The contemporary sustainability issue exemplifies how our economic activities can become, to varying degrees, destructive forces against the environment, society, and, at times, the political sphere, particularly in developing nations on the periphery. Consequently, the sustainability agenda calls for comprehensive changes across all aspects of our socio-political and economic activities, ranging from ideological shifts to organizational reforms.

10.3 Sustainability's neoliberal political logic

When the sustainability agenda first emerged in the 1970s as the "social responsibility of corporations" debate within mainstream management and economics circles, it faced significant criticism from influential proponents of neoliberal economics. Corporations investing in social responsibility and sustainability were labeled "unadulterated socialists undermining free societies." Nobel Laureate economist Milton Friedman was a prominent critic. In his 1970s essay for The New York Times Magazine, "The Social Responsibility of Business is to Increase its Profits," Friedman argued that business's focus should be solely on profit, dismissing social responsibilities as a form of socialism.

"When I hear businessmen speak eloquently about the 'social responsibilities of business in a free-enterprise system,' I am reminded of the wonderful line about the Frenchman who discovered at the age of 70 that he had been speaking prose all his life. The businessmen believe that they are defending free enterprise when they declaim that business is not concerned 'merely' with profit but also with promoting desirable 'social' ends; that business has a 'social conscience' and takes seriously its responsibilities for providing employment, eliminating discrimination, avoiding pollution and whatever else may be the catchwords of the contemporary crop of reformers. In fact, they are–or would be if they or anyone else took them seriously–preaching pure and unadulterated socialism. Businessmen who talk this way are unwitting puppets of the intellectual forces that have been undermining the basis of a free society these past decades" (Friedman 1970).

Key point:

Milton Friedman's critique of corporate social responsibility.

The rejection of corporate involvement in issues like pollution prevention and discrimination is grounded in the belief in an 'artificial economic personality.' This concept posits that economic enterprises are solely economic in nature and, therefore, should not be accountable for social and political decisions. According to Milton Friedman, since corporations are owned by profit-motivated shareholders, and managed by agents responsible only to these shareholders, it's inappropriate for corporate managers to engage in social responsibility. Friedman argues that such actions would equate to corporate managers wielding a political 'taxing' power, which he believes should be the purview of politics and government. This view is consistent with the questionable neoclassical economic ideology that distinguishes politics from economics, which Friedman explained as follows:

"This process raises political questions on two levels: principle and consequences. On the level of political principle, the imposition of taxes and the expenditure of tax proceeds are governmental functions. We have established elaborate constitutional, parliamentary and judicial provisions to control these functions, to assure that taxes are imposed so far as possible in accordance with the

> preferences and desires of the public–after all, "taxation without representation" was one of the battle cries of the American Revolution. We have a system of checks and balances to separate the legislative function of imposing taxes and enacting expenditures from the executive function of collecting taxes and administering expenditure programs and from the judicial function of mediating disputes and interpreting the law. ... Here the businessman–self-selected or appointed directly or indirectly by stockholders–is to be simultaneously legislator, executive and, jurist. He is to decide whom to tax by how much and for what purpose, and he is to spend the proceeds–all this guided only by general exhortations from on high to restrain inflation, improve the environment, fight poverty and so on and on. (Friedman 1970)".

Now, 53 years later, the world has changed, though some still believe in Friedmanian economics. At least it seems that corporations have embarked on a drive towards a sustainable world, or at least appear to give 'lip service' to a sustainable future. It has now become, in fact, a pervasive, taken-for-granted understanding among large corporations, at least at a rhetorical level, that they should invest in and spend on sustainability matters. We also see very little opposition from economists as well.

To the extent that Friedman (and others, e.g., Daly 1993) represent the principles of neoclassical and liberal economic governance, this dramatic change in the acceptance of sustainability as a corporate responsibility signifies a clear movement away from the neoclassical understanding of the social responsibilities of economic enterprises. However, despite what neoliberal economists have told us about "the nature of the firm," and despite their theories and ideologies being quite dominant and well-accepted in mainstream policy circles, the sociological and political-economic understanding (especially in critical circles) of the political role of economic enterprises has been much broader than this neoclassical economic conception. For example, since the advent of modernity and the emergence of governmentality, certain government veridictional and jurisdictional roles have been enacted within the boundaries of economic enterprises and market apparatuses (see Alawattage and Wickramasinghe 2019, 2022). From a Foucauldian perspective, organizations like factories, offices, schools, hospitals, barracks, and prisons became their own miniature legal systems, relatively independent and separate from the state but capable of exercising their own judgments, punishments, and rewards on individuals. In this sense, normalizing sanction within institutional spaces beyond the juridical processes of the sovereign state was indeed an extension of the government into the 'normal' spaces of socio-economic life, but with a new disciplinary logic (i.e., governmentality): discipline and punishment now take place within these 'normal' private social spaces, which for Foucault, disciplinary institutions operating with 'disciplinary technologies and principles', transforming the societies into 'disciplinary societies' (see Foucault 1995; Hopper and Macintosh 1993).

Key point:
Economic enterprises are not merely economic; they execute governmental roles of jurisdiction and veridiction.

Expanding on this perspective, it becomes evident that corporations embracing responsibilities for sustainability, beyond just the pursuit of profit, represent a further evolution of governmentality. This shift moves beyond the disciplinary politics of normalizing discipline and punishment (i.e., the anatomico-politics of the human body) to the biopolitics of security (see Alawattage and Wickramasinghe 2019, 2022). Indeed, this is a neoliberal approach, enhancing and empowering the role of the market and private capital in areas traditionally managed by the state. Paradoxically and ironically, this process enables private capital to assume certain political and welfare functions that neoclassical economists, like Friedman, believed should exclusively belong to the sovereign state (because, for them, it is costly for the shareholders). They argued that private capital's involvement in such matters could hinder capital accumulation. Not having a clear understanding or appreciation of this ever-increasing governance role of private capital and market apparatuses under neoliberalism, how they extend their power over every aspect of our lives, and how they absorb every aspect of political governance into it, Friedman and others initially saw this growth of social responsibility and sustainability as a threat to capital accumulation and, hence, a threat to their concept of 'freedom'—understood as the freedom to accumulate private capital. Consequently, they resisted.

Key point:
A political critique of Friedman's economic critique on corporate social responsibility.

However, their resistance would prove inconsequential as capital evolves to enhance its capacity for accumulation in various forms: economic, social, and political. This transformation positions capital as a dominant force in governance, what Hardt and Negri (2000) term the "empire". Capital is becoming akin to a state, assuming sovereignty and thus dealing with all matters traditionally managed by the political state. In the following sections, we will explore how accounting researchers have engaged with the rapid integration of sustainability as a key cross-disciplinary theme. Initially, leading economists viewed it merely as an "oxymoron" (Daly, 1993) or "pure and unadulterated socialism" (Friedman, 1970)."

Rationalizing the Oxymoron

Considering the neoclassical economic principle that a rational enterprise would only invest in activities maximizing shareholder wealth, the rise of the sustainability agenda appeared as an oxymoron, especially to those whose understanding is deeply rooted in neoclassical economic theories like agency theory and transaction cost theory. This concept seemed theoretically inexplicable. However, empirical observations revealed that companies were investing in economically irrational activities, with top executives of leading global corporations taking corporate social responsibility seriously. There was a noticeable growth in sustainability-related activities, expenditures, and reporting. For those with an economics-oriented analytical perspective, this represented a growing dependent variable requiring explanation. Based on the ontological assumption in economics that company managers, as agents of capital, should only invest in ways that contribute to maximizing shareholder wealth, this growth should correlate with its impact on financial performance. Therefore, hypotheses emerged to suggest a positive relationship between corporate social responsibility (also encompassing corporate sustainability reporting) and financial performance as a prerequisite for corporate social responsibility's continued prevalence and growth. The initial phase of academic rationalization of corporate social responsibility focused on testing these hypotheses, aiming to empirically demonstrate a neoclassical economic rationale behind the corporate world's increasing engagement in sustainability. For instance, Al-Tuwaijri et al. (2004, 447) justified their study by stating:

> As managers scramble to compete in the global economy, they must do so within societal constraints characterized by ever-increasing environmental accountability. This accountability includes heightened public scrutiny of both

the firm's environmental performance and its public disclosure of that performance. These elements of corporate environmental accountability jointly impact the firm's profitability and the value of its common equity. This study provides an integrated analysis of how management's overall strategy jointly affects (1) environmental disclosure, (2) environmental performance, and (3) economic performance. Understanding these interrelations is of increasing interest to both internal and external stakeholders in an era in which corporate environmental costs have become a significant business expense ... using a landfill to dump hazardous waste cost only $2.50 per ton in 1978, this charge rose to over $200 per ton by 1987 .... Between 1972 and 1992, total annualized environmental protection costs for US firms tripled as a percentage of Gross Domestic Product (GDP). Senior executives anticipate this trend to continue.

There is a significant number of studies conducted to assess whether "it pays to be really good" in terms of corporate social responsibility (e.g., Al-Tuwaijri et al. 2004; Alexander and Buchholz 1978; Artiach et al. 2010; Barnett and Salomon 2012). These studies have yielded mixed results, with some indicating positive, others negative, or inconclusive links between financial performance and CSR. However, the crucial aspect is not the nature of the relationship itself, but rather the methodology and underlying normative political principles of these studies. Common to these approaches is the notion that economic factors should take precedence over social and environmental considerations. This implies that the rationale for environmental and social sustainability and accountability is derived from their contributions to financial performance rather than prioritizing social and environmental protection in the calculation of economic profits. In essence, these approaches still prioritize economic criteria as the guiding principles, or the moral philosophy, in determining the merits of sustainable actions. Many economists and management consultants now argue that sustainability benefits companies mainly because it can boost profits, either directly or indirectly, or at least help mitigate losses, particularly those arising from financial penalties for non-compliance. While these messages positively encourage corporations to engage in sustainability for profit, they are underpinned by a misguided economic morality. This view suggests that sustainabil-

Key point:

The economic theory-wise oxymoron character of corporate social responsibility led to empirical testing of positive relationships between shareholder value and corporate social responsibility.

ity is important only because it can be profitable, positioning it as a means to profit rather than an end goal we all aspire to achieve. To put it simply, nothing will be profitable in an unsustainable world.

10.4 Management accounting's rationalization of sustainability

Mainstream management accounting's rationalization of sustainability adheres to the logic of financially legitimizing sustainability. Unlike being concerned with empirically 'testing' the causality between financial performance and sustainability, it emphasizes 'developing' strategic and operational frameworks to integrate sustainability into business' strategies.' This approach aims to 'create' (rather than testing) a positive correlation, or "finality" (see Norreklit 2000, 2003) between sustainability and financial performance. Most management experts now recognize sustainability as a "strategic imperative" (see Lubin and Esty 2010). The focus has shifted to integrating sustainability into various existing management models. Recent trends include adapting and updating models such as value chain analysis, balanced scorecards, and activity-based costing to incorporate sustainability issues. These popular management discourses outline a schema for embedding sustainability in management accounting, potentially leading to what I term "sustainabilizing strategy" – giving the corporation's strategy-making processes and elements a sustainable outlook by infusing sustainability concepts into management accounting frameworks and practices, as depicted in Figure 10.2.

Corporate accountability and sustainability

Corporate engagement in sustainability requires communication with a broader range of stakeholders for legitimacy, as well as for legal or institutional compliance. In accounting, 'sustainability reporting' (in contrast to institutionalization, strategizing, and operationalization) has become the most popular and evolved aspect. Indeed, it's not an exaggeration to say that the need for sustainability reporting created the managerial imperative to develop internal sustainability management systems, including emerging tools in social and environmental management accounting. This shift indicates that sustainability began penetrating the corporate world primarily as an 'accountability' requirement—an externally imposed (though not legally binding in many instances) demand to report on the environmental and social

Figure 10.2: Sustainabilizing strategy

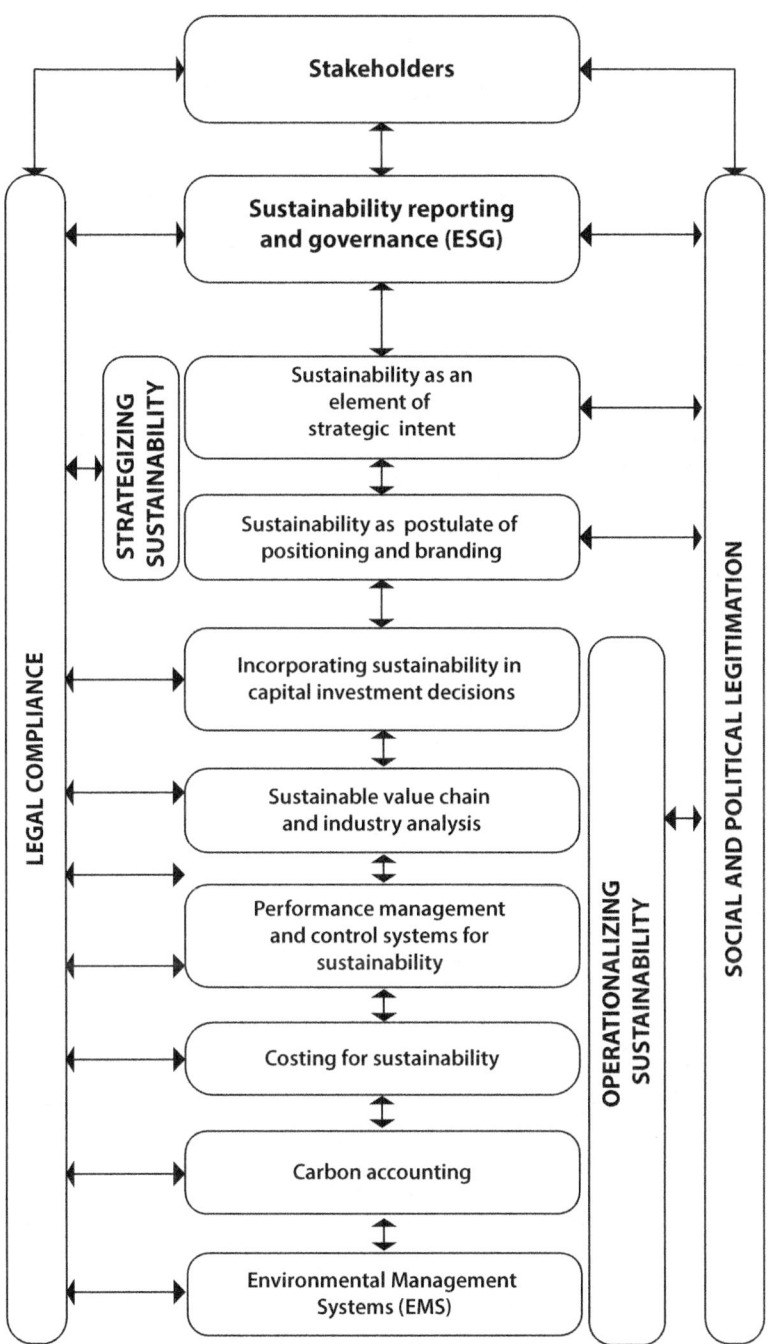

impacts of corporate activities. From this perspective, sustainability is an obligation for companies, imposed by external stakeholders, to account for how their profit-making operations affect the social and ecological environment.

The transitions to neoliberalism have profoundly impacted how we perceive corporate accountabilities. Neoliberalisation essentially amplifies the importance of free market governance logic that market capital and its individual units, such as corporations, should govern and shape lives beyond traditional business confines. This shift sees the principles of economic efficiency and capital accumulation infiltrating both the political state and civil society, reshaping them to align with capital accumulation priorities. Assuming the role of the "empire", capital has emerged as a dominant force, setting global terms and demanding reorganization in its favor (Cooper 2015; Hardt and Negri 2000; Munro 2012). In this neoliberal era, economic units, typically called 'firms', have evolved into powerful, autonomous entities. This evolution brings the accounting concept of an 'entity' into a political realm, transcending mere financial interpretation.

This transformation implies that capital and its influential agents, like multinational corporations, are no longer simply assets of shareholders. Firms now stand as independent entities, exerting influence even over their shareholders. Shareholders, in turn, are not traditional owners but rather investors in the capital market, gambling with their earnings, savings, and assets for a market return. Ownership has been reduced to a legal formality, a tradable commodity in itself in the capital market. Investors primarily profit not through direct ownership of firms but by trading their stake in stock markets. The more frequent the trading, the higher the potential profit – a concept epitomized by high-frequency trading. Thus, ownership's value lies in its circulation; the quicker it circulates, the greater the profits. In corporate shareholder structures, the conventional notion of ownership has become diluted, if not entirely irrelevant.

Simultaneously, corporations have grown extremely large, powerful, and critically influential in the global political-economic and cultural landscape, as well as in ecological matters. They have reached a status where they are 'too big to fail.' Their failures now extend beyond mere shareholder losses; they can lead to political-economic catastrophes. Thus, while corporations are instrumental in much of human civilization's progress, they have also become a primary source of insecurity and risk. Parallel to this happening, neoliberalism has changed the meaning of security and the purpose of government and governance. Instead of the state's territorial integrity, the doctrine of human security now proclaims insistently that living populations and individuals ought to constitute the new object of security. Living populations and individuals must be protected, which, when one considers biodiversity as a security issue, even constitutes non-human lives. What is sacred is no longer the sovereignty of the state but the 'life' of the individual (Gros 2014, 23) and the possibilities of reproducing the life profitably (Cooper 2015).

In neoliberal governance, therefore, corporations emerge as paradoxical entities. On one hand, they are venues where life can be profitably sustained and reproduced. On the other hand, they also represent spaces where life—in its economic, social, cultural, and even physical or ecological dimensions—is endangered, often profitably, sometimes even to the point of potential extinction.

Key point:

The political basis of why environmental, social and governance (ESG) issues became critical in the neoliberal times.

The implosion of ownership in the neoliberal era, alongside the paradoxical role of the firm as both a life-sustaining and endangering entity, has brought a new concept into the corporate accountability discourse. This concept is the 'stake' – the firm's capacity to impact collective and individual life positively or negatively. For the first time in capitalist history, the 'stake' is becoming a more crucial concept than legal ownership in terms of accountability. Notably, in popular management and accounting literature, particularly in stakeholder theory, 'stake' is defined as the capacity of stakeholders to influence the firm. However, while this capacity is important in realizing accountability, the reverse – how the firm influences collective and individual life – is more relevant and insightful in understanding recent shifts in accountability as an element of biopolitical governance. This perspective becomes especially significant in acknowledging that multinational firms have emerged as dominant forces in shaping our life processes; they have a significant 'stake' over human and non-human existence. Given their unprecedented power to affect our lives both positively and negatively, these firms have become simultaneously our allies and adversaries; they are seen as both suspects and prospects, protectors and threats.

The pluralization of corporate accountability today exemplifies a neoliberal paradox. As corporations exist in society both as suspects and prospects, they must legitimize themselves not only through financial performance but across multiple fronts. They should embrace an 'obligation' toward the sustainability of the planet and its socio-political apparatuses beyond profitability. They must demonstrate their role in safeguarding human life in all realms where they could pose a threat. Corporate accountability represents this effort of legitimization. It involves constructing narratives that explain how corporations enhance human prosperity and mitigate potential threats to life. Sustainability reporting is a crucial expression of this accountability, addressing threats ranging from economic impacts to ecological and social justice issues. Sustainability embodies this new security doctrine, with sustainability reporting operationalizing it through specific communicative actions. Consequently, firms must now justify not only their contribution to wealth accumulation through financial statements but also how they pose no (or less) threats to human and non-human life forms, now or in the future. This latter justification is (un)successfully achieved through sustainability reporting. Viewed through the lens of neoliberal biopolitics and security, the recent surge in corporate sustainability engagement and reporting, once considered an "oxymoron" or "pure unadulterated socialism," represents a biopolitical strategy to address the neoliberal security paradox inherent in the existence and growth of multinational corporations, albeit with limited success.

10.5 Integrating sustainability

Corporate sustainability reporting has grown exponentially, becoming the principal strategy for corporations to legitimize themselves within the neoliberal accountability framework. However, this growth doesn't necessarily indicate an increase in corporate sustainability. Critical accounting researchers have suggested that such reporting and its underlying frameworks might mislead and propagate incorrect notions of sustainability, often amounting to 'greenwashing'.

Side note:

At this point, it would be a good idea to read Gray et al. (2014), pages 220-232.

Despite this, some companies have begun to consider sustainability as an element of their strategy making. Influential figures in mainstream management, including consultants and corporate leaders, now see sustainability as a strategic imperative. They view it not just as an environmental challenge but also as an opportunity to enhance their market positioning and product competitiveness. This perspective, advocated by experts like Michael Porter, emphasizes sustainability as a core business strategy. For instance, Porter and Kramer (2006, 2) argue:

> Governments, activists, and the media have become adept at holding the companies to account for the social consequences of their activities. Myriad organizations rank companies on the performance of their corporate social responsibility (CSR), and, despite sometimes questionable methodologies, these rankings attract considerable publicity. As a result, CSR has emerged as an inescapable priority for business leaders in every country. ...Many companies have already done much to improve the social and environmental consequences of their activities, yet these efforts have not been nearly as productive as they could be – for two reasons. First, they pit business against society, when clearly the two are interdependent. Second, they pressure companies to think of corporate social responsibility in generic ways instead of in the way most appropriate to each firm's strategy. ... The fact is, the prevailing approaches to CSR are so fragmented and so disconnected from business and strategy as to obscure many of the greatest opportunities for companies to benefit society. If, instead, corporations were to analyze their prospects for social responsibility using the same frameworks that guide their core business choices, they would discover that CSR can be much more than a cost, a constraint, or a charitable deed–it can be a source of opportunity, innovation, and competitive advantage.

Mainstream managerial discourses have sought to incorporate sustainability in various ways. Within the management accounting remit of this chapter, their methodologies can be broadly divided into six categories:

1. Ensuring top leadership commitment through ESG: Developing new layers and apparatuses of governance to deal with sustainability, commonly propagated as ESG (environment, social, and governance).
2. Redefining elements of organizational purpose, like corporate vision and mission, to include notions of sustainability.
3. Employing sustainability as a foundational principle for strategic positioning and competitive advantage.
4. Integrating sustainability into the value chain and performance management systems.

5. Developing costing techniques for sustainability.
6. Developing and implementing environment management systems (EMS).

Applying these elements constitutes cross-border actions between the markets, organizational hierarchies, and the points of production.

Ensuring top leadership commitment

An Environmental, Social, and Governance (ESG) index is a type of stock index of corporate investment risk that assesses companies based on their performance in environmental, social, and governance (ESG) criteria. These indices provide benchmarks for the performance of investments that meet certain ESG standards. The idea is to offer investors a way to integrate these non-financial factors into their investment decisions.

Here's a breakdown of the ESG criteria:

- **Environmental:** This criterion considers how a company performs as a steward of the natural environment. It includes issues like climate change policies, energy use, waste management, and resource conservation.
- **Social:** This aspect examines how a company manages relationships with its employees, suppliers, customers, and the communities where it operates. It includes labor management, health and safety, and community engagement.
- **Governance:** This criterion assesses a company's leadership, executive pay, audits, internal controls, and shareholder rights.

Investors and investment analysts are increasingly interested in these indices as they seek to invest in companies that are not only financially sound but also responsible in their business practices or less risky in terms of the environmental and social risks that their operations can have. These indices can vary in their selection criteria and weightings, with some focusing more on certain ESG aspects than others. Examples of ESG indices include the MSCI ESG Leaders Indices, the FTSE4Good Index Series, and the Dow Jones Sustainability Indices.

In a broader sense, ESG is a market database-driven analytical framework to assess corporate performance in three interrelated dimensions: environmental performance, social performance, and reliability of governance. Given that investors (especially institutional investors) and investment analysts are increasingly concerned about sustainability in terms of various indices that the information markets provide on them, corporate top managements have to become sensitive to them and acknowledge the necessity of incorporating ESG elements into corporate top-level governance structures. Though it has the possibility of misinterpreting and misrecognizing the 'broader idea of sustainability' (see Gray et al. 2014; Milne 1996), this tendency has at least broadened the idea of corporate governance beyond the traditional stewardship or shareholder perspective to a broader stakeholder perspective.

The necessity of improving a company's ESG index assessment may lead the top leadership at the board level to implement strategic actions and policies that align with ESG principles and assessment criteria. Here are some broader initiatives that companies follow to achieve this:

1. Environmental aspect

- Setting environmental policies: The board can establish robust environmental policies that focus on reducing carbon footprint, managing waste, and ensuring sustainable use of resources.
- Green initiatives: Implementing green initiatives like renewable energy usage, eco-friendly manufacturing processes, and sustainable supply chain management.
- Regular reporting: Ensuring regular and transparent reporting on environmental impact, including disclosures about emissions, energy usage, and efforts in environmental conservation.

2. Social aspect

- Corporate social responsibility (CSR) programs: Establishing and actively supporting CSR initiatives that benefit communities, like educational programs, healthcare initiatives, and local development projects.
- Employee welfare policies: Enhancing policies related to employee welfare, diversity, and inclusion. This includes equal opportunities, anti-discrimination policies, and workplace safety measures.

- Stakeholder engagement: Actively engaging with stakeholders, including employees, customers, and local communities, to understand and address their concerns and needs.

3. Governance aspect

- Board diversity and inclusion: Ensuring the board is diverse in terms of gender, ethnicity, and experience. This promotes varied perspectives in decision-making.
- Transparency and accountability: Establishing clear governance structures and processes that ensure accountability and transparency in all corporate actions.
- Ethical conduct and compliance: Implementing a strong code of ethics and compliance, ensuring that the corporation adheres to legal standards and ethical norms in its operations.

4. Cross-cutting actions

- Sustainability integration: Integrating sustainability goals into the company's overall strategy, ensuring that ESG considerations are part of every major decision.
- Training and awareness: Conducting regular training for board members and employees to increase awareness and understanding of ESG issues and practices.
- External collaboration and reporting: Collaborating with external ESG rating agencies, auditors, and advisors for regular assessment and improvement of ESG practices. Also, ensuring comprehensive ESG reporting in annual reports and other public documents.

The common belief of ESG index providers is that by taking such actions, a corporation should not only improve its ESG index assessment but also build a sustainable, responsible, and ethical business model that adds value to all stakeholders, including investors, employees, and the community.

Envisioning sustainability

As discussed in Chapter 2, strategizing involves setting and communicating a corporation's long-term vision and direction, often through corporate vision and mission statements. These define the higher-order principles toward which corporations direct their resources and efforts, especially in the long run. By 'envisioning sustainability', I re-

Key point:

ESG is a capital market-driven assessment exercise to encourage companies to adopt certain sustainable practices to minimize social and environmental risks through sound governance.

fer to corporate efforts to integrate sustainability concepts into their strategic intents, particularly in their vision and mission statements. This approach often reflects top leadership's commitment to sustainability. Over the past decade, many large corporations reporting on sustainability have revised (and continue to revise) their vision and mission statements (and other strategic intent documents like company credos) to reflect their evolving understanding and commitment to sustainability. Figure 10.3 offers examples of this. It's important to approach the statements in Figure 10.3, or similar ones found in cor-

Figure 10.3: Examples of corporate envisioning of sustainability

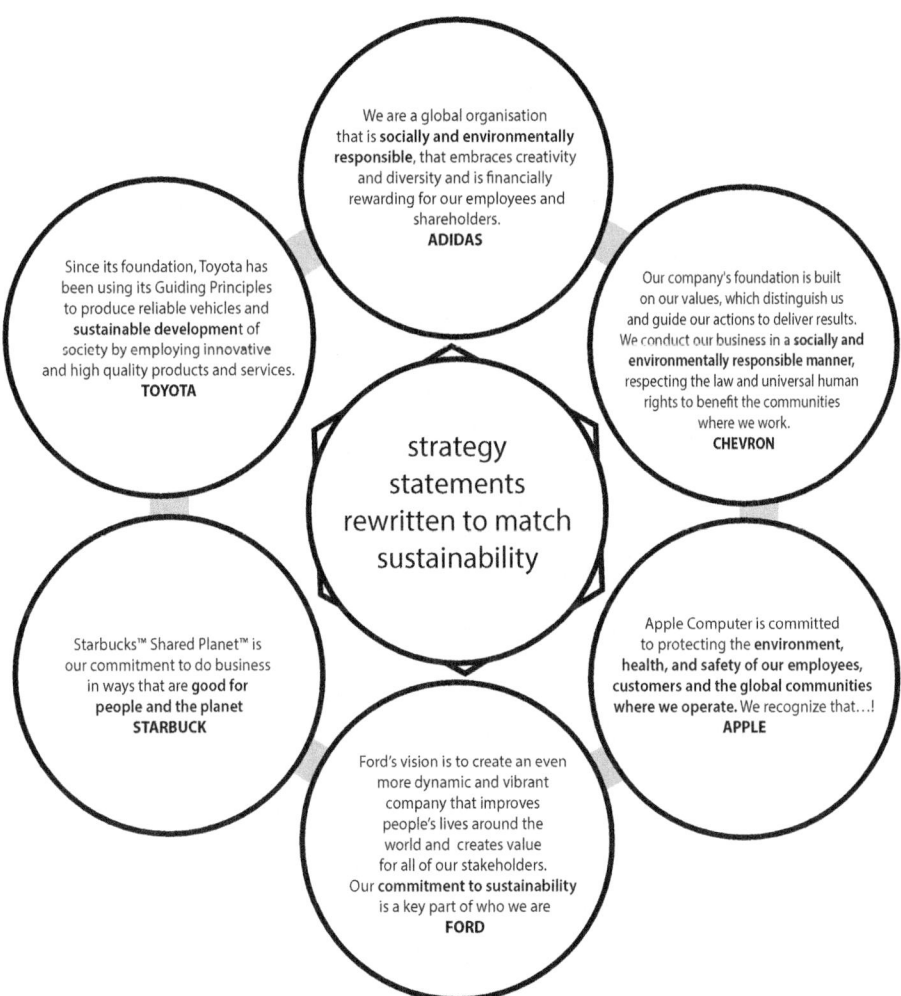

porate reports, with caution. They are aspirational and, as Gray et al. (2014, 223) note, "this is the key point – these statements will not be supported by any explanation or evidence as to why they might be true."

One of the primary motivators for companies to reframe their vision and mission around social and environmental sustainability is the reporting mandates of accrediting bodies like the Global Reporting Initiative (GRI). These organizations have explicitly outlined that companies must demonstrate a clear commitment to sustainability at the strategic level to obtain sustainability reporting accreditations. For instance, the 2021 version of GRI's reporting standards, under general disclosure, stipulates that reports must include a statement detailing "the role of the highest governance body and of senior executives in developing, approving, and updating the organization's purpose, value or mission statements, strategies, policies, and goals related to sustainable development" (p.23). In following this general disclosure requirement, based on their experiences of following the previous versions of GRI, companies would typically include the following in their sustainability reports:

Key point:

How and why corporate strategic intents are modified to accommodate sustainability.

1. A comprehensive vision and strategy for short-term, medium-term, and long-term management of significant economic, environmental, and social impacts caused by, contributed to, or directly linked to their activities, products, or services, including relationships with external entities like suppliers and local community organizations;
2. Strategic priorities and key focus areas for short and medium-term sustainability, including adherence to internationally recognized standards and their relevance to long-term organizational strategy and success;
3. Broader macroeconomic or political trends influencing the organization and its sustainability priorities;
4. Significant events, achievements, and setbacks during the reporting period;
5. Assessment of performance against set targets;
6. Prospective challenges and targets for the next year and objectives for the upcoming 3–5 years;
7. Additional elements relevant to the organization's strategic approach to sustainability.

When coupled with the companies' need to legitimize their actions through reporting (see Bebbington et al. 2008; Campbell 2000; Cho and Patten 2007), such standards provide the necessary institutional pressure for corporations to reform their strategic and operational outlooks. It appears that companies do engage in so-called 'rating games' – an attempt to legitimize their strategic and operational presence by achieving higher ratings from global institutions such as the GRI, ISO, the Dow Jones Sustainability Index, and the FTSE4Good Index (see Alawattage and Fernando 2017; Porter and Kramer 2006). In playing this 'rating game,' companies, especially those in less developed countries, employ a set of textual strategies – imitation, redefinition, innovation, and codification – to demonstrate how they meet the reporting criteria of the rating or accreditation institutions (Alawattage and Fernando, 2017). Consequently, they need to align the communicative elements of their strategic posture with the reporting standards. Changes in these companies' vision and mission statements reflect the necessity for compliance reporting, accreditation, and ratings.

Key point:

Changes to strategic intent are often driven by accreditation and rating requirements of corporate reporting.

Sustainability to postulate strategic positioning

The recent past has seen a surge in mass awareness, appreciation, and commitment towards planetary sustainability, propelled by social and traditional media coverage of environmental pollution and social impacts caused by industries. In market terms, this has led to increased demand and willingness to pay premium prices for sustainably produced products. Nielsen, a global data analytics firm, in their 2015 Global Sustainability Report titled "The Sustainability Imperative," highlights these key trends:

1. Brands demonstrating a commitment to sustainability outperform those that don't. Over the past year, sales of sustainable brands grew by over 4% globally, compared to less than 1% for others.
2. Sixty-six percent of consumers are willing to pay more for sustainable brands, up from 55% in 2014 and 50% in 2013.
3. Social responsibility is crucial for proactive reputation management. Companies with strong reputations excel in attracting top talent, investors, community partners, and, importantly, consumers.
4. Key purchasing drivers are identified as:

Key point:

Companies are keen to promote their products as 'sustainable' due to the appeal that sustainability branding has to consumers.

- Trust in the brand/company (62%)
- Health & wellness benefits (59%)
- Use of fresh, natural, or organic ingredients (57%)
- Environmental friendliness (45%)
- Commitment to social value (43%)
- Environmentally friendly packaging (41%)
- Commitment to the community (41%)

In response, companies have adopted various marketing strategies to capitalize on this sustainability premium. Nielsen's 2015 survey categorizes these tactics into three groups:

- **Claim only:** The brand indicates sustainability on product labels or packaging.
- **Marketing only:** The brand uses websites, news, and other channels to promote social/environmental impact.
- **Claim + marketing:** The brand combines product claims with sustainability in marketing.

The survey reveals that 65% of companies use "Marketing Only," 29% use "Claim + Marketing," and only 2% use "Claim Only."

10.6 Operationalizing sustainability

What I mean by 'operationalizing sustainability' is the effort by corporations to integrate various sustainability dimensions and criteria into their decision-making processes, performance evaluations, transaction processing systems, and costing practices. As depicted in Figure 10.2, within the realm of management accounting, we can identify six primary themes of operationalizing sustainability:

1. Incorporating sustainability into capital investment decisions.
2. Integrating sustainability into value-chain and industry analyses.
3. Integrating sustainability into performance management, especially balanced scorecards.
4. Adapting cost accounting to include sustainability factors.
5. Applying carbon costing methods.
6. Developing and maintaining environmental management systems

Sustainability in capital investment decisions

Although there have not been significant technical breakthroughs in developing models for capital investment decisions that can quantify and monetize the impact of investment projects on sustainability, corporate managers are showing an increasing willingness to 'consider' sustainability issues alongside financial factors in investment decisions. In the absence of quantified and monetized information on the sustainability impact of investment proposals, managers appear increasingly inclined to consider qualitative narratives and assessments, especially when they support the financial outcomes of the investment appraisal. This trend was highlighted in a survey study conducted by Vesty (2011) in Australia, which found:

- Enhancing corporate reputation is a key motivator for companies to consider sustainability in capital investment decisions. The primary method for incorporating sustainability is identifying sustainability risks in investment appraisals, along with considerations of competitive advantage, community impacts, and actions that foster employee engagement.
- Fifty-five percent of CFO respondents indicated they did not downplay qualitative data in favor of quantitative analysis.
- Preference for qualitative data was more pronounced regarding social factors than environmental ones.
- The dominant sustainability themes influencing financial capital appraisal experimentation were carbon and water accounting.
- Forty percent of CFO respondents would not automatically reject projects with negative net present values if sustainability benefits were identified.
- Sustainability managers are increasingly playing a key role in capital investment appraisals, often contributing individual sustainability reports as a separate component of the appraisal process.
- For direct investments in sustainability projects, which often require different appraisal techniques, CFOs and sustainability managers collaborate on appraisal decisions.
- While sustainability considerations are being incorporated into capital investment decisions, they have not yet become the primary decision-making criterion.

Key point:

Limited use of sustainability concerns in investment decisions.

Sustainable value chain analysis and competitive industry analysis

One key attempt to operationalize sustainability within existing strategic analysis frameworks is the reconceptualization of Michael Porter's value chain analysis. This demonstrates how the global sustainability agenda has compelled management gurus and experts to reconsider their frameworks in light of sustainability considerations. This shift could be seen as a remarketing strategy of their models in an evolving epistemic market for managerial models where sustainability has to be considered. They argue:

Key point:

How Porter and Kramer attempt to integrate their value-chain analysis with sustainability concerns.

> When a company uses the value chain to chart all the social consequences of its activities, it has, in effect, created an inventory of problems and opportunities—mostly operational issues—that need to be investigated, prioritized, and addressed. In general, companies should attempt to clear away as many negative value-chain social impacts as possible. Some company activities will prove to offer opportunities for social and strategic distinction. (Porter and Kramer 2006, 5)

Porter and Kramer's (2006) epistemic strategy in this regard is to 'insert' specific examples of the ways in which sustainability can be "considered" as an opportunity (rather than a constraint or a cost) for creating value across the value chain. Table 10.1 summarises their illustrative prescriptions.

Porter and Kramer's (2006) subsequent move involves integrating 'sustainability' into their renowned "diamond framework" of competitive context, as discussed in Chapter 2. This framework evaluates the conduciveness of national and industrial contexts in enabling firms to gain a competitive advantage. It encompasses four principal elements: context within which the firm strategy and rivalry take place, factor conditions, demand conditions, and related and supporting industries. These factors collectively shape a competitive environment conducive to the development of competitive advantages. As noted in Chapter 2, Porter utilized this framework to link firm strategies with national development policies, thus endowing his theory of competitive advantage with political significance beyond the corporate sphere. By incorporating 'sustainability' into their framework, Porter and Kramer aim to expand its political relevance as a policy

Key point:

How Porter and Kramer revise their industry analysis to incorporate sustainability concerns.

Table 10.1: Porter and Karammer's insertion of sustainability into value chain analysis

Value chain element	Examples of operational matters	Ways to consider sustainability: analyze and minimize
Inbound logistics:	Incoming materials, storage, data, collection services, customer access.	transportation impacts (e.g., emissions, congestion, logging roads)
Operations	assembly, component fabrication, branch operations	Emissions and waste; biodiversity and ecological impacts; energy and water usage; worker safety and labor relations; hazardous materials
Outbound logistics	Order processing, warehousing, report preparation	Packaging use and disposal; transportation impacts
Marketing and sales	Salesforce, promotion, advertising, proposal writing, Web site	Marketing and advertising (e.g., truthful advertising, advertising to children); pricing practices (e.g., price discrimination among customers, anticompetitive pricing practices, pricing policy to the poor); consumer information; privacy
After-sales service	Installation, customer support, complaint resolution, repair	Disposal of obsolete products; handling of consumables (e.g., motor oil, printing ink); customer privacy
Firm infrastructure	Financing, planning, investor relations	Financial reporting practices; government practices; transparency; use of lobbying to promote sustainability
Human resource management	Recruiting, training, and compensation system	Education and job training; safe working conditions; diversity and discrimination; health care and other benefits; compensation policies; layoff policies
Technology development	product design, testing, process design, material research, market research	Relationships with universities; ethical research practices (e.g., animal testing, GMOs); product safety; conservation of raw materials; recycling
Procurement	Components, machinery, advertising, and services	Procurement and supply chain practices (e.g., bribery, child labor, conflict diamonds, pricing to farmers); uses of particular inputs (e.g., animal fur); utilization of natural resources

Source: based on Porter and Kramer (2006)

planning and analysis tool. This adaptation uses the same model to gauge the conduciveness of the environment for fostering corporate sustainability. Table 10.2 encapsulates these sustainability insertions into the model.

Table 10.2: Inserting sustainability into the framework of competitive advantage of a nation

Elements of the Diamond Framework	Definition of the element	Factors that enhance firms' collective capacity to be sustainable
The context for firm strategy and rivalry	The rules and incentives that govern competition	Fair and open local competition (e.g., the absence of trade barriers, fair regulations); intellectual property protection; transparency (e.g., financial reporting, corruption: Extractive Industries Transparency Initiative); the rule of law (e.g., security, protection of property, legal system); Meritocratic incentive systems (e.g., anti-discrimination)
Local Demand Conditions	The nature and sophistication of local customer needs	The sophistication of local demand (e.g., the appeal of social value propositions: Whole Foods' customers); demanding regulatory standards (California auto emissions and mileage standards); unusual local needs that can be served nationally and globally (Urbi's housing financing, Unilever's "bottom of the pyramid" strategy).
Related and Supporting Industries	The local availability of supporting industries	Availability of local suppliers (Sysco's locally grown produce; Nestlé's milk collection dairies); access to firms in related fields; presence of clusters instead of isolated industries
Factor (Input) Conditions	Presence of high-quality, specialized inputs available to firms	Availability of human resources (Marriott's job training); access to research institutions and universities (Microsoft's Working Connections); efficient physical infrastructure; Efficient administrative infrastructure; availability of scientific and technological infrastructure (Nestlé's knowledge transfer to milk farmers); sustainable natural resources (GrupoNueva's water conservation); efficient access to capital

Source: based on Porter and Kramer (2006)

 ## Sustainable performance management with balanced scorecards

The balanced scorecards (BSC) has been a popular tool in management accounting for decades. A key response of management accounting to the sustainability imperative has been to explore how BSC can operationalize sustainability. Research into sustainability through BSC primarily addresses two major issues:

1. integrating sustainability into the BSC, and
2. establishing causal links between sustainability and other performance dimensions.

Given Kaplan's prominent association with the Balanced Scorecard (BSC), it would be insightful to explore how Kaplan and his colleagues have endeavored to integrate sustainability into BSC. However, this topic has already been discussed in Chapter 4. I recommend revisiting the section titled "Reimagining the BSC for Sustainability" in that chapter. In this segment, I will focus on the efforts of others to adapt the BSC for sustainability.

Integrating sustainability into BSC

The first issue involves integrating sustainability concerns into the strategic performance management systems represented by BSC. Proponents and followers of BSC argue that BSC's top-down hierarchical planning structure, which deduces performance measures from strategy, ensures that all business activities, including those addressing environmental and social aspects, are aligned with successful business strategy implementation. This integration implies that corporate performance management can explicitly consider the relationship between a firm's environmental, social, and economic performance. Three approaches for integrating sustainability into BSC are discussed in the literature (Figge et al. 2002):

Key point:

Different ways the BSC can be adapted to deal with sustainability concerns.

1. Integrating environmental and social aspects into the four perspectives of the balanced scorecard. This approach, akin to Porter and Kramer's (2006) suggestions relating to Porter's value chain analysis framework and diamond model of competitive advantage, involves incorporating specific sustainability issues into each of the four BSC dimensions. For example, managers might consider how internal processes could be improved to address eco-justice and eco-efficiency issues, such as mitigating discrimination and reducing carbon footprint. Figge et al. (2002, p. 274) state that:

   > Environmental/social aspects consequently become an integral part of the conventional Scorecard and are automatically integrated in its cause–effect links and hierarchically orientated towards the financial perspective and a successful conversion of a business' strategy.

2. Introducing an additional non-market perspective into the balanced scorecard. This approach recognizes that some eco-justice and eco-efficiency issues are not yet fully integrated into market and institutional processes represented by conventional BSC dimensions. Thus, an additional fifth dimension is proposed, "when environmental or social aspects

that cannot be reflected according to their strategic relevance within the four standard BSC perspectives at the same time significantly influence the firm's success from outside the market system"(Figge et al., 2002, p. 274). This fifth dimension should be considered in relation to all other dimensions and the strategic core of the BSC.
3. Deducting a derived environmental and social scorecard. This approach does not involve developing a separate BSC but extends the above two approaches. The focus is on deriving a BSC from sustainability issues related to existing dimensions and the new fifth sustainability dimension, thus augmenting the conventional BSC with this extra sustainability focus. Figge et al. (2002) explain that:

> A derived scorecard ... draws its contents from an existing BSC system and is thus predominantly used in order to coordinate, organize, and further differentiate the environmental and social aspects, once their strategic relevance and position in the cause-and-effect chains have been identified by the two approaches presented above.

Establishing causal links between sustainability and financial outcomes

The second challenge in incorporating sustainability into the Balanced Scorecard (BSC) is establishing causal links between sustainability, strategy, and other BSC aspects. Chapter 4 introduces the 'strategy map', clarifying these connections to ensure all dimensions contribute to financial improvement, as seen in a higher return on investment (see Chapter 4, especially Figure 4.7). Kaplan and McMillan's (2021) paper, "Reimagining the BSC for the ESG Era," demonstrates how these 'causalities'—or 'finalities', as Norekklit critiques BSC's concept of causality—are identified and promoted. Given your familiarity with Kaplan and colleagues' work in redefining the BSC for the ESG era from Chapter 4, I won't delve further here but recommend revisiting that section. Their approach mirrors Porter and Kramer's 2006 methodology, integrating sustainability into existing models like Porter's value chain and diamond model. It examines sustainability concerns (e.g., child labor in Figge et al.'s 2002 examples) within the BSC framework. Hence, sustainability integration in the BSC follows a similar pattern, linking sustainability issues to the BSC's overarching causality. This revisits my critique in Chapters 2 and 4 on Porter and Kramer's and Kaplan and McMillan's efforts to incorporate sustainability into value-chain analysis and the BSC, respectively. These efforts to reshape traditional management accounting and strategy frameworks in the context of sustainability often lack genuinely sustainable approaches. Instead, they seem more focused on repackaging their models in a market increasingly valuing sustainability. Despite the new sustainability-focused terminology, their fundamental ideology, prioritizing financial objectives over sustainability, remains unchanged.

Privileging financial over sustainability

Such attempts to integrate sustainability into existing performance management and strategy frameworks may bring some positive outcomes, at least in terms of the managerial acceptance and appreciation of the importance of sustainability issues. They would bring out some KPIs that translate sustainability concerns to certain performance targets and, thereby, enact some operational initiatives to deal with sustainability. However, such initiatives and enactments would be possible only to the extent that the management can effectively demonstrate a positive financial causality of such KPIs and initiatives. In other words, these attempts to integrate sustainability into the existing performance management and strategy framework limit the way in which we consider and prioritize sustainability. Sustainability is operationalized only if it can be established that a positive causality exists between solving sustainability issues and financial performance. This is because existing performance management and strategy frameworks, including BSC and value chain analysis, are too capitalistic, and they assess managerial actions and initiatives only through their contributions toward competitive positioning and shareholder wealth maximization. So, any attempt to integrate sustainability into such a framework would eventually surrender sustainability to possibilities of profits and would only operate as a tool of 'sustainability-based legitimation of financial' because the financial will always be at the top of the hierarchy of priorities. As our common sense often tells us, many of the eco-justice and eco-efficiency issues would not have a direct demonstrable positive causality toward the return on investment. Perhaps the only financial causality would be the punitive cost effect (such as penalties, loss of reputation, loss of market share etc.) that not attaining eco-justice and eco-efficien-

Key point:

Reimagining popular management accounting and strategy frameworks in light of sustainability concerns may be ideologically problematic.

cy issues would create. This means the BSC and value chain analysis-based sustainability management, as far as it is conceptualized so far, privileges the financial over sustainability.

Let's revisit Milton Friedman's and Daly's critiques of corporate social responsibility, as discussed earlier in this chapter. These economists identified a fundamental conflict: the profit motives of private capital are inherently at odds with the principles of social responsibility and sustainability. Consequently, they faced a political choice between prioritizing shareholders or social responsibility, and they chose the former. However, attempts to re-envision management accounting and strategy models appear to be veiled efforts to obscure this inherent contradiction between the economic doctrines of wealth accumulation for a few and the sustainability of everyone else.

Costing sustainability

Two primary cost accounting approaches to sustainability are prominent in the literature:

1. application of activity-based costing to allocate the costs of sustainability activities to product costs, and
2. life cycle costing.

It is important to recognize that current costing methods tend to be skewed towards accounting for 'ecological' aspects (rather than social elements) of sustainability, with a particular emphasis on accounting for greenhouse gas emissions (GHG).

Use of ABC in sustainability costing

The fundamental assumption of sustainability costing is that environmental emissions can be quantified accurately over time, much like how cost accounting systems trace and account for the financial effects of organizational transactions and events (Lemon and Pember 2014). To this end, ABC is considered effective for understanding the drivers of resource consumption, which is a crucial component in determining the extent of an organization's greenhouse gas (GHG) emissions. ABC models how resources are consumed, the reasons behind their consumption, and the parties responsible for the consumption (Lemon and Pember, 2014). Therefore, ABC can also elucidate the extent, reasons, and accountability for an organization's GHG emissions.

Numerous papers and texts attempt to explain how corporations should account for environmental emissions. However, two white papers stand out for their epistemic authority and comprehensiveness: the "Environmental Management Accounting: International Guidance Document" by the International Federation of Accountants (2005) and the "Environmental Management Accounting Procedures and Principles" by the United Nations Division of Sustainable Development (2001). The methodology advocated in these papers is essentially a blend of "natural capital inventory accounting" and "input-output analysis" (for a detailed discussion of these approaches, see Gray and Bebbington 2001; Gray et al. 1993; Lamberton 2005). Broadly, this involves tracking the environmental impact of organizational activities by tracing the physical flow of inputs, processes, activities, and outputs and then assigning monetary values to them.

Tracing the physical flows: materials flow accounting

The system theory behind tracing the physical flow of environmental impact posits that all physical inputs eventually become outputs—either as physical products or as waste and emissions. This necessitates a balance between inputs and outputs, which must be accounted for in terms of physical resources like energy, water, materials, and waste. This concept, known as physical flow accounting, is also referred to as "materials balance," "input-output balance," "mass balance," or "eco-balance." The International Federation of Accountants (2005, p. 30) recommends that organizations track all physical inputs and outputs, ensuring no significant quantities of energy, water, or other materials are unaccounted for. Many organizations conduct separate energy and water balances from other materials balances.

The accounting entity – this input-output balance can be applied at various levels: across the entire organization, within a specific manufacturing site or operational unit, to a process, machinery, product, or service line, or even beyond the organization's boundaries to include physical data from suppliers, customers, and other supply chain elements. When extended to supply chain elements, it's termed Supply Chain Environmental Management. The International Federation of Accountants (2005, p. 31) suggests that to provide a comprehensive and integrated view of "eco-balance," it's essential to trace material flows through all organizational steps—materials procurement, delivery, inventory, internal distribution, product shipping, waste collection, recycling, treatment, and disposal, etc. Such material flow ac-

Key point:

Tracing the physical flow of materials constitutes a key element of activity-based accounting of environmental impact.

counting should specifically account for:

- Raw and auxiliary materials
- Packaging materials
- Merchandise
- Operating materials, including energy
- Wastewater
- Air emissions
- Products, by-products, and packaging
- Solid and hazardous waste

Importance of accounting for physical flow: This is crucial for two reasons. Firstly, it forms the basis for the physical activity upon which the cost accounting aspect of environmental management accounting is built and implemented, offering a clear view of activities driving environmental costs. Secondly, it also establishes a foundation for environmental performance indicators (EPIs). These EPIs can be absolute, measuring resource consumption and waste/emissions generation (e.g., total freshwater used, total wastewater generated during an accounting period), or relative/normalized (e.g., freshwater consumed per output unit, wastewater generated per unit of manufactured goods or services).

 ### Tracing the monetary flow: activity-based costing of environmental impact

In this approach to costing, the objective is to identify the costs associated with environmental activities and subsequently allocate them to the relevant products (i.e., cost objects). The United Nations Division of Sustainable Development (2001, p. 75) recommends that:

Key point:

The necessity of incorporating environmentally driven costs to the cost centers and cost objects.

> Whenever possible, environment-driven costs should be allocated directly to the activity that causes the costs and to the respective cost centers and cost drivers. Consequently, the costs of treating, for example, the toxic waste arising from a product should directly and exclusively be allocated to that product.

In doing so, ABC is considered more appropriate due to its accurate representation of 'cost incidents' or the way resources are utilized by organizational activities, including environmental ones, and how these activities generate costs. This method offers a comprehensive analysis for measuring the total cost of cost objects and establishes performance metrics related to these activities. The dual utility of ABC is encapsulated in accounting literature through the concepts of "cost assignment view" and "and cost management view." This is illustrated in Figure 10.4, which focuses on the relationship between environmental activities and costs.

Figure 10.4: Environmental activity-based costing

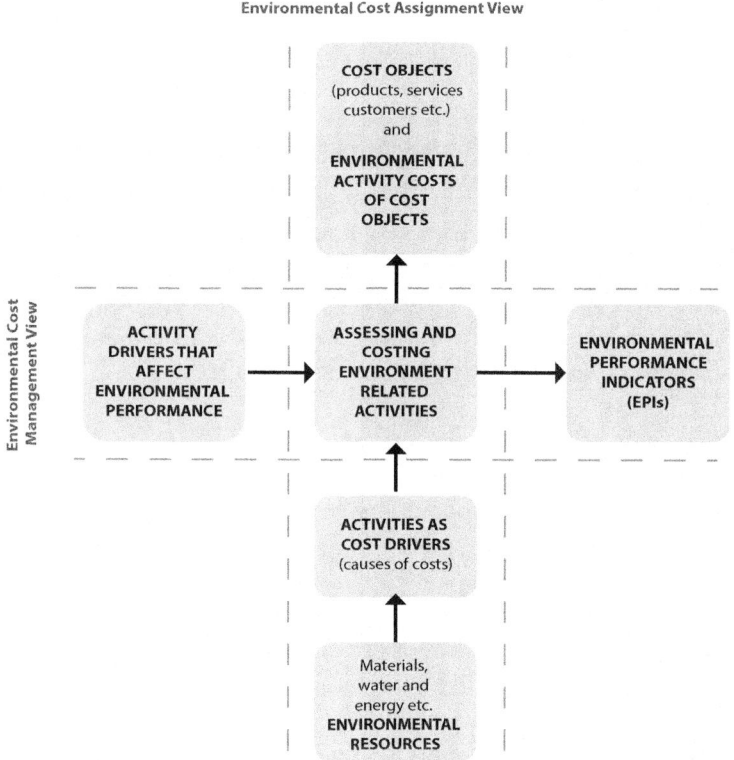

The United Nations Division of Sustainable Development (2001) states that activity-based monetary and physical flow accounting should be utilized to provide managerial insights into the volumes and nature of environment-related activities and costs. This approach enables different cost classification schema compared to traditional financial or management accounting. Such an activity and cost classification scheme should encompass elements such as:

- Waste and emission treatment.
- Preventive environmental management.
- Material purchase value of non-product outputs.
- Processing cost of non-product outputs.

Key point:

Environmental costing involves a different schema of cost classification.

According to the United Nations Division of Sustainable Development (2001), these cost categories should correlate with environmental dimensions such as:

- Air/climate
- Wastewater
- Waste
- Soil/groundwater
- Noise/vibration
- Biodiversity/landscape
- Radiation

Table 10.3 illustrates a template of this activity-cost classification scheme.

In an overall sense, therefore, costing sustainability, especially considering the approach proposed by the United Nations Division of Sustainable Development (2001), is a particular accounting approach where a specific set of environmentally related activities are identified and analyzed to assess their comparative cost impacts.

Lifecycle costing (LCC) and whole life costing (WLC)

A key point in our discussion on sustainability costing is that activity-based physical and monetary flow accounting only considers the sustainability implications of capital investment decisions as far as they are implied in the depreciation of fixed assets. LCC and WLC, in contrast, explicitly address large capital investment projects with construction elements. These are often defined as tools for assessing the total cost performance of an asset throughout its life cycle, which includes acquisition, operation, maintenance, and disposal costs (Dragos and Neamtu 2013; Langdon 2007). These tools are crucial for decision-making in the construction industry, particularly in public procurement of capital assets, and are also governed by a set of international standards, such as BS/ISO15686-5.

Both LCC and WLC operate on the premise that the purchase price of a capital asset does not fully capture the financial and non-financial benefits that an environmentally and socially preferable asset can provide, as these benefits (and costs) accumulate over the asset's life cycle. Consequently, procurement decisions based solely on purchase price may prioritize economic efficiency, potentially at the expense of

Table 10.3: Environmental activity-cost classification scheme

Environmental cost/expenditure categories	Air / Climate	Wastewater	Waste	Soil / Groundwater	Noise / Vibration	Biodiversity / Landscape	Radiation	Other	Total
1. Waste and emission treatment									
1.1. Depreciation for related equipment									
1.2. Maintenance and operating materials and services									
1.3. Related personnel									
1.4. Fees, taxes, charges									
1.5. Fines and penalties									
1.6. Insurance for environmental liabilities									
1.7. Provisions for clean up costs, remediation									
2. Prevention and environmental management									
2.1. External services for environmental management									
2.2. Personnel for general environmental management activities									
2.3. Research and development									
2.4. Extra expenditure for cleaner technologies									
2.5. Other environmental management costs									
3. Material purchase value of non- product output									
3.1. Raw materials									
3.2. Packaging									
3.3. Auxiliary materials									
3.4. Operating materials									
3.5. Energy									
3.6. Water									
4. Processing costs of non-product output									
Total of environmental expenditure									
5. Environmental revenues									
5.1. Subsidies, awards									
5.2. Other earnings									
Total of Environmental revenues									

Source: United Nations Division of Sustainable Development (2001, 19)

Key point:

Life cycle costing and whole life costing are interconnected methods of tracing the full costs of an investment decision.

environmental and social considerations. LCC typically encompasses four primary cost categories based purely on financial valuation: investment, operational, maintenance, and end-of-life disposal costs. When these fundamental cost categories are expanded to include "externalities" related to the work, service, or product, it evolves into Environmental Life Cycle Costing (ELCC). ELCC, for instance, might measure external costs of global warming contributions linked to emissions of various greenhouse gases, acidification, eutrophication, or other quantifiable impacts (Dragos and Neamtu, 2013).

WLC builds upon LCC, focusing not only on the construction, maintenance, operation, and disposal of the asset but also on client and user costs. These additional costs include project financing, land acquisition, income, and external costs (those not borne by parties to the construction contract, such as tenants). Thus, LCC is effectively a subset of WLC. This distinction is depicted in Figure 10.5.

Figure 10.5: WLC and LLC costs

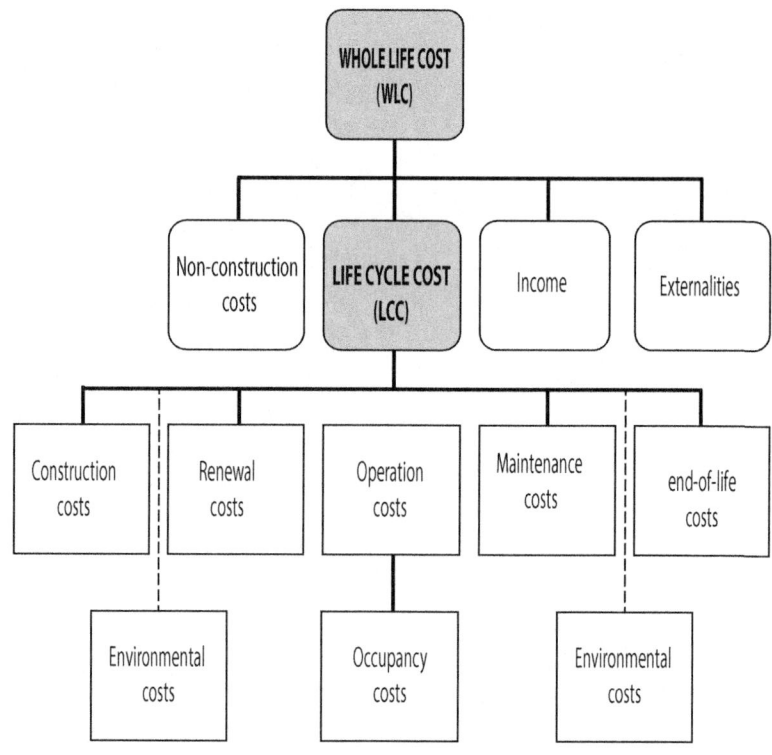

Source: Royal Institution of Chartered Surveyors (RICS) (2016, 5)

Carbon costing/accounting

Carbon accounting, also known as greenhouse gas (GHG) accounting, is the process of measuring the amounts of carbon dioxide and other GHG emissions produced by an individual, organization, event, activity, product, or asset. It is a critical tool in the fight against climate change, helping to quantify and manage carbon footprints. Carbon accounting can take various forms, associated with different regulatory and reporting initiatives, such as carbon taxes and emission trading systems. According to the Greenhouse Gas Protocol (https://ghgprotocol.org), which provides widely-adopted greenhouse gas accounting standards and tools for companies, GHG accounting can employ spend-based or activity-based methods. Often, a hybrid mixture of these methods is adopted to enhance the accuracy and comprehensiveness of carbon calculations. Carbon accounting is a diverse and ever-evolving field of study, and a comprehensive discussion about it is beyond the scope of this chapter and the book. However, based on the Greenhouse Gas Protocol, an overview of greenhouse gas accounting is provided here. For further understanding beyond these key points, you are encouraged to visit regulatory websites such as the Greenhouse Gas Protocol.

Key point:

Carbon accounting defined

The calculation process generally involves the following steps:

1. Identifying emission sources: This includes direct emissions from owned or controlled sources (Scope 1), indirect emissions from the generation of purchased energy (Scope 2), and all other indirect emissions that occur in the value chain of the reporting company (Scope 3).
2. Data collection: Gathering data on energy consumption, fuel use, and other activities leading to GHG emissions.
3. Selecting emission factors: Emission factors are used to convert activity data (like liters of fuel used or kilowatt-hours of electricity consumed) into greenhouse gas emissions, expressed in terms of CO2-equivalent.
4. Applying calculation tools: The GHG Protocol provides a range of tools and methodologies for calculating emissions.
5. Aggregation and reporting: Summing up all emissions to produce a total GHG emission inventory for the reporting entity. This report can then be used for internal management, reporting to stakeholders, or for public disclosure.
6. Setting reduction targets and strategies: Once the emissions

are understood, organizations can set targets for reduction and develop strategies to achieve these targets.
7. Tracking performance and reporting: Monitoring and regularly reporting on GHG emissions help organizations assess their performance against their targets and communicate progress to stakeholders.

Key point:

Critical elements of carbon accounting.

The GHG Protocol categorizes emissions into three 'scopes' for better management and understanding:

- Scope 1 emissions: These are direct greenhouse gas emissions from sources that are owned or controlled by the entity. This includes emissions from combustion in owned or controlled boilers, furnaces, vehicles, and emissions from chemical production in owned or controlled process equipment.
- Scope 2 emissions: These emissions are indirect greenhouse gas emissions from the consumption of purchased electricity, heat, or steam. Essentially, they stem from the generation of energy that is consumed by the entity but generated elsewhere. These emissions physically occur at the facility where the energy is generated.
- Scope 3 emissions: This is the broadest category and includes all other indirect emissions that occur in a company's value chain. These emissions are a consequence of the activities of the entity but occur from sources not owned or controlled by it. This includes emissions related to transportation, waste disposal, use

Key point:

Scopes of carbon emission accounting.

Understanding and categorizing emissions into these scopes helps organizations to comprehensively manage their carbon footprint, set and track performance targets, and comply with reporting requirements. It also assists in identifying opportunities for emission reduction, which is critical for climate change mitigation strategies.

Environmental management systems

Environmental management systems (EMS) encompass many concepts discussed in this chapter. An EMS comprises an organization's formal structures to plan, execute, manage, control, achieve, and report its environmental policies and objectives. Gray and Bebbington (2001, p. 87) describe EMS as a means for organizations to systematically harmonize and integrate their diverse environmental responses with other management and accounting systems. Like total quality management (TQM) systems, EMS aims to integrate environmental quality into an organization's operational processes and culture. It makes environmental responsibility a part of everyone's role, thereby minimizing the environmental impact of the organization's daily operations. While the specific approaches to environmental management vary based on a company's unique circumstances, the following key elements broadly define an EMS:

1. Environmental audits, surveys, and assessments: Organizations should thoroughly assess legislative, market, and industrial contexts to understand external pressures. This should be paired with an internal review of operations and processes to identify the environmental impact and prioritize mitigation efforts. Tools for these assessments include environmental audits, input-output analysis, life-cycle costing, value chain analysis, and activity-based environmental analysis.
2. Environmental objectives and policies: This includes the policy framework that outlines the company's normative approach to environmental issues. It specifies the level of corporate commitment, priority areas, legal and regulatory compliance necessities, and the foundational principles for the company's environmental approach.
3. Environmental strategies: These are specific programs, projects, and initiatives undertaken to realize environmental objectives, policies, and ways to redesign operational activities for a positive environmental impact.
4. Responsibility and accountability structure: This defines who is responsible and accountable for each element of the environmental management strategies.
5. Performance management framework: This is part of the responsibility and accountability structure, involving processes to ensure the operational implementation of environmental strategies, periodic review of outcomes, and protocols for revising plans and actions as needed. Tools like Balanced Scorecards and budgets are significant in integrating environmental aspects into the company's primary performance management system.
6. Reporting systems involve establishing transaction processing systems that accurately account for the environmental impact of day-to-day operations (e.g., recording travel mileage and energy consumption) and maintaining audit trails.

Key point:

Principal elements of EMS.

It also includes systems for compiling data into periodic reports and assessments, including sustainability reports and environmental audits by internal and external parties.

Further discussion of these elements is beyond the scope of this chapter. However, numerous texts offer detailed discussions, with Gray and Bebbington (2001) being highly recommended.

It should also be noted that EMS elements are now increasingly being integrated into enterprise resource planning (ERP) software, either as separate modules or integrated elements of other ERP modules.

Chapter summary and a concluding critique

The aim of this chapter was to discuss how management accounting has responded to the global sustainability agenda. Initially, it outlined the political contradictions underlying sustainability. The neoliberal political rationale of international organizations and corporations promoting sustainability was then explored. Prominent neoclassical economists like Friedman and Daly opposed the notion of corporate social responsibility, viewing it as "pure and unadulterated socialism" or an "oxymoron." Despite resistance from economists and policy experts, CSR grew significantly, challenging neoclassical economic views. This paradox puzzled mainstream neoclassical economics-based researchers, leading to studies testing the positive correlation between CSR and shareholder value. However, these studies yielded mixed results, unable to provide a neoclassical explanation for the growth in sustainability.

Outside mainstream neoclassical economics-based accounting studies, sustainability accounting, or social and environmental accounting, has developed various theoretical approaches, including system-theory-based, stakeholder, legitimacy, isomorphism, and political-economic explanations. The chapter didn't delve deeply into these theories but provided a brief biopolitical explanation of the sustainability agenda's growth, viewing corporate sustainability as an extension of neoliberal governmentality.

The primary focus was how management accounting has adapted to the sustainability agenda. The chapter discussed the strategic and operational modifications in management accounting for sustainability. At the strategic level, responses included extending corporate accountability, recognizing sustainability's strategic significance, and reformulating corporate vision and mission statements. At the operational level, new strategic management accounting tools and practices were employed to address sustainability, including modifications in capital investment decisions, Porterian strategy discourses, the Balanced Scorecard for sustainability performance, and new cost accounting techniques like life cycle costing, whole life costing, and activity-based costing for material flow accounting and their environmental cost classifications.

Environmental management systems were discussed as frameworks integrating accounting and management techniques.

That was the chapter summary, which must be extended to an overarching critique of management accounting's response to sustainability challenges to conclude the book with a sustainability critique of how management accounting deals with the most critical challenges of our time. Throughout this and previous chapters, you came across many occasions where management accounting scholars and practitioners attempted to revise their conceptual frameworks, techniques, and methods to incorporate sustainability. I don't suspect their motives; they seem genuinely and wholeheartedly interested in sustainability and recognize the criticality of enhancing management accounting practices accordingly.

However, the fundamental problem is that those efforts fail to recognize and acknowledge, both ideologically and pragmatically, the fundamental political contradictions upon which the (un)sustainability emerges. As we discussed at the beginning of the chapter, the political contradictions between the economy, polity, society, and ecology need to be recognized and acknowledged for a true understanding and action program of sustainability. This demands the willingness and techno-managerial acumen to appreciate sustainability beyond the economic apparatuses of capital accumulation. This is exactly what management accounting thought has failed to do so far. As a result, various attempts to incorporate sustainability into existing management accounting frameworks can be both misguiding and dangerous as the true meaning of sustainability often gets 'overcoded'. This notion of 'overcoding' is an important concept here to see what management accounting adventures of sustainabilizing management accounting do.

In Deleuze and Guattari's conception, 'overcoding' refers to the expression of the capitalist axiomatic, resulting in "phenomena of centering, unification, totalization, integration, hierarchization, and finalization" (Deleuze and Guattari 1987, 41; see also, Holmes 2007). As we have seen in the examples of management accounting adventures explained in this chapter and other chapters, this is what happens. Through various accounting measures and procedures, sustainability gets centered, unified, totalized, integrated, hierarchized, and financialized as something that can be operationalized through corporate profit motives. So, sustainability gets overcoded into ESG, something that the corporations and mainstream accounting, finance, and economics researchers can proxy sustainability based on already available market data provided by market databases. When translated into these market variables, sustainability loses its broader meaning and becomes narrowly economic. In this 'proxification', sustainability gets a different economic meaning that is far from the true meaning that the UN and other global institutions and environmental activists envisage. So, in the name of ESG, strategy gurus don't see poverty; instead, they see corporate "fortunes at the bottom of the pyramid" (Prahalad 2005). They don't see how 'poverty capital' (Roy 2010) operates; instead, they see a 'new ecosystem' from which corporations can earn extra profits (Kaplan and McMillan 2021). This could then lead us to carefully think about Milne's assertion that "sustainability is not an organizational concept and to apply it at the (capitalistic) organizational level is either very complex or very stupid" (Gray et al. 2014; Milne 1996).

Test your knowledge

1. List the four fundamental contradictory categories that underpin (un)sustainability and explain the fundamental structural logics according to which or towards which they operate.
2. Explain Chantal Mouffe's differentiation between 'the political' and 'politics'.
3. Explain what you mean by the terms "eco-efficiency" and "eco-justice". Which of these would hold the ideas of socio-political justice and ecological justice?
4. Briefly explain the grounds on which Milton Friedman propagated his critique of corporate leaders investing in corporate social responsibility projects.
5. Briefly explain this chapter's 'neoliberal reasoning' for corpo-

rate engagement in social responsibility and sustainability projects.
6. Critique the mainstream economic objection to corporate leaders investing in corporate social responsibility projects using the 'neoliberal reasoning' outlined above.
7. Explain why there was an upsurge in 'testing' the correlation between corporate financial performance and corporate social responsibility engagements.
8. List and briefly explain the different levels at which management accounting integration of sustainability takes place.
9. Briefly explain the neoliberal paradox of corporations that underpins the necessity of environmental, social, and governance (ESG) initiatives.
10. List the six key themes or levels of integrating sustainability into corporate management and accounting practices.
11. Briefly describe what you mean by ESG.
12. Briefly explain how ESG may motivate corporations to become more environmentally and socially responsible.
13. With some examples, explain how and why corporate strategic statements such as vision and mission are refined to incorporate sustainability.
14. Using Nielsen's, a global data analytics firm, survey data mentioned in this chapter as an example, explain why companies how companies mobilize sustainability as an element of 'market positioning.'
15. Using Vesty's (2011) Australian survey data as an example, briefly explain the manner in which sustainability concerns can influence capital investment decisions.
16. Briefly explain how Porter and Krammer suggest extending the value chain analysis and industry analysis frameworks to integrate sustainability concerns.
17. Using the study of Figge et al. (2002) as an example, explain the different ways that the BSC framework is refined to consider sustainability issues.
18. Briefly explain how causalities or finalities that a sustainable BSC embed could be problematic.
19. Explain the use of activity-based analysis and costing in relation to:
    a. Tracing the physical flow
    b. Tracing the monetary flow

20. Using the United Nations Division of Sustainable Development (2001) framework as a basis, list the cost categories into which environmental activity costs should be classified.
21. Briefly explain life cycle cost (LLC) and whole life cost (WLC) and their interrelationship in relation to sustainability.
22. List and briefly explain the principal elements of an Environment Management System (EMS).

Explore further

1. Read the following paper to explore the broader meaning of sustainable development.

   Bebbington, J. (2001). Sustainable development: a review of the international development, business and accounting literature. Accounting Forum, 25(2), 128-157. https://doi.org/doi:10.1111/1467-6303.00059

2. Visit the UN SDGs to explore the overall global institutional infrastructure within which the UN operationalizes its sustainability goals. Pay special attention to the importance of the corporate sector in that global project.
3. Read the book "Capitalism: As If the World Matters" by Jonathan Porritt. The author is an influential policy thinker; therefore, this book was influential in policy circles. Think of the ideas this book promotes regarding how managerialist and Western-centric they are.
4. Visit one of the following websites of ESG indexes: MSCI ESG Leaders Indices, the FTSE4Good Index Series, and the Dow Jones Sustainability Indices. Explore the methodology it follows in indexing sustainability. Critically evaluate the normative/ideological basis for this indexing exercise and how well the index captures sustainability's broader meaning.

Develop your critical argumentation skills

1. Write an argumentative essay on the following theme.

   "Sustainability is not an organizational concept, and to apply it at the (capitalistic) organizational level is either very complex or very stupid."

2. Write an argumentative essay on the following theme.

   'Sustainability involves offering organizations a new set of strategic visions, competitive strategies, and operational tactics'.

3. Write an argumentative essay on the following theme.

   When I hear businessmen speak eloquently about the 'social responsibilities of business in a free-enterprise system', I am reminded of the wonderful line about the Frenchman who discovered at the age of 70 that he had been speaking prose all his life. The businessmen believe that they are defending free enterprise when they declaim that business is not concerned 'merely' with profit but also with promoting desirable 'social' ends; that business has a 'social conscience' and takes seriously its responsibilities for providing employment, eliminating discrimination, avoiding pollution and whatever else may be the catchwords of the contemporary crop of reformers. In fact, they are – or would be if they or anyone else took them seriously – preaching pure and unadulterated socialism. Businessmen who talk this way are unwitting puppets of the intellectual forces that have been undermining the basis of a free society these past decades. (Milton Friedman 1970)

   Your essay should critically evaluate this statement first by articulating Friedman's economic arguments against corporate leaders investing in social responsibility-related matters and secondly by offering a critique drawing on alternative theoretical explanations of why corporations increasingly engage in sustainability matters.

References

Al-Tuwaijri, S. A., T. E. Christensen, and K. E. Hughes. 2004. The relations among environmental disclosure, environmental performance, and economic performance: a simultaneous equations approach. Accounting, Organizations and Society 29 (5-6):447-471.

Alawattage, C., and S. Fernando. 2017. Postcoloniality in corporate social and environmental accountability. Accounting, Organizations, and Society 60 (Supplement C):1-20.

Alawattage, C., and D. Wickramasinghe. 2019. Strategizing management accounting: liberal origins and neoliberal Trends. London: Routledge.

———. 2022. Strategizing management accounting: liberal origins and neoliberal trends. Accounting, Auditing & Accountability Journal 35 (2):518-546.

Alexander, G. J., and R. A. Buchholz. 1978. Corporate social responsibility and stock market performance. The Academy of Management Journal 21 (3):479-486.

Artiach, T., D. Lee, D. Nelson, and J. Walker. 2010. The determinants of corporate sustainability performance. Accounting & Finance 50 (1):31-51.

Barnett, M. L., and R. M. Salomon. 2012. Does it pay to be really good? Addressing the shape of the relationship between social and financial performance. Strategic Management Journal 33 (11):1304-1320.

Bebbington, J. 2001. Sustainable development: a review of the international development, business and accounting literature. Accounting Forum 25 (2):128-157.

Bebbington, J., C. Larrinaga-González, and J. M. Moneva-Abadía. 2008. Legitimating reputation/the reputation of legitimacy theory. Accounting, Auditing & Accountability Journal 21 (3).

Campbell, D. J. 2000. Legitimacy theory or managerial reality construction? corporate social disclosure in Marks and Spencer Plc corporate reports, 1969-1997. Accounting Forum 24 (1):80-100.

Cho, C. H., and D. M. Patten. 2007. The role of environmental disclosures as tools of legitimacy: A research note. Accounting, Organizations and Society 32 (7-8):639-647.

Cooper, C. 2015. Entrepreneurs of the self: the development of management control since 1976. Accounting, Organizations and Society 47:14-24.

Daly, H. E. 1993. Sustainable growth: an impossible theorem. In Valuing the Earth: Economics, Ecology, Ethics, edited by H. E. Daly and K. N. Townsend. Ma: MIT Press, 267-274.

Deleuze, G., and F. Guattari. 1987. A thousand plateaus: capitalism and schizophrenia. Minnesota: University of Minnesota Press.

Dragos, D., and B. Neamtu. 2013. Life cycle costing (LCC) in the New EU Directive Proposal. EPPPL 1:19-30.

Figge, F., T. Hahn, S. Schaltegger, and M. Wagner. 2002. The sustainability balanced scorecard – linking sustainability management to business strategy. Business Strategy and the Environment 11 (5):269-284.

Foucault, M. 1995. Discipline and punishment: the birth of the prison. 2nd Vintage Books. ed. New York: Vintage Books.

Friedman, M. 1970. The Social responsibility of business is to increase its profits. The New York Times Magazine.

Gladwin, T. N., T.-S. Krause, and J. J. Kennelly. 1995. Beyond eco-efficiency: towards socially sustainable business. Sustainable Development 3 (1):35-43.

Gray, R. 2010. Is accounting for sustainability actually accounting for sustainability…and how would we know? An exploration of narratives of organizations and the planet. Accounting, Organizations and Society 35 (1):47-62.

Gray, R., C. A. Adams, and D. Owen. 2014. Accountability, social responsibility, and sustainability: accounting for society and the environment. Harlow, Essex: Pearson Education Limited.

Gray, R., and J. Bebbington. 2001. Accounting for the Environment: Second Edition: SAGE Publications.

Gray, R., J. Bebbington, and D. Walters. 1993. Accounting for the environment: Paul Chapman [for] ACCA, Chartered Association of Certified Accountants.

Gray, R., D. Owen, and C. A. Adams. 1996. Accounting & accountability: changes and challenges in corporate social and environmental reporting. London: Financial Times/Prentice Hall.

Gros, F. 2014. The Fourth Age of Security. In the government of life: Foucault, Biopolitics, and Neoliberalism, edited by V. Lemm and M. Vatter. New York: Fordham University Press, 17-28.

Hardt, M., and A. Negri. 2000. Empire. Cambridge, Mass.; London: Harvard University Press.

Holmes, B. 2007. Escape the overcode. In Continental drift: the other side of neoliberal globalisation. https://brianholmes.wordpress.com/2007/07/20/escape-the-overcode/.

Hopper, T., and N. Macintosh. 1993. Management accounting as disciplinary practice: the case of ITT under Harold Geneen. Management Accounting Research 4 (3):181-216.

International Federation of Accountants. 2005. Environmental management accounting: international guidance document. New York: International Federation of Accountants.

Kaplan, R. S., and D. McMillan. 2021. Reimagining the balanced scorecard for the ESG Era. In Harvard Business Review, 1-12.

Lamberton, G. 2005. Sustainability accounting--a brief history and conceptual framework. Accounting Forum 29 (1):7-26.

Langdon, D. 2007. Life cycle costing (LCC) as a contribution to sustainable construction: Guidance on the use of the LCC Methodology and its application in public procurement Brussels Davis Langdon Management Consulting.

Lemon, M., and A. Pember. 2014. Environmental sustainability: activity-based costing/management. Toronto: Chartered Professional Accountants of Canada.

Lubin, D. A., and D. C. Esty. 2010. The sustainability imperative. Harvard Business Review 2010 (May):2-9.

Milne, M. J. 1996. On sustainability; the environment and management accounting. Management Accounting Research 7 (1):135-161.

Mouffe, C. 1993. The return of the political. London: Verso.

———. 1999. Deliberative democracy or agonistic pluralism? Social Research 66 (3):745-758.

———. 2000. The democratic paradox. London: Verso.

———. 2005. On the political: Abingdon ; Routledge.

———. 2013. Agonistics: thinking the world politically. London: Verso.

Munro, I. 2012. The Management of circulations: biopolitical variations after foucault. International Journal of Management Reviews 14 (3):345-362.

Norreklit, H. 2000. The balance on the balanced scorecard a critical analysis of some of its assumptions. Management Accounting Research 11 (1):65-88.

———. 2003. The balanced scorecard: what is the score? A rhetorical analysis of the Balanced Scorecard. Accounting, Organizations and Society 28 (6):591-619.

Porter, M. E., and M. R. Kramer. 2006. Strategy and society: the link between competitive advantage and corporate social responsibility. Harvard Business Review 2006 [Reprint R0612D] (December):1-15.

Prahalad, C. K. 2005. The fortune at the bottom of the pyramid: eradicating poverty through profits, enabling dignity and choice through markets. New Jersey: Wharton School Publishing.

Roy, A. 2010. Poverty capital: microfinance and the making of development: Taylor & Francis.

Thomson, I. 2007. Mapping the terrain of sustainability accounting. In Sustainability accounting and accountability, edited by J. Unerman, J. Bebbington and B. O'Dwyer. London: Routledge, 19-36.

United Nations Division of Sustainable Development. 2001. Environmental management accounting procedures and principles. New York: United Nations.

United Nations World Commission on Environment and Development. 1987. Our common future (The Brundtland Report). Oxford: Oxford University Press.

Vesty, G. 2011. The influence and impact of sustainability issues on capital investment decisions. Southbank: CPA Australia.

Index

Symbols

3D Printers 296
4Ps 80
4sihgts 243
5S 272

A

ABC 309, 340, 345, 375, 406. See also activity-based costing
   contribution to flexibility 347
   contribution to quality and continuous improvement 348
   contribution to strategic market positioning 348
   strategic significance 343
ABC/M 337
   as foundational steps toward strategic cost management 340
ABM 337, 346. See also activity-based management
absolute advantage 58
absorption costing 341
absorptive resilience 241
abstract cooperation 295, 299
accountability 232, 374, 378, 386, 389, 390, 394, 415
accountability centers 128, 130
   hierarchy of 128
accountability hierarchy
   in responsibility accounting 129
accountancy 215
   profession 11

accounting 327, 377
accounting calculations
   in corporate planning 47
   in flexible manufacturing 305, 308
   in responsibility centers 128
accounting entity 407
accounting in flexible manufacturing 308
accounting logic 131
accounting model of pricing 80, 86, 88
accounting policies. 56
accounting standards 10, 11
accounting value
   of activities performed 90
   of resources 90
accreditation institutions 397
activities 86, 87, 337, 343, 344, 345, 350
   as cost drivers 86, 87
activity analysis 309
activity-based costing 7, 10, 11, 12, 16, 29, 86, 87, 104, 110, 273, 305, 309, 339, 375, 386, 408, 409. See also ABC
   in quality costing 273
activity-based hierarchy of quality cost calculations 275
activity-based management 7, 12, 29, 110, 337, 346. See also ABM
activity-based quality costing

critical steps 274
activity centers 273
activity cost driver rates 343
activity cost drivers 309
activity-level target costs 110
actor-networks 340
actual performance 177, 330
adaptability 211, 235
adaptation 181, 183, 184
   as a resilience phase 227
adaptation advantage
   of resilience 227
adaptive innovation 243
adaptive resilience 241
adaptive structural capacity
   resilience 232
adaptivity 240
additive manufacturing (3D Printing) 306
advanced human-machine interfaces 306
advanced manufacturing technologies 341
aesthetics 255
affective labor 299
affordability 258
African Development Bank 152
agency contract 170
agency problem 170, 171
   first-best solution 174
   second-best solution 174

agency relationships 170, 171
agency theory 10, 170, 171, 384
   conception of optimum performance 172
agency theory conception of management control 170
agent 170
   risk-averse 171
   self-interest 171
   work-averse 171
agent-principal model 170
agents 384
agent's risk-return preference 173
aggregating macroeconomic, financial market, and corporate data 225
AGIL 181, 183, 194
agonistic democracy 376
airlines
   as an example of dynamic pricing 113
algorithms 112, 308
allies 20, 21, 25, 39
analysis of product requirements 109
analytics 225, 235, 305
Ananya Roy 152
anatomico-political 291
anatomico-politics of the human body 383
Ansoff 51, 52
Ansoff product-market matrix 52, 56
antagonistic principles of competition 311
anticipation
   as a resilience phase 227
anticipation advantage
   of resilience 227

appraisal costs 262, 263
aristocratic systems 13
artificial economic personality. 381
artificial intelligence 306, 308
artificial time constraining
   as a pricing technique 98
Art of War 20
Asian Development Bank 152
assemblage 338
assembly highway 302
assessing the cost efficacy of appraisal and preventive activities 279
asset procurement 100
assets 350
asset utilization 48
augmented reality (AR) 307
Australia's Modern Slavery Act, 2018 112
authentication and fraud detection technologies 307
autocratic political systems 301
automated material handling systems 303
autonomous systems 307
average cost per unit 101

B

backups 234
Bain & Company 15
balanced scorecard 7, 10, 11, 16, 26, 124, 135. See also BSC
   reimagined 150, 151
balanced scorecards 171, 180, 184, 373, 386, 398
balance sheet 130, 132
balancing between financial and

   non-financial 136, 187
barcode 308
bargaining power of buyers 62
bargaining power of supplier 62
bases of market segmentation 94
basic or element flexibilities 303
batch-and-queue 350
batch-level costs 342
BCG 21, 49, 207
   Growth-Share Matrix 49
BCG growth-share matrix 21, 24, 56
behavioral 91
behavioral segmentation 93
belief system 189, 194
   and CSR core values 195
benchmarks 127, 177
benefit orientation 93
beyond budgeting movement 334
Bhagavad Gita 219
Big Brother, 339
big-data analytics 23, 306
biodiversity 389
biopolitical/biopolitics 58, 291, 299, 313, 374, 383, 389, 390
biopolitics of security 383
black box 344
black-box 305
Board diversity and inclusion 394
Boston Consulting Group 49, 215, 227
   see also BCG 15
bottom-up approach 331
bounce back 208
boundary systems 189, 191, 194
   and CSR 195
bourgeoisie 378

brains and eyes for surveillance 340
Braverman 251
Brundtland Commission 374, 375
BSC 124, 135, 136, 137, 196. See also balanced scorecard
   as a strategic performance management system 139
   as a system of cause-and-effect relationships 143
   interdependence of the four perspectives 146
   neglect of time dimensions 145
   Norekklit's critique 145
   problematic relationship between measures 146
   reimagining for sustainability 149
   weaknesses of 148
BS/ISO15686-5 410
budget 137, 330
budgeted balance sheet 132, 334
budgeted cash flow statement 132
budgeted production 87
budgeted profit and loss account 130, 132, 334
budgeting 23, 131, 170, 171, 184, 309, 330, 333
buffer inventories 350
Burawoy 43, 111, 251
bureaucracy 13
Business.com 113
business impact analysis (BIA) 231
business planning 141
business portfolio models in corporate planning 49
business process reengineering 14, 15, 53, 56

C

calculative apparatuses of capital 327
Canon 61
capital accumulation 132, 383
   as the primary purpose of an economic enterprise 132
capital budget 333
capital expenditure plans 333
capital investment decisions 184, 398
   and sustainability 399
capitalism 298, 327
capitalistic capture 156
capital-like symbolic-analytical and communicative labor 315
capital market 388
capitalocene 155, 197
carbon accounting 413
carbon costing methods 398
carbon cycle 379
caring labor 299
Carl von Clausewitz 20
cascading 141, 187
cash budget 333
cash cow 51
cash flow estimates 333
cash flow management 230
cash flows 50, 109
cash flow statement 130, 132
catalysts 150, 155
causalities and finalities in BSC 143
causality 154
cause-and-effect relationships 143
centers of calculations 339
Chandler 45, 46

change agents 15
change management 183
Chantal Mouffe 376
charm pricing 98
circulating lives 291
circulation of labor 314
citizens 14, 21, 25
civil society 388
civil society organizations 150
cloud computing 306
clusters 311
codes of business conduct 191
codification 397
colonial capitalism 154
command-and-control 188
communicating the corporate strategy 141
communication 175, 232
communicative functionalities 177
communicative labor 295, 299
company credos 395
comparative advantage 58
comparator 177
comparison of actual performance with predetermined standards 330
compensation contract 172
competition
   as a dynamic interplay of competitive forces 23
competitive advantage 30, 57, 58, 59, 92, 291, 391, 403
   and political role of the government 58
   macroeconomic and political landscape of 58
   micro-organizational context of 58

Competitive Advantage of Nations 58
competitive advantages 400
competitive arena 351
competitive conditions 2, 14, 28, 30, 112
   new neoliberal 1
competitive context 400
competitive context analysis 61
competitive environment 193, 400
competitive industry analysis 400
competitive landscape 92
competitive market 90, 345
competitive market positioning 79, 85
competitiveness 126, 182, 311
   as a national predicament 59
competitive positioning 91
competitive strategy 291
competitive strength 50
competitive terrain 21, 22, 25, 27, 36, 37
   and strategic mapping 26
   and strategic positioning 25
   as the site of positioning 20
   time-space nature 21
   understanding the notion of 22
competitor actions 112
competitor capabilities 65
competitor response profile 61, 64
component-level target costing 108, 110, 349
computer-aided design and manufacturing 303
Computer-Aided Manufacturing International (CAM-I) 340
concept of controllability 128

conceptualizing performance 124, 138
concurrent control 175
conditionalities of resilience 225
conduct
   firms' 1, 22, 26
conduct boundaries 191
conflicts 174
conflictuality 376
conformance 254
conformance cost 271, 276
conformance cost curve 271
conquering denial 219
consultancy firms 15, 227
consultative market 218
consultocracy 13, 141, 149, 150, 152, 209, 215, 217, 219, 226, 340
   the growth of 14
   the world before 13
consultocratic discourses 232
consultocratic discourses on resilience 215
consultocratic expositions 224
consultocratic modeling 215, 224, 225, 232
consumption-as-a-service models 293
context-specific
   nature of performance 125
contextual factors 4
contextualizing v, vi
contingency planning 211, 213
continuous improvement 14, 56, 231, 256, 272
continuous improvement quality paradigm 269
contract 170

contradictions 169, 174, 239
control 14, 189, 340
   concurrent 175
   feedback 175
   feedforward 175
control apparatuses 189
controllability 128, 175, 343, 344
controlling function 331
conversion process 177
core competencies 315
core group 313
core values 189, 194
corporate capitalism 151
corporate culture 53
corporate entrepreneurs 15
corporate goals 182
corporate growth 50
corporate head office 45
corporate ideology of profit-seeking and entrepreneurship 156
corporate leadership 225
corporate mission 126, 139, 153
corporate objectives 56
corporate planning 44, 184
   emergence of 44
corporate social responsibility 149, 195. See also CSR
corporate social responsibility debate 380
corporate vision 126, 139, 153
corporations 43, 44, 45
   as as paradoxical entities of governance 389
corrective actions 330
correlation 386
corruption 378
cosmopolitan management 7

cost 252
    as accounting value of activities performed 90
    as accounting value of resources consumed 90
cost accounting 341
cost accuracy 343
cost analysis 110
cost centers 128, 130, 309, 330
cost differential 110
cost driver rates 345
cost drivers 87
cost efficiency 281, 282
cost function 374
cost incidence 87
cost incurrence 87
costing techniques for sustainability 392
cost leadership 59, 61, 79, 348, 350
cost-leadership strategy 64
    and value chain 64
cost management 325, 338
    concepts 340
    diverse nature of 338
    frameworks 340
    paradoxical nature of 337
    techniques 340
    traditional approach 327
cost management system 352
cost objects 345
cost of capital 109, 130
cost of compliance 262
cost of conformance 270
cost of externalities 100
cost of non-compliance 262
cost per factory hour 363
cost-plus pricing 86, 91

costs 126, 350
cost standards 329
cost tracing 343
cost unit 87
cost-volume-profit analysis 23, 29
COVID-19 222, 224, 226
craftsmen 328
creativity 353
creed 219
critical performance dimensions 139
critical performance variables 194
critical success factors 140
cross-cutting actions 394
CSR 149, 195, 391
cultural diversity 379
cultural-political-economic 378
cultural-symbolic 21, 26, 27
current cost 110
current strategy
    and competitory response profile 65
cushioning
    as a resilience phase 227
cushioning advantage
    of resilience 227
customer behavior 112
customer-centric circular model 294
customer perspective 140
customer satisfaction 180, 257
customization 257
cyberattacks 233
cybernetic 175
cybernetic model of management contro 176
cybernetic perspectives on management control 175

cybernetics 178
cyber-phhysical systems (CPS) 306
cybersecurity 228, 233, 234
cycle time of service offerings 294

D

Danture Wickramasinghe vii
data analytics 112, 225, 226, 228, 308
data and information infrastructure 112
database 359
data-driven flagging 228
data-driven management and decision-making 308
data-driven mindset 225
datafication 226
data protection and privacy 234
data security 228
debt management 230
defects per million opportunities (DPMO) 262
defensive 281
Deloitte 15, 113, 207, 228, 230, 232, 235
demand 58, 84, 85
demand forecasts 23, 24
    not as competitive conditions 23, 24
democracy 14, 126
demographic 91
demographic segmentation 93
departures from existing routines
    fragmental 223
    major 223
    minor 223
dependent variables
    compensation contract 173

designer creativity 108, 353
despotic labor control 111, 302
despotism 111, 378
detector 177
diagnostic control system 189, 192, 194
    and CSR 196
diamond framework/model (Porter) 58, 400, 403
differentiating activities 309
differentiation 59, 61, 79, 349, 350
differentiation strategy
    and value chain 64
different notions of flexibility in FMS 303
digital and technology resilience 233
digital communication networks 303
digitalization 8
    of technilogies 1
    of technologies 4, 8
digitalized markets 92
direct costs 86
direct expenses 86, 87
direct labor cost 86, 87
direct labor hours 86, 87
direct material cost 86, 87
disciplinary institution 328, 383
disciplinary logic 383
disciplinary principles 383
disciplinary societies 383
disciplinary technologies 383
discipline 329
discounted cash flows 130
disorganized capitalism 313
disposal and decommissioning

phase 101
diversification 53, 212, 229
divisional objectives 56
doctrinal prescriptions 219, 225, 237
doctrine of human security 389
dog 51
domains
    of strategic action 32, 79
    of strategic actions 167
    of strategizing 1, 2, 11, 26, 27, 30, 32, 36, 38
domains of strategic actions 2, 251
Donna Haraway 155
double-entry bookkeeping 327
Dow Jones Sustainability Index 397
downturn
    resilience 227
DPMO 262
dual functionality of pricing 80
dualism 259
DuPont 45, 47, 131, 133
    decomposition of ROI 47
DuPont system of ratio analysis 131
durability 255
dynamic equilibrium 194
dynamic pricing 112
    examples of 113
    issues of 114
    preconditions for 112
dynamic synthesis 259

E

eco-balance 407
eco-efficiency 379, 403, 405
eco-friendly 111
eco-justice 379, 403, 405
ecological 388, 406

ecological capital 379
ecological integrity and solidity 379
ecological justice 31, 154, 180, 390
ecology
    as a fundamental structural category 376, 379
E-commerce platforms
    as an example of dynamic pricing 113
economic growth 377
economic model of pricing 80
economic morality 385
economic performance 385
economic production quantity (EPQ) 296. See also EPQ (economic production quantity)
economic resilience 212, 213
economic whip of the market 111
economies of scale 303, 350
economy
    as a fundamental structural category 376, 377
ecosystem 149, 154, 155, 379
ecosystem players 153
Edwards Deming 269
effector 177
efficiency 126, 377
elitism 378
embracing paradox 219
emergent strategy 193
empire 298, 384, 388
employee training and awareness 234
employee welfare 180
employee welfare policies 393
end-of-life costs 100
enemies 20, 21, 39

engineering concept of resilience 211
enterprise resource planning (ERP) 108, 130. See also ERP (enterprise resource planning)
entrepreneurial human capital 299
entrepreneurialization 291
entrepreneurial self 291
entrepreneurs 156
entrepreneurship 156, 188
environment 375, 392
environmental activity-cost classification 411
environmental audits 415
environmental capital 379
environmental-centric 197
environmental disclosure 385
environmental footprint 379
environmental management systems 413
environmental objectives 415
environmental performance 385
environmental performance indicators (EPIs) 408
environmental perspective
  on management control 184
environmental policies 393, 415
environmental resilience 236
environmental strategies 415
environment management systems (EMS) 392
environment-serving organizations 51. See also ESOs
envisioning sustainability 394
episteme 10
epistemic 10

epistemic factors 10
  conceptual elements 11
  institutional elements 13
epistemic institutions 11
epistemic structure
  of neoliberal management and governance system 15
epistemic tools
  of strategizing 21
epistemic tools for strategizing 25
EPQ (economic production quantity) 296
equality 379
equilibrium 194
ERP architecture 360
ERP (enterprise resource planning) 309, 337, 340, 342, 353, 357, 359, 416
ESG 149, 153, 196, 235, 389, 391, 392
  defined 392
ESG as a market database-driven analytical framework 392
ESG index assessment 394
ESOs 51
ethical conduct and compliance 394
ethnicity 378
ethnocentric 379
EU 169
European Commission 100
events 339
eventuality 339
expansion flexibility 304
expenses 86
expository narratives 219
extension of the government into the 'normal' spaces of socio-economic life 383

external collaboration 394
external control 185
external control of organizations 185
external environment 51, 174, 182
external environmental elements 167
external failure costs 262, 264
externalities 373

F

facility-sustaining costs 343
factor conditions 58
factor endowment 58
factors of production 58
factory 43, 328, 329
factory floor 43, 44, 282
fairness 379
false economy strategy of pricing 97
federated enterprises 312
feedback and learning 141
feedback control 175
feedback mechanisms 192
feedforward control 175
Fifth Discipline 53
finalities in BSC 143
finality 154, 386
financial analysis
  in target costing 353
financial crisis 226
financial hierarchy 131
financial literacy 156
financial market 225
financial metrics 132
financial performance 384, 389
financial perspective 140

financial resilience 229
   critical elements 230
financial risk management 230
financial statement analysis 184
finite resources 375
firm
   as both a life-sustaining and endangering entity 389
firm's primary objective 81
firm strategy and structure of rivalry 58
first-best solution 174
First Industrial Revolution 306
first-order control 177
five forces model 68
fixed capital 297
flexibility 126, 188, 251, 281, 282, 289, 293, 326, 355
   multiplicity of the notion of 290
flexibility in FMS
   different notions 303
flexibilization 315
flexibilization of labor 301
flexible accumulation 289, 290, 291, 292, 313
flexible consumption 290, 292, 293, 302
   underpinning capacities of 293
flexible labor 290, 291, 292, 298, 302, 303, 316, 355
   skill flexibility 298
   time flexibility 298, 300
flexible machines 290, 291, 292, 295, 297, 300, 302, 355
flexible manufacturing 15, 289, 305, 310, 341
   political-institutional mechanisms of 310

flexible manufacturing business models 294
flexible manufacturing scheduling 355
flexible manufacturing system 292, 295, 302. See also FMS
flexible multipurpose machines 303
flexible organizations 15
flexible specialization and integration 289, 290, 292, 295, 310
flexing 334
FMS 302, 303
focal context 222, 223
focus 349
Ford 92
Fordism 44, 313
Fordist assembly line 44
Fordist mass production regime 292
Ford Motor Company 91
Ford Pinto 267
foreign direct investment 301
foresight 243
formulating policies 46
Foucauldian 383
four corner analysis 64
fragmental departures 223
fragmentation 339
fragmented and segmented markets 92
fragmented whole 339
franchising 170, 299
freedom 383
free market governance 388
French performance management system 136
FTSE4Good Index 397

full cost 86
functional departments 333
functional divisions of organizational activities 185
functional flexibility 315
functional imperatives 180, 181, 185, 186
functionalities 108, 109, 255, 258, 350, 351, 353
   as an element of survival zone 105
functional-level target costs 110
fundamental structural categories 376

G

General Electric 49
   Nine-Cell Matrix 49
generally accepted accounting principles 10
General Motors 45
General Office 45
general systems theory 51
generational conflict 375
generic strategies
   cost leadership 59
   differentiation 59
Genichi Taguchi 269
GE nine-cell matrix 21, 56
geographic segmentation 91, 93
geopolitical threats 228
GHG (greenhouse gas) 413, 414
global capitalism 111, 315
global development capital institutions 150
global governance 169
global governance institutions 169

globalization
- of markets and hierarchies 1
- of markets and organizational hierarchies 7
- of markets, hierarchies, governance, and regulations 4

globalized markets 92
global positioning technologies (GPS) 308
global regulatory institutions 111
Global Reporting Initiative (GRI) 68, 396. See also GRI
global sustainability agenda 16, 373
goal attainment 181, 183, 184, 192
goals 127, 182
good value strategy of pricing 97
governance 232
- bureaucratic 14
- globalized 7
- in ESG 392

governance hierarchy 378
governmentality 382, 383
government resilience strategies 213
grading schemes 127
graduate attributes 126
greenhouse gas accounting 413
greenhouse gas emissions (GHG) 100, 406
Greenhouse Gas Protocol 413
green initiatives 393
GRI 68, 396, 397. See also Global Reporting Initiative (GRI)
gross profit ratio 130
growth
- resilience 227

growth-share matrix 49
guidelines 127
guild masters 328
guru 152, 215
guru discourse 224
guru ideas 215, 216
guru rhetoric 219

H

Hamel Prahalad 156
hard management technologies 281
harmony 259
Harvard Business School 11, 340
Henry Ford 91
hermeneutics 222
heterogeneity 302, 339
heterogeneous 338
heterogeneous labor 298
heuristics as an element of resilience 223
hierarchical examination 329
hierarchical privilege 344
hierarchy of accountability centers 128
hierarchy of accounting measures 132
higher-order principles 126, 139, 180, 394
high-frequency trading 388
high value strategy of pricing 97
hindsight 243
historicizing v, vi
Hofstede's typology of management control 178
holism 181, 337, 338
holistic program 336, 337
homogeneity 302
horizontal value chains 307
HRM (human resource management) 186
human capital
- resilience 233

human resource management (HRM) 171
human trafficking 111
hypotheses 384

I

ideals of political, social, and ecological justice 378
ideal type 241
ideological shifts 380
ideological signification of markets 6
ILO (International Labor Organization) 112. See also International Labor Organization (ILO)
IMF (International Monetary Fund) 301
imitation 397
immaterialization of labor/immaterial labor 291, 298, 299, 301
imperfect competition 22
implosion between labor and capital 298
improvisation 222
improvisation as an element of resilience 224
Inc.com 113
incident response and recovery 234
inclusive capitalism 155, 156
inclusive ecosystem 153
inclusive growth 149, 153, 157
independence 378
indifference curve 173

indigenous rights 379
individual freedom 378
industrial and institutional infrastructure 58
industrial capitalism 44, 91, 328
industrial clusters 311
industrial engineering 329
industrial regulation 310
industrial relations 300
Industrial Revolution 13, 43
Industry 4.0 305, 307, 308, 309, 357
Industry 4.0 technologies 306
industry analysis 62, 184, 398
ineffability 259
inefficiencies 91
informational capacity for flexible consumption 295
information asymmetry 10, 171, 173
information management
    resilience 233
information symmetry 173
infrastructure 212
infrastructure-as-a-service (IaaS) 293
in-house proprietary systems 305
innovation 188, 213, 397
innovativeness 126
innumeracy
    as a pricing technique 98
input-output balance 407
inputs 177
In Search of Excellence 53
inside-out linkages 68
insight 243
institutionalized expectations and desires 127
insurance and risk transfer 230

integrated logistics 307
integration 181, 183, 184, 225
intended strategy 192, 193
interactive control system 189, 193, 194
    and CSR 196
inter-generational 375
inter-generational equity 379
internal business processes perspective 140
internal failure costs 262, 264
internal learning 177
internal product designers 352
internal rate of return 130
International Labor Organization (ILO) 112. See also ILO (International Labor Organization)
Internet of Things (IoT) 295, 306, 307
inter-organizational costing 108, 111
inter-organizational cost management systems 110
intra-generational 375
intra-generational equity 379
intrapreneurs 15
inventories
    as waste 350
inventory levels 112
inventory management 184
investment centers 47, 128
investment centres 130
investment efficiency 130
investor communication 230
ISO 397
isolation of pricing 85, 86

isomorphism 228

J

Japanese Agency for International Cooperation (JAICA) 152
Japanization 14, 280, 281, 282
Jason Moore 155
jidoka 282
JIT (just-in-time) 61, 282, 341. See also just-in-time (JIT)
job descriptions 171
job prescriptions 171
job security/insecurity 302, 316
job shops 302
joint ventures 299
judgments 383
jurisdictional 382
justice
    ecological 12, 26, 28, 30, 31, 32, 36
    social 12, 26, 28, 30, 31, 32, 36
just-in-time capitalism 313
just-in-time (JIT) 61, 341, 350. See also JIT (just-in-time)
just-in-time manufacturing 282

K

kaizen 110
kanban 281, 282, 355
Kaoru Ishikawa 270
Kaplan 11, 15, 87, 135, 137, 405
key enablers and resources 154
key performance indicators 139. See also KPIs
kin work 299
KPIs 139, 405
KPMG 207
Kramer 70, 400

L

labor contracts 314
labor costs 86
labor flexibility 303
labor flexibilization 298
labor market innovations 314
labor process 11, 14, 251, 291, 344
   as a structural element of economy 377
   definition of 43
   rganization and rationalization of 43
   strategizing the 32, 35
latency 181, 183, 184
Latour 344
laws 127
leadership 183
leadership and governance
   resilience 232
lead time 355
lean and agile principles 336
lean enterprise 350
lean manufacturing 15, 282, 340, 350, 354
lean organizations 15
learning and continuous improvement
   resilience 233
learning and growth perspective 140
learning organizations 14, 15, 53, 56
legitimacy 386
legitimization 390
leverage 48
levers of control 174, 187, 189. See also LOC (levers of control)
   and sustainability integration 195
levers of resilience 229

liberating resources 219
life 389
lifecycle 51
lifecycle costing formula 101
lifecycle costing (LCC) 99, 110, 111, 353, 410
   as a product costing technique 101
   calculative example of 103
   in asset management 100
   in asset procurement 100
   in target costing 108
   limitations of 102
life-sustaining processes 379
lifetime employment 301
limited conceptualization of the market 86
limited market conceptualization 84
limiting factor analysis 23, 29
linear programming 23, 29
linking the performance management system to corporate strategies 136, 141, 187
location detection technologies 306
LOC (levers of control) 187, 189, 194. See also levers of control
logic of responsibility accounting 133
logistics 186
long-term goals 46, 139
loyalty orientation 94

M

machine flexibility 303
machine learning 305, 308
macroeconomic 58, 225, 396

major routine breakdowns 223
management
   as an engineering task 43
management accounting
   rationalization of sustainability 386
management approach
   from administration to strategy 12
management by objectives 170
management consultancy 215
management consultancy packages 215
management control 167, 182, 184, 208
   agency theory conception of 170
   key propositions 181
   neoclassical economic perspectives on 170
   ontological condition of 169
   strategic 187
   structural functionalism in 180
management control systems 174
management gurus 14, 15, 149, 219
managerial capture 154, 156, 196, 197
managerial labor process 345
managing risks 194
managing the organization as a totality 44
manufacturing cell 302
Manufacturing Resource Planning (MRP-II) 359. See also MRP-II (Manufacturing Resource Planning)
marginal analysis 86
marginal cost 81
marginal revenue 81

marginal utility 258
market analysis 184
market and competitor analysis 109
　in target costing 353
market attractiveness 50
market-centric 290
market conditions 107
market consideration absent 90
market demand 112
market development 53
market-driven positioning 92
market-driven target costing 107, 349, 352
market dynamics 290, 291
market flexibility 305
marketing 186
marketing mix 80, 85, 292
market penetration 53, 84
markets 6, 22, 167, 326, 352
　as a fundamental reference point 290
　as a structural determinant 22
　as a structural element of economy 377
　digitalized 92, 289
　globalized 92, 289
　neoliberalized 92, 289
　political role of 383
　strategizing the 5, 6, 7, 8, 9, 11, 12, 13, 14, 18, 22, 24, 25, 26, 27, 28, 30, 31, 32, 34, 36
　virtualized 92, 289
market segmentation 92, 93
　bases of 94
market segmentation, targeting, and positioning 92. See also STP (segmentation-targeting-positioning)
market segment profile 95

market segments 93
market segments and competitor profiles 109
market share 48
market share statistics 130
market skimming 84
market skimming vs penetration pricing 99
market structures 22
market surveys 93
mass balance 407
mass customization 302
mass marketing strategy 92
mass markets 310
mass production 44, 91, 292, 350
mass production systems 302, 303
master budget/budgeting 130, 334
material costs 86
material handling flexibility 303
material requirements planning (MRP-I) 358. See also MRP-I (Material Requirement Planning)
materials balance 407
material selection
　as an element of engineering resilience 211
materials flow accounting 407
maximum allowable price 105
McKinsey 15, 53, 113, 207, 215, 227, 229, 235
McKinsey's 7S framework 53, 56
McMillan 405
measurement 189
measurement of actual performance 330
measurements 140

MEAT 100
mechanical 8
Medical Robots for Surgery 296
medicine 329
medium value strategy of pricing 97
MFD (multi-functional devices) 296
M-Form 45
microfinance 156
micro-financially indebted poor women 156
micro-organizational 58
Milton Fridman 374
Milton Friedman 380
mindful actions 243
miniature legal systems 383
minimum allowable price 105
minor departures 223
Mintzberg 20, 21, 39, 193
mission 53, 182, 190, 391, 394, 397
mission statement 56
mitigating risks 191
mitigative motive 196
mobile devices 307
modernism 298
modernity 13
modern slavery 111, 302
modular design 211
modular elements of organizational resilience 228
modularizing organizational resilience 225
monetary flow accounting 410
monitoring 235
monopolistic power 22
monopoly 22
monopoly capitalism 44, 292

monopoly conditions 92
monopoly power 90
moral philosophy 385
most economically advantageous tender 100. *See also* MEAT
MRP-II (Manufacturing Resource Planning) 359
MRP-I (Material Requirement Planning) 359
multidimensional performance management 135
multidivisional corporate conglomerates 44
multidivisional decentralized corporations 45
multi-functional device (MFD) 296
multinational corporations 388
multiple product lifecycles 298
multipurpose machines 302
multi-sector opportunities 149
multi-skilled labor 302

N

nation's competitive advantage
   six pivotal factors influencing 58
nation-states 378
natural capital 379
natural foundation 379
near-perfect quality 357
NEC 315
necessary conditions of controlability 175
neoclassical economics model of pricing 22, 80, 82
   limitations of 83
   of market strcutures
     and firm behavior 22
neoclassical economic theories 384

neoliberal 378
neoliberal biopolitics and security 390
neoliberal competitive conditions 6, 7
neoliberal governance 389
neoliberalism 388
neoliberalization 313, 388
   of politics 1, 4
neoliberalization of politics 4
neoliberalized markets 92
neoliberal markets 344
neoliberal organizations 290, 291
neoliberal paradox 389
neoliberal transformations within production systems 289
net profit ratio 130
new capitalism 313
new ecosystem 154, 155
new inclusive ecosystem 150, 153, 156
New Public Management (NPM) 6
NGOs 150, 152, 153
Nielsen 397
Nikon 61
nine-cell matrix (GE) 49
nirvana 219
non-accounting operational logic 131
non-accounting organizational hierarchies 131
non-compliance 385
non-conformance costs 276
non-confrontational competitive space 350
non-core activities 315
non-cybernetic 179

non-human lives 389
non-market perspective 403
non-resilience path 226
non-resilient survival 241
non-value added 345
non-value-added 350
normalization 329
normative political principles 385
normative prescriptions 218
Norton 87, 135, 137
numerical flexibility 316

O

objective function 81
objectives 127, 182
   in multiple dimensions 2, 20, 21, 25, 26, 27
obligation 167, 390
occasion orientation 94
OECD 212, 213, 301
oligopoly 22
ontological 384
ontological condition
   of control 169
On War 20
open-book accounting 108, 353
open system 174
operating cost 100
operating expenses 48
operational boundaries 191
operational budgets/budgeting 130, 333
operational capacity for flexible consumption 293
operational control and control systems 182, 183, 184

operational efficiency 23, 136
  as a strategy 23
operationalizing sustainability 398
operational resilience 230
  critical elements 231
operation flexibility 304
operations management 186, 333
optics 340
optimal decisions 22
optimum performance 172
organic systems 183
organizational activities
  functional division of 186
organizational-centric 197
organizational environment 184
organizational hierarchies 131
organizational hierarchy 86, 167, 326
  as a structural element of economy 377
  strategizing the 11, 14, 26, 30, 32, 34
organizational purpos 391
organizational resilience 167, 207, 208, 215, 222, 241, 291, 326
  academic discourses on 238
  capitals of 235
  consultocratic modeling approaches to 224
  differentiating academic vs consultocratic discourses on 239
  systemic and modular elements of 228
  the five capitals of 229
organizational structure 14
outputs 177
outside-in linkages 68
outsourcing 301

over charging strategy of pricing 97
overhead allocation and absorption 86
overhead costs 86
overhead expenses 86
overheads 341
oversight 243
oxymoron 374, 384, 390

P

paradox 219
particularizing v, vi
pattern in action
  strategy as a 194
pattern maintenance 181, 183, 184, 189
payback period 130
penetration 84, 99
pension shortages 302
people resilience 232
perfect competition 22
perfect quality 350
performance 132, 192, 254, 330
  as hybridity between the actual and expected 126
  coneceptualized 124
  defined 125, 126
performance and compensation contract 171
  total rent contract 171
  wage-only 171
performance appraisals 183
performance-based compensation 316
performance dimensions 192
performance management 127, 167, 184, 187, 208, 326, 398, 415
  srategic approach to 135

performance management systems 391
performance measures 177
performance optimization 243
performance outcomes 170
peripheralization 316
peripheralization of labor 314
peripheral labor market 316
personalization 257
perspective
  strategy as a 194
PEST and PESTEL analysis 52, 56
phases and capabilities of resilience 226
physical flow accounting 410
physicality 300
placeholder 291
plan
  strategy as a 194
planet 375
planning and delegation functions 331
platform-as-a-service (PaaS) 293
platform organizations 299
pluralism
  in organizational objectives 180
point of production 167, 251, 290, 291, 325, 326
policies 127, 182
policy
  formulation 46
political
  the 376
political accountability 378
political doctrines 378
political-economic
  factors behind strategic turn 3

political-economic catastrophes 388
political-economy critique
    of reimaning BSC for ESG 154
political ideologies 378
political role of the government 58
political state 388
politicizing v, vi
politics 376
polity
    as a fundamental structural category 376, 378
pool of impact investments 152, 153, 155
Porterian discourses
    sustainability implications of 68
Porterian discourses of strategy 55
Porterian ideas of strategy 337
Porterian revision of the structure-conduct-performance model 57
Porterian strategy discourses as a biopolitical hierarchy of competitiveness 67
Porter (Michael) 7, 11, 15, 21, 23, 33, 34, 39, 55, 57, 79, 85, 311, 400
Porter's five forces model of industry analysis 23, 62, 63
Porter's generic strategies 59
Porter's grand schema of strategy 66
portfolio planning models 49, 51, 56
positioning 21, 31, 33, 92, 96
    as a central concept in defining and elucidating strategies 20
    strategy as a 194
positive impact outcomes 153
post-COVID organizational conduct 224

post-Fordism 280, 289, 310, 313
post-incident analysis 233
post-industrial paradigm 313
post-Marxist 378
postmodern organizations 310
poverty capital 152, 153, 154, 155, 157
poverty capitalism 157
Prahalad 152
precariat classes of labor 317
predetermined standards 330
predictability 14
predictive analytics 224
predictive maintenance 211
predictive model 175, 177
premium strategy of pricing 97
pre-modern 13
pre-modern societies 378
pre-production phase: 101
prevention costs 262, 263
preventive control 243
preventive measures 231
price 90, 108, 109, 351
    as an element of survival zone 105
price appearance 98
price-performance ratio 258
price takers 22
pricing 79
    as a variable of marketing mix 85
    as the most critical strategic decision 80
pricing policies 56
pricing strategy 90
primary labor market 313
primary themes of operationalizing sustainability 398

prime cost 86
principal 170
principal's payoff 171, 173
private capital
    neoliberal governance role 383
    political role of 383
private information 171
privatization 5
privileging financial over sustainability 405
procedures 127
process control 255
processes of production 328
process flexibility 305
process standardization 355
processual and capability parameters of resilience 214
processual elements of traditional cost management and profit planning 331
product and process design 353
product-based approach to defining quality 254
product development 53
product flexibility 305
production flexibility 305
production or operational phase 101
production philosophy 354
production smoothing 355
production systems 11
productivity 126
product-level target costing 108, 349
product-level targets 353
product requirement analysis
    in target costing 353

product-sustaining costs 342
profit 80, 383
profitability 48, 126, 155, 390
profit and loss account 130, 132
profit centers 128, 130
profiteering 154
profit function 81, 374
profit margin 86, 91, 130
profit maximization 22, 81, 83, 86, 180
profit planning and control 330
profit variances 130
program flexibility 305
programming 184
project-based hiring 301
protectionist
   political-economic doctrines 4
protocols 127
psychographic segmentation 91, 93
psychological pricing 98
psychological resilience 210
pull strategy 90, 104
pull system of production 355
punishments 383
purchase price 100
pure unadulterated socialism 390
push strategy 90, 102, 104
PwC 207, 307

Q

QR code 308, 340
quality 108, 109, 126, 251, 281, 282, 326, 350, 351, 353, 355
   an operational definition of 261
   as an element of survival zone 105
   as a strategic imperative 280
   defined 253
   manufacturing-based approach to 255
   post-WWII discourses 269
   product-based approach to defining 254
   social constructivist approach 260
   transcendental approach to 259
   user-based approach to 257
   value-based approach 258
   zero-defect 268, 270
quality assurance systems 255
quality-centric organizational transformations 253, 355
quality circles 282
quality control 183, 184, 272
quality cost function 252
quality costing 272
   as a strategic imperative 252
   calculative elements of 253
   paradigmatic nature of 253
quality costing system 272
   defined 273
   defining the scope of a 273
quality costing techniques and methods 273
quality cost of compliance 262
quality cost of non-compliance 262
quality cost optimization model 266, 270
quality costs 262
quality costs and performance reporting and assessments of 276
quality cost variance analysis 277
quality management 252
quality paradigms 264
   continuous improvement 269
   decision variables and criteria of a 265
   traditional 265, 266
   zero-defect 269
quality transcends dualism 259
quest for resilience 219
question mark 51

R

race 378
rating games 397
rating schemes 127
rationalization of work 329
rationalizations
   strategic 31
reactive resilience 241
reactivity 240
reality judgments 177
real-time data 112
real-time information 309
real-time monitoring alerts 224
recovery
   resilience 227
redundancy 211, 234
regional conglomerations 311
regulation 14, 127, 189, 329
   by the state 5
   globalized 7
regulatory and epistemic institutions
   globalizaton and 7
regulatory compliance 225, 230, 231, 235
reimagining the BSC for sustainability 149
relations in production 43
reliability 254
Renaissance 13
rents 171

reporting criteria 397
reporting systems 415
reputational resilience 228, 232, 235, 236
required profit margin 90
research and development 333
resilience 167, 207, 219, 222
   absorptive 241
   adaptation 227
   adaptive 241
   adaptive structural capacity 232
   as a corporate character deficiency 216
   as a dialectical synthesis of reactivity and adaptivity 240
   brand reputation and climate 235
   different domains of 239
   digital and technology 233
   downturn 227
   economic 212, 213
   engineering concept of 211
   environmental 236
   financial 229
   foresight 227
   growth 227
   heuristics as an element of 223
   human capital 233
   improvisation as an element of 224
   information management 233
   leadership and governance 232
   learning and continuous improvement 233
   levers of 229
   operational 230
   organizational 241
   people 232
   processual and capability parameters of 214
   psychological 210
   reactive 241
   recovery 227
   reputational 232, 235, 236
   response 227
   social 210
   structural 232
   transformative 241
   underlying contradictions 239
resilience culture 232
resilience curve 227
resilience gap 216
resilience leadership 232
resilience modeling 225
resilience path 226
resilience phases 227
   adaptation 227
   anticipation 227
   cushioning 227
   shaping 227
resilience teams 232
resilience testing 231
resource allocation and optimization 46
resource allocation optimization 225
response planning 231
responsibility 232
responsibility accounting 128, 130, 132, 136, 170, 171, 329, 336
   key themes of 134
   weaknesses of 134
responsibility accounting system 330
retirement benefits 302
return on investment 47, 50, 64, 109, 126, 130, 153, 180, 377. See also ROI (return on investment)
   as a long-term objective 56
return on total assets 130
return per factory hour 363
revenue 126
revenue centers 128, 130
revenue function 374
rewards 383
rhizomatically 339
Richard Grimshaw case 268
Ride-sharing services
   as an example of dynamic pricing 113
rip off strategy of pricing 97
risk 194
risk assessment and identification 211, 231
risk champions 15
risk management 213
risk minimization 189
risks 14, 191
Robert Anthony 182
Robert M. Pirsig 259
Robin Cooper 104
robotics 307
robustness 211
Rochester model 170
ROI (return on investment) 47, 50, 52, 64, 129. See also return on investment
   as signature of monopoly capitalism 48
role of the market 383
root cause analysis 256
routines 222
routing flexibility 304
routinization 14, 183, 184
Royal Institution of Chartered Surveyors (RICS) 412
rules 127

S

sales growth rates 130
sales targets 333
SAP 305, 359
SBUs 45, 47, 49, 50. See also strategic business units
scale-up financing 151
scenario analysis and planning 225, 231, 233
science/scientific 329
scientific management 43, 329, 330
Scope 1 emissions 414
Scope 2 emissions 414
Scope 3 emissions 414
scorecards 140
    managerial functionalities of 137
scorecards as fundamental building blocks of performance management 137
scripted work processes 222
Sears Roebuck 45
second-best solution 174
Second Industrial Revolution 306
second-order control 177
security audits 234
segmentation 92
segmentation bases 93
segmented market positioning 341
self-interest 189
self-interested agent 171
sequential value chain model 294
setting long-term goals 46
setting objectives in multiple dimensions 25
setup times 302

shaping
    as a resilience phase 227
shaping advantage
    of resilience 228
shareholder 393
shareholder capitalism 154
shareholders 381, 388
shareholder wealth 384
share prices 130
shojinka 282
signature of monopoly capitalism 48
Simons 187
simulation 212
single-piece flow 350
single-piece production 355
Six Sigma 261
skill flexibility
    of labor 298
skimming 84, 99
Slagmulder 104
slow-growing economy 282
slumps 226
SMA v, vi, vii
    as a social science v
smart accounting 306, 307
smart-accounting 305
smart industries. 307
smart technologies 305, 307
SMA (strategic management accounting) 1
    defined 1, 2, 3, 6, 7, 8, 9, 10, 11, 12, 15, 16, 18, 19, 24, 25, 26, 27, 28, 30, 31, 33, 35, 36, 37, 39
    differentiating from other forms of accounting 28
    globalization connection 8

neoliberal connections 6
social
    in ESG 392
social and environmental
    strategizing the 26, 27, 32, 36
social and environmental management accounting 386
social and environmental perspective 154
socialized capital 377
social justice/injustice 12, 28, 29, 30, 31, 32, 36, 112, 154, 180, 302, 375, 379, 390
    in definition of SMA 30
social resilience 210
social safety nets 213
society
    as a fundamental structural category 376, 378
socio-cultural goals 379
socio-political contradictions 380
socio-technical system theories 180
soft management technologies 281
software-as-a-service (SaaS) 293
solar firms and workshop factories 312
Sony 61
sovereign power 378
sovereign state 383
sovereignty 378
Sports teams
    as an example of dynamic pricing 113
stability 14, 212
staff costs 344
stake 389
Stakeholder collaboration 237
Stakeholder engagement 394

stakeholder perspective 153
stakeholders 185, 186, 213, 386, 388, 393, 394
  categories of 185
standard cost centers 330
standard costing and variance analysis 130, 131, 171, 177, 184, 309, 329, 330, 331
standard costs 329, 330
standardization 189, 329
standardization as a basis of traditional cost management 329
standard method 329
Standard Oil 45
standard performance levels 329
standards 127, 177, 396, 397
star 51
state 383
state bureaucracy 330
state interventions 5
state ownership 5
state's territorial integrity 389
statistical process control 281
stewards 170
stewardship 393
stockholders 382
stock market performance 130
STP (segmentation-targeting-positioning) 92, 292
strategic 41
  rationalization and calculations 31
strategic action
  domains of 79
  domanis of 32
strategic actions
  domains of 167, 251, 325

strategic agency 85, 86
strategic alliances 316
strategic analysis
  of external environmental elements 11
  of organizational hierarchy and control apparatuses 11
strategic and visionary leadership 53
strategic architecture 316
strategic assumptions 65
strategic business units 45, 47, 49, 50. See also SBUs
strategic capacity 85
strategic competencies 315
strategic control 326
strategic cost management 334, 338, 354
  as an assemblage 339
strategic cost management as a holistic program 336
strategic cost management as a surveillant assemblage 336
strategic drivers 65
strategic imperatives 251, 280
strategic intents 395
strategic leaders 15
strategic learning 141
strategic management
  as a boundary-spanning activity 51
strategic management accounting v. See also SMA
strategic management accounting (SMA) 1
  defined 2, 26, 30
strategic management control 187, 291
strategic maps/mapping 21, 24, 25, 50, 143
  two-dimensional 50

strategic performance as balancing between financial and non-financial 139
strategic performance management 135, 291
  logic of 136
strategic performance management system 139, 403
strategic planning 182, 183, 184
strategic positioning 25, 28, 92, 191, 391
strategic pricing 91, 291
strategic pricing for competitive positioning 91
strategic resilience capabilities
  adaptation 227
  foresight 227
  response 227
strategic role of pricing 96
strategic thinking 225
strategic turn 2, 3–40, 334
strategic uncertainties 193, 194
strategizing 282, 394
  and UN SDGs 1, 6, 17, 20, 21, 22, 23, 25, 26, 30, 31, 32, 34, 35, 36, 39
  defined 25
  defined as a form of positioning 21
  definition 1
  domains of 30
  in traditional management accounting 1, 6, 17, 20, 21, 22, 23, 25, 26, 30, 31, 32, 34, 35, 36, 39
  organizational hierarchy 167
  point of production 290
  the labor process 7, 21, 25, 27, 30, 32, 34, 35, 39
  the market 32

the organizational hierarchy 32
the Social and Environmental 7, 21, 25, 27, 30, 32, 34, 35, 39
with quality 252
strategizing sustainability 70, 374
strategizing the labor process 208
strategizing the market 208
strategizing the organizational hierarchy 208
strategy 3, 139, 182
 a fundamental proposition of 6
 a pattern in action 194
 as a perspective 194
 as a plan 194
 as a position 194
 as coordinating multidivisional organizations 45
 as dealing with external environmental conditions 51
 as patterns of actions 20
 as perspectives 20, 26, 28
 as plans 3, 20
 as positioning 20, 21, 22, 24, 25, 26, 27, 28, 30, 31, 32, 34, 36, 39
 centralisty of defining SMA 19
 Chandler's definition 47
 definition 1
 diversification as 52
 environmental perspective of 51
 organizational discourses of 43
 Porterian discourses of 42, 55
strategy and structure 45
strategy consultants 15
strategy discourses
 military connections of 20
structural categories
 fundamental 376
structural conditions 22
structural determinism 85
structural functionalism 180, 181
structural properties of the market 85
structural resilience 232
structure-conduct-performance 85
structure-conduct-performance model 55, 85
structure of rivalry 61
subcontracting 170
suboptimal capacity utilizations 91
subordinating labor to the interests of capital 328
subsystems 51
Sun Tzu 20
super value strategy of pricing 97
supplier and partner resilience 231
supplier creativity
 in target costing 108
supplier quality management 256
suppliers 352
supply chain management software 309
supply chain/supply chain management 110, 111, 299, 337, 353
supra-system 185
surplus value 251
surveillance 329, 339, 340
surveillant assemblage 337, 339, 340
survival zone 104, 105, 109, 111, 252, 351
sustainability 12, 68, 111, 112, 126, 153, 155, 195, 212, 373, 374, 383, 384, 390, 391, 393, 400
 and target costing 108
 as a foundational principle for strategic positioning 391
 as an oxymoron 374
 as a strategic imperativ 386
 implicatons of SMA vi
 political contradictions 376
sustainability-based legitimation of financial 405
sustainability costing 410
sustainability implications of performance management 124
sustainability implications of target costing 110
sustainability management systems 386
sustainability reporting 386, 390
sustainability to postulate strategic positioning 397
sustainabilizing strategy 386
sustainable and innovative processes 154
sustainable business 379
sustainable development 378
 defined 375
sustainable value chain analysis 400
sustainablizing strategy 27
sweatshops 111
sweatshops on the periphery of global capitalism 111
SWOT analysis 52, 56, 184
symbolic-analytical labor 299
synchronization of labor with machinery 328
synthesis 241
system flexibilities 304
systemic learning 177
system monitoring 212
systems theory 174, 184, 194
systems theory conception of management control 174

T

tableau de bord 136
tactical control 183
Talcott Parson 181
talent management 233
target costing formula 104
target costing process 104, 108, 354
target costing system 90
target costing triangle 106, 352
target costs/target costing 102, 111, 291, 337, 340, 349, 350, 351, 352, 353, 373
  activity-level 110
  component-level 108, 110, 349
  defined 108, 353
  functional-level 110
  market-driven 107, 349
  product-level 108, 349
  sustainability implications of 110
  triangle 104
targeted marketing 53
targeting 92, 95
target price 109
target profit 109, 353
target return on investment 140
targets 127, 140, 330
target unit cost 109
task control 183
taxation without representation 382
techniques
  cost management 340
technology 213
technology analysis
  in target costing 353
technology, competitive conditions and strategy 9
technology roadmaps 109, 353
techno-managerial
  factors behind strategic turn 4
territorial 21, 23, 25, 27
terrorism 228
testing 386
the nature of the firm 382
theories of bureaucratic dysfunctions 180
theorizing v, vi
theory of constraints (TOC) 340, 361, 362
the political 376
Third Industrial Revolution 306
third wave of mergers 44
third-world 111
threat of new entry 62
threat of substitutes 62
throughput 303
Throughput Accounting Ratio (TPAR) 363
throughput accounting (TA) 337, 340, 361, 362
throughput contribution 363
time flexibility
  of labor 298
time flexibility of labor 300
too big to fail 388
top-down approach 331
total assets turnover 130
total quality management (TQM) 104, 269, 270, 282, 341. See also TQM (total quality management)
total rent contract 171
Toyota 282
Toyota's production system 282, 354
TQM (total quality management) 104, 269, 270, 282, 341. See also total quality management (TQM)
tracing costs 87
tracing the physical flows 407
tracking system 307
trade unions 301
traditional absorption costing 86, 309
traditional approach to performance management 128
traditional cost management 329
traditional quality paradigm 265, 266
transaction cost theory 170, 328, 384
transaction processing systems 86
transcendental approach 259
transfer pricing 184
transformative resilience 241
translating the vision 141
transparency 394
triangle of target costing 104, 106
triggers of non-routing responses 223
triple bottom line perspective 153
true cost 309, 345

U

UK Modern Slavery Act, 2015 112
Ukraine war 226
UN 112, 169
uncertainties 1, 14, 27
uncontrollable 344
uniformity 14

unionized labor 301
United Nations 111, 152. See also UN
United Nations Division of Sustainable Development 411
United Nations World Commission on Environment and Development 375
unit-level costs 342
universal marketing package 91, 92
Universal Robots UR5 295
unrecognizably dynamic change 241
UN SDGs 16, 18, 28, 29, 30, 31, 32, 68, 152, 376
unsustainability 378
usability 255
usability testing 257
usage orientation 94
US Aids 152
US competitiveness 341
utility 173

V

value 355
value-added 345
value chain 61, 63, 273, 391
value-chain analysis 63, 184, 373, 386, 398, 403
value creation 188
value engineering 108, 110, 111, 337, 353
value for money 60, 79, 140, 252
value judgment 177
value of common equity 385
value of control information 174

value proposition 79, 97, 258
 between product price and quality 97
 social dimension 68
valuing variety 219
variability 344
variance analysis 130, 131, 132, 184, 329, 334
variety 281
vendor-built 305
veridictional 382
virtual 1, 4, 8, 9, 10
virtualization
 of spaces 1, 4, 8
virtualized markets 92
vision 53, 182, 190, 391, 394, 397
vision statement 56
visual and real-time feedback information 308
volume flexibility 304
vulnerable labor 111

W

wage-only contract 171
wages 171
Wall Street Journal 113
Walter Shewhart 269
war of positioning 292
wastages 91
waste-absorbing sinks 379
waste elimination 282, 355
waste minimization 350
Waterman 53
welfareism 5
well-being 126, 233
whole life costing (WLC) 410
work-in-progress inventories 302

World Bank 152, 215, 301

X

XaaS 293
xpository narratives 215

Y

yin and yang 192

Z

zaibatsu 312
zero-defect 218, 270
 as optimum quality cost level 272
zero-defect quality level 268, 270
zero-defect quality paradigm 269
zero-hour contracts 301
zero-trauma 218, 219

Printed in Great Britain
by Amazon